Audio Effects

Theory, Implementation and Application

Joshua D. Reiss
Queen Mary University of London, United Kingdom
Andrew P. McPherson
Queen Mary University of London, United Kingdom

CRC Press
Taylor & Francis Group
Boca Raton London New York

CRC Press is an imprint of the
Taylor & Francis Group, an **informa** business

Reprint 2025
CRC Press
Taylor & Francis Group
6000 Broken Sound Parkway NW, Suite 300
Boca Raton, FL 33487-2742

ISBN: 978-0-367-24017-2

Library of Congress Cataloging-in-Publication Data

Reiss, Joshua D.
Audio effects : theory, implementation, and application / Joshua D. Reiss, Andrew P. McPherson.
pages cm
Includes bibliographical references and index.
1. Computer sound processing. 2. Sound--Recording and reproducing--Digital techniques. 3. Signal processing--Digital techniques. I. McPherson, Andrew P. II. Title.

TK7881.4.R45 2014
621.382'2--dc23 2014033468

Visit the Taylor & Francis Web site at
http://www.taylorandfrancis.com

and the CRC Press Web site at
http://www.crcpress.com

Printed and bound in India
For sale in India, Pakistan, Nepal, Bhutan, Bangladesh and Sri Lanka only.

Contents

Preface

Audio effects are used in broadcasting, television, film, games, and music production. Where once they were used primarily to enhance a recording and correct artifacts in the production process, now they are used creatively and pervasively.

The aim of this book is to describe the theory behind the effects, explain how they can be implemented, and illustrate many ways in which they can be used. The concepts covered in this book have relevance to sound engineering, digital signal processing, acoustics, audio signal processing, music informatics, and related topics.

Both authors have taught courses on this subject. We are aware of excellent texts on the use of audio effects, especially for mixing and music production. We also know excellent reference material for audio signal processing and for audio effect research. But it was still challenging to find the right material that teaches the reader, from the ground up, how and why to create audio effects, and how they are used.

That is the purpose of this book. It provides students and researchers with knowledge of how to use the tools and the basics of how they work, as well as how to create them. It is primarily educational, and geared toward undergraduate and master's level students, though it can also serve as a reference for practitioners and researchers. It explains how sounds can be processed and modified by mathematical or computer algorithms. It teaches the theory and principles behind the full range of audio effects and provides the reader with an understanding of how to analyze, implement, and use them.

We chose not to shy away from giving the math and science behind the implementations and applications. Thus, it is one of the few resources for use in the classroom with a mathematical and technical approach to audio effects. It provides a detailed overview of audio effects and example questions to aid in learning and understanding. It has a special focus on programming and implementation with industry standards and provides source code for generating plug-in versions of many of the effects.

Chapter 1 begins by covering some fundamental concepts used often in later chapters. It also introduces the notation that we use throughout. Here, we describe some essential concepts from digital signal processing, thus allowing the subject matter to be mostly self-contained, without the reader needing to consult other texts.

In Chapter 2, we introduce delay lines and related effects such as delay, vibrato, chorus, and flanging. These are some of the most basic effects, and the concept of delay lines is useful for understanding implementations of the effects introduced in later sections.

Chapter 3 then covers filter fundamentals. We chose a quite general approach here and introduce techniques that allow the reader to construct a wide variety of high-order filters. Attention is also paid to some additional filters often used in other effects, such as the allpass filter and the exponential moving average.

In Chapter 4, we explore filters in more detail, covering effects that have filters as their essential components. These include the graphic and parametric equalizer, wah-wah, and phaser.

We then move on to nonlinear effects. Chapter 5 discusses modulation, focusing primarily on tremolo and ring modulation. Chapter 6 goes into detail on dynamics processing, especially the dynamic range compressor and the noise gate. Here, much emphasis is given to correct implementation and perceptual qualities of these effects. Chapter 7 then covers distortion effects. These are concerned with the sounds that result from highly nonlinear processing, beyond the dynamics processors of the previous chapter.

Having introduced the important signal processing concepts, we can now move on to the phase vocoder and introduce several effects that do their processing in the frequency domain. This is the focus of Chapter 8.

Up to this point, none of the effects has attempted to recreate how a natural sound might be perceived by a human listener in a real acoustic space. The next three chapters deal with spatial sound reproduction and spatial sound phenomena. Chapter 9 covers some of the main spatialization techniques, starting with panning and precedence, as can be used in stereo positioning, and then moves on to techniques requiring more and more channels, vector-based amplitude panning, ambisonics, and wave field synthesis. The final technique describes binaural sound reproduction using head-related transfer functions (HRTFs) for listening with headphones.

Chapter 10 covers the Doppler effect, which is a physical phenomenon. This short chapter gives both a general derivation and details of implementation as an audio effect based on delay lines. In Chapter 11, we move on to reverberation, describing both algorithmic and convolutional approaches. Though grouped together with the other chapters concerned with spatial sound, the reverberation approaches described here do not necessarily require the processing of two or more channels of audio.

Chapter 12 is about audio production. This is, of course, a very broad area, so we focus on the architecture of mixing consoles and digital audio workstations, and how the effects we have described may be used in these devices. We then discuss how to order and combine the audio effects in order to accomplish various production challenges.

Finally, Chapter 13 is about how to build the audio effects as software plug-ins. We focus on the C++ Virtual Studio Technology (VST) format, which is probably the most popular standard and available for most platforms and hosts. This chapter (and to some extent, Chapter 12) may be read at any point, or independently of the others. It makes reference to the effects discussed previously, but the chapter is focused on practical implementation. It complements the supplementary material, which includes source code that may be used to build VST plug-ins for a large number of effects described in the book.

The text has benefitted greatly from the comments of expert reviewers, most notably Dr. Pedro Duarte Pestana. We are also deeply indebted to Brecht De Man, who revised the audio effects source code, as well as contributed several implementations. This book would also not have been possible without all of the excellent work that has been done before. We are indebted to various people whose work is frequently cited throughout the text: Julius Smith, Roey Izhaki, Udo Zoelzer, Ville Pulkki, and Sophocles Orfanidis, to name just a few. The errors and omissions are ours, whereas the best explanations are found in the works of the cited authors.

Sound examples, software plugins, and code for this book can be found on the CRC Press Web site at http://crcpress.com/product/isbn/9781466560284.

About the Authors

Joshua D. Reiss, PhD, member of IEEE and AES, is a senior lecturer with the Centre for Digital Music in the School of Electronic Engineering and Computer Science at Queen Mary University of London. He has bachelor degrees in both physics and mathematics, and earned his PhD in physics from the Georgia Institute of Technology. He is a member of the Board of Governors of the Audio Engineering Society and cofounder of the company MixGenius. Dr. Reiss has published more than 100 scientific papers and serves on several steering and technical committees. He has investigated music retrieval systems, time scaling and pitch shifting techniques, polyphonic music transcription, loudspeaker design, automatic mixing for live sound, and digital audio effects. His primary focus of research, which ties together many of the above topics, is on the use of state-of-the-art signal processing techniques for professional sound engineering.

Andrew P. McPherson, PhD, joined Queen Mary University of London as lecturer in digital media in September 2011. He holds a PhD in music composition from the University of Pennsylvania and an M.Eng. in electrical engineering from the Massachusetts Institute of Technology. Prior to joining Queen Mary, he was a postdoc in the Music Entertainment Technology Laboratory at Drexel University, supported by a Computing Innovation Fellowship from the Computing Research Association and the National Science Foundation (NSF). Dr. McPherson's current research topics include electronic augmentation of the acoustic piano, new musical applications of multitouch sensing, quantitative studies of expressive performance technique, and embedded audio processing systems. He remains active as a composer of orchestral, chamber, and electronic music, with performances across the United States and Canada, including at the Tanglewood and Aspen music festivals.

1

Introduction and Fundamentals

In digital audio signal processing and digital audio effects, we are primarily concerned with systems that take a discrete, uniformly sampled audio signal, process it, and produce a discrete, uniformly sampled output audio signal. Therefore, we start by introducing some fundamental properties of sound that are used over and over again, then how we represent it as a digital signal, and then we move on to how we describe the systems that act on and modify such signals. This is not meant to give a detailed overview of digital signal processing, which would involve discussion of continuous time signals, infinite signals, and mathematical relationships. Rather, we intend to focus on just the type of signals and systems that are encountered in audio effects, and on the most useful properties and representations. Having said that, this is also intended to be self-contained. Very little prior knowledge is assumed, and it should not be necessary to refer to more detailed discussions in other texts in order to understand these concepts.

Understanding Sound and Digital Audio

Fundamentally, all audio is composed of waveforms. Vibrating objects create pressure waves in the air; when these waves reach our ears, we perceive them as sound. With the invention of the telephone in the 19th century, audio was first encoded as an electric signal, with the changes in electric voltage representing the changes in pressure over time. Until the late 20th century, electric recording and transmission was all analog: sound was represented by a continuous waveform over time.

In this book, we will work almost exclusively with digital audio. Rather than representing audio as a continuous voltage, as in analog, the waveform will be composed of discrete samples over time. These samples can be stored, processed, and ultimately reconstructed as sound we can hear. Digital audio systems generally begin with an *analog-to-digital converter* (ADC), which captures periodic snapshots of the electrical voltage on an audio transmission line and represents these snapshots as discrete numbers. By capturing the voltage many thousands of times per second, one can achieve a very close approximation of the original audio signal. This encoding method is known

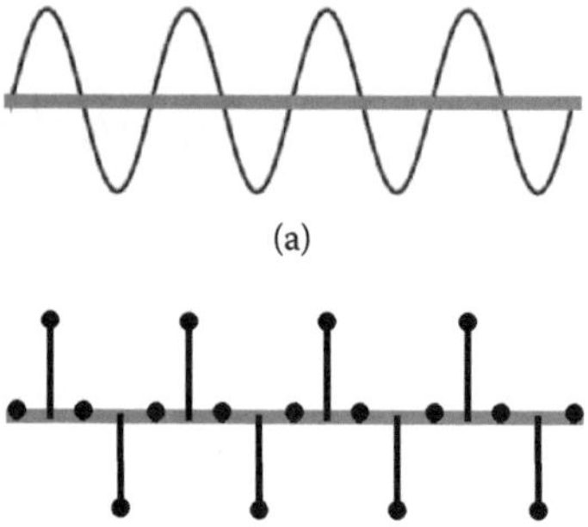

FIGURE 1.1
A continuous time signal (a), and its digital representation, found by sampling the signal uniformly in time (b).

as *pulse code modulation*, and is the encoding format used in the WAV and AIFF audio formats. Pulse code modulation is also one of the most popular forms of ADC, and certainly one of the simplest to explain.

Thus, a continuous time audio signal, such as captured from a microphone, is represented as a digital signal with uniform timing between samples (see Figure 1.1). But digital audio signals need not be derived from analog, nor even represent any physical sound. They can be completely synthetic, and generated using digital signal processing techniques. We will touch on this later in the text when discussing low-frequency oscillators (Chapter 2), phase vocoders (Chapter 8), and other concepts. It is important to note that unless additional information is stored, there is no distinction between those digital audio signals that were generated from conversion of analog signals and those that were generated from digital sound synthesis techniques (though, of course, real-world signals are likely to have more noise and more complex phenomena).

There are three important characteristics of almost any digital audio data: sample rate, bit depth, and number of channels.

Sample rate is the rate at which the samples are captured or played back. It is typically measured in Hertz (Hz), or cycles per second. In this case, one cycle represents one sample. An audio CD has a sample rate of 44,100 Hz, or 44.1 kHz. Higher sampling rates allow a digital recording to accurately record higher frequencies of sound, or to provide a safety margin in case of additional noise or artifacts introduced in the recording, processing, or playback; 48 kHz is often used in audiovisual production, and sample rates of 96 or 192 kHz are used in high-resolution audio, such as in DVD-Audio, or in professional audio production.

The *bit depth* specifies how many bits are used to represent each audio sample. The most common choices in audio are 16 bit and 24 bit. The bit depth also determines the theoretical dynamic range of the audio signal. In digital audio, amplitude is often expressed as a unitless number, representing a ratio between the current intensity and the highest (or lowest) possible intensity that can be represented. The maximum absolute value for this ratio is known as the *dynamic range*. In an ideal ADC, the dynamic range, in decibels (see below), is very roughly 6.02 times the number of bits. Thus, 16-bit audio could represent signals whose loudness ranges over 96 dB, e.g., from a quiet whisper to a loud rock concert.

The *number of channels* actually refers to the fact that audio content will often be composed of several different channels, each one representing its own signal. This is most often the case in stereo or surround sound, where each channel may represent the sound sent to each loudspeaker. Monaural audio, however, is typically encoded as a single channel. We will return to these concepts in Chapter 9.

Digital audio may be encoded with or without *data compression*. When data compression is used, sophisticated algorithms are used to encode and re-represent the data such that they take up much less space. Hence, a decoder must be used to convert the data back into time domain samples before playback. The compression can be either *lossless* (the decoded data are identical to the original data before compression) or *lossy*. Modern lossy audio compression techniques use knowledge of psychoacoustics to minimize the perceived degradation of audio that occurs when a substantial amount of the information contained in the original signal is discarded.

Data compression also introduces one more characteristic of audio data, the *bit rate*. This is the number of bits per unit of time. For lossless signals, this is simply the bit depth times the sample rate times the number of channels. For instance, CD audio would typically have a bit rate of 1,411.2 kbps (kilobits per second):

$$16\frac{\text{bits}}{\text{sample}}\cdot 44100\frac{\text{samples}}{\text{second}}\cdot 2\,(\#\,\text{channels}) = 1411200\frac{\text{bits}}{\text{second}} \tag{1.1}$$

For audio signals that have undergone lossy compression, the bit rate is usually greatly reduced. Most compression schemes, including mp3 and aac, transmit audio with a bit rate between 30 and 500 kbps.

It should be noted that there is a lot of fine detail regarding quantization, sampling, dynamic range, and lossy compression of audio data that has been omitted here. For the purpose of this text, it is sufficient to know the format and general meaning of these concepts, but the reader is also encouraged to refer to signal processing texts for more detailed discussion [1–5].

WHY 44.1 KHZ?

Perhaps the most popular sample rate used in digital audio, especially for music content, is 44.1 kHz, or 44,100 samples per second. The short answer as to why it is so popular is simple; it was the sample rate chosen for the Compact Disc and, thus, is the sample rate of much audio taken from CDs, and the default sample rate of much audio workstation software.

As to why it was chosen as the sample rate for the Compact Disc, the answer is a bit more interesting. In the 1970s, when digital recording was still in its infancy, many different sample rates were used, including 37kHz and 50 kHz in Soundstream's recordings [6]. In the late 70s, Philips and Sony collaborated on the Compact Disc, and there was much debate between the two companies regarding sample rate. In the end, 44.1 kHz was chosen for a number of reasons.

According to the Nyquist theorem, 44.1 kHz allows reproduction of all frequency content below 22.05 kHz. This covers all frequencies heard by a normal person. Though there is still debate about perception of high frequency content, it is generally agreed that few people can hear tones above 20 kHz.

This 44.1 kHz also allowed the creators of the CD format to fit at least 80 minutes of music (more than on a vinyl LP record) on a 120 millimeter disc, which was considered a strong selling point.

But 44,100 is a rather special number: $44{,}100 = 2^2 \times 3^2 \times 5^2 \times 7^2$, and hence, 44.1kHz is actually an easy number to work with for many calculations.

Working with Decibels

We often deal with quantities that can cover a very wide range of values, from very large to very small. The *decibel scale* is a useful way to represent such quantities. The *decibel* (dB) is a logarithmic representation of the ratio between two values. Typically, both values represent power, and hence, the decibel is unitless. One of these values is usually a reference, so that the decibel scale can represent absolute levels. The decibel representation of a level is then 10 times the logarithm to base 10 of the ratio of the two power quantities. Since power is usually the square of a magnitude, we can write a value in decibels in terms of the magnitudes or powers as

$$x_{dB} = 10\log_{10}\left(x^2/x_0^2\right) = 20\log_{10}\left(|x|/|x_0|\right) \tag{1.2}$$

If not specified, x_0 is usually assumed to be 1. So, for example, 1 million is 60 dB, and 0.001 is –30 dB. Whether a decibel or linear scale is used often depends just on which one best conveys the relevant information.

Level Measurements

The sound pressure measured from a source is inversely proportional to the distance from the source. Suppose a sound pressure p_1 is measured at distance r_1 from the source; then the sound pressure p_2 at distance r_2 can be calculated as

$$p_2 = p_1 r_1 / r_2 \tag{1.3}$$

Not all sources radiate uniformly in every direction. For example, a violin radiates more sound upward from the top of the instrument than from the sides or back. Measurements at different angles may therefore give different results.

The intensity I of a sound is given by the sound pressure times the particle velocity. It gives the sound power per unit area, and is measured in watts per square meter, W/m^2. Whereas pressure is proportional to the distance to the sound source, the intensity is proportional to the square of the distance to the sound source, giving a $1/r^2$ relationship.

A decibel scale is used to represent the very wide range of sound intensities that can be perceived. The sound intensity level, L_I, given in dB, is the log ratio of a given intensity I to a reference. The reference level is usually set to $I_0 = 10^{-12}$ W/m^2, which is considered to be roughly the threshold of hearing at 1 kHz.

$$L_I = 10\log_{10}(I/I_0) = 120 + 10\log_{10} I \tag{1.4}$$

Exact measurement of intensity is difficult, and the intensity values will fluctuate over time. So sound pressure level (SPL) is often used instead. The sound pressure level or sound level L_p is also given in decibels above a standard reference level, p_{ref}, of 2×10^{-5} N/m^2 = 20 μPa, the sound pressure threshold of human hearing.

$$L_p = 10\log_{10}\left(p_{rms}^2 / p_{ref}^2\right) = 20\log_{10}\left(p_{rms} / p_{ref}\right) \tag{1.5}$$

where p_{ref} is the reference sound pressure and p_{rms} is the RMS (root mean square, or square root of the average value of the squared signal) sound pressure being measured. In this text, we do not often refer to SPLs, since we will deal mostly with the processing of digital signals, where the physical sound level is not known.

For digital signals, level measurements are also given in a decibel representation. But now, decibels are measured relative to full scale, denoted dBFS. This is possible since most digital systems have a defined maximum available peak level.

Zero dBFS represents the maximum possible digital level. For example, if the maximum signal amplitude on a linear scale is 1 and the actual amplitude is 0.5, then signal level would be defined as 20 $\log_{10}(0.5/1) = -3.01$ dBFS, or 3 dB below peak level. However, if RMS measurements are used, then the definition may be ambiguous. Different conventions are used for RMS measurements. Some RMS-based level measurements set the reference level so that peak and RMS measurements of a square wave will produce the same result, all dBFS measurements will be negative, and the maximum sine wave that can be produced without clipping will have value –3.01 dBFS.

An alternative (though much less common) definition gives the reference level so that peak and RMS measurements of a sine wave will produce the same result. A full-scale sine wave would be at 0 dBFS, but a full-scale square wave would exceed this, at +3 dBFS. In audio production (see Chapter 12), meters are provided so that the user will know if maximum levels are exceeded and clipping will occur.

In Chapter 6, we will discuss some methods of estimating the levels of digital signals for use in dynamics processing. Though given on a decibel scale, these estimates are tailored to the audio effect and may be different from the dBFS value described here.

Representing and Understanding Digital Signals

The time between samples may be given as T_s so that the sampling frequency is given as $f_s = 1/T_s$. Therefore, the digital input signal may be represented as discrete sampling of a continuous signal, $x(0)$, $x(T_s)$, $x(2T_s)$, … . If we consider only the sample number, then a finite signal consisting of N samples can be represented as $x[0]$, $x[1]$, …, $x[N-1]$.*

Representing Complex Numbers

Almost always, we will have real-valued signals, and our audio effects produce real-valued results. But a lot of the math and analysis of signals and effects is actually easier to do when generalizing the discussion to complex numbers. So it is extremely useful to keep a few properties of complex numbers in mind. First, any complex number can be written in several ways:

$$x = a + bj = re^{j\theta} \tag{1.6}$$

Here, a is the real part and b is the imaginary part, and j is defined to be $\sqrt{-1}$. The complex number can be plotted as a point on a plane where the

* In this text, brackets are generally used when we refer to functions of discrete integer samples, and parentheses are used for functions of continuous time.

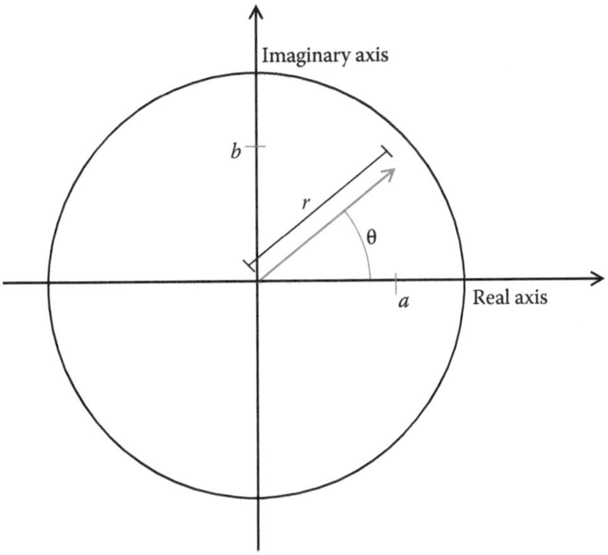

FIGURE 1.2
A complex number $a + jb = re^{j\theta}$ depicted in the complex plane. The unit circle, $\cos\theta + j\sin\theta = e^{j\theta}$ is also depicted.

x-direction is the real component and the y-direction is the imaginary one, in which case r is the magnitude of the vector from (0, 0) to (a, b), and θ is the angle between the x-axis and the vector, known as the phase. This is depicted in Figure 1.2.

Using a form of Euler's identity, $e^{j\theta} = \cos\theta + j\sin\theta$, we have

$$\begin{aligned} a &= r\cos\theta \\ b &= r\sin\theta \\ r &= \sqrt{a^2 + b^2} \end{aligned} \tag{1.7}$$

It is a bit tricky to derive the phase θ from a and b. It is not just the arctan(b/a), since this doesn't distinguish between the case when b is positive and a negative or when b is negative and a positive. That is, the arc tangent function has a range of $-\pi/2$ to $\pi/2$, but phase ranges from $-\pi$ to π. So we use the following:

$$\theta = \text{atan}\,2(b,a) = \begin{cases} \arctan(b/a) & a \geq 0, b \neq 0 \\ \arctan(b/a) + \pi\,\text{sgn}(b) & a < 0 \\ \text{undefined} & a, b = 0 \end{cases} \tag{1.8}$$

The conjugate of a complex number is simply defined as the same number, but with the sign changed on the complex component. Denoting complex conjugation by *, we then have, from (1.6),

$$x^* = a - bj = re^{-j\theta} \tag{1.9}$$

The square magnitude of a number is given by that number times its complex conjugate,

$$|x|^2 = x \cdot x^* = a^2 + b^2 = r^2 \tag{1.10}$$

Frequency and Time–Frequency Representations

Let's return to our time domain digital signal, $x[0], x[1], \ldots, x[N-1]$. There are many other ways to represent this signal. Probably the most important is the discrete Fourier transform (DFT), which is intended to represent a finite, discrete signal in terms of its frequency components.

$$X[k] = \sum_{n=0}^{N-1} x[n] e^{-jnk2\pi/N} \quad 0 \le k, n \le N-1 \tag{1.11}$$

This converts the signal from being represented in terms of a real value at sample number n to representation in terms of a complex value at frequency bin k. In the same sense that time domain sample n corresponds to discrete sample at time nT_s, frequency bin k corresponds to frequency kf_s/N. Now notice that the output involves complex numbers. More precisely, $X[k]$ gives a phase and amplitude for the frequency content from $(k - 1/2)f_s/N$ to $(k + 1/2)f_s/N$.

This transformation has a large number of properties, but for understanding digital signals, the following are the most important:

$$\begin{aligned} y[n] = x_1[n] + x_2[n] &\longleftrightarrow Y[k] = X_1[k] + X_2[k] \\ y[n] = ax[n] &\longleftrightarrow Y[k] = aX[k] \end{aligned} \tag{1.12}$$

In other words, if we add two signals together, we add their discrete Fourier transforms together, and if we multiply a signal by a constant, we multiply its discrete Fourier transforms by the same constant.

Now suppose our signal x is a complex sinusoid, $x[n] = ae^{jnl2\pi/N}$, $n = 0, 1, \ldots, N-1$, where a is some constant. Then,

$$X[k]=\sum_{n=0}^{N-1} ae^{j2\pi(l-k)n/N}=\begin{cases} a\sum_{n=0}^{N-1}1=aN & l=k \\ a\dfrac{1-e^{j2\pi(l-k)}}{1-e^{j2\pi(l-k)/N}}=0 & l\neq k \end{cases} \tag{1.13}$$

where we used a well-known identity,

$$\sum_{n=0}^{N-1} x^n=\frac{1-x^N}{1-x}.$$

So each frequency bin in a discrete Fourier transform represents the magnitude of a complex sinusoid. That implies that any finite signal can be represented as a sum of weighted sinusoids.

Finally, we can convert from the frequency representation back to the time domain using the inverse discrete Fourier transform (IDFT),

$$x[n]=\frac{1}{N}\sum_{k=0}^{N-1} X[k]e^{j2\pi nk/N} \tag{1.14}$$

The DFT allows us to represent the signal as complex-valued frequency components. Each of these has a magnitude and phase. Thus, we can plot the magnitude and phase as a function of frequency for any signal. More common than magnitude plots, however, is the power spectrum that is given as the power in each frequency bin,

$$P(k)=|X(k)|^2/N^2 \tag{1.15}$$

as a function of frequency.

The discrete Fourier transform and its inverse are very powerful tools, though very computationally intensive. But there is a lot of redundancy in the calculation. An implementation known as the fast Fourier transform (FFT) is commonly used. However, in its standard implementation, it requires that the number of samples be a power of 2.

Even with the FFT, it is still quite slow to compute over a large number of samples. Furthermore, the incoming signal may be very long or infinite, yet one would like to know the frequency content at any given time. Thus, the short-time Fourier transform (STFT) is used:

$$\mathrm{STFT}\{x[n]\} \equiv X[m,k] = \sum_{n=mR}^{N+mR-1} x[n] e^{-j(n-mR)k2\pi/N} \quad 0 \le k \le N-1 \qquad (1.16)$$

This provides estimates of the frequency content at times mR, where R is the hop size, in samples, between successive DFTs. And we often plot the *spectrogram*, $S[m,k] \equiv |X[m,k]|^2$, with S plotted as a color intensity as a function of time and frequency. The relationship between spectrogram and STFT is completely analogous to the relationship between power spectrum and DFT.

Figure 1.3 depicts the waveform, power spectrum, and spectrogram of an excerpt of a solo guitar performance.

Aliasing

An important concept, and one that will feature heavily in dealing with nonlinear processing, is aliasing. Suppose $x[n] = \cos(nl2\pi/N) = [e^{jnl2\pi/N} + e^{-jnl2\pi/N}]/2$, $n = 0, 1, \ldots, N-1$. Then,

$$\begin{aligned} X[k] &= \sum_{n=0}^{N-1} \left[e^{jnl2\pi/N} + e^{-jnl2\pi/N} \right] e^{-j2\pi kn/N} / 2 \\ &= \sum_{n=0}^{N-1} \left[e^{jnl2\pi/N} + e^{jn(N-l)2\pi/N} \right] e^{-j2\pi kn/N} / 2 = \begin{cases} N/2 & l = k \\ N/2 & l = N-k \\ 0 & l \ne k, N-k \end{cases} . \end{aligned} \qquad (1.17)$$

So a real-valued sinusoid will give two nonzero frequency components, one at k and one at $N-k$. This implies that, for real valued input signals, the frequency spectrum from $N/2$ to N is the mirror image of the spectrum from 0 to $N/2$. We can also easily show that the spectrum for an input frequency sinusoid with frequency $f + f_s$ is the same as for a sinusoid with frequency f. So if a continuous signal is sampled at a frequency f_s, then the sampled signal cannot reproduce frequencies above $f_s/2$.

In fact, when sampling at a frequency f_s, any signal at a frequency $Nf_s + f_c$ or $Nf_s - f_c$, for any integer N, will be indistinguishable from a signal at frequency f_c. As an example of this, consider Figure 1.4. A sinusoid of frequency $0.7f_s$ is sampled at frequency f_s. The samples that result could equally well represent a sinusoid of frequency $0.3f_s$. This property is known as *aliasing*, since these signals are aliases of each other.

For this reason, signals should in general, be band limited before sampling, so that they contain no frequency components greater than $f_s/2$. $f_s/2$ is known as the *Nyquist frequency*. This is also a consequence of the Nyquist–Shannon sampling theorem, which states that such band limited signals can be (in theory) completely reconstructed when sampled at a frequency of at least f_s.

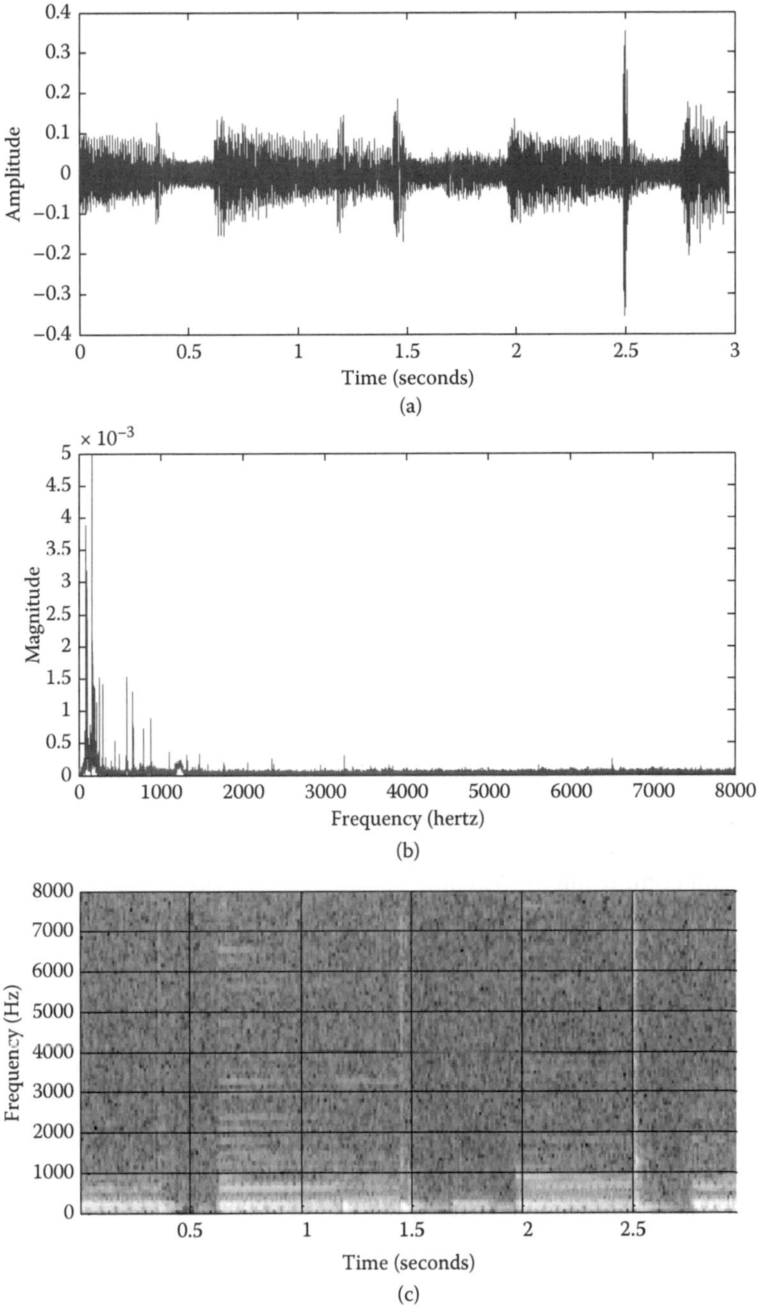

FIGURE 1.3
The time domain waveform (a), frequency domain power spectrum (b), and spectrogram of a 3 s excerpt of a solo guitar performance (c).

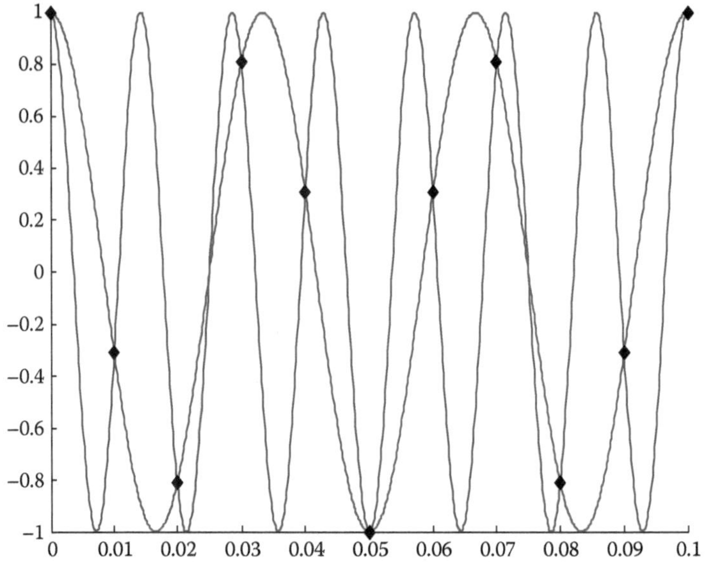

FIGURE 1.4
Two sampled sinusoids, one with frequency $0.3\,f_s$ and the other with frequency $0.7\,f_s$. They appear identical when sampled at a frequency f_s.

Modifying and Processing Digital Signals

Up to now, we've been looking at how to represent and analyze signals. But how do we modify them? We start by introducing the difference equation, a formula for computing the nth output sample based on current and previous input samples and previous output samples. A linear, time-invariant digital filter may be given as a *difference equation,*

$$y[n]=b_0x[n]+b_1x[n-1]+\ldots b_Nx[n-N]-a_1y[n-1]-\ldots a_My[n-M] \quad (1.18)$$

where x is some input signal and y is the output signal. The constants $b_0, \ldots, b_N$ and $a_0, \ldots, a_N$ are known as coefficients or multipliers. Figure 1.5 shows this as a block diagram, with the input signal entering at the top left and the output signal appearing on the right.

There are many different ways to represent this system. One of the most important is the *impulse response,* which describes the output when the input is just a single pulse:

$$h[n]=y[n],\, x[n]=\delta[n]\equiv\begin{cases}1\; n=0\\0\; n\neq 0\end{cases} \quad (1.19)$$

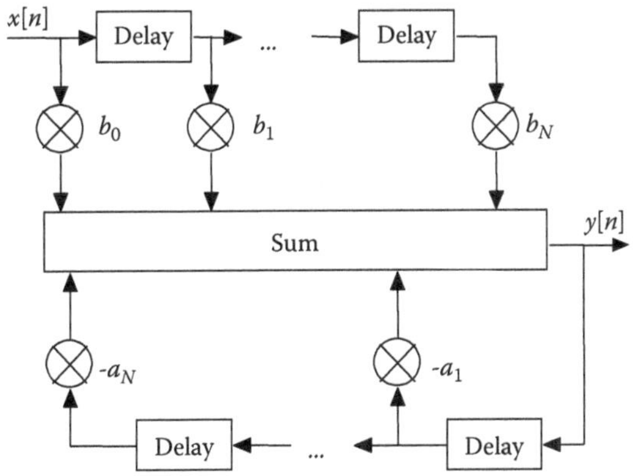

FIGURE 1.5
A time domain block diagram of a digital linear filter.

Let's quickly look at two cases, $y[n] = x[n] + 0.5y[n-1]$ and $y[n] = x[n] + 2y[n-1]$. They have the impulse responses $h[n] = 1, 0.5, 0.25, 0.125, \ldots$, and $h[n] = 1, 2, 4, 8\ldots$. In the first case, the output exponentially approaches zero, but in the second case, the output keeps growing even though the input has stopped. This first case is an example of a stable system. Whenever the impulse response converges to zero, the system is said to be stable.

Any discrete time signal can be represented as a weighted sum of delayed impulses. Since the filter is linear, the response to that signal is a weighted sum of delayed impulse responses. So the impulse response fully characterizes the system.

The *Z* Transform and Filter Representation

Another important transformation of a discrete sequence is the Z transform:

$$Z\{x[n]\} = X(z) = \sum_{n=0}^{\infty} x[n]z^{-n}, z = e^{j\omega} = e^{j2\pi f/f_s} \tag{1.20}$$

This converts the signal from being represented in terms of sample number n to representation in terms of complex number z. Note that this is related to the Fourier domain transform, of which we gave the discrete version previously. Note also that we use a normalized frequency, $\omega = 2\pi f/f_s$, so if the signal has frequency components between 0 and f_s, ω is between 0 and π, and z is between +1 and –1. This notation for normalized frequency will be used throughout this text.

For understanding digital filters, the following properties of the Z domain transform are important:

$$Z\{x_1[n]+x_2[n]\}=Z\{x_1[n]\}+Z\{x_2[n]\}=X_1(z)+X_2(z)$$
$$Z\{ax[n]\}=aZ\{x[n]\}=aX(z) \qquad (1.21)$$
$$Z\{x[n-1]\}=\sum_{n=-\infty}^{\infty}x[n-1]z^{-n}=z^{-1}\sum_{n=-\infty}^{\infty}x[n-1]z^{-(n-1)}=z^{-1}Z\{x[n]\}=z^{-1}X(z)$$

This last property states that if we delay a signal by one sample, then we multiply its z domain transform by z^{-1}. Similarly, if we delay a signal by n samples, we multiply its z domain transform by z^{-n}.

The Z domain representation allows us to redraw the block diagram as shown in Figure 1.6.

And we can transform Equation (1.18) into the Z domain,

$$Y(z)=b_0X(z)+b_1z^{-1}X(z)+\ldots b_Nz^{-N}X(z)-a_1z^{-1}Y(z)-\ldots a_Mz^{-M}Y(z) \qquad (1.22)$$

Now, we don't need to worry about what X and Y are. Equation (1.22) holds regardless of the exact nature of the input signal. We can use a little algebra to group terms involving X and terms involving Y:

$$\left[1+a_1z^{-1}+\ldots a_Mz^{-M}\right]Y(z)=\left[b_0+b_1z^{-1}+\ldots b_Nz^{-N}\right]X(z) \qquad (1.23)$$

If $M \neq N$, we can always add a few zero coefficients to the smaller of the two terms in order to set them equal. So we can now refer to N as the order of the filter. When N is large, we refer to this as a *high-order filter*. The *transfer function* is then defined as

$$H(z)=\frac{Y(z)}{X(z)}=\frac{B(z)}{A(z)}=\frac{b_0+b_1z^{-1}+\ldots b_Nz^{-N}}{1+a_1z^{-1}+\ldots a_Nz^{-N}} \qquad (1.24)$$

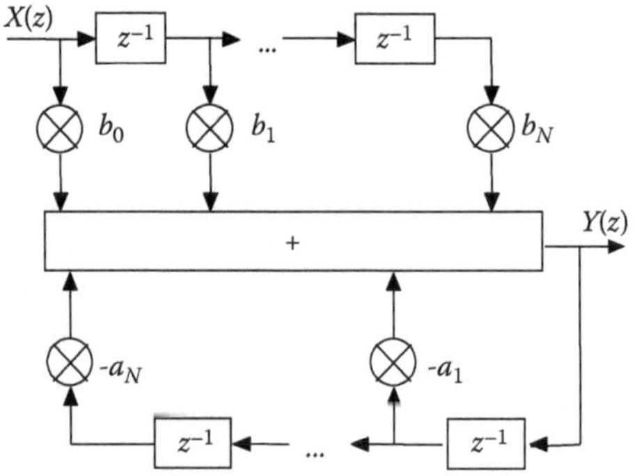

FIGURE 1.6
A Z domain block diagram of a digital linear filter.

We can rewrite this by expressing the polynomials in terms of positive powers of z (this notation is often used in this text), and factoring the polynomials,

$$H(z) = \frac{b_0 z^N + b_1 z^{N-1} + \ldots b_N}{z^N + a_1 z^{N-1} + \ldots a_N} = g\frac{(z-q_1)(z-q_2)\cdots(z-q_N)}{(z-p_1)(z-p_2)\cdots(z-p_N)} \tag{1.25}$$

This gives rise to yet another way to define the filter: in terms of its poles p_1, $p_2, \ldots, p_N$, zeros $q_1, q_2, \ldots, q_N$, and gain factor g. A *pole* is an infinite value of $H(z)$ obtained when z is set so that the denominator $A(z)$ equals zero, and a *zero* is a zero value of $H(z)$ obtained when z is set so that the numerator $B(z)$ has zero value. When poles and zeros are plotted in the complex plane, this is known as a *pole zero plot.* When all the poles have magnitude less than 1 (they are inside the unit circle), the filter will be stable. If all the zeros are inside the unit circle, the filter is said to be *minimum phase,* and minimum phase filters produce the minimum delay for a given magnitude response. That is, the impulse response described in Equation (1.19) will decay toward 0.

An important distinction needs to be made here. When the filter has no feedback, i.e., the current output does not depend on previous outputs, then it can be written as

$$\begin{aligned} y[n] &= b_0 x[n] + b_1 x[n-1] + \ldots b_N x[n-N] \\ H(z) &= b_0 + b_1 z^{-1} + \ldots b_N z^{-N} = g\frac{(z-q_1)(z-q_2)\ldots(z-q_N)}{z^N} \end{aligned} \tag{1.26}$$

Thus, all poles are located at $z = 0$ and the filter is inherently stable. This is known as a *finite impulse response* (FIR) filter. Filters containing a feedback path are known as *infinite impulse response* (IIR) filters. For a roughly equivalent magnitude response, IIR filters are usually much lower order than FIR filters.

A filter is characterized by its magnitude response, $|H(\omega)|$, and phase response, $\angle H(\omega)$, as a function of ω, where here we write the transfer function as a function of radial frequency ω rather than z. FIR filters may be designed so that they are *linear phase,* meaning that the phase response is a linear function of frequency, and thus the time domain shape of a signal may be preserved when the filter is applied. This is generally not the case for IIR filters.

To summarize, we have the following representations of a linear digital filter:

- Difference equation
- Block diagram
- Impulse response
- Transfer function

- Poles, zeros, and gain
- Magnitude and phase response

There are, of course, many other ways to represent the filter, but these are probably the most important. It is also very useful to be able to go back and forth between the different representations, since it allows us to conceptualize the filter in different ways. In Chapter 3, we will look at how various filters are designed, and in Chapter 4, we will look at some audio effects based on filter design techniques.

Digital Filter Example

At this point, it is instructive to look at an example. Consider, the following filter,

$$y[n]=4x[n]-4x[n-1]+x[n-2]-y[n-1]-y[n-2]/2 \tag{1.27}$$

This filter's current output is dependent on the current input and the two previous outputs and inputs. We can rewrite this in the Z domain as follows:

$$\begin{aligned} &Y(z)=4X(z)-4X(z)z^{-1}+X(z)z^{-2}-Y(z)z^{-1}-Y(z)z^{-2}/2 \\ &\rightarrow \\ &H(z)=\frac{Y(z)}{X(z)}=\frac{4z^2-4z+1}{z^2+z+1/2} \end{aligned} \tag{1.28}$$

We can see that it is a second-order filter, since it can be expressed with a transfer function consisting of no more than second-order polynomials in the numerator and denominator,

$$H(z)=\frac{Y(z)}{X(z)}=\frac{4z^2-4z+1}{z^2+z+1/2} \tag{1.29}$$

By factoring the polynomials, we can rewrite this transfer function in terms of zeros and poles,

$$H(z)=\frac{4\left(z-\frac{1}{2}\right)\left(z-\frac{1}{2}\right)}{\left(z-\frac{-1+j}{2}\right)\left(z-\frac{-1-j}{2}\right)} \tag{1.30}$$

So we see that there are two zeros, both located at 1/2, and two poles, located at $(-1 \pm j)/2$. The poles are complex and can be written in polar form as $e^{\pm 3j\pi/4}$.

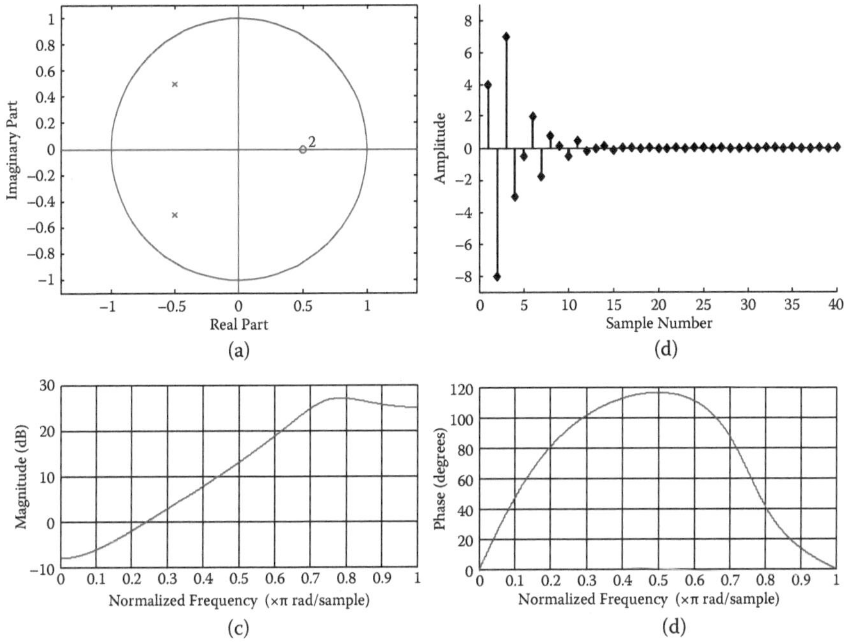

FIGURE 1.7
Pole zero plot (a), impulse response (b), magnitude response (c), and phase response (d) of a digital linear filter.

To find the impulse response of this filter, we simply enter a 1 as $x[0]$ in Equation (1.27); set all previous inputs, previous outputs, and future inputs to zero; and calculate the output values. To find the magnitude and phase response, plot $|H(\omega)|$ and $\angle H(\omega)$ as a function of ω. The pole zero plot, impulse response, magnitude (in decibels) response, and phase response for this filter are given in Figure 1.7.

It is clear from Figure 1.7c that this filter will attenuate low frequencies and boost high frequencies, with the maximum boost occurring at a normalized frequency of approximately $\omega = 0.785\pi$. For a sampling rate of 44.1 kHz, this corresponds to a frequency of approximately $f = 44.1 \times 0.785 \times 0.5 = 17.3$ kHz.

For very low and very high frequencies, this filter makes only small changes to the phase. However, for input sinusoids with normalized frequency $\omega = \pi/2$ (frequency $f = 11.025$ kHz for sampling frequency 44.1 kHz), the output signal will be a sinusoid shifted by about 116°.

Nonlinear and Time-Varying Effects

The filter described by Equation (1.18) was linear and time invariant. That is, it is linear in the sense that summing two filter outputs gives the same result as applying the filter on the sum of two signals, and scaling the filter output gives the same result as scaling the filter input. And it is time invariant in that delaying the input signal is the same as delaying the output signal. Note that these same properties applied to the Z transformation, which is one reason it is so useful for working with linear filters.

But many of the audio effects that we will encounter do not have these properties. Dynamic range compression (Chapter 6), for instance, is nonlinear, since applying a gain to the input signal is not equivalent to applying that same gain to the output signal. And many effects are not time invariant, since they incorporate a low-frequency oscillator (Chapter 2) with an explicit dependence on time.

However, this does not completely invalidate the linear representations. Most of the time-varying systems that we will encounter have relatively slow time variation, at least compared to the sampling rate. So we can consider the transfer function and other representations for a snapshot of the system, where time is held constant. Similarly, we can sometimes consider how nonlinear effects act on a given signal level, and many nonlinear effects will have a range of input signal levels where they act like a linear filter. Where appropriate, we will also apply other analysis techniques. The representations for linear, time-invariant filters are simply some of the tools at our disposal for working with almost any audio effect that we will encounter.

Problems

1. Compute the z domain representation of an impulse

$$x(n)=\begin{cases}1 & n=0\\ 0 & n\neq 0\end{cases}$$

and of a step function

$$x(n)=\begin{cases}1 & n\geq 0\\ 0 & n<0\end{cases}$$

2. Show that the IDFT of the DFT gives the original signal.
3. Show that the spectrum for an input frequency sinusoid with frequency $f+f_s$, where f_s is the sample rate, is the same as for a sinusoid with frequency f.
4. Explain the difference between FIR and IIR digital filter designs. Which is computationally less expensive? Which usually exhibits the lower overall latency? Which better preserves the phase relationships of the original signal? Why?

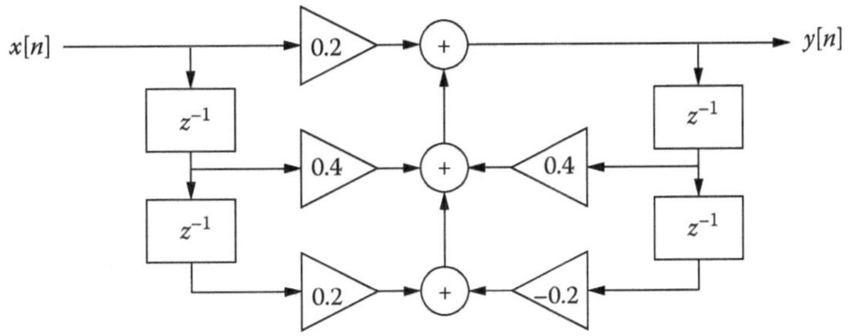

FIGURE 1.8
Example block diagram.

5. a. Write the difference equation corresponding to the block diagram in Figure 1.8. Is this an FIR or IIR filter? Why?
   b. From the difference equation, take the Z transform and derive the transfer function $H(z) = Y(z)/X(z)$.
   c. What are the values of $H(z)$ at $z = e^{j0} = 1$ and $e^{j\pi} = -1$? Roughly, how does this filter affect the frequency content of the input signal?

2

Delay Line Effects

Delay lines are the fundamental building blocks of many of the most important effects. They are rather easy to implement, and only small changes in how they are used allow many different audio effects to easily be constructed. In this chapter, we look at some common effects that are built using delay lines.

Delay

Delay is a simple effect with powerful applications. In the simplest case, adding a single delayed copy of a sound to itself can enliven an instrument's sound in a mix or, at longer delay times, allow a performer to play a duet with himself or herself. Many familiar effects, including chorus, flanging, vibrato, and reverb, are also built on delays.

Theory

Basic Delay

The basic delay plays back an audio signal after a specified *delay time.* Depending on the application, the delay time might range from a few milliseconds to several seconds or longer. Figure 2.1 shows a block diagram of the basic delay. It is common to mix the delayed output with the original input, thereby producing two copies of the sound. For this reason the basic delay is also sometimes known as an *echo* effect (though as we will see, the perception of echo also depends on the delay time).

We can express the output audio samples $y[n]$ as a function of the input samples $x[n]$, the delay time N (expressed in samples), and the gain g of the delayed signal:

$$y[n] = x[n] + gx[n - N] \tag{2.1}$$

Delay is a *linear, time-invariant* effect. To show linearity, consider two signals $x_1[n]$ and $x_2[n]$. Let $y_1[n]$ and $y_2[n]$ be the delayed output of each signal

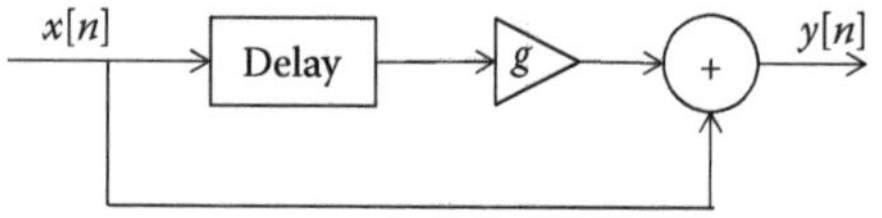

FIGURE 2.1
Diagram of the basic delay unit, or an echo device. The box marked "delay" is commonly known as a delay line.

individually. If we delay the sum of the signals, we find that the output is the sum of the individual delayed signals:

$$\begin{aligned} y[n] &= (x_1[n]+x_2[n])+g(x_1[n-N]+x_2[n-N]) \\ &= (x_1[n]+gx_1[n-N])+(x_2[n]+gx_2[n-N])=y_1[n]+y_2[n] \end{aligned} \tag{2.2}$$

Time invariance implies that shifting the input in time produces an identical shift in the output. Consider taking the delay of $x_d[n] = x[n - M]$ for some number of samples M:

$$y_d[n]=x[n-M]+gx[n-M-N]=y[n-M] \tag{2.3}$$

Using the Z transform, we can also find the frequency response of the basic delay:

$$Y(z)=X(z)+gz^{-N}X(z) \Rightarrow H(z)=\frac{Y(z)}{X(z)}=1+gz^{-N}=\frac{z^N+g}{z^N} \tag{2.4}$$

Since the transfer function $H(z)$ has no poles outside the unit circle, the basic delay must be *stable* in all cases; i.e., a bounded input will always produce a bounded output.

Delay with Feedback

The simple "feedforward" delay is limited in application, producing only a single echo. Most audio delay units also have a feedback control (sometimes called regeneration), which sends a scaled copy of the delay output back to the input, as shown in Figure 2.2. Feedback causes the sound to repeat continuously, and assuming a feedback gain less than 1, the echoes will become quieter each time. Though the echoes are theoretically repeated forever, they will eventually become so quiet as to be below the ambient noise in the system and thus be inaudible.

To find the time domain difference equation for delay with feedback, it helps to consider the signal $d[n]$ at the output of the delay line:

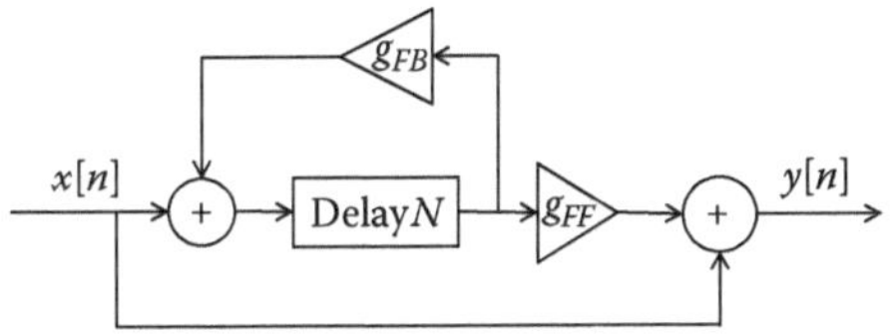

FIGURE 2.2
Diagram of the basic delay unit with feedback.

$$y[n] = x[n] + g_{FF}d[n] \quad \text{where} \quad d[n] = x[n-N] + g_{FB}d[n-N] \tag{2.5}$$

The form of $d[n]$ is similar to the delayed output signal $y[n-N]$, which lets us substitute and write $y[n]$ directly in terms of $x[n]$:

$$\begin{aligned} y[n-N] &= x[n-N] + g_{FF}d[n-N] \\ d[n] &= \frac{g_{FB}}{g_{FF}}y[n-N] + \left(1 - \frac{g_{FB}}{g_{FF}}\right)x[n-N] \\ \Rightarrow y[n] &= g_{FB}y[n-N] + x[n] + (g_{FF} - g_{FB})x[n-N] \end{aligned} \tag{2.6}$$

Taking the Z transform, we can find the frequency domain transfer function:

$$\begin{aligned} Y(z) - g_{FB}z^{-N}Y(z) &= X(Z) + (g_{FF} - g_{FB})z^{-N}X(z) \\ H(z) = \frac{Y(z)}{X(z)} &= \frac{1 + z^{-N}(g_{FF} - g_{FB})}{1 - z^{-N}g_{FB}} = \frac{z^N + g_{FF} - g_{FB}}{z^N - g_{FB}} \end{aligned} \tag{2.7}$$

Thus, the system has poles at the N complex roots of g_{FB}. As with the basic delay, delay with feedback is linear and time invariant. The above transfer function implies the effect will be stable whenever the poles are inside the unit circle, that is, when $|g_{FB}| < 1$. This result aligns with intuition, in that only when the feedback gain is less than 1 will the echoes grow softer over time.

Other Delay Types

Slapback Delay

A *slapback delay* is identical to a basic delay without feedback and with a relatively short delay time, typically between 60 and 150 ms. The delayed copy is perceived as a separate sound that appears immediately after the original sound. A longer delay, where there is a noticeable gap between the original and delayed sounds, is often referred to as an *echo*.

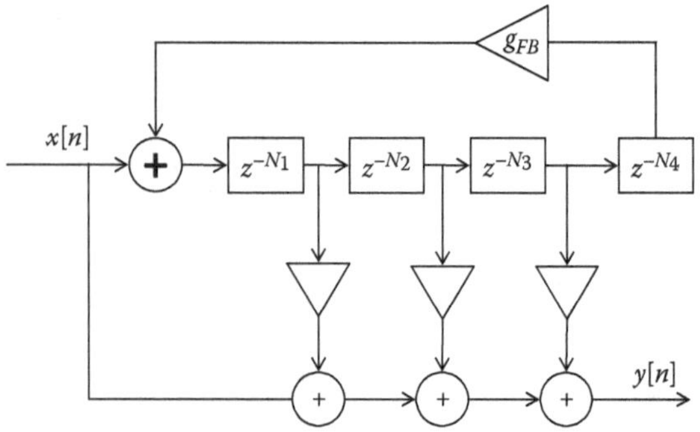

FIGURE 2.3
Flow diagram of a three-tap delay. If the last delay value is zero, and only the third tap is used, the system is equivalent to the basic delay.

Multitap Delay

In a standard delay with or without feedback, the time between copies is always the same, since the output signal is taken after the signal reaches the end of the delay line. Multitap delay provides more flexibility by taking several additional outputs in the middle of the delay line, where the signal has been delayed only part of the total time. This process is known as "tapping" the delay line, following the analogy of adding taps along a water pipe to get water at various locations. Multitap delay is commonly labeled according to the number of taps; for example, a four-tap delay would have four total outputs at various points on the delay line. The delay between each tap is typically not the same, so multitap delays allow more complex patterns to be created that can add interesting rhythmic qualities to an instrument. A diagram of multitap delay is shown in Figure 2.3.

The multitap delay is a more general case of the basic delay design. The multitap delay can be further generalized by allowing feedback from the tap outputs to the beginning of the delay line as well. In this case, care must be taken with the feedback gains to avoid creating an unstable system.

Ping-Pong Delay

Ping-pong delay is a multichannel delay-based effect that produces a bouncing sound from one channel to the other, hence the name. It is implemented as a delay with feedback with at least two distinct delay lines (Figure 2.4). Each delay line may be driven by a separate input, or only one input can be used. The output of each delay line, rather than feeding back to itself, attaches to the input of the opposite delay line. In its two-channel configuration, ping-pong delay produces a sound that bounces between left and right channels in a stereo track.

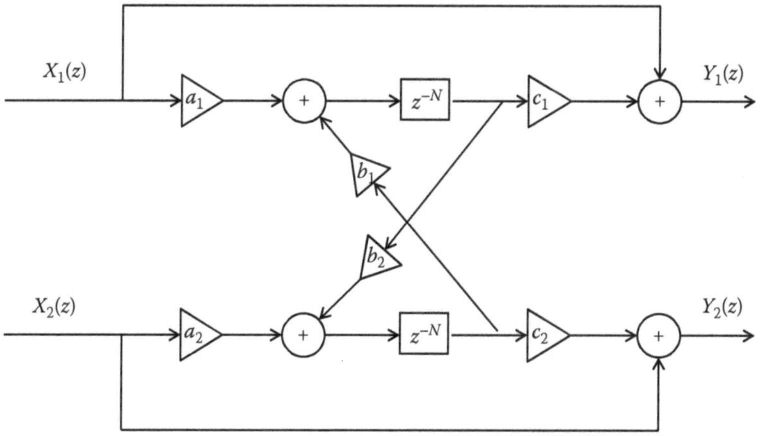

FIGURE 2.4
Flow diagram of a ping-pong delay unit.

Implementation

Basic Delay

Before the days of digital audio, delays were one of the more cumbersome effects to implement, relying on physical audiotape or analog "bucket brigade device" integrated circuits to store and retrieve audio signals. In the digital realm, delay is one of the simplest effects. Audio samples are stored in a preallocated memory *buffer* as they arrive, while previously stored samples are read from the buffer once the delay time has elapsed. In other words, in a simple delay, each sampling period includes one read operation (retrieving the delayed signal) and one write operation (storing the current signal). When the end of the memory buffer is reached, the system should loop around to the beginning of the buffer. In signal processing, this process is known as a *circular buffer,* and it is quite efficient. Programming considerations for circular buffers are discussed in Chapter 13.

Variations

Delay with feedback is implemented identically to a simple delay, but rather than storing the raw input signal in the memory buffer, the sum of the input signal and the delayed, scaled output is stored ($x[n] + g_{FB}x[n-N]$ in Figure 2.2). Ping-pong delay uses two independent memory buffers and, hence, two read operations and two write operations for each sample.

Multitap delay uses a single memory buffer with multiple *read pointers.* At each sample, the current input is written into a slot in the buffer (the *write pointer*), but samples are read back from multiple locations in the buffer (the read pointers). The spacing in memory between the pointers determines the difference in their delay times. This process is further discussed in Chapters 10 and 13.

Delay Line Interpolation

Digital delays are implemented using a memory buffer of discrete audio samples. To change the delay time, we change the distance in the buffer between where samples are written and where they are read back. However, many effects, including the flanger and chorus, require a delay that changes over time. To achieve a smooth variation in delay, rounding to the nearest-integer number of samples is usually not good enough.

Delay becomes more complex when a noninteger number of samples is required. Consider a simple delay with a length of 0.5 samples. From Equation (2.1) we have

$$y[n] = x[n] + gx[n - 0.5] \Rightarrow y[1] = x[1] + gx[0.5] \tag{2.8}$$

However, $x[n]$ is defined only for integer n, so $x[0.5]$ does not exist. Strictly speaking, it is not correct to think of $x[0.5]$ as "halfway between" $x[0]$ and $x[1]$. However we might ask what the result would be if $x[n]$ were converted from discrete to continuous time, shifted half a sampling period, then reconverted to discrete time. An excellent discussion of the underlying mathematics of this process, which is based on sinc functions ($sin(n)/n$), can be found in [3]. Interestingly, exact reconstruction of fractional sample values requires knowledge of the entire signal (i.e., $x[n]$ from $n = -\infty$ to ∞), which is clearly impossible in a real-time audio context.

In practice, fractional delays in audio are implemented using interpolation or allpass filters [7]. Interpolation involves using a weighted combination of surrounding samples to approximate the fractional sample value. Interpolation involves estimating a value of a continuous function, given discrete points, and can be used to estimate values between points on a delay line. Polynomial interpolation is where the function is estimated to be an Nth-order polynomial, $x(t) = c_N t^N + c_{N-1} t^{N-1} + \ldots c_1 t^1 + c_0$.

If values out of the delay line closest to the required point are read, this is zeroth-order, or nearest-neighbor, interpolation. It is probably the least computationally expensive approach. However, the output now has abrupt jumps between values. The quality of this approach is quite poor. Clicking in the output may be heard as the delay length changes, also known as *zipper noise*.

Linear interpolation, or first-order interpolation, is implemented by connecting two known samples by a straight line and then reading the desired value from that line. This is given in the following equation:

$$x(t) = (n + 1 - t)x[n] + (t - n)x[n + 1], \quad n \le t < n + 1 \tag{2.9}$$

Linear interpolation is simple to calculate and produces much better results than nearest-neighbor interpolation. However, it is still only a rough approximation to the ideal continuous time case, and it can introduce noise and aliasing into the signal. In many cases, audibly better quality will be obtained with a more computationally complex interpolation method.

One such method is second-order polynomial interpolation. Consider three successive samples, $x[n-1]$, $x[n]$, and $x[n+1]$. We would typically use these samples if we are trying to interpolate a value of x near $x[n]$. Let's define a new function, $y(\tau) = x(t)$, where $\tau = t - n$. Thus, $x[n-1]$, $x[n]$, and $x[n+1]$ become $y[-1]$, $y[0]$, and $y[1]$. Assuming that these points are on a second-order polynomial, we have the following three equations:

$$\begin{aligned} y[-1] &= c_2(0-1)^2 + c_1(0-1) + c_0 \\ y[0] &= c_2 0^2 + c_1 0 + c_0 \\ y[1] &= c_2(0+1)^2 + c_1(0+1) + c_0 \end{aligned} \tag{2.10}$$

where c_0, c_1, and c_2 are the coefficients of some second-order polynomial. This can be solved to give

$$\begin{aligned} c_0 &= y[0] \\ c_1 &= \left(y[1] - y[-1]\right)/2 \\ c_2 &= \left(y[1] - 2y[0] + y[-1]\right)/2 \end{aligned} \tag{2.11}$$

So our interpolated values are

$$\begin{aligned} x(t) = y(\tau) &= c_2\tau^2 + c_1\tau + c_0 \\ &= \left(x[n+1] - 2x[n] + x[n-1]\right)(t-n)^2/2 + \left(x[n+1] - x[n-1]\right)(t-n)/2 + x[n] \\ &= \frac{(t-n-1)(t-n)x[n-1] - 2(t-n-1)(t-n+1)x[n] + (t-n)(t-n+1)x[n+1]}{2} \end{aligned} \tag{2.12}$$

Cubic interpolation requires more computation, but it can give better results with lower added noise resulting from inaccuracies than the ideal sinc-function case. There are many forms of cubic interpolation; a detailed discussion is available in [8]. The simplest case uses the four samples surrounding the interpolated location:

$$x(t) = c_3(t-n)^3 + c_2(t-n)^2 + c_1(t-n) + c_0 \quad \text{for} \quad n \le t < n+1 \tag{2.13}$$

where the coefficients are given by

$$\begin{aligned} c_3 &= -x[n-1] + x[n] - x[n+1] + x[n+2] \\ c_2 &= x[n-1] - x[n] - a_0 \\ c_1 &= x[n+1] - x[n-1] \\ c_0 &= x[n] \end{aligned} \tag{2.14}$$

Code Example

The following C++ code fragment, adapted from the code that accompanies this book, shows the implementation of a basic delay with feedback, and without interpolation.

```
// Variables whose values are set externally:
int numSamples;       // How many audio samples to process
float *channelData;  // Array of samples, length numSamples
float *delayData;     // Our own circular buffer of samples
int delayBufLength;  // Length of our delay buffer in samples
int dpr, dpw;         // Read/write pointers into delay buffer

// User-adjustable effect parameters:
float dryMix_;        // Level of the dry (undelayed) signal
float wetMix_;        // Level of the wet (delayed) signal
float feedback_;      // Feedback level (0 if no feedback)

for (int i = 0; i < numSamples; ++i)
{
    const float in = channelData[i];
    float out = 0.0;

    // The output is the input plus the contents of the
    // delay buffer (weighted by the mix levels).

    out = (dryMix_ * in + wetMix_ * delayData[dpr]);

    // Store the current information in the delay buffer.
    // delayData[dpr] is the delay sample we just read, i.e.
    // what came out of the buffer. delayData[dpw] is what
    // we write to the buffer, i.e. what goes in

    delayData[dpw] = in + (delayData[dpr] * feedback_);

    if (++dpr >= delayBufLength)
        dpr = 0;
```

```
    if (++dpw >= delayBufLength)
        dpw = 0;

    // Store output sample in buffer, replacing the input
    channelData[i] = out;
}
```

This example assumes that a single channel of input audio data is present in the `channelData` array. In a real-time effect, `channelData` will hold only the most recent block of audio samples, rather than the entire input signal. To implement the delay, we write each input sample into `delayData` at a position indicated by the write pointer `dpw`, while reading a delayed sample previously written into the buffer using read pointer `dpr`.

`delayData` is a circular buffer: after each sample is processed, `dpr` and `dpw` are incremented, and when either of them reaches the end of the buffer, it is reset back to position 0. Notice that there is no parameter for the delay length in this code example. It is the difference between the read and write pointers `dpr` and `dpw` that determines the delay length. These values are initialized elsewhere in the effect. More details and a more extensive code example can be found in Chapter 13.

Applications

Delays are a very common effect in music production. Even a single basic delay, without feedback, has many uses. A common use is to combine an instrument's sound with a short echo (for example, around 50–100 ms) to create a doubling effect. This can create a wider, more lively sound than the original single version. If the original and delayed copies are panned differently in a stereo mix, short delays can also help make the mix sound "bigger." More complex arrangements including feedback and multiple taps can start to simulate the sound of a reverb unit, though reverb (covered in Chapter 11) typically creates more complex patterns than can be simulated with simple delays.

Longer delays become less subtle once the original and delayed copies are easily perceived as two separate acoustic events. One common trick is to synchronize the delay time with the tempo of the music, such that the delayed copies appear in rhythm with the track [9]. If the delay time is especially long, for example, equal to one or more bars of music, a musician can play over himself or herself and develop elaborate harmonies and textures.

Sampler and looper pedals are fundamentally based on the delay, with additional features to be able to define the start and end of an audio segment, which then can loop continuously. Other features are possible, including the ability to mix additional sounds onto a loop that was previously recorded, to play a loop backwards, or to have multiple simultaneous loops. Some

FRIPPERTRONICS AND CRAFTY GUITARISTS

Robert Fripp (King Crimson, The League of Crafty Guitarists, League of Gentlemen, solo artist…) is known as one of the greatest and most influential guitarists of all time. Evolving out of his work with Brian Eno in 1973, he devised a tape looping technique to layer his guitar sounds in real-time. It used two reel-to-reel tape recorders. The tape traveled from the supply reel of one recorder to the take-up reel of the second one. Then the tape from the second machine is fed back to the first one, and the delay can be changed by adjusting the distance between the two machines. Furthermore, it also provided a recording of the complete overlayed recording, and could be used in live performance. Fripp's girlfriend later named this technique 'Frippertronics,' though we would describe it as a time varying delay with feedback. Also among Robert Fripp's more unusual contributions are many of the sounds for the Windows Vista operating system.

Many other famous guitarists are also known for music technology innovations. For instance, Tom Scholz of the band Boston designed a wide range of novel guitar effects devices, including the Rockman amplifier. But one of the most famous guitarists is also one of the people who most influenced music technology, Les Paul. His solid body electric guitar designs were some of the first and most popular, and he is credited with many innovations in multitrack recording.

standard delay pedals will include basic looper capability, though often limited to a single loop of a few seconds at most.

Vibrato Simulation

Vibrato is defined as a small, quasi-periodic variation in the pitch of a tone. Traditionally, vibrato is not an audio effect but rather a technique used by singers and instrumentalists. On the violin, for example, vibrato is produced by rhythmically rocking the finger back and forth on the fingerboard, slightly changing the length of the string. However, vibrato can be added to any audio signal through the use of *modulated delay lines*.

Vibrato is characterized by its *frequency* (how often the pitch changes) and *width* (total amount of pitch variation). On acoustic instruments, especially wind instruments, vibrato is often accompanied by some degree of amplitude modulation or tremolo (Chapter 5), with the pitch and amplitude of the signal changing in synchrony.

Theory

The vibrato effect works by changing the playback speed of the sampled audio. The effect of playback speed is familiar to many listeners: playing a sound faster raises its pitch, and playing it slower lowers the pitch. To add a vibrato, then, the playback speed needs to be periodically varied to be faster or slower than normal.

Implementation of the vibrato effect is based on a modulated delay line, a delay line whose delay length changes over time under the control of a *low-frequency oscillator* (LFO), as shown in Figure 2.5. Unlike other delay effects, the input signal $x[n]$ is not mixed into the output.

Delay alone does not introduce a pitch shift. Suppose the length $M[n]$ of the delay line does not change. Then at every sampling period n, exactly one sample $x[n]$ goes in and one sample $y[n - M]$ comes out. The sound will be delayed but otherwise identical to the original. But now suppose that the length $M[n]$ decreases each sample by an amount Δm:

$$M[n] = M_{\text{max}} - (\Delta m)n \tag{2.15}$$

Examining the output of the delay line, we can see that each new input sample n moves the output by $(1 + \Delta m)$ samples:

$$y[n] = x\left[n - M_{\text{max}} + (\Delta m)n\right] = x\left[(1 + \Delta m)n - M_{\text{max}}\right] \tag{2.16}$$

In other words, the playback rate from the buffer is $(1 + \Delta m)$ times the input rate. Correspondingly, the frequencies in the input signal $x[n]$ will all be scaled upwards by a factor of $(1 + \Delta m)$. For similar reasons, if the length of the delay line *increased* each sample ($\Delta m < 0$), the frequencies of the output signal would all be scaled down compared to the original.

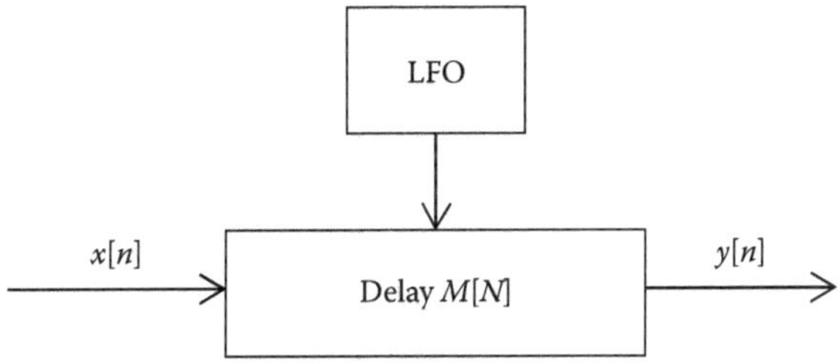

FIGURE 2.5
Modulated delay and pitch shift.

Notice that the pitch shift is sensitive only to the change in delay Δm, not its initial value M_{max}. We can generalize to write that pitch shift is dependent on the *derivative* (or, in discrete time, *first difference*) of delay length, with increasing length producing lower pitch:

$$f_{ratio}[n] = \left(\frac{f_{out}}{f_{in}}\right)[n] = 1 - \left(M[n] - M[n-1]\right) \tag{2.17}$$

To create a vibrato effect, then, the delay is periodically lengthened and shortened.

Interpolation

Strictly speaking, Equation (2.16) is defined only for integer samples of x, i.e., when $(1 + \Delta m)n - M_{max}$ is an integer. In general, this is not always the case for a modulated delay line where delay lengths change gradually from sample to sample, so *interpolation* must be used to approximate noninteger values of x. See the earlier section on fractional delay for a more detailed discussion of interpolation and its implementation.

Implementation

Though Equation (2.17) suggests that arbitrary pitch shifts are possible by choosing the rate Δm at which the delay length varies, real-time audio effects are limited by two practical considerations. First, real-time effects must be *causal*, which implies that the delay length $M[n]$ must be nonnegative. If we want to increase the pitch of a sound, this means that for any finite initial delay M_{max}, $M[n]$ will eventually reach 0, at which point it will no longer be possible to maintain the pitch shift. The second consideration is that computer systems have finite amounts of memory. To decrease the pitch of a sound, $M[n]$ must steadily increase, which requires an ever greater memory buffer to hold the delayed samples. Because the output is being played more slowly than the input, eventually it will be impossible to hold all the intervening audio in memory.

To satisfy these two considerations, the *average change* in delay length over time must be 0. In a vibrato effect, the delay length varies periodically around a fixed central value, producing periodic pitch modulation, but a sustained increase or decrease in pitch is not possible. In Chapter 8, we will examine a technique for real-time pitch shifting using the phase vocoder.

Low-Frequency Oscillator

The delay effect described earlier can be characterized as a linear, time-invariant filter. But many of the audio effects that we will encounter are not time invariant. That is, the effect acts like a filter, but now the output

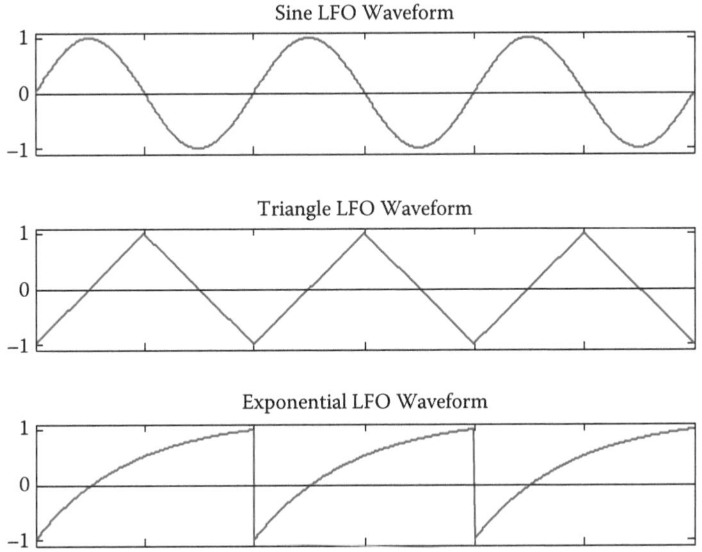

FIGURE 2.6
Three commonly used low-frequency oscillator (LFO) waveforms.

as a function of input depends on the time or, in discrete form, the sample number. This is most often accomplished by driving the effect (making some parameters explicitly a function of time) with a low-frequency oscillator (LFO). This is the case for vibrato and the other delay line-based effects described in the following sections.

LFOs do not have a formal definition, but they may be considered to be any periodic signals with a frequency below 20 Hz. They are used to vary delay lines or as modulating signals in many synthesizers, and they will be used in many of the effects featured later in the book. Like their audio frequency counterparts, LFOs typically use periodic waveforms such as sine, triangle, square, and sawtooth waves. However, any type of waveform is possible, including user-defined waveforms read from a wave table.

Figure 2.6 depicts three of the most commonly used waveforms. Different LFO waveforms are preferred for different effects. In the vibrato effect, the delay length is typically controlled by a sinusoidal LFO:

$$M[n] = M_{avg} + W\sin(2\pi nf/f_s) \tag{2.18}$$

where M_{avg} is the average delay (for real-time effects, it is chosen so that $M[n]$ is always nonnegative), W is the width of the delay modulation, f is the LFO frequency in Hz, and f_s is the sample rate. The rate of change from one sample to the next can be approximated by the continuous time derivative:

$$
\begin{aligned}
M[n] - M[n-1] &= W\left[\sin\left(2\pi n f / f_s\right) - \sin\left(2\pi (n-1) f / f_s\right)\right] \\
&\approx 2\pi f W \cos\left(2\pi n f / f_s\right)
\end{aligned}
\tag{2.19}
$$

We can then find the frequency shift for the vibrato effect:

$$
f_{ratio}[n] = 1 - \left(M[n] - M[n-1]\right) \approx 1 - 2\pi f W \cos\left(2\pi n f / f_s\right) \tag{2.20}
$$

Notice that in the implementation of the LFO, W indicates the amount that the delay length changes, not the amount of pitch shift. Equation (2.20) shows that pitch shift depends on both W and f, such that for the same amount of delay modulation, a faster LFO will produce more pitch shift. As Figure 2.7 demonstrates, this is an expected result, since increasing the frequency of a sine wave while maintaining its amplitude will result in a greater derivative.

Given the desired amount of maximum pitch shift and an LFO frequency, we can calculate the approximate required amount of delay variation:

$$
W = \left(f_{ratio}[n] - 1\right) / 2\pi f \tag{2.21}
$$

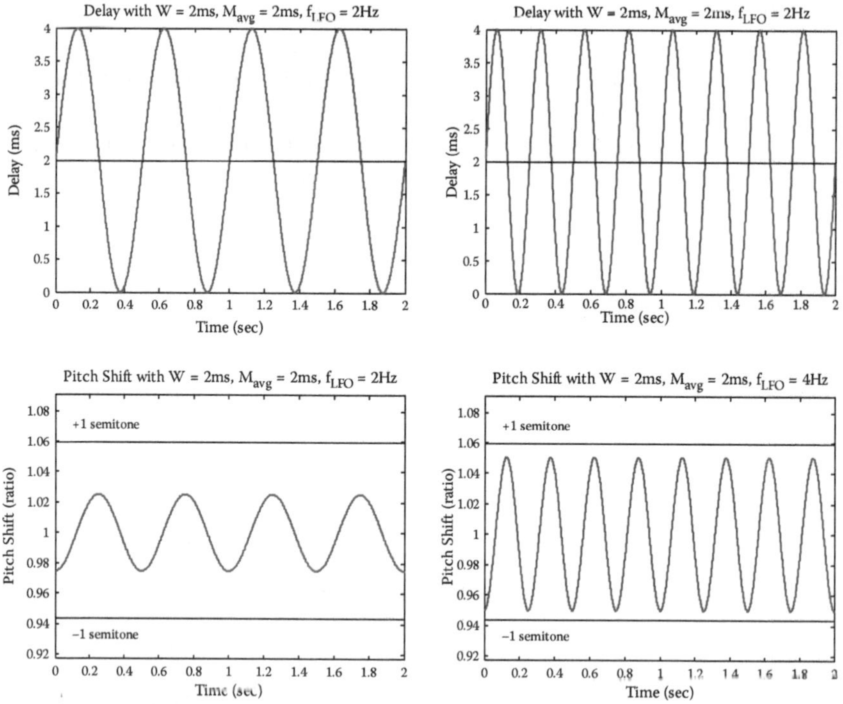

FIGURE 2.7
Vibrato in operation. The LFO waveform on top and the pitch shift on bottom, for LFO frequency 2 Hz (left) and 4 Hz (right).

From this, we can also find the average delay $M_{avg} \geq W$ needed to keep the effect causal. In all but the most extreme cases, M_{avg} will be small enough that no delay will be perceptible at the output of the vibrato effect.

Parameters

The vibrato effect is completely characterized by *LFO frequency, LFO waveform,* and *vibrato (pitch shift) width.* The pitch shift parameter is used to calculate the amount of delay modulation, which is what ultimately produces the vibrato effect. A typical violin vibrato has a frequency on the order of 6 Hz, with frequency variation of around 1% (i.e., approximately 0.99 to 1.01 in frequency ratio) [1]. With a sinusoidal LFO, these settings would produce a delay variation W of 0.265 ms in either direction. By way of comparison, two notes a semitone apart differ in frequency by $\sqrt[12]{2} \approx 1.059$, or 5.9%.

Sinusoidal waveforms are best for emulating normal instrumental vibrato, but other waveforms can be used for special effects. For example, a triangle waveform (Figure 2.8a) has only two slopes (rising and falling), and accordingly, the pitch will jump back and forth between two fixed

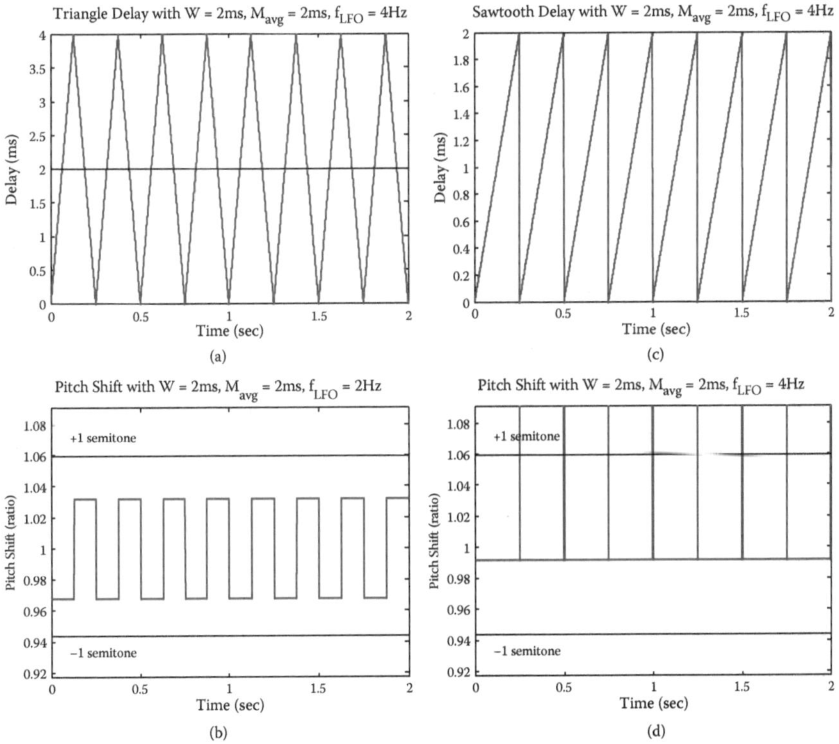

FIGURE 2.8
Triangular (a) and sawtooth LFOs (b), with corresponding pitch shift (c and d).

values (Figure 2.8c). A rising sawtooth wave (Figure 2.8b) approximates a pitch-lowering effect since the derivative of delay length is usually positive. However, the periodic discontinuities (Figure 2.8d) in the sawtooth waveform produce artifacts that degrade the quality of the result, so this technique is not normally used for pitch shifting.

Code Example

The following C++ code fragment, adapted from the code that accompanies this book, implements a vibrato with sinusoidal LFO and linear interpolation.

```
// Variables whose values are set externally:
int numSamples;       // How many audio samples to process
float *channelData; // Array of samples, length numSamples
float *delayData;    // Our own circular buffer of samples
int delayBufLength; // Length of our delay buffer in samples
int dpw;              // Write pointer into the delay buffer
float ph;             // Current LFO phase, always between 0-1
float inverseSampleRate; // 1/f_s, where f_s = sample rate

// User-adjustable effect parameters:
float frequency_;    // Frequency of the LFO
float sweepWidth_;   // Width of the LFO in samples

for (int i = 0; i < numSamples; ++i)
{
    const float in = channelData[i];
    float interpolatedSample = 0.0;

    // Recalculate the read pointer position with respect to
    // the write pointer. A more efficient implementation
    // might increment the read pointer based on the
    // derivative of the LFO without running the whole
    // equation again, but this makes the operation clearer.
    float currentDelay = sweepWidth_ * (0.5f +
                              0.5f * sinf(2.0 * M_PI * ph));

    // Subtract 3 samples to the delay pointer to make sure
    // we have enough previous samples to interpolate with
    float dpr = fmodf((float)dpw
                  - (float)(currentDelay * getSampleRate())
                  + (float)delayBufLength - 3.0,
                  (float)delayBufLength);

    // Use linear interpolation to read a fractional index
    // into the buffer. Find the fraction by which the read
    // pointer sits between two samples and use this to
    // adjust weights of the samples
```

```
    float fraction = dpr - floorf(dpr);
    int previousSample = (int)floorf(dpr);
    int nextSample = (previousSample + 1) % delayBufLength;
    interpolatedSample = fraction*delayData[nextSample]
        + (1.0f-fraction)*delayData[previousSample];

    // Store the current information in the delay buffer.
    delayData[dpw] = in;

    // Increment the write pointer at a constant rate. The
    // read pointer will move at different rates depending
    // on the settings of the LFO, the delay and the
    // sweep width.
    if (++dpw >= delayBufLength)
        dpw = 0;

    // Store the output sample in the buffer, replacing the
    // input. In the vibrato effect, the delayed sample is
    // the only component of the output (no mixing with the
    // dry signal)
    channelData[i] = interpolatedSample;

    // Update the LFO phase, keeping it in the range 0-1
    ph += frequency_*inverseSampleRate;
    if(ph >= 1.0)
        ph -= 1.0;
}
```

The code exhibits many similarities to the basic delay in the previous section. One notable difference is that the read pointer `dpr` is now fractional, taking noninteger values. Accordingly, `dpr` cannot be directly used to read the circular buffer `delayData`, since arrays in C++ can be accessed only at integer indices. In this example, the variable `fraction` holds the noninteger component of the read pointer `dpr`; it is used to calculate a weighted average between the two nearest samples in the circular buffer (`previousSample` and `nextSample`). Notice how the index of the sample following `dpr` is calculated:

```
int nextSample = (previousSample + 1)% delayBufLength;
```

The % sign is a *modulo operator.* This means that if the expression (`previousSample + 1`) exceeds `delayBufLength`, it will be wrapped around to the beginning of the buffer. The use of modulo arithmetic is needed to implement a circular buffer.

For the vibrato effect, no feedback or mixing with the original signal is used, so many of the parameters in the basic delay example are not found here. In the complete code example that accompanies this book, a choice of LFO waveforms and interpolation types is offered.

Applications

Vibrato, when used by vocalists or instrumentalists, can add a sense of warmth and life to a musical line. The width and frequency of vibrato and their evolution over time are important expressive decisions for many performers. Vibrato can also help an instrument or voice stand out from an ensemble. A single musical note will contain energy at discrete, harmonically related frequencies, but by varying the pitch back and forth, a single note can use more of the frequency spectrum.

Vibrato is sometimes used to cover slight errors in pitch, as it is easier to perceive a steady pitched sound as being out of tune than one containing vibrato. However, the use of vibrato to cover pitch errors is generally considered poor musical practice.

The vibrato audio effect is not as flexible as a performer's natural vibrato, since the LFO operates at a constant rate and width regardless of the musical material. Also, a simple vibrato implementation does not synchronize with the beginnings and endings of individual notes as a performer would. More advanced implementations do, though, such as can be found in some synthesizers.

Though it is possible to imagine a vibrato effect with a pedal or other control to give the user more flexibility over the LFO, this is rarely seen in practice. Nonetheless, even a fixed-frequency vibrato can add warmth and body to the sound of an instrument, especially when used with reverberation.

Flanging

Flanging is a delay-based effect originally developed using analog tape machines 50 years ago (see [1] and references therein). It refers to the flange or outer rim of the open-reel tape recorders in common use in studios at the time. To create the flanging effect, two tape machines are set up to play the same tape at the same time. Their outputs are mixed together equally, as shown in Figure 2.9.

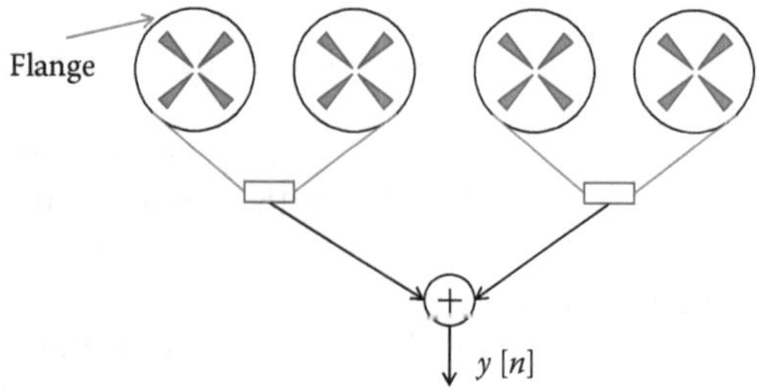

FIGURE 2.9
Two tape machines configured to produce a flanging effect.

KEN'S FLANGER

Flanging is an unusual name for an audio effect, and it is certainly not a common word in music or signal processing. The flange refers to a rim or edge, especially on a tape reel. Producers were known to manipulate the flange of a tape reel to achieve nice effects on many early tape recordings. One of the earliest known examples of producing a sound similar to the modern flanger is "The Big Hurt" by Tony Fisher, recorded in 1959.

But the origin of the name of the audio effect is an unusual one, and has been well documented by Beatles' historians Bill Biersach and Mark Lewisohn [10].

In 1966, the Beatles recorded *Revolver* at Abbey Road. The studio technician Ken Townsend later said that "they would relate what sounds they wanted and we then had to go away and come back with a solution … they often liked to double-track their vocals, but it's quite a laborious process and they soon got fed up with it. So, after one particularly trying night-time session doing just that, I was driving home and suddenly had an idea."

What Townsend devised was not the modern flanging, but the closely related chorus effect, or artificial double tracking (ADT). But it is implemented using the same approach, slowing down and speeding up a tape machine. The seemingly random variations in speed (and hence also pitch) mimic the effect of a singer trying to harmonize with the original.

John Lennon loved the effect, and asked George Martin, the Beatles' producer, to explain it. As Martin recalled, "I knew he'd never understand it, so I said, 'Now listen, it's very simple. We take the original image and split it through a double vibrocated sploshing flange with double negative feedback … .' He said, 'You're pulling my leg, aren't you?' I replied, 'Well, let's flange it again and see.' From that moment on, whenever he wanted it he'd ask for his voice to be 'flanged,' or call out for 'Ken's flanger'" [11].

If the two machines played perfectly in unison, the result would simply be a stronger version of the same signal. Instead, the operator lightly touches the flange of one of the tape machines, slowing it down and thereby lowering the pitch. This action also causes the tape machine to fall slightly behind its counterpart, creating a delay between them. The operator then releases the flange and repeats the process on the other machine, which causes the delay to gradually disappear and then grow in the opposite direction. The process is repeated periodically, alternately pressing each flange.

If too much delay accumulates between the machines, the mixed output will no longer be heard as a single signal but as two distinct copies. For this reason, the delay must be kept well below the threshold of echo perception (see Chapter 9), i.e., only a few milliseconds in each direction, so the result is heard as a single sound rather than two separate sounds.

The flanging effect has been described as a kind of "whoosh" that passes through the sound. The effect has also been compared to the sound of a jet passing overhead, in that the direct signal and the reflection from the ground arrive at a varying relative delay. And when the delay is modulated rapidly, an audible Doppler shift may be heard [1] (see Chapter 10).

Theory

Principle of Operation

The flanger is based on the principle of constructive and destructive interference. If a sine wave signal is delayed and then added to the original, the sum of the two signals will look quite different depending on the length of the delay. At one extreme, when the two signals perfectly align in phase, the output signal will be double the magnitude of the input. This is *constructive interference.* At the other extreme, when the delay causes the two signals to be perfectly out of phase, they cancel each other out: an increase in one signal is precisely balanced by a decrease in the other, so they will sum to zero. This is *destructive interference.*

Typical audio signals contain energy at a large number of frequencies. For any given delay value, some frequencies will add destructively and cancel out (*notches* in the frequency response) and others will add constructively (*peaks*). Peaks and notches by themselves do not make a flanger: it is the *motion* of these notches in the frequency spectrum that produces the characteristic flanging sound. As the following sections show, the motion of the peaks and notches is achieved by continuously changing the amount of delay (Figure 2.10).

Basic Flanger

A block diagram of a basic flanger is shown in Figure 2.11. Its operation is closely related to the basic delay discussed previously, with the key difference that the amount of delay varies over time. It is also closely related to the vibrato that was depicted in Figure 2.5. The input/output relation for the flanger can be expressed in the time domain as

$$y[n] = x[n] + gx\left[n - M[n]\right] \tag{2.22}$$

The delay length $M[n]$ varies under the control of a separate low-frequency oscillator, discussed in the following sections. This structure is known as a

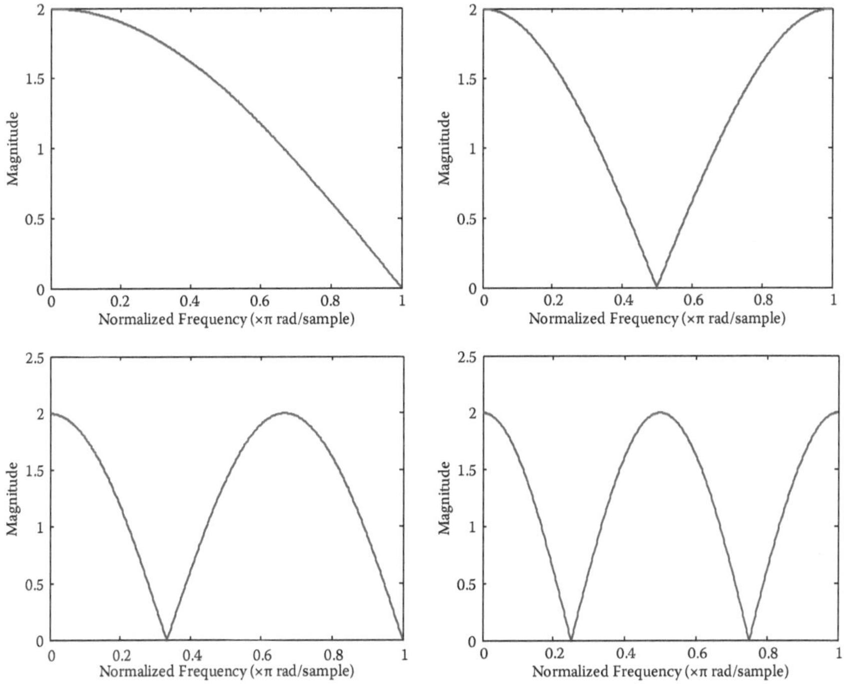

FIGURE 2.10
The magnitude response of a flanger with depth set to 1 and delay times set to one, two, three, and four samples.

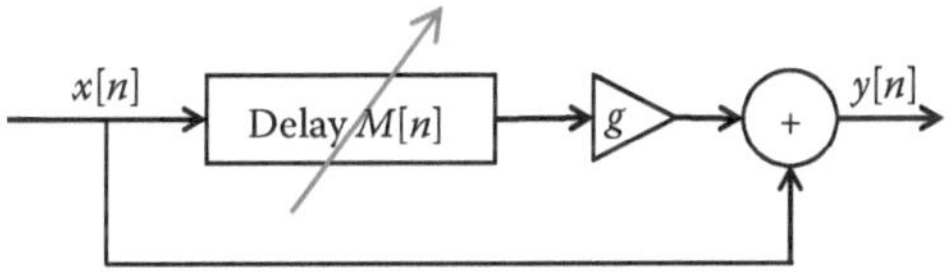

FIGURE 2.11
Block diagram of a basic flanger without feedback. The delay length $M[n]$ changes over time.

feedforward comb filter, since the delayed signals feed forward from the input to the output (with no feedback). To see why this difference equation results in a comb filter, we should consider its Z transform and transfer function:

$$Y(z) = X(z) + gz^{-M[n]}X(z) \Rightarrow H(z) = \frac{Y(z)}{X(z)} = 1 + gz^{-M[n]} \tag{2.23}$$

To find the frequency response of the flanger for each frequency ω, we substitute $e^{j\omega}$ for z and find the magnitude of the transfer function:

$$
\begin{aligned}
H(e^{j\omega}) &= 1 + ge^{-j\omega M[n]} = 1 + g\cos(\omega M[n]) - jg\sin(\omega M[n]) \\
\left|H(e^{j\omega})\right| &= \sqrt{\left(1+ge^{-j\omega M[n]}\right)\left(1+ge^{j\omega M[n]}\right)} = \sqrt{1+2g\cos(\omega M[n])+g^2}
\end{aligned}
\tag{2.24}
$$

Notice that the frequency response is periodic: for $g > 0$, we have M peaks in the frequency response, located at the frequencies when the cosine term reaches its maximum value:

$$\omega_p = 2\pi p/M \quad \text{where} \quad p = 0, 1, 2, \ldots, M-1 \tag{2.25}$$

Likewise, for $g > 0$, there are M notches (minima) in the frequency response. These are located where the cosine term reaches its minimum value:

$$\omega_n = (2n+1)\pi/M \quad \text{where} \quad n = 0, 1, 2, \ldots, M-1 \tag{2.26}$$

The pattern of peaks and notches is shown in Figure 2.12. The equations show that a larger delay $M[n]$ produces more notches and a lower frequency for the first notch. As $M[n]$ varies, the notches sweep up and down through

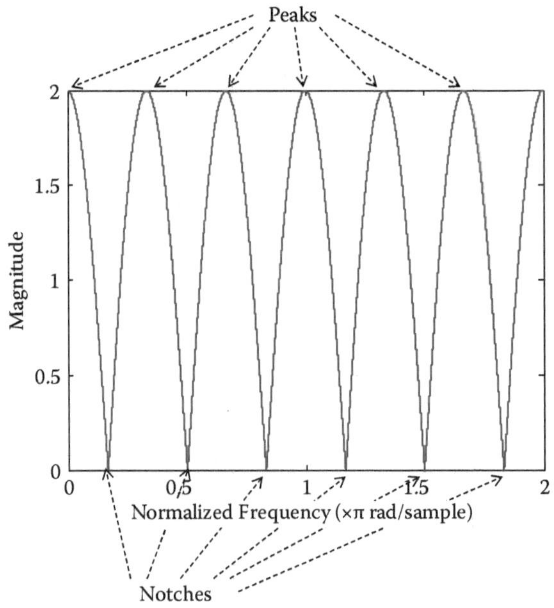

FIGURE 2.12
The frequency response of a simple flanger with a six-sample delay and depth set to 1. The locations of the six peaks and six notches over the whole frequency range from 0 to 2π are shown.

the frequency range. The notches are regularly spaced at intervals of f_s/M Hz where f_s is the sampling rate. Their pictorial resemblance in Figure 2.12 to the teeth of a comb is what gives this structure the term *comb filter.* Chapter 4 will examine *phasing,* an effect that produces similar moving notches in the frequency response that are not regularly spaced.

The depth of the notches depends strongly on the gain g of the delayed signal. When $g = 0$, the frequency response is perfectly flat, as we would expect since $g = 0$ corresponds to no delayed signal. When g is between 0 and 1 (or greater than 1), notches appear in the spectrum, but their depth is finite and depends on the value of g. When $g = 1$, the notches are infinitely deep, as the frequency response exactly equals 0 at the notch frequencies w_n. For this reason, $g = 1$ produces the most pronounced flanging effect.

Low-Frequency Oscillator

The characteristic sound of the flanger comes from the *motion* of regularly spaced notches in the frequency response. For this reason it is critical that the length of the delay $M[n]$ changes over time. Typically, $M[n]$ is varied using a low-frequency oscillator (LFO). The LFO can be one of several waveforms, including sine, triangle, or sawtooth, with sine being the most common choice. Typical delay lengths for the flanger range from 1 to 10 ms, corresponding to notch intervals ranging from 1000 Hz down to 100 Hz. Further details on LFO parameters are discussed in the "Parameters" section below.

Flanger with Feedback

Just as feedback could be added to the basic delay, some flangers incorporate a feedback path that routes the scaled output of the delay line back to its input, as shown in Figure 2.13. Feedback on the flanger is also sometimes referred to as *regeneration.* As with the delay effect with feedback, using feedback in the flanger will result in many successive copies of the input signal spaced several milliseconds apart and gradually decaying over time (Figure 2.14). However, since the delay times in the flanger (typically less than 20 ms) are below the threshold of echo perception (roughly 50–70 ms), these copies are not heard as independent sounds but as coloration or filtering of the input sound.

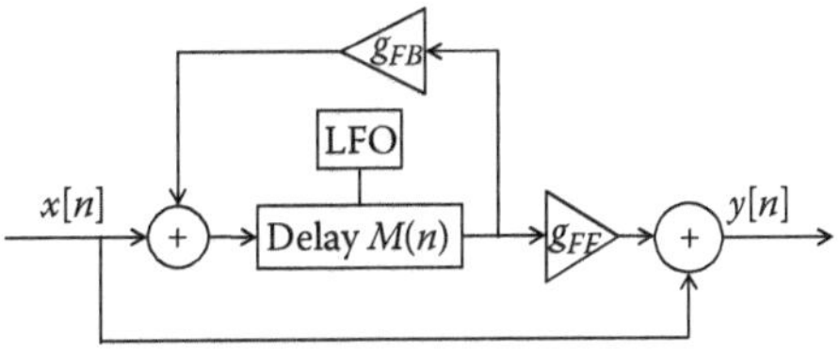

FIGURE 2.13
Flanger with feedback. Delay in all flangers is controlled by a low-frequency oscillator (LFO).

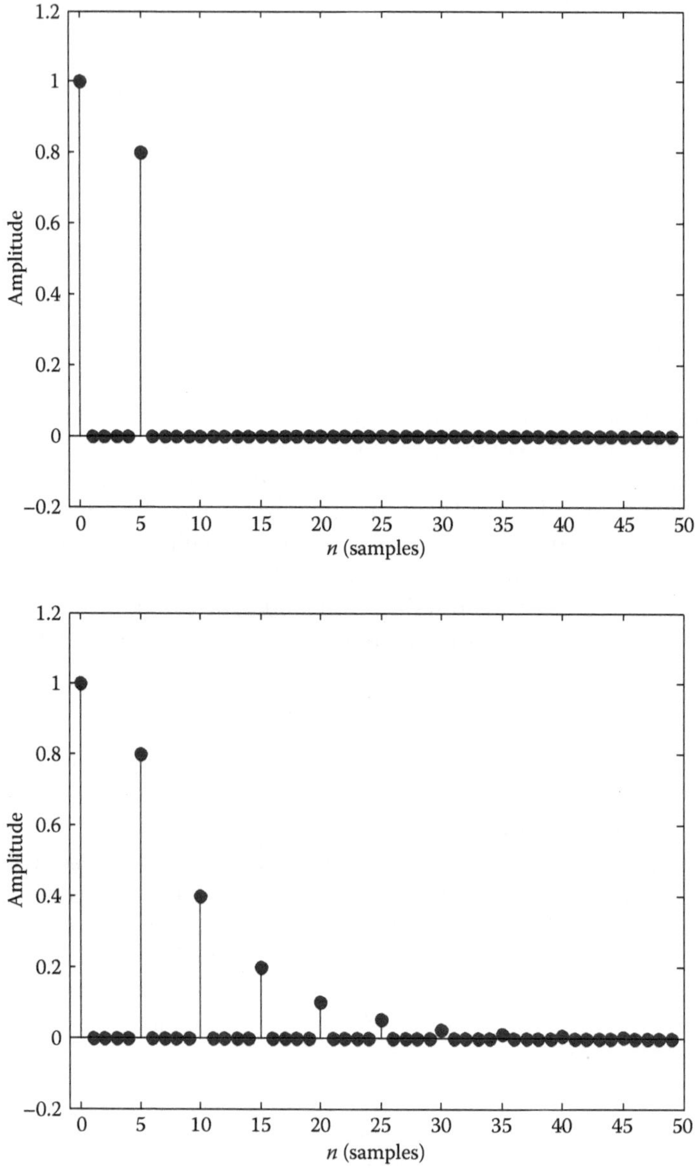

FIGURE 2.14
Impulse responses for a comb filter (i.e., delay effect) with a five-sample delay. On top, $g = 0.8$ and no feedback. On bottom, $g_{FF} = 0.8$ and $g_{FB} = 0.5$.

The difference equation and frequency response for a flanger with feedback can be derived similarly to the delay with feedback:

$$y[n] = g_{FB}y[n - M[n]] + x[n] + (g_{FF} - g_{FB})x[n - M[n]]$$
$$H(z) = \frac{Y(z)}{X(z)} = \frac{1 + z^{-M[n]}(g_{FF} - g_{FB})}{1 - z^{-M[n]}g_{FB}} = \frac{z^{M[n]} + g_{FF} - g_{FB}}{z^{M[n]} - g_{FB}} \quad (2.27)$$

We can see that when the feedback gain $g_{FB} = 0$, these terms exactly match the basic flanger without feedback, as expected. In addition to the zeros of $H(z)$, which are similarly located to the flanger without feedback, the transfer function has poles at the complex roots of g_{FB}. If $g_{FB} < 1$, these will remain inside the unit circle and the system will be *stable*. This is an intuitive result: feedback gains less than 1 mean that the delayed copies of the sound will gradually decay, where a gain of 1 or more means they will grow (or at least persist with significant amplitude) indefinitely.

The effect of feedback is to make the peaks and notches sharper and more pronounced. Its sound is often described as intense or metallic, and as the feedback gain approaches 1, the pitch f_s/M resulting from the delay line can overwhelm the rest of the sound.

Stereo Flanging

A stereo flanger is constructed of two monophonic flangers that are identical in all settings except the *phase* of the low-frequency oscillator. Typically, the two oscillators are in *quadrature phase,* where one leads the other by 90°. In a stereo flanger, the same signal can be used as the input to both channels, or separate signals can be used for each input. The outputs are typically panned fully to the left and right of a stereo mix.

Properties

Because the flanger (with or without feedback) is composed entirely of delays and multiplication, it is a *linear* effect. However, because the properties of the delay line vary over time independently of the input signal, it is *time variant,* unlike the standard delay: shifting the input signal in time by N samples does not necessarily produce the identical output shifted by N samples, since the delay line length may have changed. The basic flanger is always *stable,* where the flanger with feedback is stable if and only if the feedback gain $g_{FB} < 1$.

Common Parameters

The typical flanger effect contains several controls that the musician can adjust.

Depth (or Mix)

The *depth* control affects the amount of delayed signal that is mixed in with the original. $g = 0$ produces no effect, whereas $g = 1$ produces the most pronounced flanging effect. Higher depth settings ($g > 1$) produce a louder overall sound due to scaling up the delayed signal, but the flanging effect becomes less pronounced: only when the original and delayed copies exactly match in amplitude can perfect cancelation of the notch frequencies occur.

Delay and Sweep Width

The term *delay* is potentially misleading in the flanger since the length of the delay line varies over time under the control of a low-frequency oscillator. The delay control parameter on a flanger affects the minimum amount of delay $M[n]$. The value of the LFO is added to produce larger time-varying values. *Sweep width* controls the total amplitude of the low-frequency oscillator, such that the maximum delay time is given by the sum of the delay and sweep width controls (Figure 2.15).

As the delay is decreased, the first notch becomes higher in frequency. The delay control thus sets the highest frequency the first notch will reach. If it is set to zero, the notches will disappear entirely when the LFO reaches its minimum value: when the original and delayed signals are exactly aligned, no cancelation will take place at any frequency. Similarly, the sum of the delay and sweep width controls determines the lowest frequency the first notch will reach.

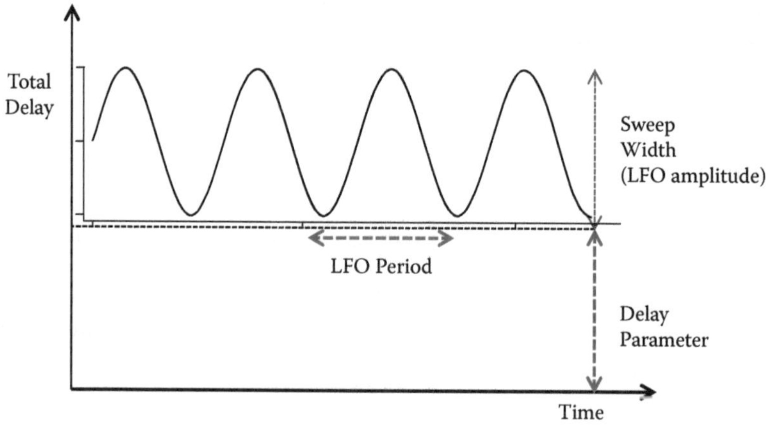

FIGURE 2.15
The maximum delay is the sum of the *sweep width* and *delay* parameters. The delay changes over time according to the *sweep rate*.

Speed and Waveform

These controls affect the behavior of the LFO controlling the delay length. The *speed* control sets the LFO frequency and typically ranges from 0.1 Hz (10 s per cycle) to 10 Hz. *Waveform* is usually chosen from one of several predefined values, including sine, triangle, sawtooth, or exponential (triangular in log frequency). Many flangers do not offer this control and always use a sinusoidal LFO. In this case, the total delay $M[n]$ is given by

$$M[n] = M_0 + \frac{M_W}{2}\left[1 + \sin\left(2\pi f_{LFO} n / f_s\right)\right] \tag{2.28}$$

where M_0 (in samples) is given by the delay control, M_W (in samples) is given by the sweep width control, f_{LFO} (in Hertz) is given by the speed control, and f_s (in Hertz) is the sampling frequency. We can see that the value of $M[n]$ varies from M_0 at minimum to $M_0 + M_W$ at maximum, consistent with the expected behavior of these controls.

Feedback (or Regeneration)

The basic flanger has only a feedforward path, in which the delayed signal is added to the original. In a flanger with feedback, the *feedback/regeneration* control sets the gain g_{FB} between output and input of the delay line. Possible values are in the range [0, 1), i.e., strictly less than 1, to maintain stability. In practice, values close to 1 are rarely used except for special effects. Even when the system is mathematically stable, large gains at the peaks can result in clipping distortion depending on the level of the input.

Inverted Mode (or Phase)

On some flangers, the feedforward gain g or g_{FF} can be altered in polarity. *Inverted mode* is typically selected with a switch; when activated, g ranges from 0 to –1 instead of 0 to 1, in which case, the peaks and notches in the frequency response will trade places; the lowest peak will occur at $f = f_s/2M$ Hz and the lowest notch at $f = 0$ (DC). Because of the notch at DC, the bass response in the inverted mode is poor, producing a thinner sound unless M is very large (which reduces the frequency of the lowest peak). The different color of the inverted mode flanger can be useful in some musical situations.

Implementation

Buffer Allocation

The flanger, like all delay-based effects, is typically implemented digitally using *circular buffers* (see Chapter 13). Memory allocation and deallocation are highly time-consuming in comparison to basic audio calculations. Since the length of the delay changes with the phase of the LFO, the buffer is preallocated to be large enough to accommodate the maximum amount of delay at any point in the LFO cycle, for any settings of the delay and sweep width parameters.

The actual length of delay at any time is controlled by the distance between the read pointer and write pointer in the buffer. In a typical implementation, the write pointer will move at a constant speed, advancing one sample in the buffer for each input sample. Moving the read pointer faster than this rate will decrease the amount of delay, while moving it slower will increase the delay.

Interpolation

Since the delay of the flanger changes by small amounts each sample, it will inevitably take fractional values. As discussed previously in this chapter, mathematically exact *fractional delay* involves calculations requiring knowledge of the complete signal extending to infinity in both directions. This is clearly impractical, so approximations based on low order polynomial interpolation are used that are suitable for real-time computation. Interpolation is always used when calculating the delayed signal of the flanger.

Code Example

The following C++ code fragment, adapted from the code that accompanies this book, implements a flanger with feedback.

```
// Variables whose values are set externally:
int numSamples;       // How many audio samples to process
float *channelData; // Array of samples, length numSamples
float *delayData;    // Our own circular buffer of samples
int delayBufLength; // Length of our delay buffer in samples
int dpw;              // Write pointer into the delay buffer
float ph;             // Current LFO phase, always between 0-1
float inverseSampleRate; // 1/f_s, where f_s = sample rate

// User-adjustable effect parameters:
float frequency_;    // Frequency of the LFO
float sweepWidth_;   // Width of the LFO in samples
float depth_;        // Amount of delayed signal mixed with
                     // original (0-1)
float feedback_;     // Amount of feedback (>= 0, < 1)

for (int i = 0; i < numSamples; ++i)
{
    const float in = channelData[i];
    float interpolatedSample = 0.0;
```

```
    // Recalculate the read pointer position with respect to
    // the write pointer.
    float currentDelay = sweepWidth_ * (0.5f +
                                0.5f * sinf(2.0 * M_PI * ph));

    // Subtract 3 samples to the delay pointer to make sure
    // we have enough previous samples to interpolate with
    float dpr = fmodf((float)dpw
                - (float)(currentDelay * getSampleRate())
                + (float)delayBufLength - 3.0,
                (float)delayBufLength);

    // Use linear interpolation to read a fractional index
    // into the buffer.
    float fraction = dpr - floorf(dpr);
    int previousSample = (int)floorf(dpr);
    int nextSample = (previousSample + 1) % delayBufLength;
    interpolatedSample = fraction*delayData[nextSample]
        + (1.0f-fraction)*delayData[previousSample];

    // Store the current information in the delay buffer.
    // With feedback, what we read is included in what gets
    // stored in the buffer, otherwise it's just a simple
    // delay line of the input signal.
    delayData[dpw] = in + (interpolatedSample * feedback_);

    // Increment the write pointer at a constant rate.
    if (++dpw >= delayBufLength)
        dpw = 0;

    // Store the output in the buffer, replacing the input
    channelData[i] = in + depth_ * interpolatedSample;

    // Update the LFO phase, keeping it in the range 0-1
    ph += frequency_*inverseSampleRate;
    if(ph >= 1.0)
        ph -= 1.0;
}
```

This code example is nearly identical to the code for vibrato. The main differences appear at the end of the example, where feedback is used on the delay buffer and the original (dry) signal is mixed with the output:

```
delayData[dpw] = in + (interpolatedSample * feedback_);
// [...]
channelData[i] = in + depth_ * interpolatedSample;
```

For this reason, the flanger also has feedback and depth parameters where the vibrato example did not. This example code for the flanger could be used with slight modifications and different parameter values (mainly longer delay time) to implement a chorus. Complete flanger and chorus examples accompany this book, including variable LFO waveform and stereo options.

Applications

The flanger originated as a way of conveniently simulating the double-tracking effect on vocals, but its application goes well beyond the voice. Flanging is commonly used as a guitar effect (where it can be implemented with analog or digital electronics) and is often applied to drums and other instruments. The frequency of the LFO can be aligned to the tempo of the music for beat-synchronous effects.

Resonant Pitches

Recall that audio signals of a single pitch are typically composed of *harmonically related* sinusoids, i.e., integer multiples of a fundamental frequency. Because the peaks and notches in the flanger frequency response are always uniformly spaced, they can impose a discernible resonant pitch on the audio signal. The effect is similar to being inside a resonant tube whose length changes over time according to the amount of delay [1]. The resonance effect is particularly strong when feedback is used and when the depth control is at its maximum.

Avoiding Disappearing Instruments

The notches in a flanger are spaced at regular intervals in frequency, much like the harmonics of a musical instrument, where the signal consists of regular multiples of a fundamental frequency. If a flanger is applied to an instrument sound and the notches happen to line up precisely with the instrument's harmonics, it is possible for the instrument to disappear entirely. In practice, the effect will never be perfect and the instrument will not be completely eliminated, but strange amplitude modulation effects could take place as the notches sweep up and down. This problem does not occur when flanging is applied to more noise-like signals, such as drums. Flanging can also be used on an entire mix, where the frequency content is likely to be complex enough to avoid these modulation effects.

Flanging versus Chorus

The flanger and the chorus are nearly identical in implementation, both being based on modulated delay lines. The primary difference is that the chorus uses longer delay times (30 ms is a typical value) to accentuate the perception of multiple instruments playing together. Flanging and chorus are used in similar situations, but because of the greater delay between copies of the sound and corresponding perception of multiple instruments, chorus is somewhat less likely to be used on complex audio sources such an entire mix.

Chorus

In music, the chorus effect occurs when several individual sounds with similar pitch and timbre play in unison. This phenomenon occurs naturally with a group of singers or violinists, who will always exhibit slight variations in pitch and timing, even when playing in unison. These slight variations are crucial to producing the lush or shimmering sound we are accustomed to hearing from large choirs or string sections. The chorus audio effect simulates these timing and pitch variations, making a single instrument source sound as if there were several instruments playing together.

Theory

Basic Chorus

Figure 2.16 shows a block diagram of a basic chorus, in which a delayed copy of the input signal is mixed with the original. As with the flanger and vibrato effect, the delay length varies with time (modulated delay line). The input/output relationship can be written as

$$y[n] = x[n] + gx[n - M[n]] \tag{2.29}$$

Notice that this formula is identical to the basic flanger presented in the previous section. In general, the chorus effect is nearly identical to the flanger, using the same structure with different parameters. The main difference is the *delay length*, which in a chorus is usually between 20 and 30 ms, in

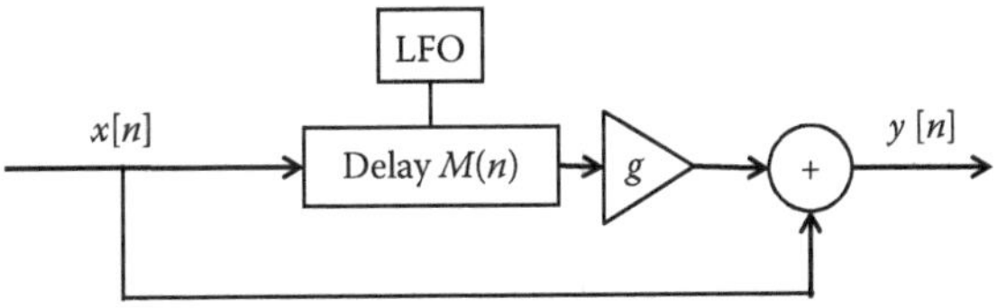

FIGURE 2.16
The flow diagram for the chorus effect including its LFO dependence. The delay changes with time.

contrast to delays between 1 and 10 ms in the flanger. We saw previously that the flanger produces patterns of *constructive* and *destructive interference*, resulting in a frequency response characterized by evenly spaced peaks and notches:

$$\left|H(e^{j\omega})\right| = \sqrt{1+2g\cos(\omega M[n])+g^2} \tag{2.30}$$

with the peaks (points of maximum frequency response) located at

$$\omega_p = 2\pi p/M \quad \text{where} \quad p = 0, 1, 2, \ldots, M-1 \tag{2.31}$$

and the notches (minimum frequency response) at

$$\omega_n = (2n+1)\pi/M \quad \text{where} \quad n = 0, 1, 2, \ldots, M-1 \tag{2.32}$$

Thus, the *comb filtering* produced by the flanger also occurs in the chorus. However, the longer delay $M[n]$ substantially alters its perceived effect. At a sample rate of 48 kHz, a 30 ms delay corresponds to $M = 1440$ samples. There will therefore be 1440 peaks and 1440 notches in the frequency response, each located at intervals of f_s/M (recalling that $\omega = 2\pi$ corresponds to the sampling frequency f_s). Thus, a peak will occur every 33.3 Hz, with notches likewise spaced every 33.3 Hz. These are close enough together that the characteristic sweeping timbre of the flanger is no longer perceptible. In particular, any sense that the comb filter has a definite pitch (owing to its regularly spaced peaks) will be lost at such close spacing. Nonetheless, though the sound is different from the flanger, this comb filtering is an important part of the sonic signature of the chorus effect.

Considered a different way, a delay on the order of 20–30 ms begins to approach the threshold where two separate sonic events can be perceived, though a clear perception of an echo requires a longer delay still (100 ms or more). So the chorus can also be heard as two separate copies of the same sound, whose exact timing relationship changes over time as $M[n]$ changes. Both understandings are mathematically correct; the only difference lies in human audio perception.

Low-Frequency Oscillator

In the chorus, as in the flanger, the delay length $M[n]$ varies under the control of a low-frequency oscillator. Several waveforms can be used for the LFO, with sinusoids being the most common. In comparison to the flanger, slower LFO sweep rates (3 Hz or less) but higher LFO sweep widths (5 ms or more) are typically used. As with all modulated delay effects, interpolation is used to calculate the output of the delay line whenever $M[n]$ is not an integer.

Pitch-Shifting in the Chorus

The wider sweep width (delay variation) in the chorus has an important consequence on the pitch of the delayed sound. As was shown for the vibrato effect, changing the length of a delay line introduces a *pitch shift* into its output, where lengthening the delay scales all frequencies in a signal down, and reducing the delay scales them up. Recall the formula for pitch shift as a function of LFO frequency f, sweep width W, and sample rate f_s:

$$f_{ratio}[n] \approx 1 - 2\pi fW\cos(2\pi nf/f_s) \tag{2.33}$$

Given that the cosine function ranges from –1 to 1, we can find the maximum pitch shift for any given set of parameters as

$$f_{ratio,\max} = 1 + 2\pi fW \tag{2.34}$$

For f = 1 Hz and sweep width W = 10 ms, this results in a pitch ratio of 1.063 (6.3% variation), slightly more than a semitone (5.9%) in either direction. This is a noticeable amount of tuning variation between the original and delayed copies of the signal, which can simulate and even exaggerate the natural variation in pitch between musicians playing in unison. Note that in comparison to the vibrato effect, the chorus mixes the original and delayed copies, so a single pitch shift is not heard.

Multivoice Chorus

The basic chorus can be considered a *single-voice chorus* in that it adds a single delayed copy to the original signal. A *multivoice chorus*, by contrast, involves several delayed copies of the input signal mixed together, with each delayed copy moving independently. Figure 2.17 shows a diagram for an arrangement with two delayed copies (*dual voice*). Each individual voice can be analyzed identically to the basic chorus described in the preceding sections, but the sum total of all voices will produce a more complex, richer tone suggest-

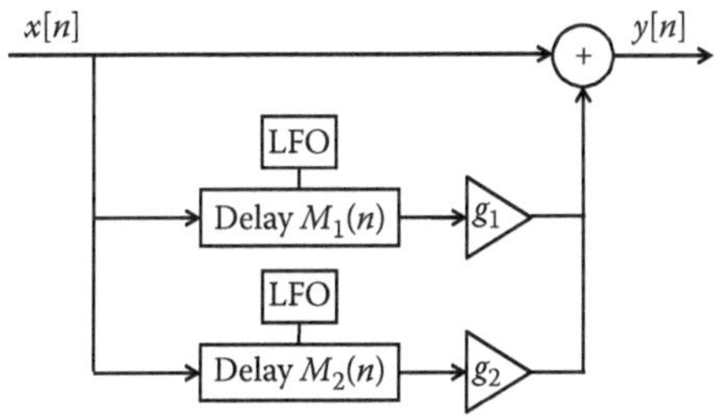

FIGURE 2.17
A multivoice chorus diagram.

ing multiple instruments played in unison. The "Implementation" section below discusses control strategies for the voices in a multivoice chorus.

Stereo Chorus

Stereo chorus is a variation on multivoice chorus, where each delayed copy of the signal is panned to a different location in the stereo field. When two voices are used, the delayed signals are typically panned completely to the left and right, with the original signal in the center. In this case, the two voices are usually run in quadrature phase: each LFO has the same sweep rate and same sweep width, but they differ in phase by 90°. When more than two voices are used, they may be spread evenly across the stereo field or split into two groups, with one group panned hard left and the other group panned hard right.

Properties

The chorus is implemented identically to a flanger without feedback, so it shares the same properties. Notably, since delay and mixing are linear operations, the chorus is a linear effect (for any number of voices). The delay $M[n]$ changes over time under the control of the LFO, so the chorus is a time-variant effect: an input signal applied at one time may produce a different result than the same signal applied at a different time if the LFO phase differs. Since the chorus never involves feedback, it is always stable, with a bounded input producing a bounded output.

Common Parameters

Chorus effects have several user-adjustable controls.

Depth (or Mix)

As with the flanger, the depth controls affect the amount of delayed signal(s) that are mixed in with the original. $g = 0$ produces no effect, whereas $g = 1$ produces the most pronounced chorus effect. Higher depth settings ($g > 1$) make the delayed copies louder than the original, a setting rarely found in practice as it produces a weaker chorus effect than $g = 1$. Some simple chorus effects may not have this control (always setting g to 1). Confusingly, the term *depth* is also sometimes used to refer to sweep width, or the amount of variation in the delay. When examining an existing chorus effect, it is thus important to find out what the depth control means.

Delay and Sweep Width

The *delay* parameter on the chorus controls the minimum amount of delay $M[n]$. Typical values are on the order of 20 to 30 ms, and this setting represents one of the primary differences between flanger and chorus. The *sweep width* (which is sometimes called *sweep depth,* but should not be confused with *depth/mix*) controls the amount of additional delay added by the LFO. In other words, sweep width controls the amplitude of the LFO, and the maximum delay is given by the sum of delay and sweep width. The relationship between the delay and sweep width parameters is depicted in Figure 2.15. Typical values for sweep width range from 1–2 to 10 ms or more. A larger sweep width will result in more pitch, creating a warbling effect, whereas changing the delay parameter will not affect the pitch modulation.

Speed and Waveform

As in the flanger, the *speed* (or *sweep rate*) sets the number of cycles per second of the LFO controlling the delay time. In addition to producing a more quickly oscillating chorus effect, higher speed will produce more pronounced pitch modulation for the same sweep width, since the delay line length will be changing more quickly over time. Typical values in the chorus are slower than in the flanger, ranging from roughly 0.1 to 3 Hz.

The *waveform* control selects one of several predefined LFO waveforms, including sine, triangle, sawtooth, or exponential (triangular in log frequency). In addition to controlling how the voices move in time, each waveform will affect the type of pitch modulation. For example, the derivative of a sine wave is a cosine, which is always changing, so the pitch is always changing as well. A triangular waveform, though, has only two discrete slopes, so the pitch will jump back and forth between two fixed values. Many chorus effects do not offer a waveform parameter and always use a sine LFO. As with the flanger, this results in a total delay $M[n]$ given by

$$M[n] = M_0 + \frac{M_W}{2}\left[1 + \sin\left(2\pi f_{LFO} n / f_s\right)\right] \tag{2.35}$$

where M_0 (in samples) is given by the *delay* control, M_W (in samples) is given by the *sweep width* control, f_{LFO} (in Hertz) is given by the speed control, and f_s (in Hertz) is the sampling frequency. $M[n]$ thus varies from M_0 to $M_0 + M_W$.

Number of Voices

As discussed in the previous section, a multivoice chorus uses more than one delayed copy of the input sound, simulating the effect of more than two instruments being played in unison. Many chorus units give the option of choosing the number of voices. In a simple implementation, each voice could be controlled by the same LFO, but with a different phase. The delay time will be different for each voice since they are at different points in the waveform, but they will remain synchronized to one another over time. More complex implementations can use different LFO waveforms and speeds for each voice.

Other Variations

When multiple instruments play in unison, the variations between them are likely to be more random than periodic. Instead of using a fixed-speed LFO, the delay time between voices could be changed in a more irregular, quasi-random fashion (keeping in mind that abrupt changes in delay will produce audible pitch artifacts). Another variation is to modulate the amplitude of each voice to model the fact that musicians playing in unison will not all have the same relative loudness.

Summary: Flanger and Chorus Compared

The chorus and flanger effects are nearly identical in structure. The main differences are in the parameter settings: the chorus uses a longer delay time than the flanger and often a larger sweep width. These together produce more sense of separation between the original and delayed copies of the signal and more pitch modulation. The chorus tends to use a lower speed or sweep rate than the flanger, though there is a significant area of overlap. One structural difference is that the flanger can use feedback to produce a more intense effect, whereas this is almost never found in the chorus. On the other hand, the chorus can use more than one delayed copy of the sound (multivoice chorus), where the flanger uses only one copy (except in a stereo flanger). When chorus and flanger effects are implemented in stereo, the same procedure is used in both cases, panning one delayed copy to the left and one to the right, though a multivoice chorus with more than two delayed copies allows further variations on this procedure.

Problems

1. Suppose we want to delay a signal by 2.5 samples. Briefly explain two different methods of calculating the new signal and their relative advantages and disadvantages.
2. Consider a signal $x[0] = 0.8$, $x[1] = 0.4$, $x[2] = 0.1$, $x[3] = -0.15$, $x[4] = -0.4$. Use zero-, first-, and second-order interpolation to estimate the value $x[1.7]$.
3. a. Draw a block diagram for delay with feedback. Label the input $x[n]$, output $y[n]$, and any other commonly used parameters.

   b. Under what conditions is the system stable? Why?
4. A delay without feedback produces notches at 300 and 900 Hz. List at least three other frequencies where notches will also be present,

and explain why. For a sample rate of 48 kHz, how many samples of delay could produce this comb filter?

5. There are two microphones on a guitar, one close microphone placed only 5 cm away, picking up the direct sound, another placed 1.5 m away from the guitar, picking up the room sound. How much delay should be added to the close microphone to align the two signals?
6. a. Draw a block diagram of a basic flanger. Now draw a block diagram of a flanger incorporating feedback or regeneration.
   b. Derive the frequency response of a flanger without feedback.
   c. Based on your block diagram in part (a), write the difference equation(s) for a flanger *with* feedback, relating the output $y[n]$ to the input $x[n]$. Define any other variables you use in your equation(s).
   d. Describe whether or not the flanger is *linear, time invariant,* and *stable.* Explain why, and whether the answer depends on parameter settings or whether feedback is used.
7. Define the following parameters for a flanger: *depth, delay, sweep width,* and *sweep rate.* Describe the effect of varying their settings.
8. Why do we not hear an echo when flanging is applied?
9. How does chorus differ from flanger in terms of the LFO settings and use of feedback?
10. Suppose we implement the flanger with a circular buffer. We may hear artifacts as the delay length changes. Explain why this occurs and suggest a solution to overcome it.
11. a. Starting with the template in Figure 2.18, draw a block diagram for a ping-pong delay with mono input and stereo output. Label the inputs $x_1[n]$ and $x_2[n]$, the outputs $y_1[n]$ and $y_2[n]$, and any other commonly used parameters.
    b. Give the transfer function and difference equation for ping-pong delay. That is, find $Y_1(z)$ and $Y_2(z)$ in terms of $X_1(z)$ and $X_2(z)$.

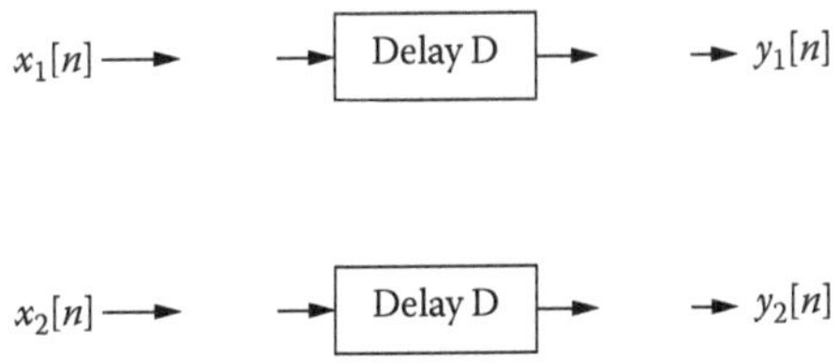

FIGURE 2.18
Template for a ping-pong delay.

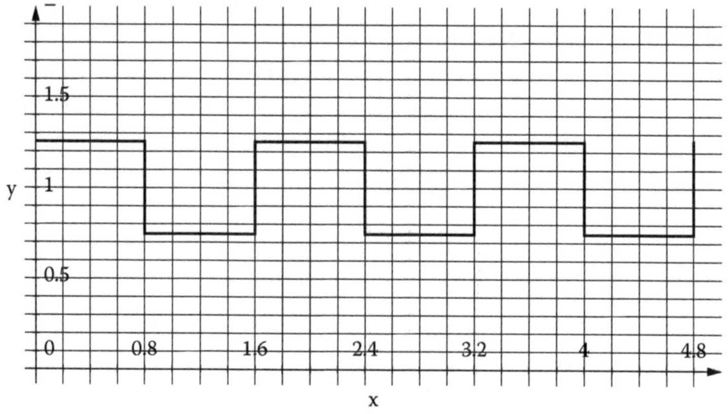

FIGURE 2.19
Relative pitch at the output of a vibrato unit.

c. Suppose the ping-pong delay was extended to four-channel output, with the input sound bounced sequentially around them. Draw a block diagram for this arrangement.

d. With delays of length D, how large does the total buffer need to be (in samples) for the two- and four-channel ping-pong delays?

12. a. For a vibrato effect, suppose that the delay time is given by $d(t) = M + W\sin(2\pi ft)$, where M is the average delay, W is the sweep width, and f is the LFO frequency. If $M = 5$ ms and $f = 6$ Hz, find the value of W needed to give a maximum pitch shift of 1.03 (roughly half a semitone). You can leave the result as a fraction.

b. The plot in Figure 2.19 shows the relative pitch at the output of a vibrato unit. What LFO waveform was used to produce this result, and why?

3

Filter Design

Filters are the basis for many types of audio effects. In this chapter, we'll look at the basics of designing digital filters. We will show how many of the most important digital filters can be derived from the simplest possible designs. Several types of filters are commonly used in audio effects for manipulating the frequency content of the signal. These filters, in their ideal form, are depicted in Figure 3.1. They can be summarized as follows.

Low-pass, high-pass, and band-pass filters: The first class of filters aims to totally eliminate certain frequency ranges from the signal. The low-pass filter passes low frequencies below some *cutoff frequency* ω_c while eliminating all frequencies above the cutoff. The high-pass filter is a mirror image of this. It passes all frequencies above the cutoff frequency ω_c and eliminates all frequencies below it. Band-pass filters pass a range of frequencies. They are defined by the *center frequency* ω_c and the *bandwidth* B, which specify the location and width of the *pass band*, respectively. Frequencies above and below this pass band are blocked. The inverse of the band-pass filter is the *band stop filter*, which blocks frequencies in its *stop band* while passing frequencies above and below.

Shelving, peaking, and notch filters: This class of filters does not aim to entirely eliminate any frequencies, but rather to adjust the relative gain of specific portions of the frequency spectrum. Shelving filters come in two forms, *low shelving* and *high shelving* filters. They are analogous to low-pass and high-pass filters, but instead of eliminating high or low frequency, they provide a boost or cut on the shelf region and leave all other frequency content unaffected. Peaking and notch filters are analogous to band-pass and band stop filters in that they affect only a narrow range of the spectrum. They apply a boost or cut to a specific frequency band while leaving the area around it unchanged. Like band-pass and band stop filters, peaking and notch filters are often specified by a center frequency and bandwidth. The center frequency defines the location of maximum gain in a peaking filter, or minimum gain in a notch filter. The bandwidth defines the size of the region around the center frequency. The gain is also typically a parameter in peaking and notch filter design. These will be explained in detail later in the chapter.

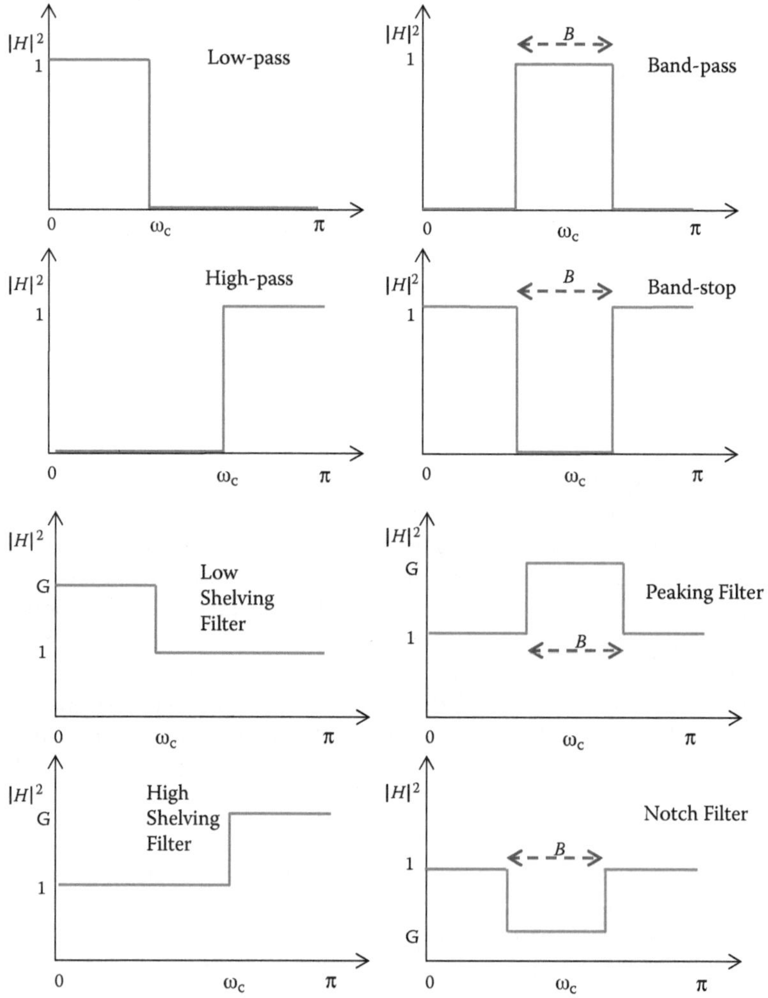

FIGURE 3.1
Ideal filters.

In Chapter 4, we will see how these filters are used in audio effects such as equalizers. But let us first study their general behavior. In practice, we cannot achieve the perfectly sharp cutoff between pass band and stop band shown in Figure 3.1, and in fact, a perfectly sharp cutoff would not be aesthetically desirable. Rather, in audio contexts, we usually desire a smooth transition between regions. As we will see, the *order* of a filter (a rough measure of its complexity) also determines how sharp the cutoff is between pass band and stop band. Audio effects most commonly use low-order filters, which have the benefits of simpler design and less susceptibility to error.

In the following sections, we will begin with a very simple prototype filter and gradually generalize it to more complex designs. We will show that all the common classes of filters can be constructed by a series of operations on this simple prototype, and that we can alter the frequency spectrum of a signal almost arbitrarily just by applying combinations of such filters.

Filter Construction and Transformation

In this section, we look at how a simple filter can be constructed, and how it can be extended or transformed into other designs. We keep most of the discussion regarding transformations quite general, so that they apply to high-order as well as low-order designs. There is a fair amount of math in this section, and we don't skip the details. However, readers can skip ahead to the next section on popular IIR (infinite impulse response) filter design, if just interested in how these transformations are used to generate the various filter designs from Figure 3.1.

Simple Prototype Low-Pass Filter

Consider averaging every two consecutive samples. In the time domain, the output is given as

$$y[n] = (x[n] + x[n-1])/2 \tag{3.1}$$

This equation produces a low-pass filter. To see why, let's consider its response at very low and very high frequencies. For a very low frequency input, the signal hardly changes from sample to sample. In fact, if the input signal has frequency 0, $x[n] = A\cos(2\pi 0 n/f_s)$, then it is constant. This is known as DC input, since direct current electrical signals have this quality. For DC input, the output of this filter is identical to the input.

Now suppose we have a very high frequency signal, at half the sampling frequency. So $x[n] = A\cos(2\pi(f_s/2)n/f_s) = A\cos(\pi n)$. Thus, the signal switches sign from sample to sample, and the output of this filter is zero.

Let's look at this filter in the frequency domain. Recall from Chapter 1 that we can express this in the Z domain as $Y(z) = (X(z) + z^{-1}X(z))/2$. Its transfer function, written in positive powers of z, is

$$H(z) = \frac{z+1}{2z} \tag{3.2}$$

and the square magnitude of this transfer function is

$$|H(z)|^2 = \frac{1+z}{2z}\frac{1+z^{-1}}{2z^{-1}} = \frac{1+z+z^{-1}+1}{4} = \frac{1+\cos\omega}{2} \tag{3.3}$$

Hence, this acts as a low-pass filter, allowing low frequencies to pass through to the output, but removing high-frequency content. You can easily see that for $f = 0$, $H(z = 1) = 1$, and for $f = f_s/2$, $H(z = -1) = 0$. But what happens halfway, at $f = f_s/4$? Here, $\omega = 2\pi f/f_s = \pi/2$, and we see that $|H(z = j)|^2 = 1/2$.

We call this the cutoff frequency of our low-pass filter. Generally, the cutoff frequency is where the frequency response makes the transition between two values. There are various ways a cutoff frequency may be formally defined, but one of the most effective, and the one we will use in this chapter, is that it is the frequency at which the square magnitude is halfway between its low and high value (in this case, halfway between 0 and 1).

High-Order Prototype Low-Pass Filter

Sometimes we want a sharp roll-off at the cutoff frequencies. Let's return to our simple low-pass filter. It has one zero at $z = -1$ and one pole at $z = 0$. Replace the pole at 0 by N points given by

$$p_n = j\tan(\alpha_n/2) \tag{3.4}$$

where α_n assumes ranges over the values between $-\pi/2$ and $\pi/2$, $\alpha_n = ((2n - 1)/N - 1)\pi/2$, $n = 1, 2, \ldots, N$. So our Nth-order prototype filter is

$$\begin{aligned} H_P(z) &= \prod_{n=1}^{N} \frac{1}{2\cos\gamma_n}\frac{z+1}{z - j\tan\gamma_n} \\ \gamma_n &= \frac{\pi((2n-1)/N-1)}{4}, \quad n = 1, 2, \ldots, N \end{aligned} \tag{3.5}$$

These filters have the same cutoff frequency and same behavior at DC and Nyquist as the first-order filter. But now the poles result in a very sharp transition at $\omega = \pi/2$. In fact, the square magnitude is now

$$|H_P(z)|^2 = \frac{1}{1+\tan^{2N}(\omega/2)} \tag{3.6}$$

The pole zero plot and square magnitude are shown in Figure 3.2 for a fourth-order prototype low-pass filter.

We now have a high-order filter, composed of first-order sections. In what follows, we will show how each of those first-order sections may be transformed to create other types of high-order filters.

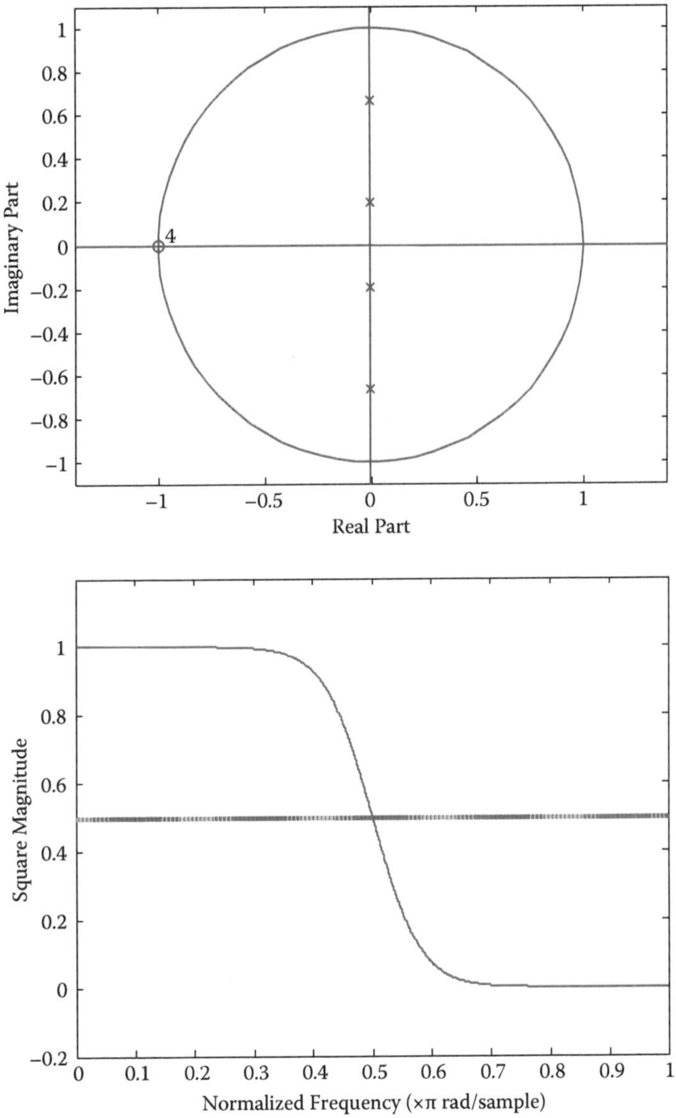

FIGURE 3.2
Pole zero plot (top) and square magnitude response for a fourth-order prototype low-pass filter.

Changing the Gain at the Cutoff Frequency

Consider another transformation, given by

$$F(z) = \frac{z - \alpha}{1 - \alpha z} \tag{3.7}$$

This has a few important properties. Every value inside the unit circle is mapped to a value inside the unit circle, those outside are mapped to values outside the unit circle, and those on the unit circle stay on the unit circle. So we can view this transfer function as preserving stability. Furthermore, it maps $z = 1$ to 1 and $z = -1$ to -1.

Suppose that at some frequency ω_G we have

$$\left| H_P\left(z = e^{j\omega_G}\right) \right|^2 = G^2 \tag{3.8}$$

Then from (3.6),

$$(1/G^2 - 1)^{1/2N} = \tan(\omega_G/2) \tag{3.9}$$

We now use F to map this frequency ω_G to $\pi/2$, so that the square magnitude of $H(F(z))$ at $\omega = \pi/2$ is the same as the square magnitude of $H(z)$ at $\omega = \omega_G$. That is, we need the transformation

$$F\left(z = e^{j\pi/2}\right) = e^{j\omega_G} \tag{3.10}$$

From (3.7) and (3.10) we have

$$\alpha = \frac{e^{j\omega_G/2} - je^{-j\omega_G/2}}{e^{j\omega_G/2}j - e^{-j\omega_G/2}} = \ldots = \frac{\tan(\omega_G/2) - 1}{\tan(\omega_G/2) + 1} = \frac{(1/G^2 - 1)^{1/(2N)} - 1}{(1/G^2 - 1)^{1/(2N)} + 1} \tag{3.11}$$

Thus, to change the gain at the cutoff frequency $\pi/2$, we replace each first-order section, $H_P(z) = k(z - q)/(z - p)$, from our prototype filter with the following:

$$\begin{aligned} H(F(z)) &= k\frac{F(z) - q}{F(z) - p} \\ &= k\frac{z(1 + \alpha q) - (q + \alpha)}{z(1 + \alpha p) - (p + \alpha)} \end{aligned} \tag{3.12}$$

where

$$\alpha = \frac{(1/G^2 - 1)^{1/(2N)} - 1}{(1/G^2 - 1)^{1/(2N)} + 1}$$

Shifting the Cutoff Frequency

So far, our cutoff frequency has been set to $\pi/2$. We would like to be able to set the cutoff frequency to any value between 0 and π. This would allow us to change the location that provides the transition between where frequencies are passed and blocked.

Consider another transformation, given by

$$F_{\omega_c \to \pi/2}\left(z = e^{j\omega_c}\right) = e^{j\pi/2} \tag{3.13}$$

where, as before,

$$F_{\omega_c \to \pi/2}(z) = \frac{z - \beta}{1 - \beta z} \tag{3.14}$$

This transfer function will map some new cutoff frequency ω_c to the cutoff frequency of our prototype filter, $\pi/2$, as shown in Figure 3.3.

By putting (3.13) into (3.14) and solving for β,

$$\beta = \frac{e^{j\omega_c} - e^{j\pi/2}}{1 - e^{j\omega_c} e^{j\pi/2}} = \ldots = \frac{1 - \tan(\omega_c/2)}{1 + \tan(\omega_c/2)} \tag{3.15}$$

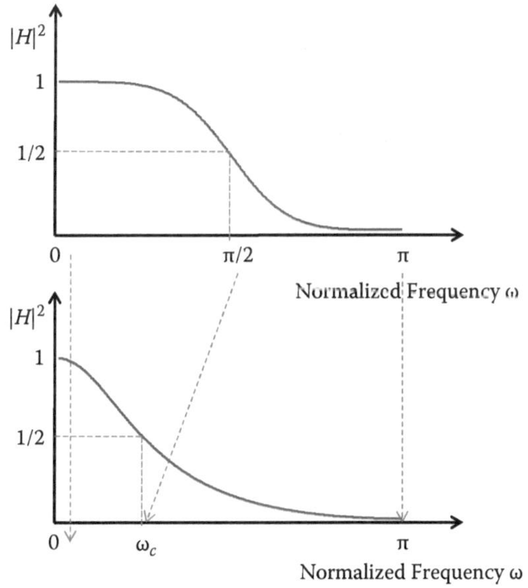

FIGURE 3.3
Shifting the center frequency of a low-pass filter.

Let us consider any first-order section (the transfer function can be written as first-order polynomials), $H(z) = k(z-q)/(z-p)$. To change the cutoff frequency, we replace $H(z)$ with

$$H_{\omega_c \to \pi/2}(z) = k\frac{z(1+\beta q)-(q+\beta)}{z(1+\beta p)-(p+\beta)} \tag{3.16}$$

where β is defined as in (3.15).

Creating a Shelving Filter

We can construct a low shelving filter by transforming our prototype filter such that the square magnitude response is transformed from H^2 to $(G^2-1)H^2+1$, depicted in Figure 3.4. This transformation changes the extreme square magnitudes 0 and 1 of a low-pass design to 1 and G^2.

Recall that the poles will push up the magnitude response for nearby frequencies, and the zeros will pull it down. For the low shelving filter, we want to keep the poles on the imaginary axis, giving a sharp cutoff frequency. But now we shift the zeros so that, for each first-order section, $H(z=1) = g = G^{1/N}$ and $H(z=-1) = 1$. That is, if the first-order section of a prototype low-pass filter is written as

$$H_{LP} = k\frac{z-q}{z-p} \tag{3.17}$$

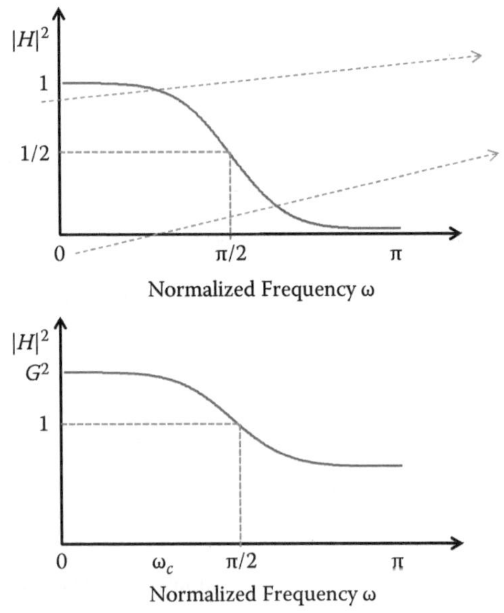

FIGURE 3.4
Shelving filter transformation.

then the first-order section of the low shelving filter becomes

$$H_{LS} = \frac{1}{2}\frac{[1+p+g(1-p)]z-[1+p-g(1-p)]}{z-p} \tag{3.18}$$

So $H_{LS}(1) = g, H_{LS}(-1) = 1$. The pole zero plot and square magnitude response for a fourth-order low shelving filter are shown in Figure 3.5. The poles still produce a sharp transition at the cutoff frequency, and the filter reaches its minimum at $\omega = \pi$. But the zeros are all inside the unit circle, far from $\omega = \pi$, so that the square magnitude response does not drop to zero. What the pole zero plot does not show, however, is the constant k, which is used to normalize the filter so that the response ranges from G to 1.

Inverting the Magnitude Response

For a high-pass filter, we want $|H(z = 1)|^2 = 0$, $|H(z = -1)|^2 = 1$, and $|H(z = \omega_c)|^2 = G^2$. So we simply apply the transformation $F_{HP}(z) = -z$. This transformation is shown in Figure 3.6.

$$F_{HP}(H(z)) = k\frac{-z-q}{-z-p} = k\frac{z+q}{z+p} \tag{3.19}$$

Simple Low-Pass to Band-Pass Transformation

Now we want to create a band-pass filter from our simple filter with center frequency $\pi/2$. We would like to transform the frequency range 0 to π to the frequency range $-\pi$ to π. If this transformation is applied to the input before a low-pass filter is applied, then our low-pass filter becomes a band-pass filter, as shown in Figure 3.7. To do this, consider a transfer function $F(z)$ with the following constraints:

$$\begin{aligned}
F(z) &= -\frac{z^2+\alpha_1 z+\alpha_2}{\alpha_2 z^2+\alpha_1 z+1} \\
F\left(z = e^{j0}\right) &= e^{-j\pi} = -1 \\
F\left(z = e^{j\omega_l}\right) &= e^{-j\pi/2} = -j \\
F\left(z = e^{j\omega_c}\right) &= e^{j0} = 1 \\
F\left(z = e^{j\omega_u}\right) &= e^{j\pi/2} = j \\
F\left(z = e^{j\pi}\right) &= e^{j\pi} = -1
\end{aligned} \tag{3.20}$$

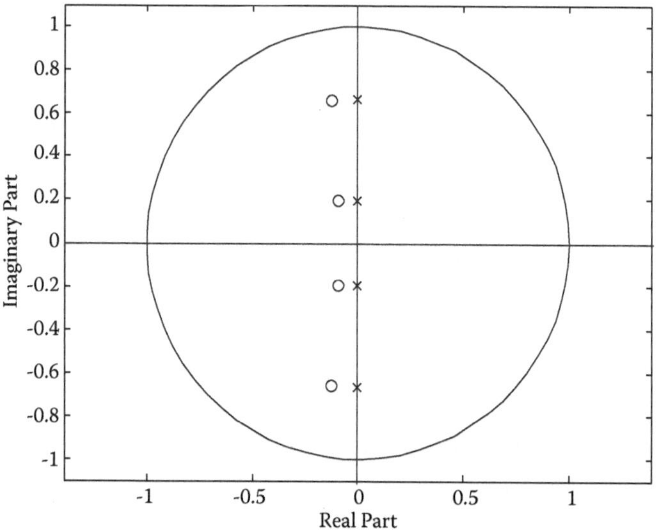

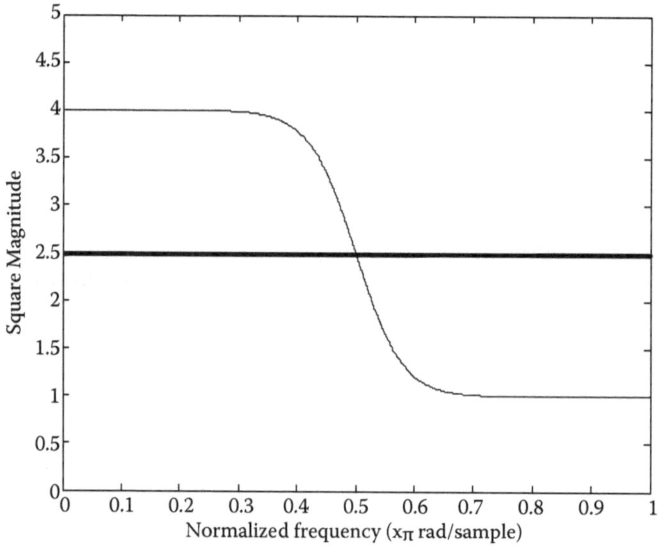

FIGURE 3.5
Pole zero plot (top) and square magnitude response for a fourth-order prototype low shelving filter (bottom). Compared to our prototype filter, it moves the zeros toward the pole positions on the imaginary axis.

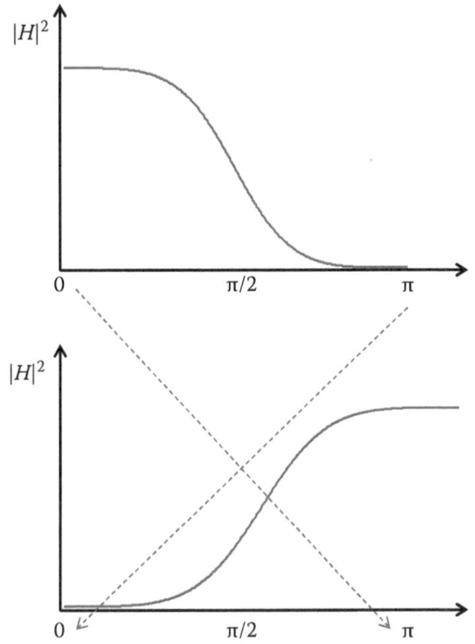

FIGURE 3.6
Reversing the z domain to turn a low-pass into a high-pass filter.

F will move the lower and upper cutoff frequencies to $\pm\pi/2$, where our prototype low-pass filter has its cutoff frequency, and it will move the center frequency to 0, where our prototype low-pass filter has gain equal to 1.

We can solve Equation (3.20) to arrive at

$$H_{BP}(z) = H\big(F(z)\big) = k\frac{z^2 - z(1+q)\cos\omega_c + q}{z^2 - z(1+p)\cos\omega_c + p} \tag{3.21}$$

This transfer function has second-order polynomials in the numerator and the denominator. So, our first-order section has now become a second-order section.

Popular IIR Filter Design

It is possible to design *finite impulse response* (FIR) filters, where the output is dependent only on current and previous inputs, and not on previous outputs, that is, to design the filters whose ideal forms were depicted in Figure 3.1. However, FIR designs either give poor approximations to the ideal forms or

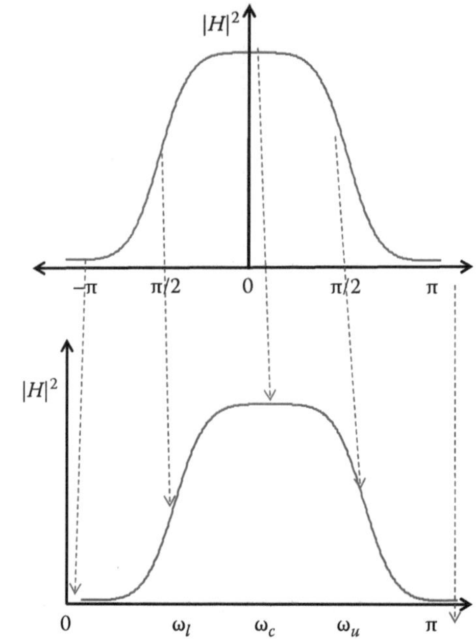

FIGURE 3.7
Transforming a low-pass filter into a band-pass filter.

must be very high order, and hence introduce significant delay and computational issues. Thus, preferred designs are usually *infinite impulse response* (IIR) filters, where output is fed back to the input. This section will use the transformations from the previous section to construct such filters.

We now have everything we need to construct many of the most popular audio filters. We first construct a high-order prototype filter with prescribed gain at $\pi/2$. Then we show how we can use the transformations just described to turn this prototype filter into the filters given in Figure 3.1. In each case, will give an example of the lowest order where cutoff frequency or bandwidth is defined using Equation (3.35).

Low Pass

As mentioned, a low-pass filter has a transfer function H_{LP} with magnitude 1 at frequency 0 and magnitude 0 at frequency $\omega = \pi$ ($f = f_s/2$). That is, the magnitudes of the lowest frequencies are unaffected, and the highest frequencies are eliminated. At some cutoff frequency ω_c, it has magnitude G_c, and this represents the transition where frequencies below ω_c are considered passed, and above this are rejected.

In order to generate a high-order low-pass filter, we first generate our high-order prototype filter. Then by applying these transformations to each first-order section in our high-order prototype filter, we can generate a high-order low-pass filter.

We first use Equation (3.12) to transform each first-order section in the Nth-order prototype filter such that each first-order section has magnitude $G_c^{1/N}$, rather than $(1/2)^{1/(2N)}$, at $\omega = \pi/2$ (that is, the whole filter has square magnitude G_c^2, rather than 1/2 at $\omega = \pi/2$). Then we apply Equation (3.16) to shift the cutoff frequency so that each first-order section has magnitude $G_c^{1/N}$ at ω_c, rather than at $\pi/2$.

Consider a simple first-order case where we define the gain at the cutoff frequency such that the square magnitude is the average of the two extremes, $G_c^2 = (0^2 + 1^2)/2 = 1/2$.

We start with

$$H(z) = \frac{z+1}{2z} \tag{3.22}$$

At $\omega = \pi/2$, this filter has square magnitude 1/2. That is, this definition of gain at the cutoff is the same definition used in the prototype filter. So there is no need to change the gain at the cutoff frequency.

Now we shift the cutoff frequency from $\pi/2$ to ω_c,

$$H_{LP}(z) = \frac{(1-\beta)}{2}\frac{z+1}{z-\beta} \tag{3.23}$$

where

$$\beta = \frac{1-\tan(\omega_c/2)}{1+\tan(\omega_c/2)}$$

This simplifies to

$$H_{LP}(z) = \frac{(z+1)\tan(\omega_c/2)}{z\left(\tan(\omega_c/2)+1\right)+\tan(\omega_c/2)-1} \tag{3.24}$$

Figure 3.8 shows a pole zero plot and square magnitude response of a first-order and a fourth-order low-pass filter with cutoff frequency of $\pi/4$. In both cases, the zeros are at –1. Notice that, for the fourth-order design, the poles are placed on the arc of a circle so as to pull down the magnitude sharply at ω_c.

High Pass

A high-pass filter has a transfer function H_{HP} with magnitude 0 at frequency $\omega = 0$, magnitude 1 at frequency $\omega = \pi$, and magnitude G_c at some cutoff frequency ω_c.

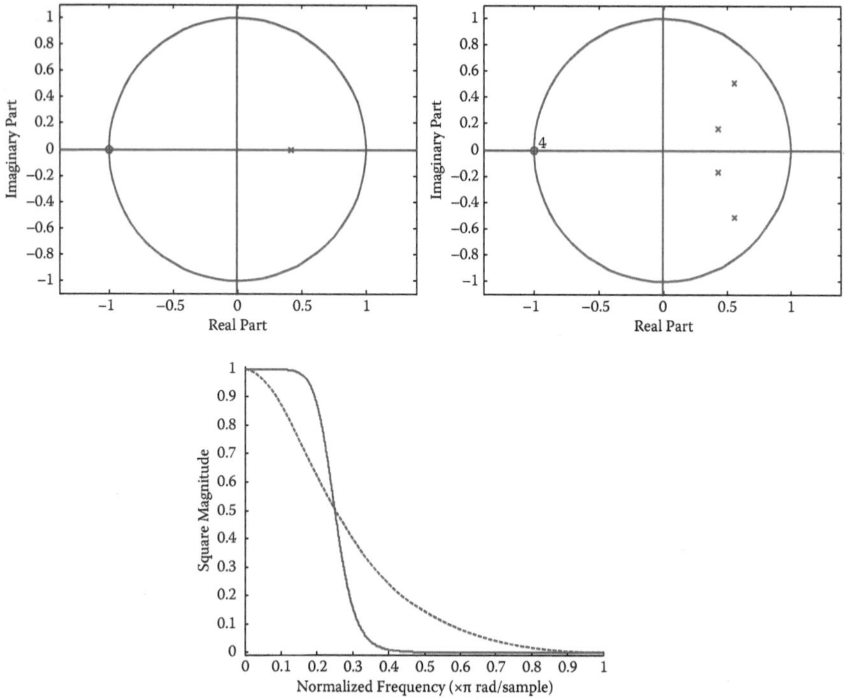

FIGURE 3.8
Pole zero plot for first-order (top left) and fourth-order (top right) low-pass filters with center frequency $\omega_c = \pi/4$. On bottom, square magnitude response for the first-order (solid line) and fourth-order (dash-dot line) filters.

To generate a high-pass filter with cutoff frequency ω_c, we begin with the high-order prototype filter. Next we transform each first-order section, such that it has magnitude $G_c^{1/N}$ at $\omega = \pi/2$. Then we invert the magnitude response of each of these sections, and shift the cutoff frequency of each section from $\pi/2$ to ω_c.

Let us again consider the first-order case where $G^2 = 1/2$. There is no need to change the gain at the cutoff frequency, so we begin with Equation (3.22). Then we invert the magnitude response using Equation (3.19), giving

$$H_{HP,\omega_c=\pi/2}(z) = \frac{1}{2}\frac{z-1}{z} \tag{3.25}$$

And now we shift the cutoff frequency,

$$H_{HP}(z) = \frac{1}{2}\frac{(1+\beta)(z-1)}{z-\beta} \tag{3.26}$$

where

$$\beta = \frac{1 - \tan(\omega_c/2)}{1 + \tan(\omega_c/2)}$$

which reduces to

$$H_{HP}(z) = \frac{z - 1}{(\tan(\omega_c/2) + 1)z + \tan(\omega_c/2) - 1} \tag{3.27}$$

Figure 3.9 shows a pole zero plot and square magnitude response of a first-order and a fourth-order low-pass filter with cutoff frequency of π/4. These are identical to the low-pass filters, except now the zeros have been moved from –1 to +1, giving maximal attenuation at the low frequencies.

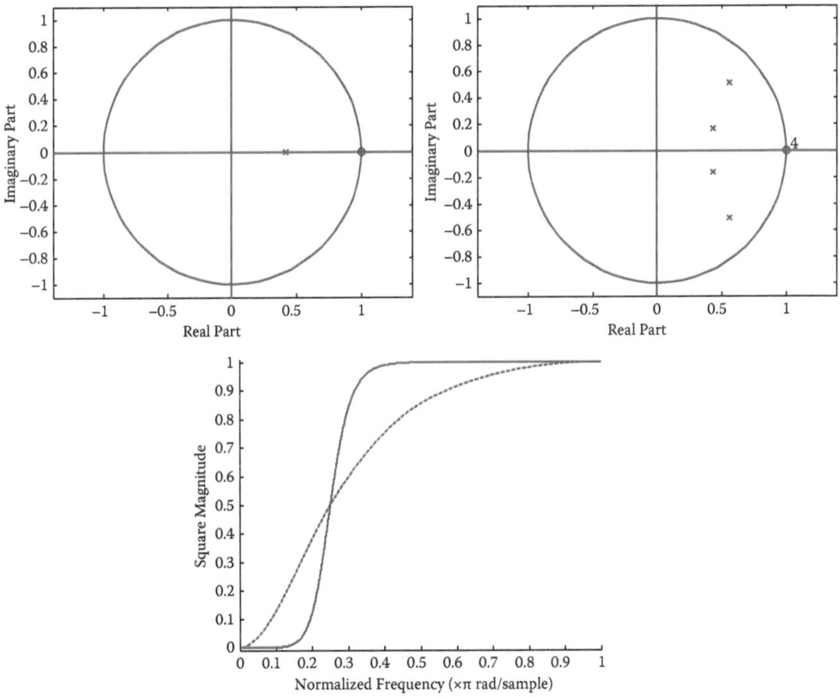

FIGURE 3.9
Pole zero plot for first-order (top left) and fourth-order (top right) high-pass filters with center frequency $\omega_c = \pi/4$. On bottom, square magnitude response for the first-order (dash-dot line) and fourth-order (solid line) filters.

Low Shelf

A low shelving filter has a transfer function H_{LS} with magnitude G at frequency $\omega = 0$ (representing the low shelf), magnitude 1 at frequency $\omega = \pi$, and magnitude G_c at some cutoff frequency ω_c.

As earlier, we start with our high-order prototype filter. We will change the gain at the cutoff frequency to some value g. We will transform the range of square magnitudes of the prototype filter to the range of square magnitudes of the shelving filter. That is, we want the extreme square magnitudes, 0 and 1, of the low-pass filter, 0 and 1, to map to the extreme square magnitudes of the low-pass filter, 1 and G^2, with g^2 mapping to G_c^2. Thus,

$$\frac{g^2-0}{1-0}=\frac{G_c^2-1}{G^2-1}\rightarrow g^2=\frac{G_c^2-1}{G^2-1} \tag{3.28}$$

So for each first-order section of an Nth-order prototype filter, we apply Equations (3.12) and (3.28) to change the gain at the cutoff frequency to this new value $g^{1/N}$. Then we transform each section to a shelving filter using Equation (3.18), and use Equation (3.16) to shift the cutoff frequency to ω_c.

Consider again our example first-order filter with the gain at the cutoff frequency defined such that the square magnitude is the average of the two extremes $G_c^2 = (G^2 + 1^2)/2$. Then Equation (3.28) simplifies to

$$g^2=\frac{(G^2+1)/2-1}{G^2-1}=1/2 \tag{3.29}$$

And as with the low-pass filter, this choice of cutoff frequency is the same as that used in the prototype filter.

Now we create the shelf,

$$H_{LS,\omega_c=\pi/2}(z)=\frac{1}{2}\frac{z[1+G]+G-1}{z} \tag{3.30}$$

And finally, we shift the cutoff frequency,

$$H_{LS}(z)=\frac{1}{2}\frac{z(1+G+(1-G)\beta)-[1-G+(1+G)\beta]}{z-\beta} \tag{3.31}$$

where

$$\beta=\frac{1-\tan(\omega_c/2)}{1+\tan(\omega_c/2)}$$

which reduces to

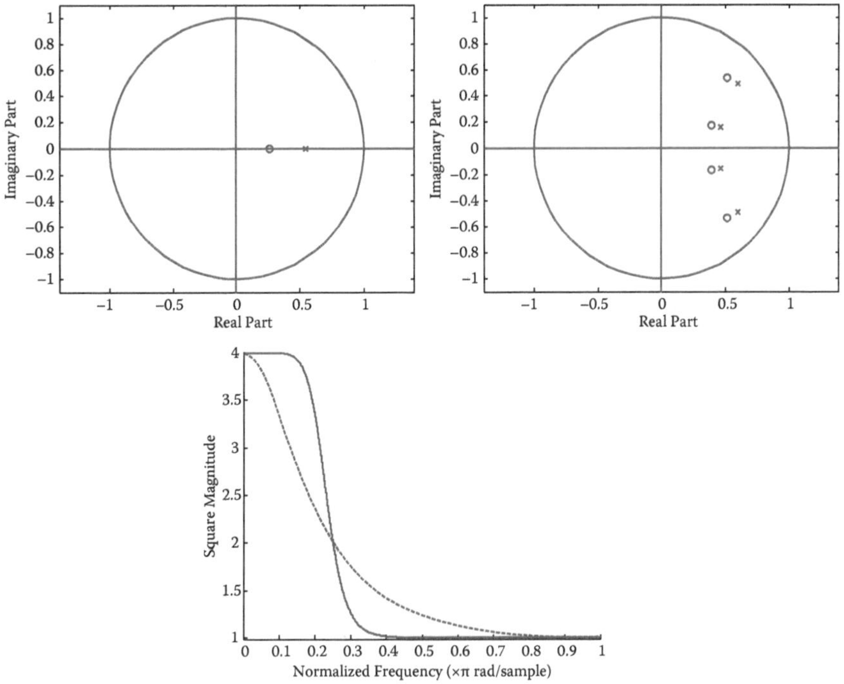

FIGURE 3.10
Pole zero plot for first-order (top left) and fourth-order (top right) low shelving filters with center frequency $\omega_c = \pi/4$ and gain at center frequency $G = 2$. On bottom, square magnitude response for the first-order (dash-dot line) and fourth-order (solid line) filters.

$$H_{LS}(z) = \frac{(1 + G\tan(\omega_c/2))z + G\tan(\omega_c/2) - 1}{(1 + \tan(\omega_c/2))z + \tan(\omega_c/2) - 1} \tag{3.32}$$

In Figure 3.10, we've given a pole zero plot and square magnitude response of a first-order and a fourth-order low shelving filter with cutoff frequency of $\pi/4$. By placing the poles slightly closer to 1 than the zeros, it has the effect of pushing up the low frequencies. If the poles and zeros were farther apart, then the shelf would be higher (larger value of G). If the zeros were placed closer to 1 than the poles, then the shelf would be at a value $G < 1$.

High Shelf

A high shelving filter has a transfer function H_{HS} with magnitude 1 at frequency $\omega = 0$, magnitude G at frequency $\omega = \pi$ (representing the high shelf), and magnitude G_c at some cutoff frequency ω_c.

As earlier, we will change the square magnitude at the cutoff frequency of each first-order section of an Nth-order prototype filter, from $(1/2)^{1/N}$ to $g^{2/N}$, where g^2 is defined as in (3.28). Then we transform each section to a shelving filter, invert the magnitude response, and shift the cutoff frequency to ω_c.

For our first-order filter, the procedure is the same as with the low shelf, giving Equation (3.30) after we transform this to a shelving filter. Inverting the magnitude response then gives

$$H_{LS}(z) = \frac{1}{2}\frac{z[1+G]-G+1}{z} \tag{3.33}$$

And after shifting the cutoff frequency, we arrive at

$$H_{HS}(z) = \frac{(G+\tan(\omega_c/2))z+\tan(\omega_c/2)-G}{(1+\tan(\omega_c/2))z+\tan(\omega_c/2)-1} \tag{3.34}$$

First- and fourth-order high shelving filters are depicted in Figure 3.11. Compared with the low shelving filter, the pole and zero positions have been switched. Note that the pole zero plots are also equivalent to a low shelving filter with $G < 1$; only the constant term would be different.

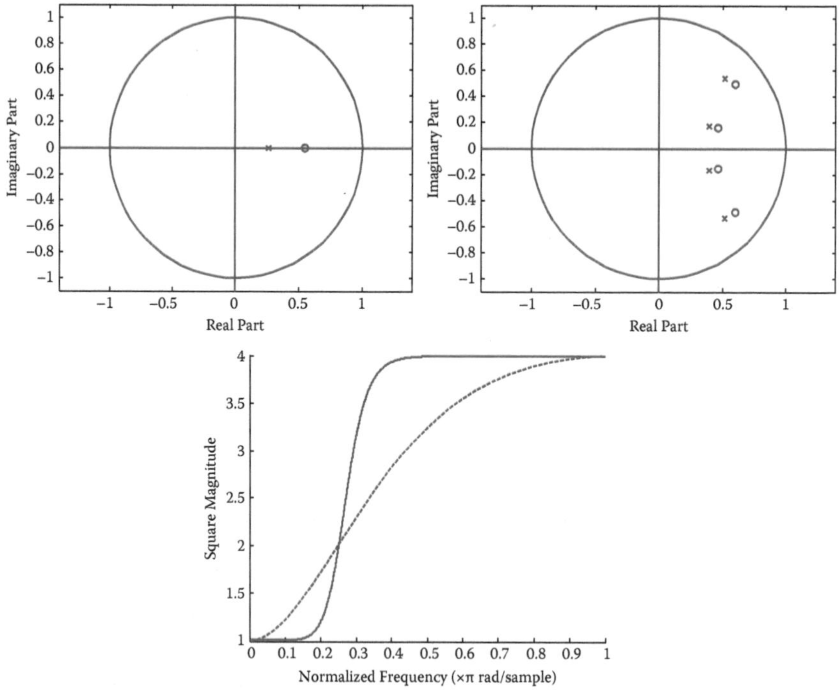

FIGURE 3.11
Pole zero plot for first-order (top left) and fourth-order (top right) high shelving filters with $\omega_c = \pi/4$ and $G = 2$. On bottom, square magnitude response for the first-order (dash-dot line) and fourth-order (solid line) filters.

Gain at Bandwidth

The band-pass, band stop, peaking, and notch filters have additional parameters that relate to bandwidth. We previously specified that the center frequency is where the filter reaches its maximum or minimum value, and cutoff frequency is where the square magnitude is halfway between its two extremes, but what about bandwidth? Well, the gain at bandwidth is defined similarly to the gain at the cutoff frequency. That is, G_B is defined using the arithmetic mean of the extremes of the square magnitude response, $G_B^2 = (1 + G^2)/2$. So

$$G_B^2 - 1 = (G^2 - 1)/2 = G^2 - G_B^2 \tag{3.35}$$

This is thus the simplest definition, and one we will use in examples that show how to generate simple low-order filters. Note, however, that we will introduce an alternative definition later when we discuss parametric equalizers in Chapter 4.

Band-Pass Filters

For a band-pass filter, $H_{BP}(\omega = 0) = 0$, $H_{BP}(\omega = \pi/2) = 0$, and $H_{BP}(\omega = \omega_c) = 1$, and for the upper and lower cutoff frequencies, $|H_{BP}(\omega = \omega_l)| = |H_{BP}(\omega = \omega_u)| = G_c$. Bandwidth is defined as $B = \omega_u - \omega_l$. So this filter is designed to pass only a range of frequencies around the cutoff frequency and to suppress all other content. To design a high-order band-pass filter, we consider each first-order section of our prototype filter. We change the gain at the cutoff frequency to G_c using Equation (3.12), then shift the cutoff frequency to the bandwidth with Equation (3.16), where ω_c in Equation (3.16) is replaced with B. Finally, we transform this to a band-pass filter using Equation (3.21).

For our first-order filter with the gain at the cutoff frequencies defined such that the square magnitude is the average of the two extremes $G_c^2 = (0^2 + 1^2)/2 = 1/2$, again there is no need to change the gain at the cutoff frequency of the prototype low-pass filter.

So we now shift the center frequency of the prototype filter to B.

$$H(z) = \frac{(z+1)\tan(B/2)}{z(\tan(B/2)+1)+\tan(B/2)-1} \tag{3.36}$$

Then we transform to a band-pass filter with bandwidth B and center frequency ω_c, which gives

$$H_{BP}(z) = \frac{\tan(B/2)(z^2-1)}{(\tan(B/2)+1)z^2 - 2\cos\omega_c z + 1 - \tan(B/2)} \tag{3.37}$$

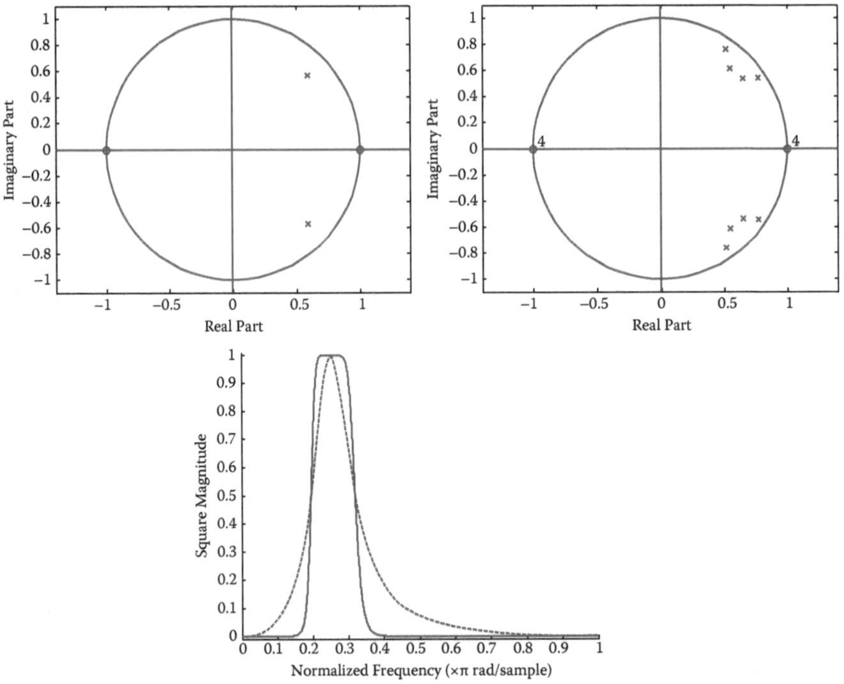

FIGURE 3.12
Pole zero plot for second-order (top left) and eighth-order (top right) band-pass filters with $\omega_c = \pi/4$ and $B = \pi/8$. On bottom, square magnitude response for the first-order (dash-dot line) and fourth-order (solid line) filters.

Band-pass filters are shown in Figure 3.12. Note that these are twice the order of the previous examples (second and eighth, as opposed to first and fourth) since the band-pass transformation doubles the order of the filter. Now there are zeros at both 1 and –1, but poles surround the center frequency, allowing for a sharp transition from attenuating to passing frequency content. If the bandwidth is increased, then the distance of the poles from the center frequency would also increase.

Band-Stop Filters

For a band stop filter, $H_{BP}(\omega = 0) = 1$, $H_{BP}(\omega = \pi/2) = 1$, and $H_{BP}(\omega = \omega_c) = 0$, and bandwidth is $B = \omega_u - \omega_l$, where $|H_{BP}(\omega = \omega_l)| = |H_{BP}(\omega = \omega_u)| = G_c$. So this filter is designed to suppress a range of frequencies around the center frequency and to pass all other content.

To design a band stop filter, we again start with the prototype filter. For each first-order section, we change the gain at the cutoff frequency. Then we invert the magnitude response, shift the cutoff frequency, and transform this to a band-pass filter. This is similar to the design of a high-order band-pass filter, except that by inverting the magnitude response using Equation (3.19), the resultant filter has band stop behavior.

For our first-order filter with the gain at the upper and lower cutoff frequencies given as $G_c^2 = 1/2$, there is no need to change the gain at the cutoff frequency. So, starting with the prototype, we invert the magnitude response, and then shift the cutoff frequency, as in the high-pass filter, giving

$$H_{HP}(z) = \frac{z-1}{(\tan(B/2)+1)z + \tan(B/2) - 1} \tag{3.38}$$

Then we transform to a band-pass filter with bandwidth B.

$$H_{BS}(z) = \frac{z^2 - 2z\cos\omega_c + 1}{(\tan(B/2)+1)z^2 - 2\cos\omega_c + 1 - \tan(B/2)} \tag{3.39}$$

The pole zero plots of the band stop filters in Figure 3.13 are very similar to the band-pass filters in Figure 3.12. But now the zeros have been moved from

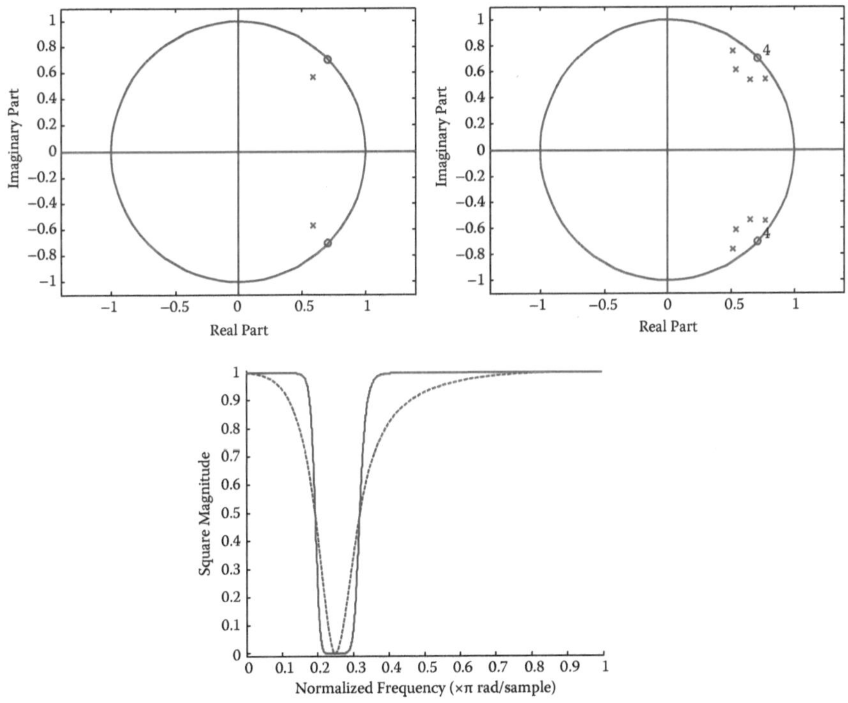

FIGURE 3.13
Pole zero plot for second-order (top left) and eighth-order (top right) band stop filters with $\omega_c = \pi/4$ and $B = \pi/8$. On bottom, square magnitude response for the first-order (dash-dot line) and fourth-order (solid line) filters.

+1 and –1 to $\cos\omega_c + j\sin\omega_c$ and $\cos\omega_c - j\sin\omega_c$. This has the effect of the poles and zeros canceling out far from the center frequency (leaving the magnitudes unaffected), and having the zeros dominate at the center frequency (attenuating the magnitude to zero).

Peaking and Notch Filters

For a peaking or notch filter, $H_{PN}(\omega = 0) = 1$, $H_{PN}(\omega = \pi/2) = 1$, and $H_{PN}(\omega = \omega_c) = G$, and for the upper and lower cutoff frequencies, $|H_{PN}(\omega = \omega_l)| = |H_{PN}(\omega = \omega_u)| = G_c$ [12]. Bandwidth is defined as $B = \omega_u - \omega_l$. When G is greater than 1, this filter provides a boost around ω_c and is known as a peaking filter. When G is less than 1, this filter attenuates the frequency content near ω_c and is known as a notch filter. Clearly, if $G = 0$, the filter completely removes frequency content near ω_c and is a band stop filter.

To design a high-order peaking or notch filter, we consider each first-order section of our prototype filter. We use Equations (3.12) and (3.28) to change the gain at the cutoff frequency. Next we transform this to a shelving filter using Equation (3.18). Then we shift the cutoff frequency to the bandwidth with Equation (3.16), where ω_c in Equation (3.16) is replaced with B. Finally, we transform this to a band-pass filter using Equation (3.21).

For our first-order filter with the magnitude of the transfer function at bandwidth defined as we defined the magnitude at the cutoff frequency for the shelving filter, we can follow the same steps as were taken with the shelving filter to give Equation (3.32), except now the center frequency is replaced by the bandwidth B.

$$H_{LS}(z) = \frac{(1 + G\tan(B/2))z + G\tan(B/2) - 1}{(1 + \tan(B/2))z + \tan(B/2) - 1} \tag{3.40}$$

Then we transform to a band-pass filter with bandwidth B.

$$H_{PN}(z) = \frac{(G\tan(B/2) + 1)z^2 - 2z\cos\omega_c + 1 - G\tan(B/2)}{(\tan(B/2) + 1)z^2 - 2z\cos\omega_c + 1 - \tan(B/2)} \tag{3.41}$$

The pole zero and square magnitude plots for first- and fourth-order designs are shown in Figure 3.14.

To summarize, when we use the simple definition of bandwidth or cutoff frequency, the standard filters mentioned above all have relatively straightforward forms for first-order designs (where bandwidth is not specified) and second-order designs (for band-pass, band stop, and peaking/notch filters). These are given in Table 3.1.

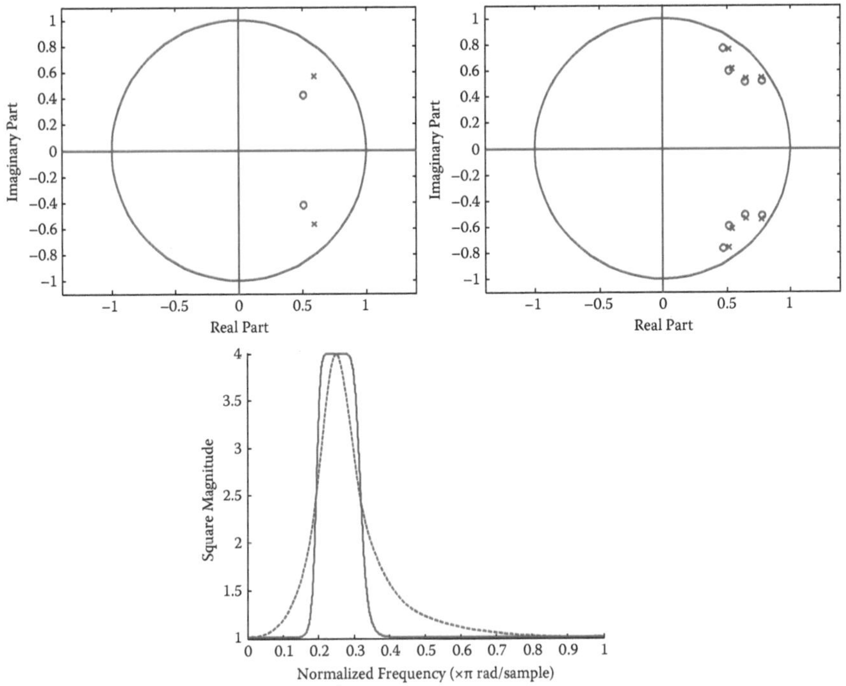

FIGURE 3.14
Pole zero plot for second-order (top left) and eighth-order (top right) peaking filters with $\omega_c = \pi/4$, $B = \pi/8$, and $G = 2$. On bottom, square magnitude response for the first-order (dash-dot line) and fourth-order (solid line) filters.

The Allpass Filter

In addition to the filter types discussed so far, there is one more type that commonly appears in audio effects. This is the *allpass filter,* and it passes all frequencies with no amplification or attenuation. That is, the magnitude of the gain is 1 at all frequencies. But if the gain doesn't change, what does the filter do? The answer lies in the *phase* of the signal. The allpass filter introduces a frequency-dependent phase shift that is useful for many effects, especially the *phaser* (Chapter 4). Also, a simple delay is a type of allpass filter, since it changes the phase but not the magnitude of each frequency component. Figure 3.15 is a plot of the magnitude and phase response of another possible allpass filter.

TABLE 3.1

Transfer Functions of Common First- and Second-Order Filters, and Their Equivalent Forms Based on Simpler Filters

	Transfer Function	Equivalence
First-order low-pass (H_{LP})	$\frac{\tan(\omega_c/2)+\tan(\omega_c/2)z^{-1}}{1+\tan(\omega_c/2)-[1-\tan(\omega_c/2)]z^{-1}}$	—
First-order high-pass (H_{HP})	$\frac{1-z^{-1}}{1+\tan(\omega_c/2)-[1-\tan(\omega_c/2)]z^{-1}}$	$1 - H_{LP}(z)$
First-order low-shelf (H_{LS})	$\frac{1+G\tan(\omega_c/2)-[1-G\tan(\omega_c/2)]z^{-1}}{1+\tan(\omega_c/2)-[1-\tan(\omega_c/2)]z^{-1}}$	$GH_{LP}(z) + H_{HP}(z)$
First-order high-shelf (H_{HS})	$\frac{\tan(\omega_c/2)+G+[\tan(\omega_c/2)-G]z^{-1}}{1+\tan(\omega_c/2)-[1-\tan(\omega_c/2)]z^{-1}}$	$H_{LP}(z) + GH_{HP}(z)$
Second-order band-pass (H_{BP})	$\frac{\tan(B/2)-\tan(B/2)z^{-2}}{1+\tan(B/2)-2\cos\omega_c z^{-1}+[1-\tan(B/2)]z^{-2}}$	—
Second-order band-stop (H_{BS})	$\frac{1-2\cos\omega_c z^{-1}+z^{-2}}{1+\tan(B/2)-2\cos\omega_c z^{-1}+[1-\tan(B/2)]z^{-2}}$	$1 - H_{BP}(z)$
Peaking or notch filter (H_{PN})	$\frac{1+G\tan(B/2)-2\cos\omega_c z^{-1}+[1-G\tan(B/2)]z^{-2}}{1+\tan(B/2)-2\cos\omega_c z^{-1}+[1-\tan(B/2)]z^{-2}}$	$GH_{BP}(z) + H_{BS}(z)$

The allpass filter may be given as

$$H(z) = \pm\frac{a_N z^N + a_{N-1}z^{N-1}\ldots + a_1 z + 1}{z^N + a_1 z^{N-1}\ldots + a_{N-1}z + a_N} \tag{3.42}$$

We can easily check that this has the allpass property

$$\begin{aligned}|H(z)|^2 &= \frac{a_N z^N + a_{N-1}z^{N-1}\ldots+1}{z^N + a_1 z^{N-1}\ldots + a_N}\cdot\frac{a_N z^{-N} + a_{N-1}z^{-N+1}\ldots+1}{z^{-N} + a_1 z^{-N+1}\ldots + a_N}\frac{z^N}{z^N} \\ &= \frac{a_N z^N + a_{N-1}z^{N-1}\ldots+1}{z^N + a_1 z^{N-1}\ldots + a_N}\cdot\frac{a_N + a_{N-1}z\ldots + z^N}{1 + a_1 z\ldots + a_N z^N} = 1\end{aligned} \tag{3.43}$$

If we look at any first-order section from this high-order filter, it can be written in the form

$$H_n(z) = \pm\frac{zc^* - 1}{z - c} \tag{3.44}$$

and we see that for a pole at c, there is a corresponding zero at $1/c^*$.

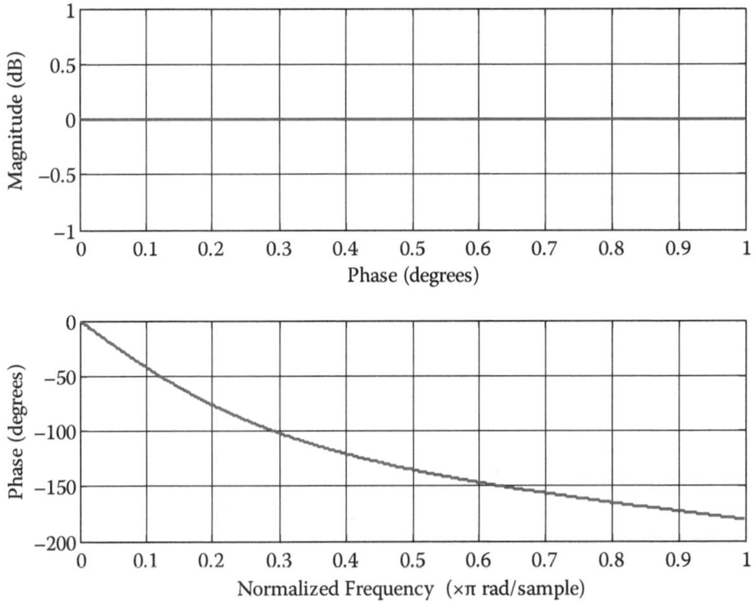

FIGURE 3.15
The magnitude and frequency response for a particular allpass filter (first order, cutoff frequency of $\omega_c = \pi/4$). All frequencies have unity gain but a different phase shift.

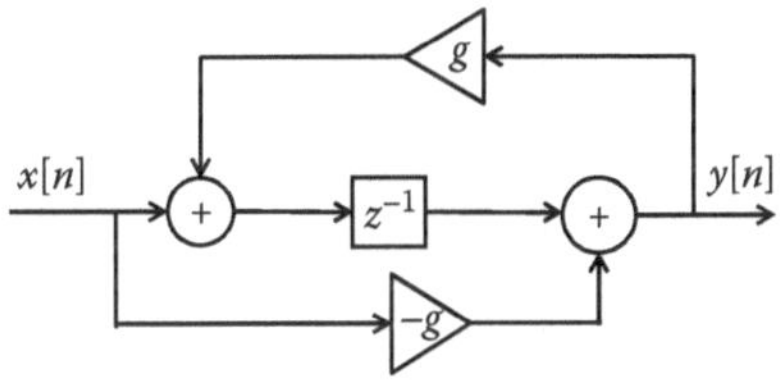

FIGURE 3.16
The block diagram for the first-order digital allpass filter.

A digital allpass filter can be created rather simply with a single sample delay and two gain blocks. Figure 3.16 shows the block diagram; note that the feedforward and the feedback gain are identical in magnitude but opposite in sign.

This is only a first-order allpass filter, as in the following equation:

$$H(z) = -\frac{zg-1}{z-g} \tag{3.45}$$

It is simply a version of Equation (3.44) with real-valued coefficients.

More complicated, higher-order versions with multiple delay blocks must be constructed in order to create an arbitrary phase response. See Chapter 4 for how this is accomplished with the phaser.

Applications of Filter Fundamentals

Exponential Moving Average Filter

Let's now take a look at one simple, but very important filter. The exponential moving average filter, also known as a smoothing filter or one-pole moving average filter, is given by

$$y[n] = \alpha y[n-1] + (1-\alpha)x[n] \tag{3.46}$$

where α is the amount of decay between adjacent samples. For instance, if α is 0.75, the value of each sample in the output signal is three-quarters of the previous output and one-quarter of the new input. The higher the value of α, the slower the decay. This filter is often used to smooth the effect of processing a signal, or to derive a smoothly changing estimate of signal level. As we will see in Chapter 6, it features prominently in dynamics processing.

The transfer function is

$$H(z) = \frac{(1-\alpha)z}{(z-\alpha)} \tag{3.47}$$

which gives one zero at zero, one pole at α, and gain of $(1-\alpha)$. We can also find the square magnitude response and, after a bit of manipulation, the phase response,

$$\begin{aligned} |H(z)|^2 &= \frac{1-\alpha}{1-\alpha z^{-1}}\frac{1-\alpha}{1-\alpha z} = \frac{(1-\alpha)^2}{1-2\alpha\cos\omega+\alpha^2} \\ \angle H(z) &= \tan^{-1}\frac{\alpha\sin\omega}{1-\alpha\cos\omega} \end{aligned} \tag{3.48}$$

where $\omega = 2\pi f/f_s$ is normalized radial frequency.

The impulse response of this filter is

$$y[n] = \alpha^n(1-\alpha) \tag{3.49}$$

Now consider the step function,

$$x[n] = \begin{cases} 1 & n \geq 0 \\ 0 & n < 0 \end{cases}.$$

The step response of this filter is

$$y[n] = 1 - \alpha^n \quad \text{for} \quad x[n] = 1, n \geq 1 \tag{3.50}$$

The time constant τ is defined as the time it takes for this system to reach $1 - 1/e$ of its final value, i.e., $y[\tau f_s] = 1 - 1/e$. Thus from (3.50) we have

$$\alpha = e^{-1/(\tau f_s)}, \quad \tau = -1/\left(f_s \ln \alpha\right) \tag{3.51}$$

This is an important filter, since it can be used to very simply smooth a signal. Generally, one gives the time constant τ, finds α from (3.51), and implements the filter in the time domain using (3.46). Note that this particular filter is primarily used for smoothing a signal in the time domain, and not explicitly for modifying frequency content. It simply provides a smooth output that can still quickly respond to sudden changes in the input.

Loudspeaker Crossovers

Low-pass, high-pass, and band-pass filters are commonly used in *crossover networks* (or just *crossovers*) for loudspeakers. Larger hi-fi speakers almost always use more than one speaker driver to cover the entire audio frequency range. *Woofers* are large drivers (4–15 in. diameter) used for the lower frequencies, and *tweeters* are smaller cone- or dome-shaped drivers (0.5–2 in. diameter) used for the higher frequencies. Some speakers also include a third *midrange* driver to cover the frequencies between woofer and tweeter. Others use a single freestanding *subwoofer* to cover the lowest bass frequencies for the entire audio system; since the human ear cannot localize low bass frequencies, a single large subwoofer can be used to cover the low-frequency content for a stereo or surround sound system, which allows the remaining speakers to be smaller and less expensive.

For a speaker to work properly, the same signal cannot be sent to every driver. Woofers reproduce high frequencies poorly and with significant distortion, and sending bass frequencies to a tweeter can cause mechanical damage. The role of the crossover is to divide the audio signal into two or three frequency ranges that are sent to each driver. In a speaker with a woofer and tweeter (*two-way*), the crossover consists of a low-pass filter for the woofer

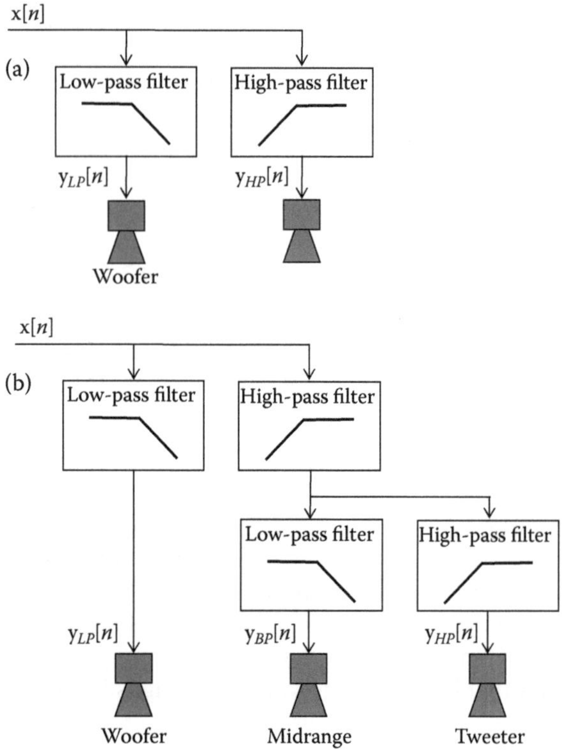

FIGURE 3.17
A loudspeaker crossover separates the incoming audio signal into several different frequency bands so that each loudspeaker is provided with content within a preferred frequency range. Two-way (a) and three-way (b) loudspeaker crossovers are depicted.

and a high-pass filter for the tweeter (Figure 3.17a). The two filters have the same cutoff frequency (typically around 1–3 kHz), which means that any given input frequency should go either to the woofer or to the tweeter, but not both. Of course, practical filters do not have perfectly sharp cutoffs, so there will always be a gradual transition between the two drivers. The gradual transition is a desirable property in practice, and very few crossovers use filters higher than fourth order. Second-order filters are most commonly used in crossovers, and the occasional first-order design can also be found.

When woofer, midrange, and tweeter are used (a *three-way* speaker), there are two crossover points to consider: the transition between the woofer and the midrange and that between the midrange and tweeter. In practice, a three-way crossover looks like 2 two-way crossovers in series (Figure 3.17b). A low-pass filter is used for the woofer and a high-pass filter for the rest of the signal. The output of the high-pass filter is then split again into midrange and tweeter components. (An equivalent way to understand the operation is that the woofer has a low-pass filter, the midrange a band-pass filter, and the tweeter a high-pass filter.) The woofer–midrange crossover frequency is typically in the range 200 Hz–1 kHz, and the midrange–tweeter crossover in the range 2–4 kHz.

In the early days of loudspeakers, crossovers were built using high-power capacitors and inductors that could operate directly on the output of an audio power amplifier. This is still a common practice, but increasingly, self-powered speakers such as studio monitors will perform the crossover filtering on the line-level audio signal and use a separate power amplifier for each driver; this process is known as *biamplification* for a two-way speaker or *triamplification* for a three-way speaker. Crossovers at line level can generally have lower distortion and tighter component tolerances, and they can be more sophisticated in correcting slight imperfections in the frequency responses of the drivers.

Good crossover design can be as important as the quality of the drivers in determining the sound of a finished loudspeaker. Many subtle design variations are possible, which are discussed in detail in [13]. Crossovers are easily implemented digitally using the basic filters presented in this chapter, the main practical constraint being that there must be at least one DAC channel and one amplifier for every driver (e.g., six channels for a stereo three-way speaker).

Problems

1. Design a second-order peaking filter for a 48 kHz signal with center frequency 6 kh and gain of 6 dB, and bandwidth of 1 kHz. Assume bandwidth is defined as when the square magnitude is the average of the two extremes, $G_B^2 = (1 + G^2)/2$, where G is the linear gain.
2. Consider the second-order filter having transfer function

$$H(z) = \frac{r^2z^2 - 2r\cos\theta z + 1}{z^2 - 2r\cos\theta z + r^2}$$

   Show that it is an allpass filter; that is, show that $|H(z)| = 1$. Find the zeros of the filter as a function of the poles.
3. Consider the exponential moving average filter. Find the cutoff frequency if it is defined as where the square magnitude is halfway between the two extremes, $|H(z = 1)|^2$ and $|H(z = -1)|^2$.
4. Consider the moving average window

$$y[n] = \frac{1}{W}\sum_{i=0}^{W-1} x[n-i]$$

What are the transfer function, impulse response, and step response of this filter? Define the time constant as was done for the exponential moving average, the time it takes for this system to reach $1 - 1/e$ of its final value, i.e., $y[\tau f_s] = 1 - 1/e$.

If the time constant of the moving average window is set equal to the time constant of the exponential moving average, what is the relationship between W and α?

5. An out-of-band shelving filter has unity gain at center frequency ω_c, bandwidth B, and magnitude G at frequency 0 and at $f_s/2$. It may be constructed by converting the prototype to a shelving filter, reversing the filter, shifting the cutoff frequency to the bandwidth, and then transforming this to a band-pass filter. A second-order design could also be constructed by manipulating other filter designs. Give the transfer function for a second-order out-of-band shelving filter.

4

Filter Effects

In a sense, any audio effect could be considered a *filter* in that every effect performs mathematical operations on the input signal that produce some change in the content. This chapter, however, is concerned with effects based on the canonical types of filters defined in Chapter 3: low-pass, high-pass, band-pass, peaking/notch, shelving, and allpass filters. The effects that fall into this category are *equalizers*, a broad class of effects that adjust the frequency balance of the input audio signal; *wah-wah*, a musical effect typically used on guitar that is based on a peaking filter; and the *phaser*, an effect based on allpass filters that produces a sweeping, spacious sound similar to the flanger (Chapter 2).

Equalization

Equalization (EQ) is one of the most common audio effects. It is the process of adjusting the relative strength of different frequency bands within a signal. The name *equalization* comes from the desire to obtain a flat (equal) frequency response from an audio system by compensating for nonideal equipment or room acoustics. Peaks or troughs in the frequency response of a system are often described as "coloration" of the sound, and equalization can be used to remove this coloration [14–16].

Equalization covers a broad class of effects, ranging from simple tone controls to sophisticated graphic and parametric equalizers. All EQ effects are based on filters, and most equalizers consist of multiple subfilters, each of which affects a single frequency band. In the following, we will go through the steps of designing an equalizer out of such subfilters and discuss the properties these subfilters should have.

Theory

Equalizers range in complexity from simple two-knob tone controls to complex multiband graphic and parametric equalizers, but at a fundamental level, all designs are based on the same collection of filter structures. Equalizer design therefore depends heavily on choosing the correct parameters for each filter, keeping in mind which parameters should be fixed by the design and which should be user-adjustable.

Two-Knob Tone Controls

Most stereo systems feature *tone controls*, which provide a simple and quick way to adjust the sound to suit the listener's taste and compensate for the frequency response of the room. Tone controls are the simplest and possibly most common equalization system. A basic version consists of two knobs, typically labeled "bass" and "treble." These knobs are used to control the *gain* of low and high frequencies, respectively, through the use of *shelving filters*. Figure 4.1a shows a block diagram of a typical implementation.

Recall from Chapter 3 that shelving filters come in *low* and *high* shelf configurations. A low shelving filter has adjustable gain at low frequencies and unity gain at high frequencies; it is used in the bass control. The reverse is true for the high shelving filter, used in the treble control. Tone controls commonly use first-order shelving filters, which produce a gradual 6 dB/octave transition between low and high frequencies (Figure 4.2).

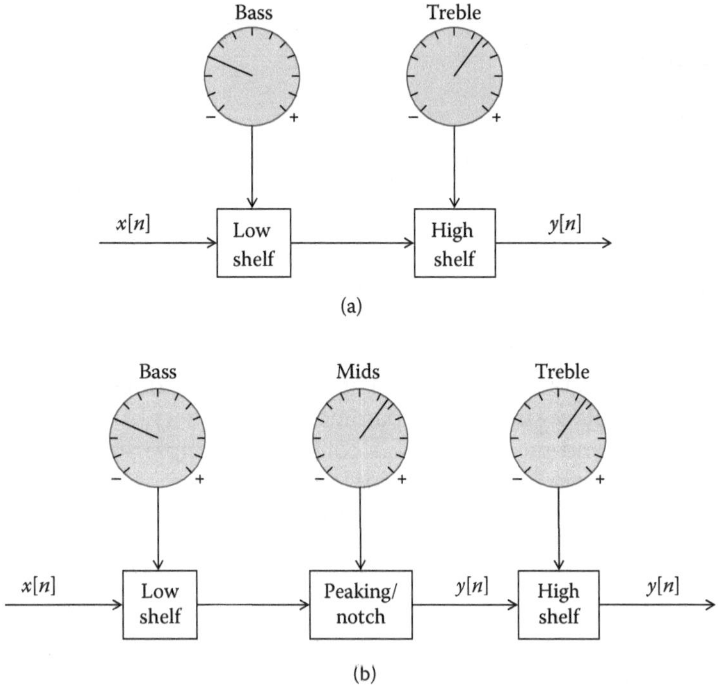

FIGURE 4.1
(a) Bass and treble tone controls implemented as a low shelving filter and high shelving filter placed in series. (b) Three tone controls, including a peaking/notch filter to adjust the midrange.

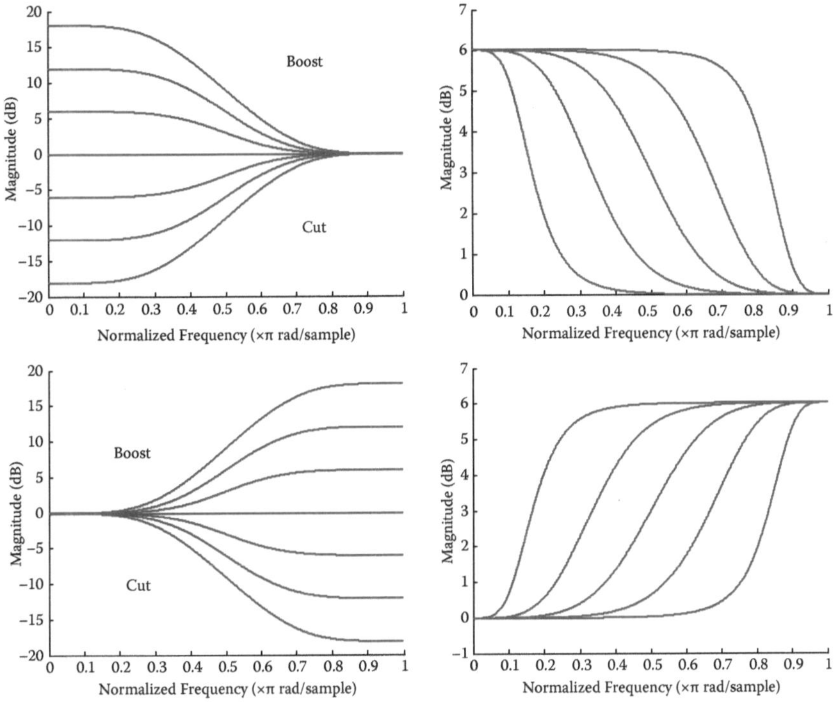

FIGURE 4.2
Frequency response of a low shelving filter (top) and a high shelving filter (bottom), for varying the gain (left) or varying the center frequency (right).

We can use the procedure described in Chapter 3 to design the shelving filters. However, now we would like the gain at the cutoff frequency, G_c, to be $\sqrt{G}$, where G is the gain of the shelf. That way, a low shelf and high shelf with the same cutoff frequency ω_c and gain G will produce a constant gain G across all frequencies. The transfer function for the low shelving filter is as follows:

$$H_{LS}(z) = \frac{\left[G\tan(\omega_c/2)+\sqrt{G}\right]z + G\tan(\omega_c/2)-\sqrt{G}}{\left[\tan(\omega_c/2)+\sqrt{G}\right]z+\tan(\omega_c/2)-\sqrt{G}} \tag{4.1}$$

And for the high shelving filter:

$$H_{HS}(z) = \frac{\left[\sqrt{G}\tan(\omega_c/2)+G\right]z+\sqrt{G}\tan(\omega_c/2)-G}{\left[\sqrt{G}\tan(\omega_c/2)+1\right]z+\sqrt{G}\tan(\omega_c/2)-1} \tag{4.2}$$

In each case, the maximum gain of the shelf, G, is adjustable. Where $G > 1$, the bass (low-shelf case) or treble (high-shelf case) will be boosted; where $G < 1$, it will be cut. Typical tone controls have an adjustment range of ±12 dB, corresponding to approximately $0.25 < G < 4$ for each filter. The *cutoff frequency* ω_c is usually fixed. The values for bass and treble vary by manufacturer, but typically the bass control uses a lower ω_c than the treble control. Cutoff frequencies for the bass control might range from 100 to 300 Hz, and the treble control from 3 to 10 kHz.

Three-Knob Tone Controls

In two-knob tone controls, the *midrange* frequencies (between bass and treble) are usually left unchanged. On some units, in addition to control of the bass and treble, there may be a midrange or mid control. This control is usually implemented as a *peaking* or *notch filter*. Its transfer function is derived in Chapter 3, where again, we define the gain at bandwidth to be $\sqrt{G}$:

$$H_{PN}(z) = \frac{\left[\sqrt{G} + G\tan(B/2)\right]z^2 - 2\sqrt{G}\cos\omega_c z + \sqrt{G} - G\tan(B/2)}{\left[\sqrt{G} + \tan(B/2)\right]z^2 - 2\sqrt{G}\cos\omega_c z + \sqrt{G} - \tan(B/2)} \tag{4.3}$$

The peaking or notch filter is depicted in Figure 4.3.

The knob on the midrange control affects the gain G at center frequency, which generally takes the same range of values as the bass and treble controls (e.g., $0.25 < G < 4$). The center frequency ω_c is generally fixed to be midway between the bass and treble controls, and the bandwidth B is chosen so that the midrange control affects the frequencies that are left unadjusted by the bass and treble controls.

Presence Control

Some systems, including many guitar amplifiers and mixing consoles, will have a presence knob or button in addition to the tone controls mentioned above. This controls a peaking filter in the upper midrange frequencies. The transfer function for the peaking filter is identical to the midrange control described in the previous section, but the center frequency and the *quality factor* or Q (defined as center frequency over bandwidth) are higher, such that the presence control affects roughly the 2–6 kHz frequency band, where the human ear is very sensitive. The presence control is intended to simulate the effect of an instrument being physically present in the same room as the listener, and it can help bring out an instrument in a mix without changing its overall level.

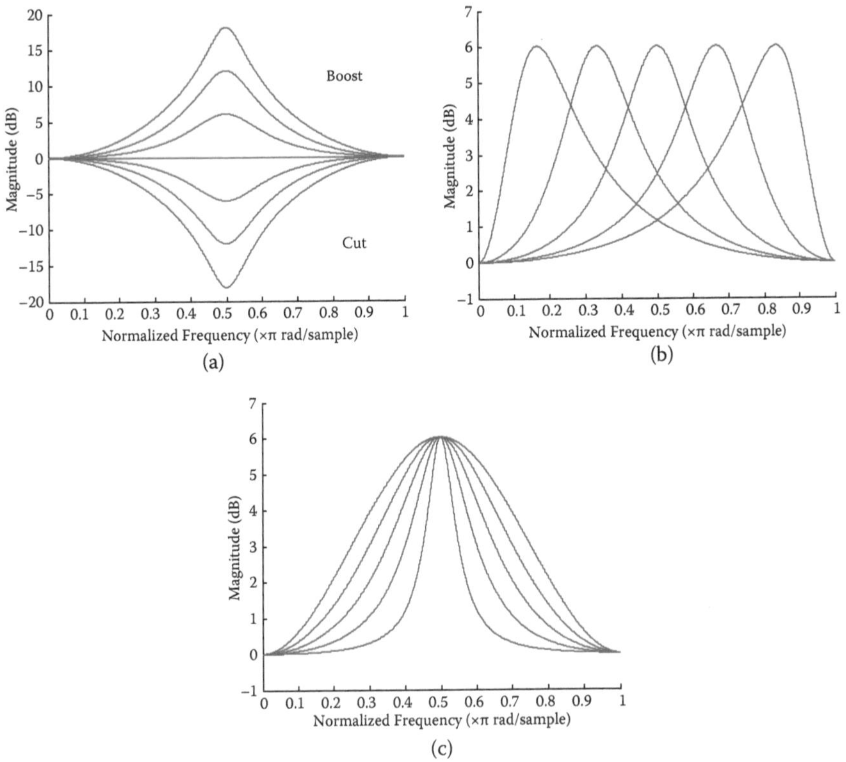

FIGURE 4.3
Magnitude responses for a peaking or notch filter when adjusting gain (a), center frequency (b), and bandwidth (c).

Loudness Control

Many stereo amplifiers feature a "loudness" control, either as a knob or an on–off button. In this context, *loudness* has a different meaning than *volume* or *amplitude* (which refer to the total sound pressure level (SPL) produced by the audio system). The sensitivity of human hearing is heavily dependent on frequency: for the same SPL, midrange frequencies will be perceived to be louder than very low or very high frequencies.

Figure 4.4 shows a plot of *equal loudness contours* for human hearing. Each curve indicates the SPL required to maintain the same perceived loudness (equivalent to 90 phon, 80 phon, …, 10 phon, where 1 phon = 1 dBSPL at a frequency of 1 kHz) across all frequencies. Notice that the curves become flatter as overall SPL increases. This means that especially at low listening levels, bass and treble need to be boosted with respect to the midrange to be perceived as equally loud.

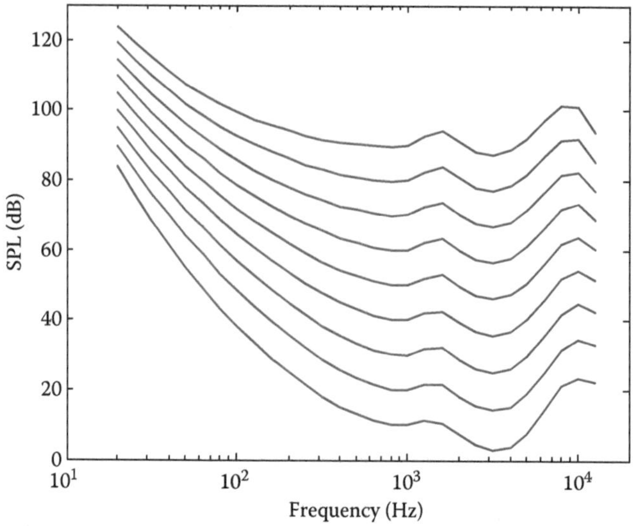

FIGURE 4.4
Equal loudness contours by phon (90 phon, top curve; 10 phon, bottom curve), as given in the ISO 226 standard. Each curve represents the sound pressure level (SPL) required for which a listener will perceive a constant loudness when presented with pure steady tones across the frequency range.

The loudness control is therefore designed to boost the low and high frequencies of the input signal. Two *shelving* filters (one for bass, one for treble) can be used for this purpose. When the loudness control is implemented as a continuous knob, its setting controls the *gain* of the low- and high-frequency shelves, with the midrange gain fixed at 1. When it is implemented as a button, it switches between flat frequency response (no boost) and an inverse of the A-weighting loudness curve, which is a rough approximation of the equal loudness, contours near 40 phon. Thus, it is used to boost that frequency content that we perceive to have additional attenuation at low listening levels.

Graphic Equalizers

The graphic equalizer is a tool for precisely adjusting the gain of multiple frequency regions. In contrast to the simple two- or three-knob tone control, a graphic equalizer can provide up to 30 controls for manipulating the frequency response. Structurally, a graphic EQ is simply a set of filters, each with a fixed center frequency. The only user control is the amount of boost or cut in each frequency band, which is often controlled with vertical sliders. The term *graphic* refers to the fact that the position of the sliders' knobs can be understood as a graph of the equalizer's magnitude response versus frequency. In other words, the position of the sliders resembles the frequency response itself, which makes the graphic equalizer intuitive to use despite the number of controls.

The basic unit of the graphic equalizer is the *band*. A band is a region in frequency defined by a *center frequency* ω_c and a *bandwidth* B or *quality factor* Q. Recall that these three terms are related by $Q = \omega_c/B$.

The gain of each band is controllable by the user. Typical gains range from –12 dB to +12 dB ($0.25 < G < 4$), with 0 dB ($G = 1$) meaning no change or flat. The same peaking or notch filter found in the midrange tone control, Equation (4.3), can be used to create a single band of a graphic equalizer.

The center frequency ω_c and bandwidth B are not user-adjustable. To choose the right values for these parameters, we must consider the relationship between the bands.

Bands in a Graphic Equalizer

The bands in a graphic equalizer are usually distributed logarithmically in frequency, to match human perception. Let us denote the normalized lower and upper cutoff frequencies of the ith band with $\omega_{l,i}$ and $\omega_{u,i}$, respectively. As earlier, bandwidth is the difference between the upper and lower cutoff frequencies, $B_i = \omega_{u,i} - \omega_{l,i}$.

The frequency bands are adjacent [17], so the upper cutoff of band i will be the lower cutoff of band $i + 1$, $\omega_{u,i} = \omega_{l,i+1}$. That is, input audio frequencies below this cutoff will be primarily affected by the gain control for band i, where input frequencies above it will be primarily affected by the gain control for band $i + 1$.

The logarithmic distribution of the frequency bands can be specified using a fixed ratio R between each band, so $\omega_{l,i+1} = R \cdot \omega_{l,i}$, $\omega_{u,i+1} = R \cdot \omega_{u,i}$, or $B_{i+1} = R \cdot B_i$. We also consider the geometric mean of the two cutoff frequencies, $\omega_{M,i} \equiv \sqrt{\omega_{l,i}\omega_{u,i}}$, where you can see that we have the same relationship for the distribution of these values, $\omega_{M,i+1} = R \cdot \omega_{M,i}$.

Two common designs are *octave* and *one-third-octave* graphic equalizers. An octave is a musical interval defined by a doubling in frequency, so octave graphic equalizers will have the ratio $R = 2$ between each band. In a one-third-octave design, each octave contains three bands, which implies $R^3 = 2$ or $R \approx 1.26$. So starting at 100 Hz, an octave spacing would have geometric mean frequencies at 200, 400, 800 Hz, etc., and a one-third-octave spacing would have filters centered at 126, 159, 200 Hz, etc.

The number of bands is determined by their spacing and the requirement to cover the entire audible spectrum. Octave graphic equalizers usually have 10 bands, ranging from 31 Hz at the lowest to 16 kHz at the highest. One-third-octave designs have 30 bands ranging from 25 Hz to 20 kHz. These frequencies, shown in Table 4.1, are standardized by the International Organization for Standardization (ISO) [18].

TABLE 4.1

The ISO Standard for Octave and One-Third-Octave Frequency Bands

Octave Bands			One-Third-Octave Bands		
Lower Frequency f_l (Hz)	Geometric Mean Frequency f_M (Hz)	Upper Frequency f_u (Hz)	Lower Frequency f_l (Hz)	Geometric Mean Frequency f_M (Hz)	Upper Frequency f_u (Hz)
22	31.5	44	22.4	25	28.2
			28.2	31.5	35.5
			35.5	40	44.7
44	63	88	44.7	50	56.2
			56.2	63	70.8
			70.8	80	89.1
88	125	177	89.1	100	112
			112	125	141
			141	160	178
177	250	355	178	200	224
			224	250	282
			282	315	355
355	500	710	355	400	447
			447	500	562
			562	630	708
710	1000	1420	708	800	891
			891	1000	1122
			1122	1250	1413
1420	2000	2840	1413	1600	1778
			1778	2000	2239
			2239	2500	2818
2840	4000	5680	2818	3150	3548
			3548	4000	4467
			4467	5000	5623
5680	8000	11,360	5623	6300	7079
			7079	8000	8913
			8913	10,000	11,220
11,360	16,000	22,720	11,220	12,500	14,130
			14,130	16,000	17,780
			17,780	20,000	22,390

The bandwidth can be easily related to the geometric mean of the cutoff frequencies,

$$\omega_{M,i} \equiv \sqrt{\omega_{l,i}\omega_{u,i}} = \sqrt{R}\cdot\omega_{l,i} = \omega_{u,i}/\sqrt{R}$$
$$\rightarrow B_i = \omega_{u,i} - \omega_{l,i} = \left(\sqrt{R} - 1/\sqrt{R}\right)\omega_{M,i} \tag{4.4}$$

Note that the geometric mean of the cutoff frequencies of a filter, $\omega_{M,i}$, is not usually the true center frequency where the filter reaches its maximum or minimum value, $\omega_{c,i}$. From Chapter 3 and a bit of trigonometry, we can find a relationship between the upper and lower cutoff frequencies and the center frequency of a band-pass, band stop, peaking, or notch filter,

$$\tan^2\left(\omega_{c,i}/2\right) = \tan\left(\omega_{u,i}/2\right)\tan\left(\omega_{l,i}/2\right) \tag{4.5}$$

However, the geometric mean is usually quite close to the center frequency. Thus, the bandwidth scales roughly proportionally with the center frequency, and higher bands will have a larger bandwidth than lower ones. Since $Q = \omega_c/B$, this is another way of saying that the Q factor is nearly constant for each band in a graphic equalizer. From (4.4), we can estimate Q as

$$Q = \omega_{c,i}/B_i \sim \omega_{M,i}/B_i$$
$$= 1/\left(\sqrt{R} - 1/\sqrt{R}\right) = \frac{\sqrt{R}}{R-1} \tag{4.6}$$

for an octave (10-band) equalizer, $Q = \sqrt{2} \approx 1.41$ since $R = 2$. For a third-octave (30-band) equalizer, we find $Q \approx 4.32$ since $R = \sqrt[3]{2} \approx 1.26$.

Ideally, the subfilter for the ith band has magnitude of the desired gain G_i inside the band and gain at bandwidth $\sqrt{G}$, so that at the cutoff frequency, when $G_i = G_{i+1} = G$, we have

$$\left|H_{i+1}\left(e^{j\omega_{L,i+1}}\right)H_i\left(e^{j\omega_{U,i}}\right)\right| = G \tag{4.7}$$

The individual filters are high-order low shelving filters, as derived previously.

We base our design on the lower cutoff frequencies, so that we express other parameters as

$$\omega_{u,i} = R\omega_{l,i}$$
$$B_i = \omega_{u,i} - \omega_{l,i} = (R-1)\omega_{l,i} \tag{4.8}$$
$$\omega_{C,i} = 2\tan^{-1}\sqrt{\tan(\omega_{u,i}/2)\tan(\omega_{l,i}/2)}$$

So the design of a graphic equalizer is as follows:

1. Choose the distribution of filters, i.e., set R for octaves, one-third octaves, etc.
2. Choose the first lower cutoff frequency.
3. From this, find bandwidth and center frequency.
4. For a given gain, generate the peaking/notch filter.
5. Find next lower cutoff frequency.
6. Repeat steps 3–5 until the whole frequency range is covered.

This procedure could equally have been performed with band-pass filters rather than peaking/notch filters. However, then the filters would have been arranged in parallel, not series.

Parametric Equalizers

The parametric equalizer is perhaps the most powerful and flexible of the equalizer types. Where each band of a graphic equalizer is adjustable only in gain, each band in a parametric equalizer has three adjustments: *gain*, *center frequency*, and Q (or bandwidth). Most parametric equalizer bands are implemented with the same peaking/notch filter we have previously seen, Equation (4.3). Notice that the three controls relate directly to the parameters G, ω_c, and B (where $B = \omega_c/Q$).

Since each band is more complex on a parametric equalizer compared to a graphic equalizer, a complete parametric equalizer unit will typically have fewer bands (an EQ section on a mixing console might have one or two bands; a dedicated rack-mount unit, four or six bands).

In addition to the gain, center frequency, and Q controls, some bands may have a switch to act as a shelving filter rather than the typical peaking/notch filter. In shelving mode (Figure 4.2), gain G is applied to all frequencies below the center frequency (*low shelving filter*, sometimes used in the lowest-frequency band) or to all frequencies above the center frequency (*high shelving filter*, sometimes used in the highest-frequency band). These shelving filters are similar to those found in the basic tone control, but where the tone control usually uses first-order shelving filters, the parametric equalizer uses either first- or second-order filters.

Summary

Every equalization effect, from the simplest tone control to the most complex parametric EQ, is based on the same set of filter types. The main differences between them are the number of individual subfilters and the controls presented to the user. First- and second-order filters are most commonly used in

WHO INVENTED THE PARAMETRIC EQUALIZER?

Early filters included bass and treble controls without adjustable center frequency, bandwidth, and cut or boost. So sound engineers could only make broad, overall changes to a signal. When graphic equalizers arrived, engineers were still limited to the constraints imposed by the number and location of bands.

In the 1960s Harold Seidel of Western Electric and Bell Telephone devised a tunable parametric filter. Daniel Flickinger then introduced an important tunable equalizer in early 1971. His circuit allowed arbitrary selection of frequency and cut/boost level in three overlapping bands over the entire audio spectrum.

In 1966, Burgess Macneal and George Massenburg began work on a new recording console for International Telecomm Incorporated. During the building of the console, Macneal and Massenburg, who was still a teenager, conceptualized an idea for a sweep-tunable EQ that would avoid inductors and switches. Soon after, Bob Meushaw, a friend of Massenburg, built a three-band, frequency adjustable, fixed-Q equalizer.

When asked who invented the parametric equalizer, Massenburg stated, "Four people could possibly lay claim to the modern concept: Bob Meushaw, Burgess Macneal, Daniel Flickinger, and myself … . Our (Bob's, Burgess', and my) sweep-tunable EQ was born, more or less, out of an idea that Burgess and I had around 1966 or 1967 for an EQ … . By 1969 I was spending all of my time designing circuitry sufficient to get to an elegant user interface: we perceived this as three controls adjusting, independently, the parameters for each of three bands for a recording console … . I remember agonizing over the topology for the EQ for months, and asking everyone I knew for help. I wrote and delivered the AES paper on Parametrics at the Los Angeles show in 1972 [19] … it's the first mention of 'Parametric' associated with sweep-tunable EQ … what I'm proudest of is less in designing devices alone and more in exploring the ever-expanding applications and uses of gear, and then applying that knowledge to designs."

George Massenburg went on to win many awards for both his technical contributions to recording technology and his critically acclaimed recordings. And today, the parametric equalizer is pervasive in audio signal processing, and a fundamental tool in digital filtering techniques as well [20].

all equalizers, as these provide sufficient flexibility while minimizing complexity and artifacts sometimes found in higher-order filters. The next section discusses the practical implementation of the required filters for each type of equalizer.

Implementation

General Notes

All types of equalizers discussed in this chapter were originally analog effects, and their digital implementation follows the analog designs as closely as possible. Infinite impulse response (IIR) filters are used throughout. Partly this is to emulate analog models, but processing delay is also a concern whenever any effect is used in live performance. While the maximum allowable total delay in an audio system may be a matter of discussion, it is safe to require each individual device to have the lowest possible processing delay, to allow cascading of several devices. This suggests using minimum phase IIR filters (see Chapter 1) instead of linear phase FIR filters, which typically exhibit higher latency for the same performance.

While some simple equalization effects such as the presence control can be implemented with a single filter section, most effects require two or more independent filters (referred to here as subfilters) to produce the overall result. In the case of the graphic equalizer, 30 or more subfilters might be used, and the way they are connected to one another becomes extremely important. Two topologies are commonly used: *parallel* connections, where audio is processed independently through several subfilters and the results added together, and *cascade* (or *series*) connections, where the output of one subfilter becomes the input to the next one. The optimal choice for each type of equalizer is discussed in the following sections.

Tone Control Architecture

The two-knob tone control is implemented with a low shelving filter for the bass and a high shelving filter for the treble. First-order filters are used to create smooth (6 dB/octave) transitions between affected and unaffected frequency regions. When a third midrange knob is used, it is often created from a second-order peaking/notch filter. Cascade connections are most commonly used for these controls, as shown in Figure 4.1b.

See Chapter 3 for details of implementing each subfilter. Calculating the output of a first-order IIR filter requires not only the current input sample $x[n]$, but also the previous input $x[n-1]$ and the previous output $y[n-1]$. The second-order peaking/notch filter also requires values for $x[n-2]$ and $y[n-2]$. Therefore, a complete three-knob tone control will require 11 stored previous values.

Calculating Filter Coefficients

The coefficients for each filter in the tone control depend on the settings of the three knobs. As seen in Equations (4.1) to (4.3), calculating the coefficients requires a complex series of operations, including trigonometric functions and floating-point division, all of which are more computationally expensive than multiplication. It is therefore advisable to recalculate the filter coefficients only when the knob positions change. The calculated coefficients can then be stored and recalled each time they are needed to process new audio samples.

Presence and Loudness Architecture

The presence control can be implemented with a single peaking/notch filter with a center frequency around 4 kHz and a Q of approximately 1. This corresponds to a bandwidth of 4 kHz, thus covering the 2–6 kHz frequency range. The presence knob adjusts the gain of this band; as with all peaking/notch filters, the gain outside of the band is 1.

The loudness control is architecturally nearly identical to the two-knob tone control. A low shelving and a high shelving filter are connected in cascade mode (Figure 4.1a). Their cutoff frequencies are fixed by design (100 Hz in the bass and 8 kHz in the treble are typical values), just as the cutoff frequencies are fixed in the tone control. However, a single knob or button controls the pass band gain of both filters. The midrange gain remains at 1.

Graphic Equalizer Architecture

The graphic equalizer can be considered a generalization of the basic tone control with more bands; however, it is often implemented differently. The bass and treble controls in a basic tone control are connected in cascade, with each control affecting part of the frequency range and leaving the rest unaffected. A cascade of peaking/notch filters can be used in the graphic equalizer, but it involves the series connection of up to 31 subfilters, which can have unexpected harmful effects.

The discussion in this chapter has focused mostly on the *magnitude response* of each filter, but *phase distortion* needs to be considered as well. Every IIR filter will have a nonlinear phase response with respect to frequency, and when filters are connected in cascade, the phase response of each section will add. In some cases, the combined phase shifts can produce audible artifacts that color the sound. FIR filters, which are less commonly used in equalization, can have linear phase, avoiding this particular form of distortion. However, FIR filters typically have a longer *group delay* for the same filter performance, so cascading many FIR filters in series might produce an audible delay between input and output.

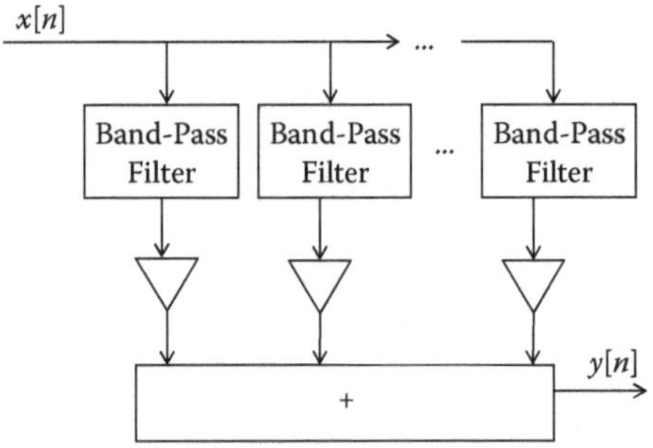

FIGURE 4.5
A diagram of a graphic equalizer, implemented with band-pass filters placed in parallel, with *N* bands of control.

Instead of using a cascade of peaking/notch filters, graphic equalizers often use a collection of band-pass filters arranged in *parallel*, as shown in Figure 4.5. The audio input is split and sent to the input of every band-pass filter. Each filter allows only a small frequency band to pass through. The center frequencies and bandwidths are configured so that if all the outputs were added together, the original signal would be reconstructed. The controls on the graphic equalizer are then implemented by changing the gain of each band-pass filter output before the signals are summed together.

Parallel connection of band-pass filters avoids the accumulating phase errors (and, potentially, *quantization noise*) found in the cascade. It also has a secondary benefit: the coefficients of each band-pass filter depend only on their center frequency and Q and do not change with the setting of the gain sliders. Coefficients can therefore be calculated once when the effect is initialized, given information on the *sample rate*. Changing gain involves changing only a single number that multiplies the output of the band-pass filter.

Parametric Equalizer Architecture

A single section of a parametric equalizer is created from a second-order peaking/notch filter (or in certain cases, a second-order shelving filter). When multiple sections are used, they are always connected in cascade so that the effects of each subfilter are cumulative. Even though the parametric equalizer is among the most complex for the user to control, its implementation is no more complex than a simple tone control. Also like the tone control, filter coefficients should be recalculated every time the user changes any knob, but for reasons of efficiency should *not* be recalculated for every audio sample.

Code Example

Implementing a parametric equalizer includes two main tasks: first, the coefficients of the IIR filter must be calculated whenever the user changes the center frequency, gain, or bandwidth, and second, the filter must be applied to each audio sample. This code shows the calculation of coefficients. For efficiency, it is run only when the user updates the controls.

```
void ParametricEQFilter::makeParametric(const double freq,
                                        const double Q,
                                        const double
                                         gainFactor)
{
    // Limit the bandwidth so we don't get a nonsense result
    // from tan(B/2)
    const double bandwidth = jmin(discreteFrequency / Q,
                                  M_PI * 0.99);
    const double two_cos_wc = -2.0*cos(discreteFrequency);
    const double tan_half_bw = tan(bandwidth / 2.0);
    const double g_tan_half_bw = gainFactor * tan_half_bw;
    const double sqrt_g = sqrt(gainFactor);

    // setCoefficients() takes arguments: b0, b1, b2, a0,
    // a1, a2. It will normalise the filter by a0 to allow
    // standard time-domain implementations

    setCoefficients (sqrt_g + g_tan_half_bw, /* b0 */
                     sqrt_g * two_cos_wc, /* b1 */
                     sqrt_g - g_tan_half_bw, /* b2 */
                     sqrt_g + tan_half_bw, /* a0 */
                     sqrt_g * two_cos_wc, /* a1 */
                     sqrt_g - tan_half_bw /* a2 */);
}
```

This code is based on the JUCE `IIRFilter` class, which implements a generic two-pole, two-zero IIR filter. The `ParametricEQFilter` object is a subclass of IIRFilter that implements the coefficients for a parametric equalizer. `setCoefficients()` saves the values of the six coefficients so they can later be used to calculate output samples. `jmin()` is a simple macro provided by JUCE to return the minimum of two numbers.

The following code applies the filter to a block of audio samples for a single channel.

```
int numSamples;      // How many audio samples to process
float *channelData; // Array of samples, length numSamples
float coefficients[6]; // Previously calculated filter
                       // coefficients
float x1, x2, y1, y2;  // Previous input/output values

for (int i = 0; i < numSamples; ++i)
{
    const float in = channelData[i];

    float out = coefficients[0] * in /* b0 */
    + coefficients[1] * x1 /* b1 */
```

```
        + coefficients[2] * x2 /* b2 */
        - coefficients[4] * y1 /* a1 */
        - coefficients[5] * y2; /* a2 */

    x2 = x1;
    x1 = in;
    y2 = y1;
    y1 = out;

    channelData[i] = out;
}
```

Here, `coefficients` is an array containing the values `b0`, `b1`, `b2`, `a0`, `a1`, and `a2`, as previously calculated and stored using `setCoefficients()`. Notice that `a0` is not used in this calculation. When the coefficients are set, they are normalized so `a0 = 1`, eliminating the need for it in further calculations. The variables `x1`, `x2`, `y1`, and `y2` hold the last two inputs and outputs, respectively. For example, if `in` represents $x[n]$, then `x1` represents $x[n-1]$ and `x2` represents $x[n-2]$.

Applications

Graphic Equalizer Application

Graphic equalization is more commonly found in live performance and recording studios than in most home stereo systems. One common use of graphic equalization is to "tune" a room, adjusting the equalizer to roughly compensate for resonances in the room or imperfections in the frequency response of the speakers [21]. The goal is to achieve a desired frequency response, flattening out extremes, reducing coloration in the sound, and achieving greater sonic consistency among performance venues. However, graphic equalizers are occasionally found in consumer stereo systems and even in digital music player software, where they can be used as a more flexible form of tone control for adjusting the sound to taste.

Parametric Equalizer Application

Parametric equalizers allow the operator to add peaks or notches at arbitrary locations in the audio spectrum. Adding a peak can be useful to help an instrument be heard in a complex mix (see also the presence control earlier in the chapter), or to deliberately add coloration to an instrument's sound by boosting or reducing a particular frequency range [22]. Notches can be used to attenuate unwanted sounds, including removing power line hum (50 or 60 Hz and sometimes their harmonics) and reducing feedback. To remove artifacts without affecting the rest of the sound, a narrow bandwidth would be used. To deliberately add coloration to an instrument's sound by reducing a particular frequency range, a wider bandwidth might be used.

Wah-Wah

The sound of the *wah-wah* effect resembles its name: wah-wah is a filter-based effect that imparts a speech-like quality to the input sound, similar to a voice saying the syllable "wah." Wah-wah is most commonly known as a guitar effect that was popularized by Jimi Hendrix, Eric Clapton, and others in the late 1960s. However, its origins go back to the early days of jazz, when trumpet and trombone players achieved a similar sound using mutes.

The wah-wah audio effect uses a band-pass or peaking filter whose center frequency is changed by a foot pedal. In some pedals, the mix between original and filtered signal can be controlled by a separate knob, as shown in Figure 4.6 [23].

Theory

Basis in Speech

In speech, *formants* are the peaks in the frequency spectrum when a human voice utters a sound, and are due to resonances in the vocal tract. For many vowel sounds, at least three formants can be easily identified. Humans listen

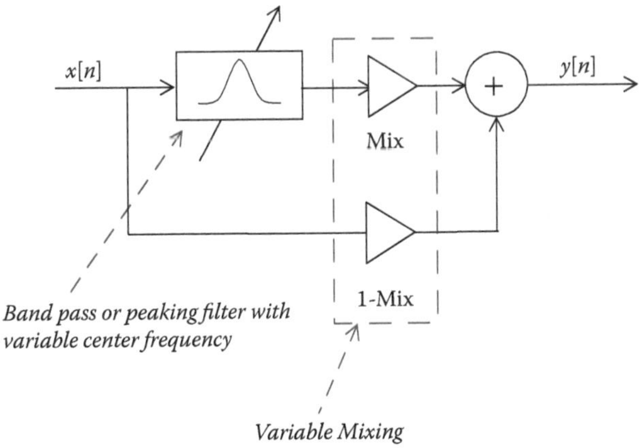

FIGURE 4.6
General wah-wah effect block diagram.

for and assign meaning to the relative spacing of the first three formants of the human vocal tract.

Formants are distinct from the *fundamental frequency* (or pitch) of the voice, which is the frequency at which the vocal folds vibrate. We hear and notice the fundamental frequency, but in most languages its exact location is not important when assigning meaning to vocal sounds. We also notice relative shifts of the fundamental frequency, but these are often associated with emotional states, such as when someone's voice goes up in pitch when under stress. But the relative positioning of formants, especially the first two formants, represents important information in how we interpret vowel sounds.

The wah-wah effect gives a voice-like quality to an input signal by simulating the formants found in speech [23]. The first formant of the [u] vowel is roughly located around 300 Hz, and the first two formants of the [a] vowel are located at approximately 750 and 1200 Hz. Therefore, the wah-wah simulates the transitions between vowels by adjusting the center frequency of its filter in roughly this range (the exact range depends on the manufacturer and model of pedal, but a range between 400 and 1200 Hz is typical). Wah-wah could be considered a simple form of speech synthesizer, though not close enough to be truly mistaken for a vowel sound.

Basic Wah-Wah

Figure 4.6 shows a block diagram of the wah-wah effect. A single second-order filter is typically used, with several possible variations: peaking, band-pass, or resonant low-pass filters. As discussed previously, a peaking filter will boost the midrange frequencies while leaving all other frequencies with a gain of 1, and a band-pass filter will boost the midrange frequencies and gradually roll off the low and high frequencies to 0. A *resonant low-pass* filter will pass the low frequencies with a gain of 1, create a peak with magnitude G_c in the midrange around the cutoff frequency ω_c, and gradually roll off the high frequencies to 0. A second-order resonant low-pass filter is given below:

$$H_{LP,\mathrm{Res}}(z)=\frac{\Omega_c^2(z^2+2z+1)}{\left[\Omega_c^2+\Omega_c/G_c+1\right]z^2+2\left[\Omega_c^2-1\right]z+\Omega_c^2-\Omega_c/G_c+1} \tag{4.9}$$

where $\Omega_c = \tan(\omega_c/2)$. The magnitude response of this filter is shown in Figure 4.7.

The gain and Q of the filter are generally fixed by design, but the center frequency is adjustable under the control of a foot pedal. As mentioned, the center frequency commonly takes a range of around 400–1200 Hz. Above and below this range, the effect loses its vocal quality. A *mix* control is sometimes used to vary the intensity of the effect by mixing between the filtered

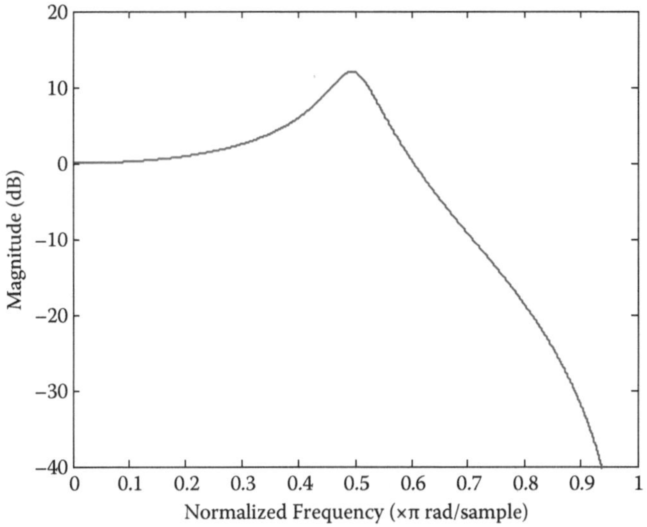

FIGURE 4.7
Magnitude response of a resonant low-pass filter, with magnitude 12 dB ($G_c \sim 20$) at $\omega_c = \pi/2$.

THE SERENDIPITOUS INVENTION OF THE WAH-WAH PEDAL

The first wah-wah pedal is attributed to Brad Plunkett in 1966, who worked at Warwick Electronics Inc., which owned Thomas Organ Company. Warwick Electronics acquired the Vox name due to the brand name's popularity and association with the Beatles. Their subsidiary, Thomas Organ Company, needed a modified design for the Vox amplifier, which had a midrange boost, so that it would be less expensive to manufacture.

In a 2005 interview [24], Brad Plunkett said, I "came up with a circuit that would allow me to move this midrange boost … . As it turned out, it sounded absolutely marvelous while you were moving it. It was okay when it was standing still, but the real effect was when you were moving it and getting a continuous change in harmonic content. We turned that on in the lab and played the guitar through it … . I turned the potentiometer and he played a couple licks on the guitar, and we went crazy.

"A couple of years later … somebody said to me one time, 'You know Brad, I think that thing you invented changed music.'"

and unfiltered signals. In the case of a peaking filter, this function could be equivalently implemented by changing the gain at the center frequency.

Auto-Wah

For the standard wah-wah, as used commonly on guitar pedals, the player manually controls the center frequency. In the *auto-wah* effect, the center frequency is controlled automatically. Two variations of auto-wah are commonly found. In the first, the center frequency sweeps back and forth following a *low-frequency oscillator* (LFO) with an adjustable frequency, typically around 1–2 Hz. The range of filter center frequencies is similar to that of the basic wah-wah, but it is often adjustable by the user.

In the second auto-wah variation, the center frequency is automatically adjusted according to the amplitude of the input signal. This arrangement is sometimes known as an *envelope follower,* and when used on a guitar, it produces a moving resonance on every note. Louder signals push the center frequency upward (toward the "ah" sound). The sensitivity of this process is typically a user-adjustable parameter, as are the *attack time* and *release time* of the envelope. More details on envelope calculation can be found in Chapter 6.

Tremolo-Wah

If the LFO-controlled auto-wah is combined with a periodic change in amplitude (*tremolo;* Chapter 5), the result is an effect known as *tremolo-wah.* The effect is generally equivalent to placing a tremolo and auto-wah effect in series:

$$y[n] = w[n]g[n] \text{ where } g[n] = 1 + \alpha\cos(\omega n) \tag{4.10}$$

where $y[n]$ is the output of the entire tremolo-wah, $w[n]$ is the output of the auto-wah section, $g[n]$ is a time-varying gain factor, and ω is normalized frequency $2\pi f/f_s$ as usual. $g[n]$ may also be calculated on a logarithmic scale since the human sensitivity of loudness follows a logarithmic relation. The same LFO can be used to control both amplitude and wah center frequency, but often the two move independently with different frequencies, or with the same frequency but out of phase.

Other Variations

The standard wah-wah pedal has only one resonant peak, in contrast to the two or three identifiable formants in most vowel sounds. By adding additional resonances, even more vocal-like sounds from a wah-wah effect are possible. Some pedals use a second peaking filter circuit whose center frequency moves around in a different manner than in the main filter, for example, following the second formant in the "oo" and "ah" vowels. This produces an effect much closer to human speech.

WAH-WAH AND WACKA-WACKA

The wah-wah effect is incredibly expressive. It is associated with whole genres of music, and it can be heard on many of the most influential funk, soul, jazz, and rock recordings over the past 50 years.

Jimi Hendrix would sometimes use the wah-wah effect while leaving the pedal in a particular location, creating a unique filter effect that did not change over time. However, in "Voodoo Child (Slight Return)," Hendrix muted the strummed strings while rocking the pedal, creating a percussive effect. The sweeping of the wah-wah pedal is more dramatic in the louder verses and the chorus, emphasizing the song's blues styling.

The wacka-wacka sound that Hendrix created soon became a trademark of a whole subgenre of 1970s funk and soul. Melvin "Wah-Wah Watson" Ragin, a highly respected Motown session musician, is renowned for his use of the wah-wah pedal, especially on the Temptations' "Papa Was a Rolling Stone." This distinctive wacka-wacka funk style soon became a feature of urban black crime dramas, such as in Isaac Hayes's "Theme from Shaft," Bobby Womack's score to "Across 110th Street," and Curtis Mayfield's "Superfly."

Another unusual use of the wah-wah pedal can be heard on the Pink Floyd song "Echoes." Here, screaming sounds were created by plugging in the pedal back to front; that is, the amplifier was connected to the input and the guitar was connected to the pedal's output.

Of course, use of wah pedals is not reserved just to guitar. Bass players have used wah-wah pedals on well-known recordings (Michael Henderson playing with Miles Davis, Cliff Burton of Metallica, etc.). John Medeski and Garth Hudson use the pedals with Clavinets. Rick Wright employed a wah-wah pedal on a Wurlitzer electric piano on the Pink Floyd song "Money," and Dick Sims used it with a Hammond organ. Miles Davis's ensembles used it to great extent, both on trumpet and on electric pianos. The wah-wah is frequently used by electric violinists, such as Boyd Tinsley of the Dave Matthews Band. Wah-wah pedals applied to an amplified saxophone also feature on albums by Frank Zappa and David Bowie.

Implementation

Filter Design

As with equalization, wah-wah nearly always uses second-order IIR filters. Two of the filter types used in the wah-wah are the same as those found in the various types of equalizer. The peaking/notch filter is used in the parametric EQ, and a passable wah-wah effect can be obtained from a parametric EQ by choosing large gain (up to 12 dB) and high Q (values from 2–10 are typical) and varying the center frequency. The band-pass filter, used in some wah-wah implementations, is also found in the graphic EQ. Again, a high Q is often used. The design and implementation of these filters are the same as in the equalizers.

Most analog wah-wah pedals for guitar use band-pass filters. Analog synthesizers typically use resonant low-pass filters to achieve similar effects. Resonant low-pass filter coefficients can be calculated similarly to more commonly used second-order low-pass filters, but substituting a higher Q. Values from 2 to 10 might be found in the wah-wah, compared to 0.71 in a standard Butterworth low-pass filter. The resonant low-pass filter creates a peak in the frequency response at the *cutoff frequency*, which is responsible for the wah effect.

As with the equalizers, the filter coefficients should be recalculated if and only if the center frequency (or cutoff frequency) has changed. Changing the mix control in the basic wah-wah (Figure 4.6) does not require recalculating the filter. In any variation of the auto-wah, the center frequency changes each sample and continuous recalculation of the coefficients is inevitable. However, the computational load can be reduced by recalculating the coefficients less frequently than for each audio sample. For example, at a sample rate of 44.1 kHz, recalculating the coefficients every 16 samples will still update the center frequency over 2700 times per second, improving efficiency without any significant difference in audio quality.

Low-Frequency Oscillator

In one variant of the auto-wah, an LFO controls the center frequency of the filter. Typical parameters include *LFO frequency, LFO waveform, minimum frequency,* and *sweep width.* Not all parameters will be user-adjustable; some will be fixed by design. LFO frequency (f_{LFO}) is the number of cycles per second the center frequency oscillates; typical values range from 0.2 to 5 Hz. LFO waveform controls the shape of the center frequency variation; sinusoidal waveforms are most common in the auto-wah. Minimum frequency (f_{min}) sets the lowest center frequency for the filter, typically no less than around 250 Hz and often higher to maintain the vocal effect. Sweep width (W), expressed in Hz, is the difference between the minimum and maximum center frequencies across an entire oscillation. The center frequency of the filter over time with sinusoidal LFO and sample rate f_s can be written as

$$f_c[n] = f_{\min} + 0.5W\left(1+\cos\left(2\pi f_{LFO} n/f_s\right)\right) \tag{4.11}$$

Further considerations on LFO implementation can be found in Chapter 2.

Envelope Follower

The envelope follower variant of the auto-wah scales the center frequency of the filter proportionally to the level of the input signal. The instantaneous value of each sample is a poor measure of a signal's level, so a *level detector* must be used to calculate a local average value. Level detectors based on the exponential moving average are discussed in detail in Chapter 6, and the same types of level detectors used in the compressor can be used in the envelope follower wah. A common level detector has a variable *attack time* τ_A and *release time* τ_R; its operation is given by

$$y_L[n] = \begin{cases} \alpha_A y_L[n-1] + (1-\alpha_A) x_L[n] & x_L[n] > y_L[n-1] \\ \alpha_R y_L[n-1] + (1-\alpha_R) x_L[n] & x_L[n] \le y_L[n-1] \end{cases} \tag{4.12}$$

where $\alpha_A = e^{-1/(\tau_A f_s)}$, $\alpha_R = e^{-1/(\tau_R f_s)}$, and $x_L[n]$ is the absolute value of the input signal. Attack time and release time are often user-adjustable parameters. The other parameters in the envelope follower wah are minimum frequency and sweep width, which work analogously to the LFO case. We can therefore write the center frequency f_c as a function of the level detector value $y_L[n]$:

$$f_c[n] = f_{\min} + W y_L[n] \tag{4.13}$$

$y_L[n]$ is taken to always be positive, and assuming the input signal is scaled to have a maximum value of 1, the center frequency will reach a maximum value of $f_{min} + W$, just as with the LFO auto-wah.

Analog Emulation

Musicians often become attached to particular brands of wah-wah pedals to achieve their signature sound. Even when the gain, center frequency, and Q of a digital filter are tuned identically to the analog case, the sound may still be subtly different. Part of the distinct sound of many analog wah pedals comes from nonlinear distortion introduced by the electronic components, especially the iron-core inductors used in the resonant filters. Nonlinear distortion, discussed in Chapter 7, adds new *harmonic* and *intermodulation* frequency components to the output signal that were not present in the input. Precise replication of these effects requires detailed numerical simulation of the behavior of each circuit element, which is beyond the scope of this text. References for further reading on analog modeling are given in [25].

Phaser

The *phase shifter* (or *phaser*) creates a series of *notches* in the audio spectrum where sound at particular frequencies is attenuated or eliminated. The flanger (Chapter 2) also produces its characteristic sound from notches, and in fact, the flanger can be considered a special case of phasing. However, where the flanger is based on delays, the phaser uses *allpass filters* to create phase shifts in the input signal. When the allpass-filtered signal is mixed with the original, notches result from destructive interference. Where the flanger always generates evenly spaced notches, the phaser can be designed to arbitrarily control the location of each notch, as well as its number and width. As with the flanger, though, the phaser's characteristic sound comes from the sweeping motion of the notches over time.

Theory

Basic Phaser

The notches needed for the phaser are most often implemented using allpass filters. Allpass filters, whose design is discussed in Chapter 3, pass all frequencies with no change in magnitude, but they introduce a frequency-dependent phase lag. The output of the allpass filter is then added to the original signal, as in Figure 4.8. The relative level of the filtered signal can be adjusted by a depth (or mix) control.

Mixing the original and filtered signals creates notches in the frequency response according to the principle of *constructive* and *destructive interference,* just as in the flanger. At certain frequencies, the allpass filters will introduce a phase shift of 180° or an odd multiple thereof (540°, 900°, etc.). This is equivalent to inverting the input, and when the original and filtered signals are added together with equal weight (depth = 1), they will cancel completely, resulting in a notch at those frequencies. Frequencies near the notch, which experience nearly 180° of phase shift, will also be attenuated.

The pure delay used in the flanger can also be considered an allpass filter with *linear phase*: a delay produces no change in magnitude for any frequency, but it produces a phase lag proportional to the input frequency. Therefore, the phase response of a pure delay hits odd multiples of 180°

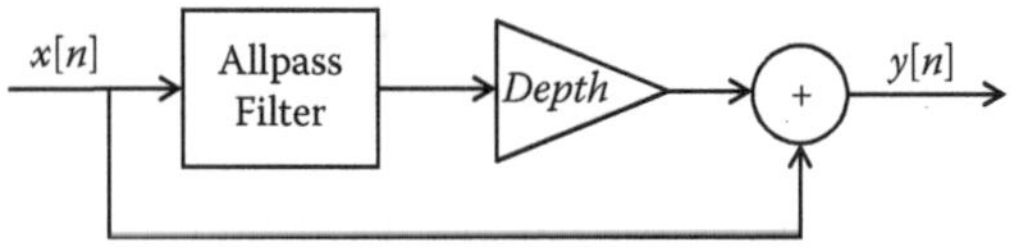

FIGURE 4.8
A phaser, also known as a phase shifter.

(–180°, –540°, –900°, –1260°; the negative value indicates that the output phase lags the input) at evenly spaced frequencies, and the notches will also appear at evenly spaced frequencies.

IIR allpass filters (Chapter 3), as with all IIR filters, are not linear phase, so the phase shift they create is not a linear function of frequency. By changing the order, *Q*, and center frequency of the filter, many variations in notch location and width are possible. The number of notches is determined by the number of times the phase crosses an odd multiple of 180°, which in turn is determined by the order of the filter. However, another useful property of allpass filters is that a cascade (series connection) of several allpass filters is itself an allpass filter. Phaser effects thus often consist of several simpler allpass filters in series, where the total phase lag is the sum of each filter's phase response.

Low-Frequency Oscillator

As with the chorus and flanger effects, an LFO produces a periodic change in notch location over time. It does this by changing the center frequencies of the allpass filters. But where the chorus and flanger commonly use sinusoidal or triangular LFO waveforms, the phaser often changes the notch frequencies in an *exponential* pattern over time. This more closely corresponds to human hearing, where perceived pitch is an exponential function of frequency. Example LFO waveforms are discussed later in the "Implementation" subsection.

Phaser with Feedback

As with the flanger, some phasers incorporate feedback (sometimes called *regeneration*) between the allpass filter output and input, as shown in Figure 4.9. As with other effects incorporating feedback, the *feedback gain* of the phaser must be strictly less than 1 to maintain stable operation. The effect of feedback is to increase the *Q* of the allpass filters, making the phase transitions steeper and, therefore, making the notches sharper.

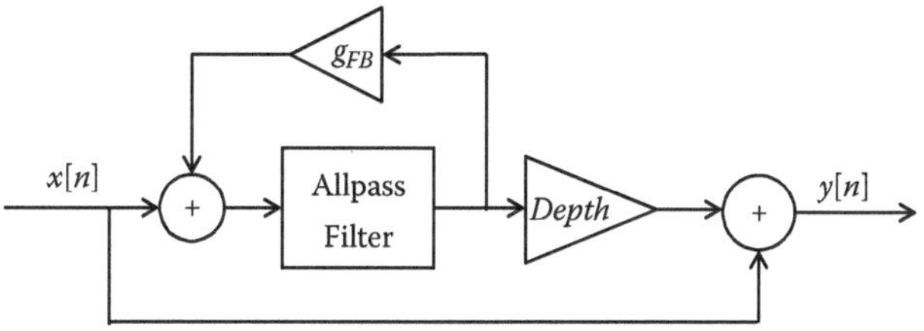

FIGURE 4.9
A phaser with feedback. The feedback gain can be positive or negative, but must have a magnitude strictly less than 1.

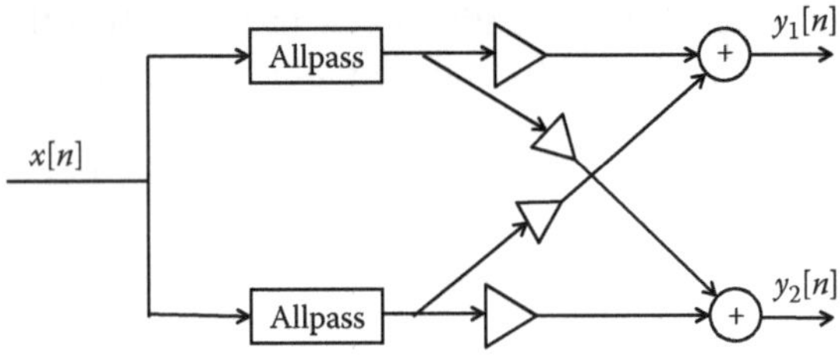

FIGURE 4.10
A generalized diagram of a stereo phaser with feed-across gains.

Stereo Phaser

Just as with stereo flangers and chorus units, a stereo phaser can be created from two monophonic phasers with different filter settings, creating notches at different frequencies. Typically, the notches are controlled by two low-frequency oscillators in quadrature phase, where the output of one oscillator trails the other by 90°.

An optional addition is to selectively mix the outputs of each filter, which can create additional notches (Figure 4.10). The phaser effect can even be created acoustically with no mixing at all: each *feed-across* gain is set to zero, and each output is sent to a separate speaker. In this *spatial phaser* arrangement, notches exist at different points in the room where the signal from each speaker cancels out in the air. Moving around the room will change the location of the notches.

Implementation

Allpass Filter Calculation

The phaser uses first-order or second-order IIR allpass filters whose center frequencies vary over time, as shown in Figure 4.11a. A first-order allpass has 0° phase lag at 0 Hz and a total phase lag of 180° at high frequencies. By itself, a single first-order section is not enough to create a moving notch in the phaser. A second-order allpass has a total phase of 360° at high frequencies. Since the phase lag increases monotonically with frequency, a single second-order section produces a single notch at the frequency with 180° phase lag (which is the cutoff frequency of the allpass filter), as shown in Figure 4.12a. To achieve more notches, multiple allpass sections are placed in series.

A common analog phaser design uses four first-order allpass filter sections in series (or, equivalently, two second-order sections). This produces 720° of total phase shift and therefore two notches (at 180° and 540°). In a typical design, all four first-order allpass filters might have the same center frequency (that is, the frequency at which the phase lag is 90°). This does not mean that both notches fall at the same frequency. Rather, the total phase lag

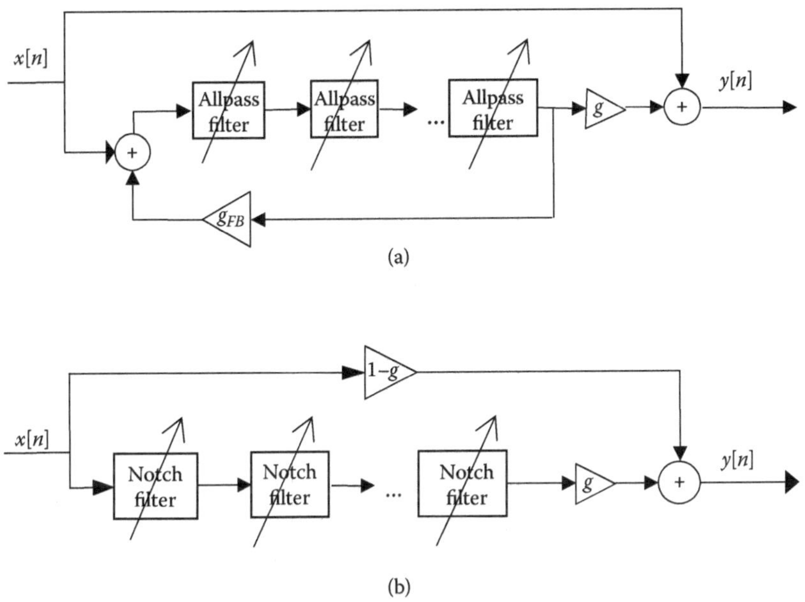

FIGURE 4.11
Two approaches to implementing a phaser: phasing with time-varying allpass filters and optional feedback (a) and phasing with notch filters (b).

is the sum of the contributions of each filter, and the notches occur where this sum reaches 180° and 540°. Therefore, in this four-section design, the notches fall where the phase shift of each individual filter is 45° or 135° (Figure 4.12b).

If six first-order allpass sections are used instead, the total phase lag is 1080° and three notches will result (180°, 540°, 900°). Again, each section can be tuned to an identical center frequency, but the notches will occur in different locations than in the four-section design (Figure 4.12c), this time occurring where each filter contributes 30°, 90°, or 150° of phase lag.

The transfer functions for an allpass filter were derived in Chapter 3. We can rewrite these transfer functions, replacing the arbitrary constants by terms relating to how the filter modifies the phase. A first-order allpass filter may be given as

$$H(z)=\frac{z\left[\tan(\omega_c/2)-1\right]+\tan(\omega_c/2)+1}{z\left[\tan(\omega_c/2)+1\right]+\tan(\omega_c/2)-1} \tag{4.14}$$

For a second-order design, we can write the allpass filter [5] as

$$H(z)=\frac{\left[1-\tan(B/2)\right]z^2+2z\cos\omega_c+1+\tan(B/2)}{\left[1+\tan(B/2)\right]z^2+2z\cos\omega_c+1-\tan(B/2)} \tag{4.15}$$

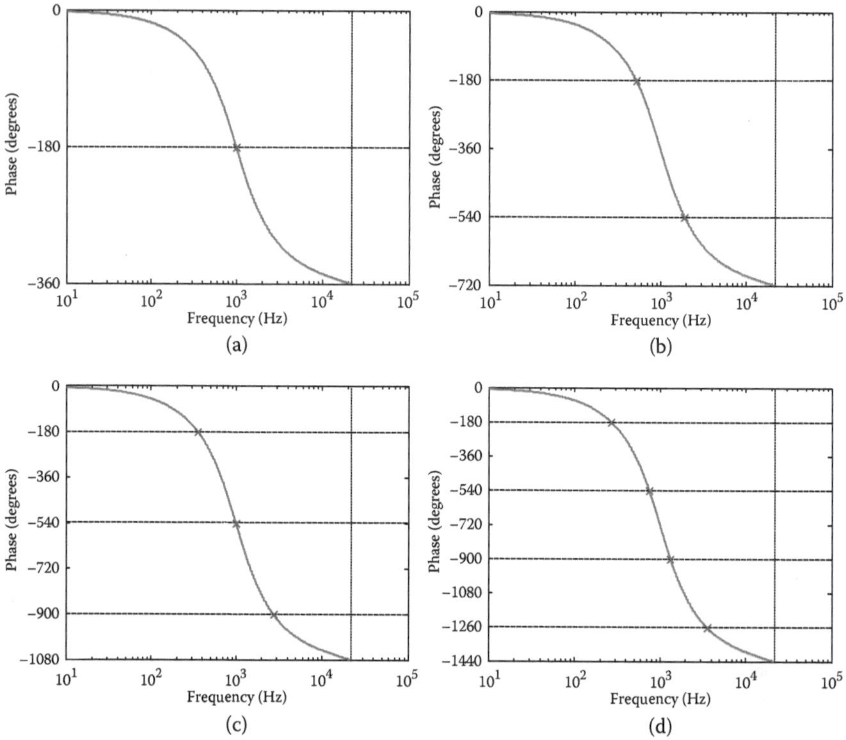

FIGURE 4.12
Allpass filter phase and phaser notch locations for different numbers of second-order allpass filters. Center frequency is 1 kHz and sampling frequency is 44.1 kHz; (a), (b), (c), and (d) represent one, two, three, and four second-order sections, respectively.

Here, the cutoff frequency ω_c is where the phase response reaches 180° and the bandwidth B is the difference between the two frequencies where the phase response reaches 90° and 270°. Note that Equation (4.15) conforms with the format of any allpass filter given in Chapter 3.

Alternate Implementation

An alternate approach to phaser design uses a set of notch filters (Figure 4.11b) in place of the allpass sections (Figure 4.11a). The notch filters can be implemented as a cascade of second-order IIR sections, similar to a parametric equalizer with high Q and gain 0 at the center frequency of each section. This implementation does not require the filter output to be mixed with the direct sound since the notches are created directly; however, a mix can still be used to vary the intensity of the effect. As with the allpass implementation, the center frequency of the notch filters is varied with a low-frequency oscillator.

LFO Waveform

Just as with the flanger, the sound of the phaser results from how the notch frequencies change over time. In contrast to sinusoidal low-frequency oscillators commonly found in other effects, exponential motion of the notch frequencies is often used in the phaser. Specifically, a waveform that is triangular in the log-frequency domain can be used.

$$\begin{aligned} \ln\left(f_c[n]\right) &= \ln(f_{\min}) + \ln(W)triangle(\omega_{LFO}n) \\ f_c[n] &= f_{\min}W^{triangle(\omega_{LFO}n)} \end{aligned} \tag{4.16}$$

where f_{min} is the minimum center frequency, $\omega_{LFO} = 2\pi f_{LFO}/f_s$ is the normalized LFO frequency, and $W = f_{max}/f_{min}$ is defined as the ratio of the maximum to minimum frequency. Note that this definition of W differs from the wah-wah effect described earlier in the chapter. Here we define the triangle waveform to take a range of values between 0 and 1 over a complete oscillation:

$$triangle(t) = \begin{cases} t/\pi & 0 \le t < \pi \\ 2 - t/\pi & \pi \le t < 2\pi \end{cases} \tag{4.17}$$

Analog and Digital Implementations

Filters implemented digitally (*discrete time*) behave slightly differently from their analog (*continuous time*) counterparts, due to the fact that frequency is unbounded in the continuous time domain but restricted to the $[0, 2\pi)$ range in discrete time. Techniques exist to convert continuous time prototype filters into discrete time equivalents, including the *bilinear transform* with prewarping. However, even with these methods, the responses of the continuous and discrete filters diverge near the Nyquist frequency.

Figure 4.13 shows the differences between the continuous and discrete filter phase responses and the resulting effect on phaser notch location. For an allpass center frequency $f_c = 3$ kHz and four second-order sections, the highest notch is 2.5 semitones (15%) lower in discrete time than it would be in an analog implementation. When $f_c = 10$ kHz, the top notch is 12.8 semitones (52%) lower, over an octave of difference. Fortunately, the range of center frequencies used in the phaser rarely extends much beyond 1 to 2 kHz (though individual notch locations may be higher), so the differences present only a minor concern when emulating analog phasers.

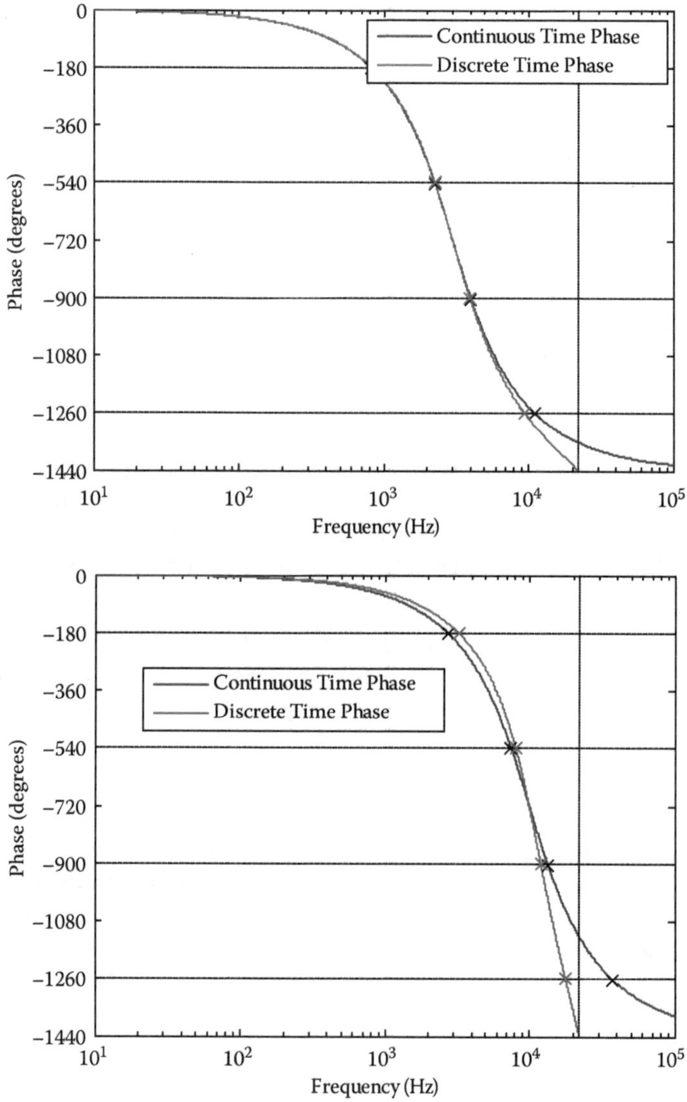

FIGURE 4.13
Continuous time (analog) and discrete time (digital) allpass filters produce different notch locations when used in the phaser, particularly at high frequencies. Both plots depict the phase response and notch locations for four second-order allpass sections and 44.1 kHz sampling frequency. Top, center frequency is 3 kHz, and bottom, center frequency is 10 kHz.

Common Parameters

Depth (mix/level): The depth controls the amount of allpass filtered signal that is added to the output. At a depth of zero, only the original signal appears at the output. At a depth of 1, the mix between original and filtered signals is equal, producing the deepest notches. Some phasers will use *depth* to refer to what this book labels *sweep width,* the frequency range in which the notches move, so it is important to know the convention used by any particular phaser unit.

Sweep width (range): This parameter controls the frequency range across which the notches sweep. Possible variations include fixing the minimum frequency location and using the sweep width to change the maximum frequency, or offering separate controls for minimum and maximum frequency.

Feedback/regeneration: This control adjusts the feedback gain between output and input of the allpass filter section (Figure 4.9). The value must be strictly less than 1 to avoid instability. Using feedback can produce sharper, more pronounced notches.

LFO frequency: Sometimes labeled *speed* or *rate,* this changes the rate at which the notches move up and down in frequency. Its effect and use is similar to the flanger and chorus. As with those effects, the control sets how many times per second the notches sweep across their range. The actual speed at which the notches move (in Hz per second) will also depend on the sweep width and LFO waveform.

Code Example

The following C++ code fragment, adapted from the code that accompanies this book, implements a phaser with feedback, a user-selectable number of allpass sections, and adjustable LFO waveform.

```
int numSamples;          // How many audio samples to process
float *channelData;      // Array of samples, len. numSamples
float ph;                // Current phase of the LFO (0-1)
float lastFilterOutput; // Output of the filter last sample,
                         // for implementing feedback
OnePoleAllpassFilter **allpassFilters;
                          // Objects handling a first-order
                          // allpass filter
float inverseSampleRate; // Defined as 1.0/(sample rate)
int sc;                   // Sample count, used to decide
                          // when to update the coefficients

float depth_;           // Depth of the phaser effect (0-1)
float feedback_;        // Amount of feedback (>= 0, < 1)
```

```
float lfoFrequency_;  // Frequency of the LFO
float baseFrequency_; // Lowest point in the sweep of the
                      // allpass center frequency
float sweepWidth_;    // Width of the LFO (in Hz)
int waveform_;        // Identifier of what type of waveform
                      // to use (sine, triangle, ...)
int filtersPerChannel_;     // How many allpass filters
int filterUpdateInterval_;  // How often to update the
                            // allpass coefficients

for (int sample = 0; sample < numSamples; ++sample)
{
    float out = channelData[sample];

    // If feedback is enabled, include the feedback from the
    // last sample in the input of the allpass filter chain.
    if(feedback_ != 0.0)
        out += feedback_ * lastFilterOutput;

    for(int j = 0; j < filtersPerChannel_; ++j)
    {
        // First, update the current allpass filter
        // coefficients depending on the parameter settings
        // and the LFO phase. Recalculating the filter
        // coefficients is much more expensive than
        // calculating a sample. Only update the
        // coefficients at a fraction of the sample rate;
        // since the LFO moves slowly, the difference won't
        // generally be audible.
        if(sc % filterUpdateInterval_ == 0)
        {
          allpassFilters[j]->makeAllpass(inverseSampleRate,
                                 baseFrequency_ +
                                 sweepWidth_ *
                                 lfo(ph, waveform_));
        }
        out=allpassFilters[j]->processSingleSampleRaw(out);
    }

    lastFilterOutput = out;

    // Add the allpass signal to the output
    // depth = 0 --> input only ; depth = 1 --> evenly
    // balanced input and output
    channelData[sample] = (1.0f-0.5f*depth_) *
                          channelData[sample] +
                          0.5f*depth_*out;
```

```
    // Update the LFO phase, keeping it in the range 0-1
    ph += lfoFrequency_ * inverseSampleRate;
    if(ph >= 1.0)
        ph -= 1.0;
    sc++;
}
```

At the core of this code is an array of C++ objects `allpassFilters`, which each implement a single first-order allpass filter. Even if every filter has the same coefficients, we need to maintain separate objects for each filter since the filter must keep track of previous input and output samples in order to calculate its output. The code above passes each sample through each filter in succession, eventually arriving at the sample `out`, which is mixed with the original input `channelData[sample]` to produce the phaser effect. The `depth_` parameter controls the relative balance of these two signals, with `depth_ = 1` producing an even mix between them and, therefore, the most pronounced phaser effect.

As in the earlier parametric equalizer example, it is not efficient to recalculate the filter coefficients at every single audio sample, and the LFO will change value slowly enough that recalculating once every few samples will be sufficient. The variable `sc` stores how many samples have elapsed since the coefficients were last recalculated, and `filterUpdateInterval_` indicates how often they should be recalculated. A value of 16 or 32 would strike an appropriate balance between efficiency and smoothness of effect.

The function `lfo()` implements one of several LFO waveforms depending on the value of the `waveform_` variable. `waveform_` will take one of several predefined values, for example, 0 corresponding to a sine, 1 to a triangle wave, 2 to a square wave, or 3 to a sawtooth wave.

The expression `allpassFilters[j]->processSingleSampleRaw(out)` runs the following code for each allpass filter object:

```
float OnePoleAllpassFilter::processSingleSampleRaw(
                                  const float sampleToProcess)
{
    // Process one sample, storing the last input and output
    y1 = (b0 * sampleToProcess) + (b1 * x1) + (a1 * y1);
    x1 = sampleToProcess;
    return y1;
}
```

Here, `x1` and `y1` keep track of the last input and output $x[n-1]$ and $y[n-1]$, respectively. `b0`, `b1`, and `a1` are coefficients of the filter, as calculated by the `makeAllpass()` function in the previous code block.

Problems

1. Which one of the three diagrams in Figure 4.14 would *not* produce a working graphic equalizer, and why?
2. Suppose a graphic equalizer is implemented with six filters having an octave spacing between filters. The first (the one with the lowest center frequency) filter has a lower cutoff frequency at 375 Hz. Find the lower cutoff frequency, upper cutoff frequency, bandwidth, and center frequency of the fourth filter.
3. a. Draw a magnitude response plot showing the frequency response of each band in a 10-band, one-octave graphic EQ with a lowest center frequency of 30 Hz. Assume the controls are all set to flat.
   b. Draw a block diagram of the implementation of this filter.
4. a. How do graphic equalizers differ from parametric EQs and basic tone controls?
   b. What are the primary controls in a graphic EQ?
   c. What are the primary controls in a parametric equalizer, and what do they do?
5. (Difficult) In a peaking or notch filter, as used for parametric equalization, find a formula for the lower cutoff frequency as a function of bandwidth and center frequency.
6. Explain why wah-wah could be considered a special case of parametric equalization. (What is the main effect of moving the pedal on a wah-wah box?)
7. Define three of the main parameters of a phaser—depth, sweep width, and speed—and describe the effect of varying their settings.
8. a. How does a flanger differ from a phaser in implementation?
   b. One of the diagrams in Figure 4.15 is the frequency response of a flanger, and the other is the frequency response of a phaser. Identify which is which, and explain why.
9. Explain how a phaser may be implemented using allpass filters to create notches in the frequency spectrum.

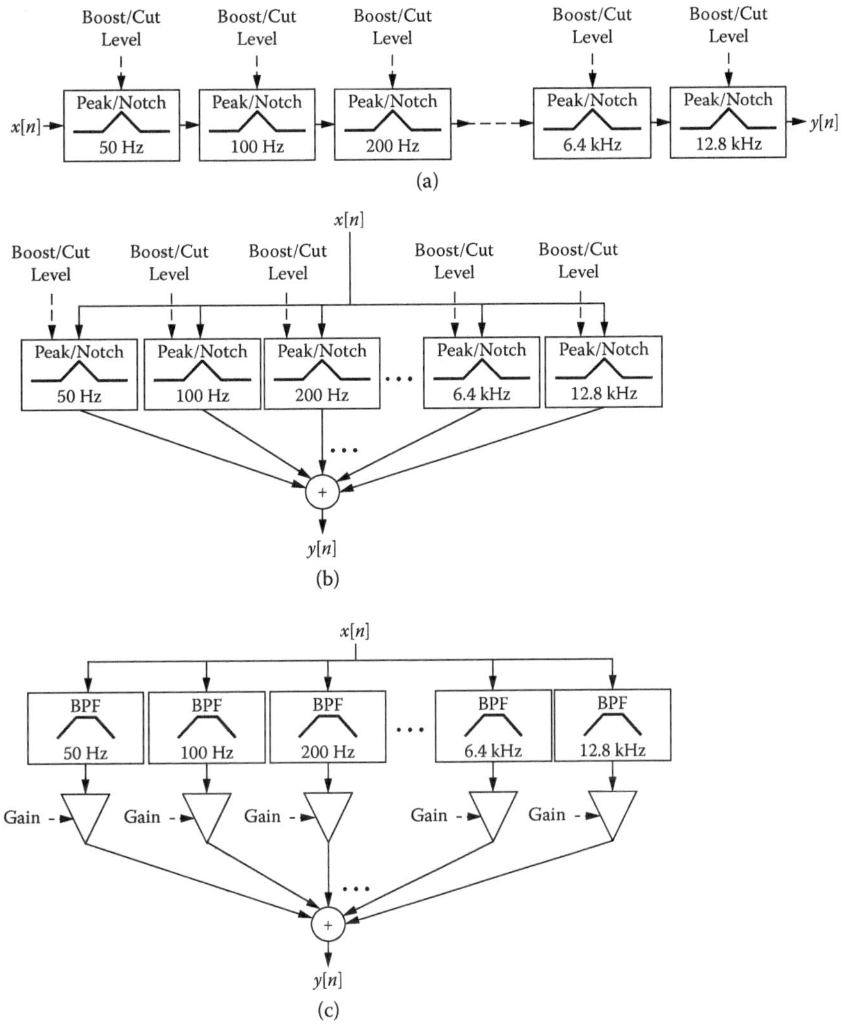

FIGURE 4.14
One of these three does *not* represent a graphic equalizer.

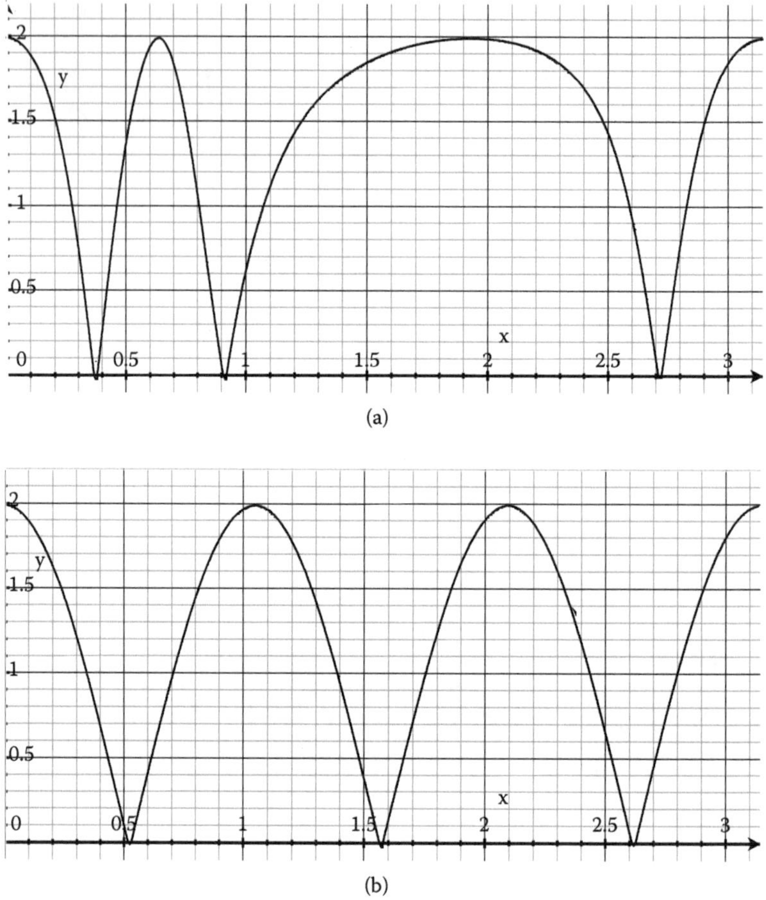

FIGURE 4.15
One of these is the frequency response of a flanger; the other is the frequency response of a phaser.

5

Amplitude Modulation

The term *modulation* refers to the variation of one signal by another. *Amplitude modulation* specifically refers to one signal changing the amplitude (or gain) of another. There are two common uses of amplitude modulation in digital audio effects: *tremolo* and *ring modulation*. Though mathematically similar, their musical effects are quite different.

Another type of modulation is *frequency modulation*, the periodic variation in frequency (pitch) of a signal. Frequency modulation is used in the *vibrato* effect discussed in Chapter 2; this chapter is devoted solely to amplitude modulation effects.

Tremolo

Tremolo is a musical term that literally means "trembling." It typically refers to a style of playing involving fast repeated notes, for example, fast repeated bow strokes on a violin, rolls on a percussion instrument, or continuous rapid plucks on a mandolin. The tremolo audio effect simulates this playing style by periodically modulating the amplitude of the input signal, so a long sustained note comes out sounding like a series of short rapid notes. The effect is commonly used on electric guitar, and tremolo was built into some guitar amplifiers as early as the 1940s. Tremolo is also one of the more straightforward effects to implement digitally.

Theory

Tremolo, as depicted in Figure 5.1, results from multiplying the input signal $x[n]$ with a periodic, slowly varying signal $m[n]$:

$$y[n] = m[n]\,x[n] \tag{5.1}$$

The simplest interpretation of this equation is to consider the tremolo as a variable gain amplifier whose gain at sample n is given by $m[n]$. When $m[n] > 1$, the output amplitude is greater than the input amplitude, and similarly, $m[n] < 1$ reduces the level of the output signal relative to the input.

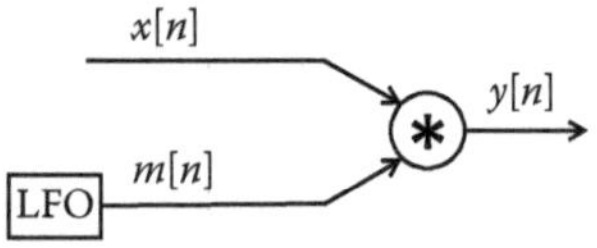

FIGURE 5.1
The tremolo multiplies the input signal by a low-frequency oscillator that changes its gain.

Low-Frequency Oscillator

The characteristic sound of the tremolo comes from the fact that the gain changes periodically over time. The modulating signal $m[n]$ is generated by a *low-frequency oscillator* (LFO):

$$m[n] = 1 + \alpha \cos \omega_{LFO} \tag{5.2}$$

Here, α is the *depth* of the tremolo and $\omega_{LFO} = 2\pi f_{LFO}/f_s$ is the normalized frequency of the oscillator, where f_s is the sampling frequency. f_{LFO} typically ranges from 0.5 to 20 Hz. Figure 5.2 shows an example of tremolo applied to an audio waveform. A depth of 0 produces no effect; a depth of 1 produces

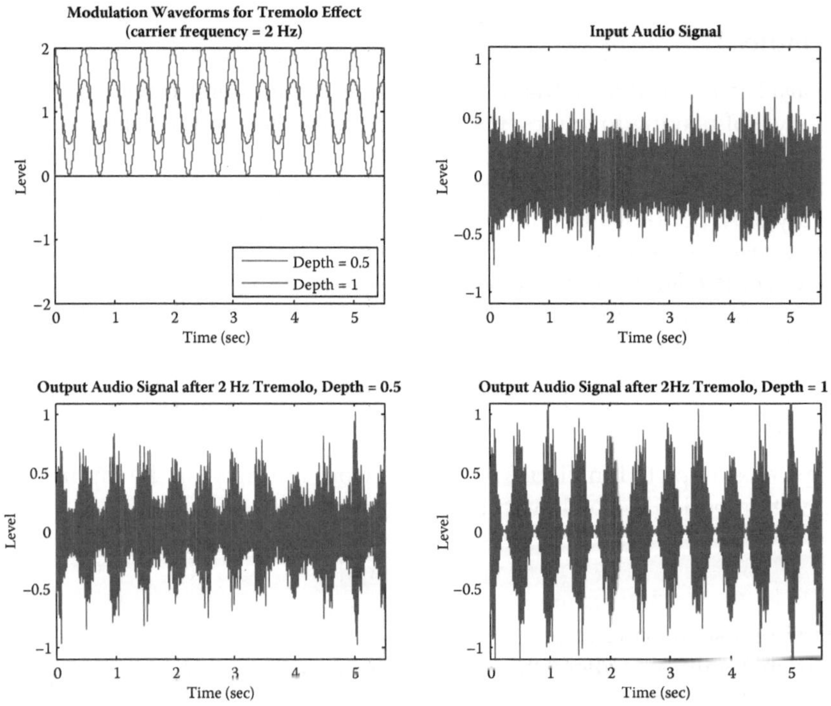

FIGURE 5.2
Tremolo applied to an audio signal, with two different values of the depth parameter.

the most pronounced tremolo by having the minima of $m[n]$ reach 0. Both frequency and depth are typically user-adjustable controls.

Some tremolo units also allow the LFO waveform to be selected by the user. In addition to sine waves, triangular and square waveforms are sometimes used. Square waves, with their abrupt transition between high and low, produce a stuttering effect in contrast to the smoother transitions of the sine wave LFO.

Properties

Tremolo is a simple effect consisting of a single multiplication per sample. Because multiplication is a *linear* operation, the tremolo is also linear. Tremolo is *time variant* on account of the low-frequency oscillator: delaying the input signal and passing it to the tremolo will not produce the same result as delaying the output of the tremolo by the same amount, because the gain of the tremolo changes with the LFO phase. Because a bounded input signal always produces a bounded output, the tremolo is a *stable* effect for all parameter settings. Tremolo is *memoryless* since each output sample depends on only the current input sample and not any previous inputs.

Implementation

The original tremolo units were based on *voltage-controlled amplifier* (VCA) circuits built from vacuum tubes, in which a time-varying voltage from the LFO would change the gain of the audio signal. Digital implementation of the tremolo is very simple, using only a single multiplication for each audio sample (not including the computation of the LFO). The most complex implementation aspect is the LFO. In particular, keeping track of the phase of the LFO is critical. One could imagine the following pseudocode implementation, where `f` and `alpha` are adjustable parameters:

```
for(n = 0; n < numSamples; n++)
{
    m[n] = 1.0 + alpha*cos(2*pi*f*n/fs);
    y[n] = m[n]*x[n];
}
```

Assume this code is running in real time (as $x[n]$ arrives). It will produce accurate results unless the user changes the value of `f` midway through. Suppose at time $n = N$, there is a step change in the frequency `f`. Then the value inside the `cos()` function will jump from sample $N-1$ to N, producing a noticeable artifact in the result (Figure 5.3 top).

Instead, the desired behavior is that the tremolo changes frequency but maintains continuity (Figure 5.3 bottom). We achieve this by recording the phase of the LFO at each sample. Recall that frequency is the derivative of

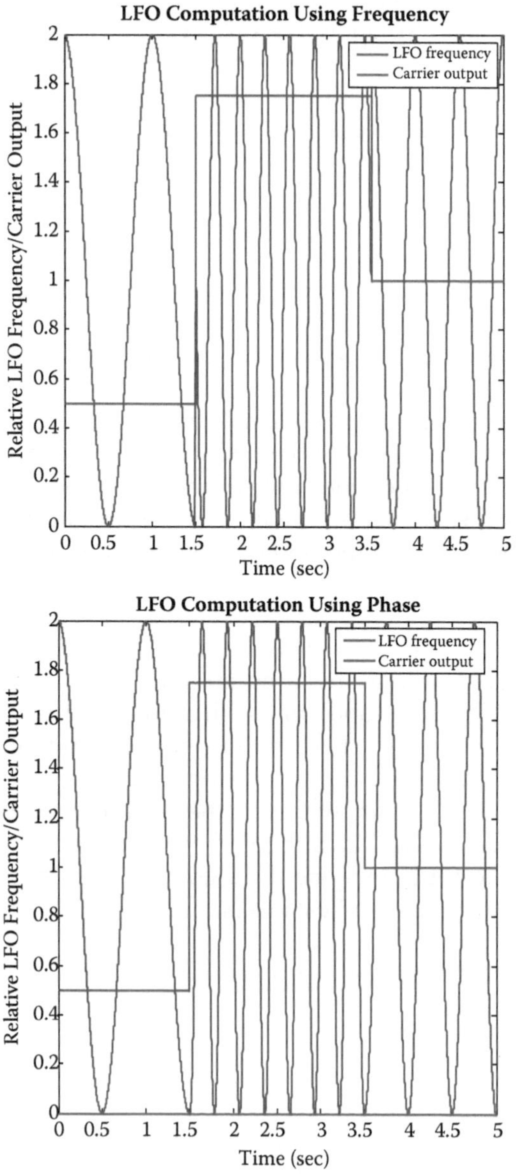

FIGURE 5.3
Tremolo showing LFO output with frequency-based computation (top) and phase-based computation (bottom).

phase, so by incrementing the phase by the right amount of each sample, we cause the LFO to run at the expected frequency while making it robust to frequency changes:

```
phase = 0;
for(n = 0; n < numSamples; n++)
{
    m[n] = 1.0 + alpha*cos(phase);
    y[n] = m[n]*x[n];
    phase = phase + 2*pi*f/fs;
}
```

Audio Rate and Control Rate

Because the LFO value changes very little from one audio sample to the next, total computation can be reduced by updating the LFO value less frequently. For example, the LFO value could be recalculated only once every 64 audio samples without noticeable loss of quality. In computer music, signals that update less frequently in this manner are called *control rate* signals (in comparison to *audio rate* signals, which are updated every sample). However, given the simplicity of the tremolo, control rate updating of the LFO is unlikely to be necessary except on the smallest of mobile or embedded processors.

Code Example

The following C++ code fragment, adapted from the code that accompanies this book, implements a basic tremolo effect.

```
int numSamples;          // How many audio samples to process
float *channelData;      // Array of samples, len. numSamples
float ph;                 // Current phase of the LFO (0-1)
float inverseSampleRate; // Defined as 1.0/(sample rate)

float depth_;          // Depth of the tremolo effect (0-1)
float frequency_;      // Frequency of the LFO
int waveform_;         // Identifier of what type of waveform
                       // to use (sine, triangle, ...)

for (int i = 0; i < numSamples; ++i)
{
    const float in = channelData[i];

    // Ring modulation is easy! Just multiply the waveform
    // by a periodic carrier
```

```
    channelData[i] = in * (1.0f - depth_ *
                                   lfo(ph, waveform_));

    // Update the carrier and LFO phases, keeping them in
    // the range 0-1
    ph += frequency_*inverseSampleRate;
    if(ph >= 1.0)
        ph -= 1.0;
}
```

The code uses the variable `ph` to keep track of the current phase of the LFO. The tremolo effect itself is simply a change in volume modulated by the value of the LFO. This tremolo example includes a choice of LFO styles, as implemented in the `lfo()` function.

```
float lfo(float phase, int waveform)
{
    switch(waveform)
    {
       case kWaveformTriangle:
            if(phase < 0.25f)
                return 0.5f + 2.0f*phase;
            else if(phase < 0.75f)
                return 1.0f - 2.0f*(phase - 0.25f);
            else
                return 2.0f*(phase-0.75f);
       case kWaveformSquare:
            if(phase < 0.5f)
                return 1.0f;
            else
                return 0.0f;
       case kWaveformSquareSlopedEdges:
            if(phase < 0.48f)
                return 1.0f;
            else if(phase < 0.5f)
                return 1.0f - 50.0f*(phase - 0.48f);
            else if(phase < 0.98f)
                return 0.0f;
            else
                return 50.0f*(phase - 0.98f);
       case kWaveformSine:
       default:
            return 0.5f + 0.5f*sinf(2.0 * M_PI * phase);
    }
}
```

Here, `waveform` takes one of several predefined values (`kWaveformTriangle`, `kWaveformSine`, etc.), and the values returned are all scaled to the range 0 to 1.

Ring Modulation

Tremolo is a rhythmic effect, with the LFO inducing periodic amplitude changes in the input signal. The human ear is capable of distinguishing discrete rhythmic events up to a rate of about 10–20 events per second [26]. As the LFO frequency increases above this threshold, the amplitude modulation will cease to be perceived as rhythmic pulses and begin to be heard as a change in timbre.

Ring modulation is an effect that multiplies the input signal by a periodic *carrier* signal, producing unusual, sometimes discordant sounds. Uniquely among common audio effects, the output sounds tend to be *nonharmonic* (not containing multiples of a fundamental frequency) for even the simplest of input sounds. Because of the strangeness of these nonharmonic outputs, the ring modulator is not widely used in music production.

Theory

The basic input/output relation of the ring modulator is identical to that of the tremolo:

$$y[n] = m[n]x[n] \tag{5.3}$$

where $x[n]$ is the input signal (usually from a musical instrument) and $m[n]$ is the modulating carrier signal. All the same properties of the tremolo apply (i.e., $m[n]$ can be thought of as changing the gain of $x[n]$). However, the characteristic sound of the ring modulator results from the particular properties of the input and carrier signals. Consider a simple case, where each of the signals is a single sinusoid,

$$x[n] = \cos(\omega n), m[n] = \cos(\omega_c n) \tag{5.4}$$

The cosine of the sum or difference of two angles may be given by $\cos(A + B) = \cos(A)\cos(B) - \sin(A)\sin(B)$ and $\cos(A - B) = \cos(A)\cos(B) + \sin(A)\sin(B)$. So,

$$m[n]x[n] = \cos(\omega_c n)\cos(\omega n) = \left[\cos((\omega_c - \omega)n) + \cos((\omega_c + \omega)n)\right]/2 \tag{5.5}$$

In other words, multiplying two sinusoids together results in *sum and difference frequencies*. For example, if our input was a 400 Hz sine wave and the carrier was a 100 Hz sine wave, the result would not be the original frequencies at all, but instead would be sinusoids at 300 and 500 Hz. This is illustrated in Figure 5.4. Note that using sine instead of cosine in the above

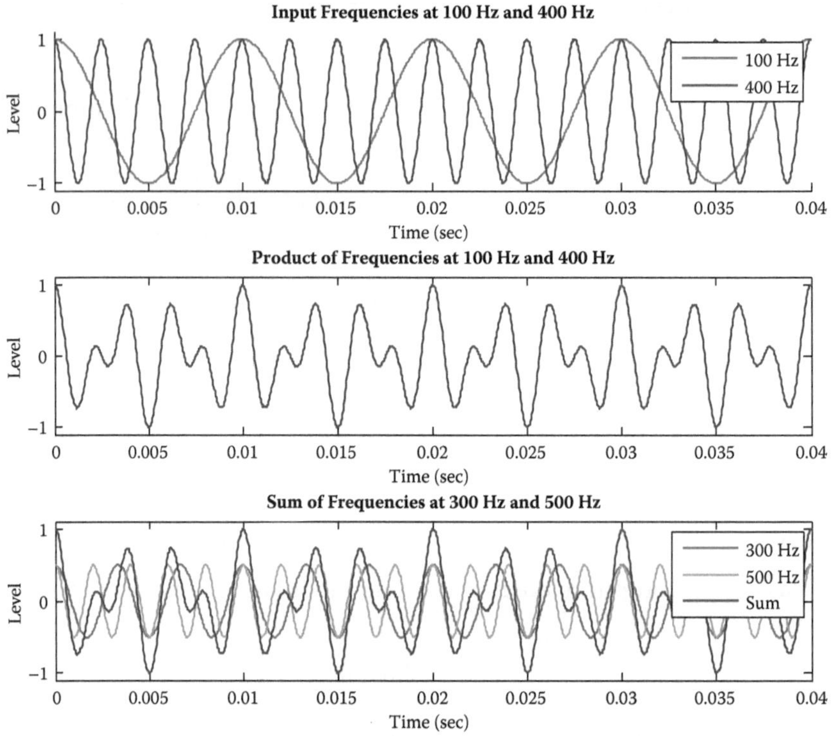

FIGURE 5.4
Multiplying sinusoids at 400 and 100 Hz results in sum and difference components at 500 and 300 Hz, respectively.

equations changes the phase of the results but not the essential sum and difference effects.

Musical instrument signals are composed of many superimposed frequencies. For a single note, these frequencies tend to be harmonically related, or integer multiples of some fundamental frequency. We can thus refine the simple example above to an input $x[n]$ containing k harmonically related sinusoids, each with a different strength a and a phase offset ϕ. The carrier $m[n]$ remains the same:

$$x[n]=\sum_{i=1}^{k} a_i \cos(i\omega n+\phi_i), \quad m[n]=\cos(\omega_c n) \tag{5.6}$$

As in Equation (5.5), trigonometric identities give us the following result:

$$m[n]x[n]=\sum_{i=1}^{k} a_i\left[\cos\left((i\omega+\omega_c)n+\phi_i\right)+\cos\left((i\omega-\omega_c)n+\phi_i\right)\right]/2 \tag{5.7}$$

In other words, the frequencies present in the modulated output signal will be $\omega - \omega_c$, $\omega + \omega_c$, $2\omega - \omega_c$, $2\omega + \omega_c$, $3\omega - \omega_c$, $3\omega + \omega_c$, etc. Except in the special case where the carrier frequency ω_c is a multiple of the instrument's fundamental frequency ω, these output frequencies will no longer be integer multiples of ω. This shows why the ring modulator produces nonharmonic output sounds. The result holds even for more complex real-world musical signals that typically contain a small amount of inharmonicity.

Modulation in the Frequency Domain

Another way of understanding the ring modulation effect is to consider its behavior in the frequency domain by examining its Z transform. Multiplication in the time domain is equivalent to *convolution* in the frequency domain:

$$y[n] = m[n]x[n] \Rightarrow Y(z) = M(z)*X(z) \tag{5.8}$$

Convolving two signals can be thought of as a process of gradually sliding one signal past the other and multiplying the two together at every offset (Figure 5.5).

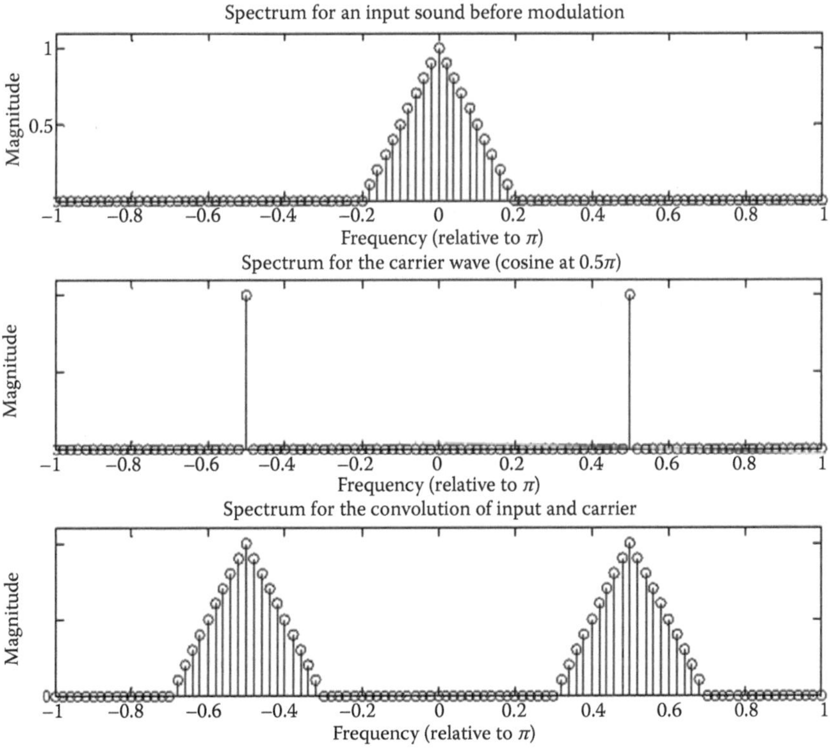

FIGURE 5.5
An example convolution of input and carrier signals.

Perception

The frequency of the carrier signal $m[n]$ typically ranges from 10 Hz to 1 kHz or more. At the very bottom of the range, the ring modulator produces a rhythmic warbling effect similar to the tremolo, and the sounds tend to become more unusual as the frequency increases. Why should the same effect produce a perception of rhythm at low carrier frequencies and a change in timbre at high carrier frequencies? The answer has to do with the properties of the human ear.

The ear can be modeled as a *filterbank* of many band-pass filters, each sensitive to a narrow range of frequencies (similar to a short-time Fourier transform). The resolution of the filterbank is not infinite, and if two tones are

FOURIER IN THE EAR

The cochlea is a coiled cavity within the inner ear that is primarily responsible for much of our auditory system. Within the cochlea is the basilar membrane, a filmy structure that divides the cochlea and vibrates with incoming sound energy. The width of the basilar increases from the base (entrance) to apex (end), while the width of the cochlear cavity decreases.

The basilar membrane has thousands of basilar fibers embedded within. These fibers affect the local stiffness in the membrane. The membrane starts thick and stiff, but becomes thinner and more flexible toward its apex. When sound waves travel along the basilar membrane, sound energy is dissipated at the place along the membrane that has the same natural resonant frequency. The stiff fibers will resonate with high frequencies, and the more flexible fibers resonate at lower frequencies.

The hair cells along the length of the basilar membrane detect this vibration and convert it into electrical potentials for transmission to the brain. There are also outer hair cells that contract in response to signals from the brain. This allows the brain to adjust or tune the stiffness of the membrane, thus providing a feedback mechanism to enhance the resolution of frequency content.

Together, the basilar membrane and hair cells give a continuum of natural resonance from high frequencies at the base to low frequencies at the apex. This distributes the energy over space as a function of frequency. (The distribution is logarithmic, which also accounts for why we hear sound on a log scale.) Thus, the cochlea acts as a filterbank, performing a Fourier decomposition of the incoming sound.

Interestingly, this is a reversal of the normal frequency representation, since the highest frequencies appear at the entrance to the cochlea, and the lowest frequencies at the rear.

close enough in frequency to fall within the *critical bandwidth* of hearing, the ear will be unable to distinguish them as separate signals [27]. In this case, the perceptual result will be a single tone exhibiting *beating*, or changing amplitude. This is the effect of the tremolo. At high carrier frequencies, the ring modulator will produce tones that are separated by more than the critical bandwidth, which is typically on the order of 15–20% of each band's center frequency (much more accurate formulae are available in [27]). For moderate carrier frequencies between these extreme cases, where the tones are separated by an amount roughly equal to the critical bandwidth, the perceived result is often described as *roughness*: neither clear beating nor obviously separable tones.

As mentioned above, one special case occurs when the carrier and the input fundamental frequency are multiples of one another. In this case, the output frequencies will be harmonically related, though with different frequencies emphasized. The result will be a sound with a more clearly identifiable pitch, lacking the strangeness of most ring modulator sounds. However, since the carrier frequency is usually fixed, this effect can only occur for the few notes that match its pitch.

Low-Frequency Oscillator

As with the tremolo, the ring modulator requires an LFO to generate the carrier signal $m[n]$. The implementation is similar but not identical to the tremolo:

$$m[n] = 1 - \alpha + \alpha\cos(n\omega_c) \tag{5.9}$$

Here, as in the tremolo, α controls the depth of the effect. It takes a range of 0 to 1, with $\alpha = 0$ producing no effect, $\alpha = 1$ producing a pure ring modulator effect, and $\alpha = 0.5$ producing an equal balance between the two. Notice that at the maximum depth ($\alpha = 1$), the carrier reduces to a simple sinusoid:

$$m[n] = \cos(n\omega_c) \tag{5.10}$$

In comparison to the tremolo, this carrier lacks an offset term. If the offset was present ($m[n] = 1 + \cos(\omega_c n)$), the output $y[n]$ would also contain the original frequency components of $x[n]$. To see why, substitute this alternate definition of $m[n]$ into Equation (5.3). In no case does the carrier frequency itself (ω_c) appear in the output. For this reason, this type of modulation is known as *suppressed carrier* modulation.

Variations

Typical ring modulators take one input for connecting an instrument, and have one control for setting the frequency of the LFO. Sinusoidal LFOs are most commonly used, but more complex waveforms can be used as well. Since complex periodic waveforms can be modeled as the sum of sinusoids, the output quickly becomes quite dense as each term interacts with each other one:

$$x[n]=\sum_{i=1}^{k} a_i \cos(i\omega n+\phi_i), \quad m[n]=\sum_{h=1}^{l} b_h \cos(h\omega_c n+\phi_{c,h}) \tag{5.11}$$

$$m[n]x[n]=\sum_{i=1}^{k}\sum_{h=1}^{l}\frac{a_i b_h}{2}\left[\cos\left((i\omega+h\omega_c)n+\phi_i+\phi_{c,h}\right)+\cos\left((i\omega-h\omega_c)n+\phi_i-\phi_{c,h}\right)\right]$$

Another variation is to use two input signals in place of a carrier. The two signals are multiplied, producing new frequency components depending on the spectral content of the two inputs. If the same signal is used for both inputs, the output is the square of the input, which produces a type of nonlinear distortion (Chapter 7) but otherwise lacks the characteristic nonharmonic qualities of the ring modulator.

Implementation

Early ring modulators used "analog multiplier" circuits to modulate the two signals. These were expensive and typically had less than perfect accuracy, adding a certain amount of extra nonlinearity to the output. Digital implementation of the ring modulator is trivial, consisting of a single multiplication per sample. However, the sound of classic analog units will result in part from the nonlinearity of the multiplier circuits, so these effects would need to be simulated if replicating an individual unit's sound were desired.

Another consideration in digital ring modulation is *aliasing*. Depending on the frequency content of the input and the carrier, the sum and difference frequencies at the output may extend beyond the Nyquist frequency, $f_s/2$. If this happens, these frequencies will be aliased, adding yet another layer of inharmonicity to the output. Aliasing can be avoided by strictly band-limiting the input or carrier signals such that the maximum frequency term $k\omega + \omega_c$ remains below the Nyquist frequency. If low-pass filtering the input is not desirable, the signals can be *upsampled* in advance and the modulation performed at a higher sampling rate. The output is then low-pass filtered before being *downsampled* back to the original rate.

Code Example

The following C++ code fragment implements a basic ring modulator.

```
int numSamples;          // How many audio samples to process
float *channelData;      // Array of samples, len. numSamples
float ph;                 // Current phase of the LFO (0-1)
float inverseSampleRate; // Defined as 1.0/(sample rate)
```

```
float carrierFrequency_;       // Frequency of the oscillator

for (int i = 0; i < numSamples; ++i)
{
    const float in = channelData[i];

    // Ring modulation is easy! Just multiply the waveform
    // by a periodic carrier
    channelData[i] = in * sinf(2.0 * M_PI * ph);

    // Update the carrier phase, keeping it in the range 0-1
    ph += carrierFrequency_*inverseSampleRate;
    if(ph >= 1.0)
        ph -= 1.0;
}
```

THAT SCI-FI SOUND

Ring modulation was popular in early electronic music, and one of the first examples of its use was in the Melochord, an instrument built by the electronic music pioneer, Harald Bode, in 1947. But ring modulation really came of age as a special effect in science fiction film and television.

In 1956, Louis and Bebe Barron were commissioned to do twenty minutes of sound effects for the sci-fi movie *Forbidden Planet*. After creating some initial samples, the producers were sufficiently impressed to ask the husband and wife team to compose the entire score. This was one of the first electronic scores for a major film, and made heavy use of ring modulators that were built by Louis and Bebe. They treated each ring modulator as a different "actor," with a unique voice and behavior. As they explained on the sleeve notes for the soundtrack album, "We created individual cybernetics circuits for particular themes and leit motifs, rather than using standard sound generators. Actually, each circuit has a characteristic activity pattern as well as a 'voice.'"

Ring modulation was also used heavily by the BBC Radiophonic Workshop, a sound effect unit of the BBC well-known for innovations in sound synthesis and effects. For the voice of the Daleks, first used in 1963, Brian Hodgson applied a 30 Hz modulation, among other effects, to give a harsh buzzing sound to the voices. Ring modulation has been applied to almost every Dalek voice since, and a Moog ring modulator has also been used to generate as a special effect on the voices of another *Doctor Who* villain, the Cybermen.

The ring modulator has become synonymous with sci-fi sound effects. It is easily recognizable in classic productions, such as *The Outer Limits* and *The Hitchhiker's Guide to the Galaxy*. Today, it's an essential sound effect in television, film, and game audio production.

As the code indicates, ring modulation is a simple effect to implement digitally. Each incoming sample is multiplied by the output of an audio frequency oscillator whose frequency is given by `carrierFrequency_`. The variable `ph` keeps track of the phase of the oscillator at each sample. The main differences between the ring modulation code and the earlier tremolo code example are that the carrier is in the audio frequency range rather than the LFO range, and that waveform takes values between –1 and 1 rather than between 0 and 1.

Applications

The ring modulator's sound is found relatively rarely in music compared to most other well-known audio effects. When it is used, it is often made less strange by mixing in the original instrument sound (low values for the depth control). When a small amount of ring-modulated sound is mixed into an otherwise clean instrument, it can add an interesting roughness to the track.

The iconic use of ring modulation was not in music but in television and movies, especially early science fiction. Because the information in speech is contained in the overall shape of the spectrum and not in the fundamental frequency of the voice [28], ring modulation maintains intelligibility while scrambling the identity of the original speaker.

Problems

1. a. When two frequency components of equal amplitude are added together, as could be the case in ring modulation, when is beating, separate tones, or roughness perceived in the output?

   b. Assuming critical bandwidth is 20% of the center frequency, give approximate equations for the conditions for beating, separate tones, or roughness when two sinusoids with frequencies f_1 and f_2 are added together?

   c. Which of the three conditions in part (b) is most likely to be heard for each of the combinations: 300 and 500 Hz tones, 500 and 495 Hz tones, and 500 and 580 Hz tones?

2. Derive the following result, which was mentioned in the discussion on ring modulation:

   If

$$x[n] = \sum_{i=1}^{k} a_i \cos(i\omega n + \phi_i), \quad m[n] = \cos(\omega_c n),$$

then

$$m[n]x[n] = \sum_{i=1}^{k} a_i[\cos((i\omega + \omega_c)n + \phi_i) + \cos((i\omega - \omega_c)n + \phi_i)] / 2.$$

3. An input signal containing frequencies at 500 and 900 Hz is modulated by a carrier at 200 Hz. What are the frequencies that will appear in the output?
4. A signal containing only two frequency components is modulated by a third carrier frequency. At the end of this process, the output frequencies are 200, 400, 1100, and 1300 Hz. What were the original frequencies of the signal and the frequency of the carrier?

6

Dynamics Processing

Dynamic audio effects apply a time-varying gain to the input signal. The applied gain is typically a nonlinear function of the level of the input signal (or a secondary signal). Dynamic effects are most often used in order to modify the amplitude envelope of a signal. They often compress or expand the dynamic range of a signal.

In this chapter, we will focus on two of the most common forms of dynamics processing, dynamic range compression and expansion, as well as their more extreme forms, limiting and noise gates.

Dynamic Range Compression

Dynamic range compression (or just compression) is concerned with mapping the perceived dynamic range of an audio signal to a smaller perceived range. Dynamic range compressors achieve this goal by reducing the high signal levels while leaving the quieter parts untreated. Dynamic range compression should not be confused with data compression as used in audio codecs, which is a completely different concept.

Our goals here are to describe how a compressor is designed and to discuss how the different design choices affect the perceived sonic characteristics of the compressor, considering both technical and perceptual aspects. We first provide an overview of the basic theory, paying special attention to the adjustable parameters used to operate a dynamic range compressor. Then the principles of its operation are described, including detailed discussion of digital implementation based on classic analog designs. Next, different methods and implementations are given for a complete design. Applications of compressors are then discussed, along with the artifacts that may result with their use.

Theory

Compressor Controls

A compressor has a set of controls directly linked to compressor parameters through which one can set up the effect. The most commonly used compressor parameters may be defined as follows.

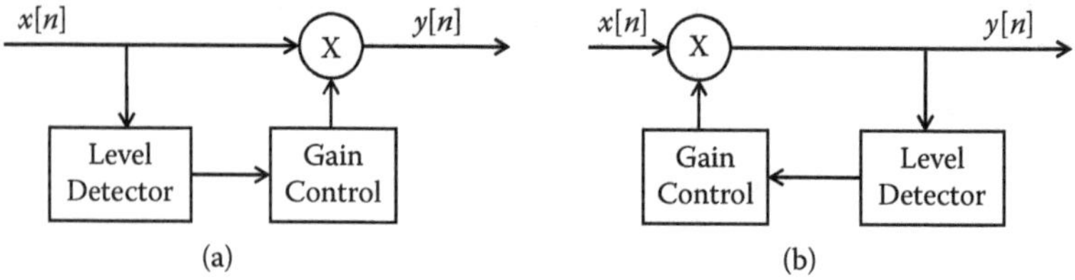

FIGURE 6.1
Flow diagram of a feedforward (a) and feedback (b) compressor.

A *compressor* is essentially a variable gain control, where the amount of gain used depends on the level of the input. Attenuation is applied (gain less than 1) when the signal level is high, which in turn makes louder passages softer, reducing the dynamic range. The basic scheme, implemented as either a feedforward or a feedback device, is shown in Figure 6.1.

Threshold defines the level above which the compressor is active. Whenever the signal level overshoots this threshold, the level will be reduced.

Ratio controls the input/output ratio for signals overshooting the threshold level. It determines the amount of compression applied. A ratio of 3:1 implies that the input level needs to increase by 3 dB for the output to rise by 1 dB.

A compressor's input/output relationship is often described by a simple graph, as in Figure 6.2. The horizontal axis corresponds to the input signal level, and the vertical axis is the output level, where level is measured in decibels. A line at 45° through the origin corresponds to a gain of 1, so that any input level is mapped to exactly the same output level. The ratio

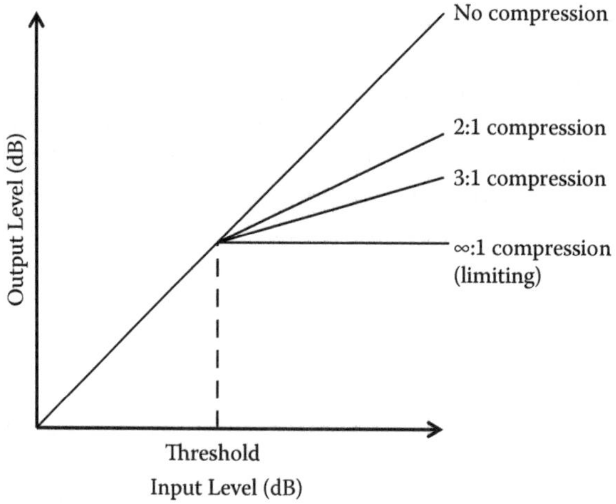

FIGURE 6.2
Compressor input/output characteristic. The compressor weakens the signal only when it is above the threshold. Above that threshold, a change in the input level produces a smaller change in the output level.

describes how the compressor changes the slope of that line above the threshold value. The distance between the highest and lowest output levels defines the dynamic range of the output.

Limiting is simply an extreme form of compression where the ratio is very high (often described as 20:1 or higher), and thus the input/output relationship becomes very flat. This places a hard limit on the signal level.

Attack and release times, also known as time constants, control the speed at which a compressor reacts to a change in signal level. Instantaneous compressor response, as described in [29], is not usually sought because it introduces distortion on the signal.

The attack time defines the time it takes the compressor to decrease the gain to the level determined by the ratio once the signal overshoots the threshold. The release time defines the time it takes to bring the gain back up to the normal level once the signal has fallen below the threshold.

Figure 6.3 shows how the attack and release times affect an example input. There is overshoot when the signal level increases, since it takes time for the gain to decrease, and attenuation when the input signal returns to the initial level, since it takes time for the gain to increase. As shown, the release time is generally longer than the attack time.

A *makeup gain* control is usually provided at the compressor output. The compressor reduces the level (gain) of the signal, so that applying a makeup gain to the signal allows for matching the input and output loudness levels.

The *knee width* option controls whether the bend in the response curve has a sharp angle or a rounded edge. The knee is the threshold-determined point where the input/output ratio changes from unity to a set ratio. A sharp transition is called a hard knee and provides a more noticeable compression. A softer transition, where, over a transition region on both sides of the threshold, the ratio gradually grows from 1:1 to a user-defined value, is called a soft knee. It makes the compression effect less perceptible. Depending on the signal, we can use hard or soft knee, with the latter being preferred when we want less obvious (transparent) compression.

A compressor has a set of additional controls, most of which are found in most modern compressor designs. These include a *hold* parameter, *sidechain filtering*, *look-ahead*, and many more. However, in this chapter, we will focus primarily on the parameters mentioned above.

Signal Paths

The signal entering the compressor is split into two copies. One is sent to a variable gain amplifier (the gain stage) and the other to an additional path, known as a sidechain, where the gain computer, a circuit controlled by the level of the input signal, applies the required gain reduction to the gain stage. The copy of the signal entering the sidechain has its bipolar amplitude converted into a unipolar representation of level. When the level of the signal is determined by its absolute value (instantaneous signal level), this is known

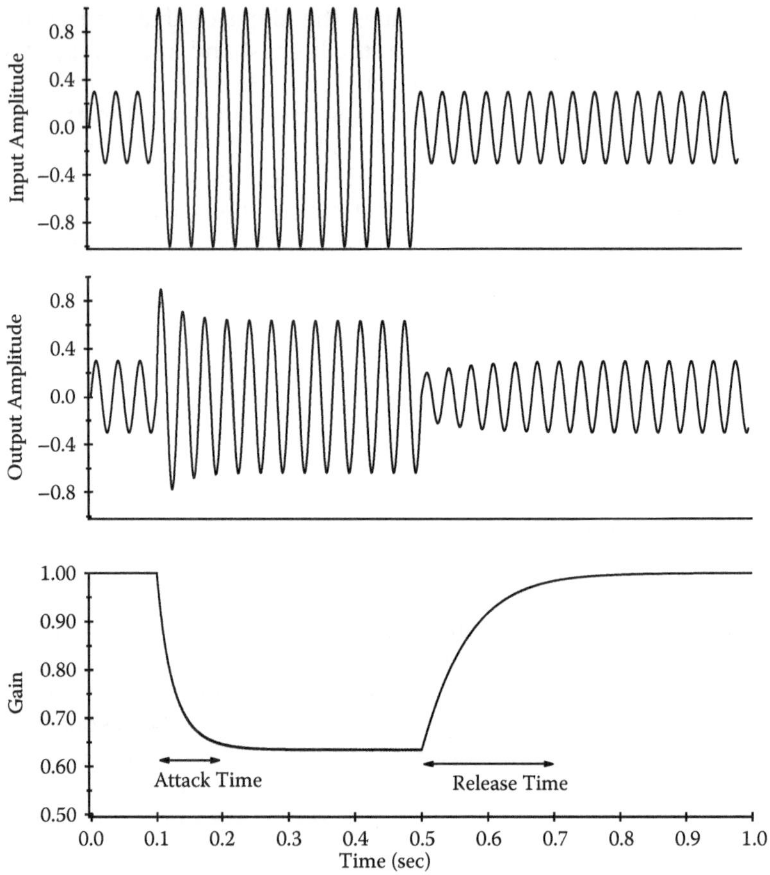

FIGURE 6.3
Effect of a compressor on a signal. Only the middle portion of input is above the compressor's threshold.

as peak sensing. An alternative is to use root mean square (RMS) sensing and determine the signal level by RMS value.

The Gain Stage

The gain stage is responsible for attenuating the input signal by a varied amount of decibels (dB) over time. The heart of every compressor is the element that applies this gain reduction: a voltage-controlled amplifier (VCA) that attenuates the input signal according to an external control signal (*c*) coming from the sidechain. Building a VCA with analog components is nontrivial, and thus many approaches have been applied [30]. Optical compressors such as the Teletronix LA-2A use a light-dependent resistor (LDR) as the bottom leg of a voltage divider located within the signal path. The control voltage is used to drive a light source that with increasing brightness will lower the resistance of the LDR and, therefore, apply the necessary gain reduction. A similar approach is taken by the Universal Audio 1176 compressor, but instead of using an LDR, it uses the drain-to-source resistance of a field effect transistor (FET compressor). The control voltage could then be applied to the gate terminal in order to lower the FET's resistance [31]. An even earlier approach used in so-called variable mu compressors such as the Fairchild 670 exploited the fact that altering the grid-to-cathode voltage would change the gain of a tube amplifier. More modern compressor designs make use of specialized integrated VCA circuits. These are much more predictable than the earlier approaches and offer improved specifications (such as less harmonic distortion and a higher usable dynamic range).

In a solely digital design, one can model an ideal VCA as multiplying the input signal by a control signal coming from the sidechain (sidechain refers to any signal path in an audio effect that doesn't produce the output signal; see Chapter 12). If $x[n]$ denotes the input signal, $y[n]$ the output signal, and $c[n]$ the control signal, then $y[n] = c[n] \cdot x[n]$. In addition, makeup gain is often used to add a constant gain back to the signal in order to match output and input levels. In a digital compressor we can easily implement a makeup gain by multiplying the compressor's output by a constant factor corresponding to the desired makeup gain value. So, representing the signals in either the linear or decibel domains, where M is the makeup gain,

$$\begin{aligned} y[n] &= x[n] \cdot c[n] \cdot M \\ y_{dB}[n] &= x_{dB}[n] + c_{dB}[n] + M_{dB} \end{aligned} \tag{6.1}$$

The Gain Computer

The gain computer is the compressor stage that generates the control signal. The control signal determines the gain reduction to be applied to the signal. This stage involves the threshold T, ratio R, and knee width W parameters. These define the static input/output characteristic of compression. Once the signal level exceeds the threshold value, it is attenuated according to the ratio.

The compression ratio is defined as the reciprocal of the slope of the line segment above the threshold,

$$R = \frac{x_G - T}{y_G - T} \quad \text{for} \quad x_G > T \tag{6.2}$$

where the input and output to the gain computer, x_G and y_G, and the threshold T are all given in decibels. The static compression characteristic is described by the following relationship:

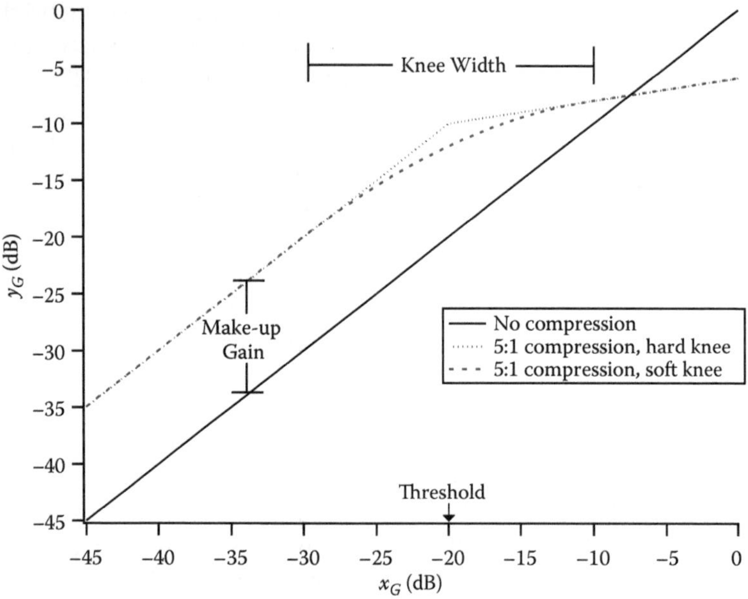

FIGURE 6.4
Static compression characteristic with makeup gain and hard or soft knee.

$$y_G = \begin{cases} x_G & x_G \le T \\ T + (x_G - T)/R & x_G > T \end{cases} \tag{6.3}$$

In order to smooth the transition between compression and no compression at the threshold point, we can soften the compressor's knee. The width W of the knee (in decibels) is equally distributed on both sides of the threshold. Figure 6.4 presents a compression gain curve with a soft knee.

To implement this, we replace Equation (6.3) with the following piecewise, continuous function:

$$y_G = \begin{cases} x_G & 2(x_G - T) < -W \\ x_G + (1/R - 1)(x_G - T + W/2)^2/(2W) & 2|(x_G - T)| \le W \\ T + (x_G - T)/R & 2(x_G - T) > W \end{cases} \tag{6.4}$$

When the knee width is set to zero, the soft knee becomes a hard knee.

Level Detection

The level detection stage is used to provide a smooth representation of the signal's level and may be applied at various places in the sidechain. The gradual change of gain is due to the attack and release times. The process of properly setting up these times is crucial to the performance of the compressor since unpleasant artifacts are often associated with the choice of these compressor parameters.

The attack and the release times are usually introduced through a smoothing detector filter. We can simulate the time domain behavior of the filter in the digital domain with a digital one-pole filter,

$$y[n] = \alpha y[n-1] + (1-\alpha)x[n] \tag{6.5}$$

where α is the filter coefficient, $x[n]$ is the input, and $y[n]$ is the output. The step response of this filter is

$$y[n] = 1 - \alpha^n \quad \text{for} \quad x[n] = 1, n \geq 0 \tag{6.6}$$

The time constant τ is defined as the time it takes for this system to reach $1 - 1/e$ of its final value, i.e., $y[\tau f_s] = 1 - 1/e$. Thus, from (6.6) we have

$$\alpha = e^{-1/(\tau f_s)} \tag{6.7}$$

Alternate definitions for the time constant are often used [8]. For instance, if one considers rise time for the step response to go from 10 to 90% of the final value,

$$0.1 = 1 - \alpha^{\tau_1 f_s},\ 0.9 = 1 - \alpha^{\tau_2 f_s} \to \tau_2 - \tau_1 = \tau \ln 9 \tag{6.8}$$

Another alternative is to relate the attack and release time to the amount of decibel gain change; e.g., if the attack and release times are specified relative to 10 dB, then an 8 ms attack time implies that the compressor will take 8 ms to reduce the gain from 0 to –10 dB.

In analog detectors the filter is typically implemented as a simple series resistor capacitor circuit, with τ = RC. Equations (6.5) and (6.7) may then be found by digital simulation using a step-invariant transform [5]. The advantage of this approach over other digital simulation methods such as the bilinear transform is that we preserve the analog filter topology with the capacitor's voltage as the state variable. Therefore, we will not experience any clicks and pops once we start varying the filter coefficients over time.

RMS Detector

The RMS detector is useful when we are interested in a smoothed average of a signal. Level detection may be based on a measurement of the RMS value of the input signal [32], which is defined as

$$y_L{}^2[n] = \frac{1}{M} \sum_{m=-M/2}^{M/2-1} x_L{}^2[n-m] \tag{6.9}$$

However, this is generally unsuitable for real-time implementations since it enforces a latency of $M/2$ samples. In the implementation of real-world effects this measurement is often approximated by filtering the squared input signal with a first-order low-pass infinite impulse response (IIR) filter and taking the square root of the output [33]. This is also commonly found in analog RMS-based compressors [5]. The difference equation of the RMS detector with smoothing coefficient becomes

$$y^2[n] = \alpha y^2[n-1] + (1-\alpha)x^2[n] \tag{6.10}$$

We can find RMS detectors in some compressors at the beginning of the sidechain. In [34], it was shown that Equation (6.10) produces behavior generally equivalent to Equation (6.5), save for a scaling of the time constant. Therefore, we will focus on the various options for the peak detector.

Peak Detector

The analog peak detector circuit, as commonly found in analog dynamic range controls, is given in Figure 6.5. If we are not required to simulate a particular type of diode, we can idealize it by assuming that it can supply infinite current once the voltage across the diode becomes positive and completely blocks when reverse biased. This significantly simplifies the calculation [34]:

$$\frac{dV_C}{dt} = \frac{\max(V_{in} - V_C, 0)}{R_A C} - \frac{V_C}{R_R C} \tag{6.11}$$

The capacitor is charged through resistor R_A according to a positive voltage across the diode but continually discharged though R_R. Taking α_A as the attack coefficient and α_R as the release coefficient, calculated according to

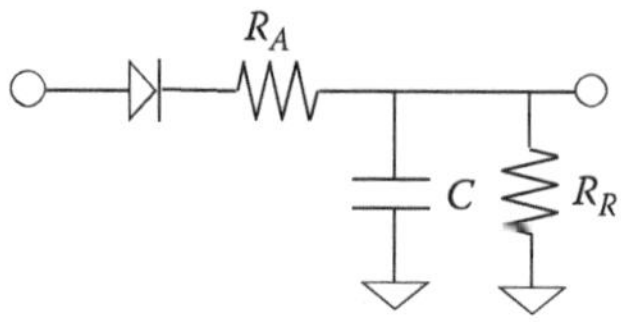

FIGURE 6.5
Peak detector circuit.

Equation (6.7) from the attack and release times $\tau_A = R_A C$ and $\tau_R = R_R C$, we can simulate the ideal analog peak detector with

$$y_L[n] = \alpha_R y_L[n-1] + (1-\alpha_A)\max\left(x_L[n] - y_L[n-1], 0\right) \tag{6.12}$$

Although used in many analog compressors, and some digital designs [35], this circuit has a few problems. When $x_L[n] \geq y_L[n-1]$, the step response is

$$y[n] = (1-\alpha_A)\sum_{m=0}^{n-1}(\alpha_R + \alpha_A - 1)^m \to \frac{1-\alpha_A}{2-\alpha_R-\alpha_A} \approx \frac{\tau_R}{\tau_R + \tau_A} \tag{6.13}$$

where we used the series expansion of the exponential function. Equation (6.13) implies that we will get a correct peak estimate only when the release time constant is considerably longer than the attack time constant. Another side effect is that the attack time also gets slightly scaled by the release time: there will be a faster attack time than expected when we use a fast release time. Both problems are illustrated in Figure 6.6.

In order to accomplish a program-dependent release behavior (autorelease), some analog compressors use a combination of two release time constants in their peak detectors. One such design is found in the famous SSL Stereo Bus Compressor. It uses two release networks stacked on top of each other. The much earlier Fairchild compressors and similar tube compressors used similar designs. When used in a compressor, the peak detector with dual time constant automatically increases the release time once the compression continues for a longer time period. This gives the desirable property

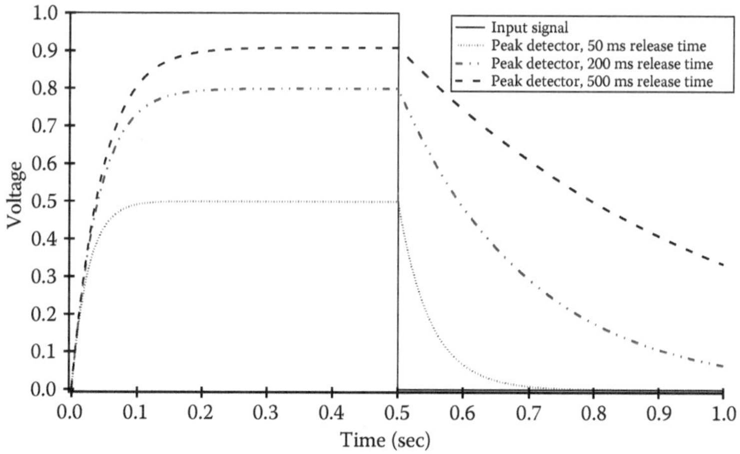

FIGURE 6.6
Output of the analog peak detector circuit for different release time constants. Attack time = 50 ms.

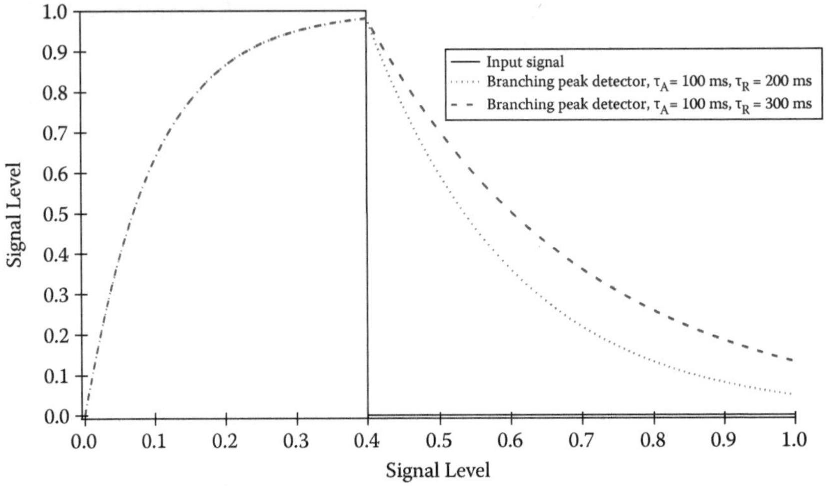

FIGURE 6.7
Output of the branching peak detector for different release time constraints.

of a shorter release time after compressing transients and a longer release time for steady-state compression. However, this type of peak detector suffers from the same level problems.

Level-Corrected Peak Detectors

A more modern, digital design decouples the attack and release, and provides a branch to the difference equation,

$$y_L[n] = \begin{cases} \alpha_A y_L[n-1] + (1-\alpha_A)x_L[n] & x_L[n] > y_L[n-1] \\ \alpha_R y_L[n-1] + (1-\alpha_R)x_L[n] & x_L[n] \le y_L[n-1] \end{cases} \tag{6.14}$$

This peak detector, also used in [5, 35], now simply switches coefficients between the attack and the release phase. As shown in Figure 6.7, it does not suffer from the level differences caused by different time constants exhibited by the standard peak detector circuit.

There are many other choices for the peak detector, both described in the literature and implemented in commercial designs. A detailed description of these, along with an assessment of their performance, is provided in [30].

Implementation

Considering the classic audio effects (equalization, delay, panning, etc.), the dynamic range compressor is perhaps the most complex one. There is no single correct form or implementation, and there is a bewildering variety of design choices. This explains why every compressor in common usage behaves and sounds slightly different and why certain compressor models have become audio engineers' favorites for certain types of signal. Analysis of compressors is difficult because they represent nonlinear time-dependent systems with memory. The gain reduction is applied smoothly and not instantaneously, as would be the case with a simple static nonlinearity. Furthermore, the large number of design choices makes it nearly impossible to draw a generic compressor block diagram that would be valid for the majority of real-world compressors. Some differ in topology, others introduce additional stages, and some simply differ from the precise digital design because these deviations add character to the compressor. However, we can describe the main parameters of a compressor unit and specify a set of standard stages and building blocks that are present in almost any compressor design.

Feedback and Feedforward Design

There are two possible topologies for the sidechain, a feedback or feedforward topology. In the feedback topology the input to the sidechain is taken after the gain has been applied. This was used in early compressors and had the benefit that the sidechain could rectify possible inaccuracies of the gain stage.

The feedforward topology has the sidechain input before the gain is applied. This means that the sidechain circuit responsible for calculating the gain reduction, the gain computer, will be fed with the input signal. Therefore, it will have to be accurate over the whole of the signal's dynamic range, as opposed to a feedback type compressor where it will have to be accurate over a reduced dynamic range since the sidechain is fed with the compressor's output. This bears no implications for digital design, but it should be taken under consideration if designing an analog feedforward compressor. Most modern compressors are based on the feedforward design.

By combining Equations (6.1) and (6.3) we can calculate the control signal either from the input or from the output of the compressor, leading to the two topologies of feedforward and feedback compression (Figure 6.8a and b).

The feedback design has a few limitations, such as the inability to allow a look-ahead function or to work as a perfect limiter due to the infinite negative amplification needed. From Equations (6.1) and (6.3), when $x_L > T$, the control signal for the feedback compressor is calculated as

$$c_{dB}[n] = (1 - R)(y_G[n-1] - T) \tag{6.15}$$

where we have assumed a hard knee and no attack or release. A limiter (with a ratio of ∞:1) would need infinite negative amplification to calculate

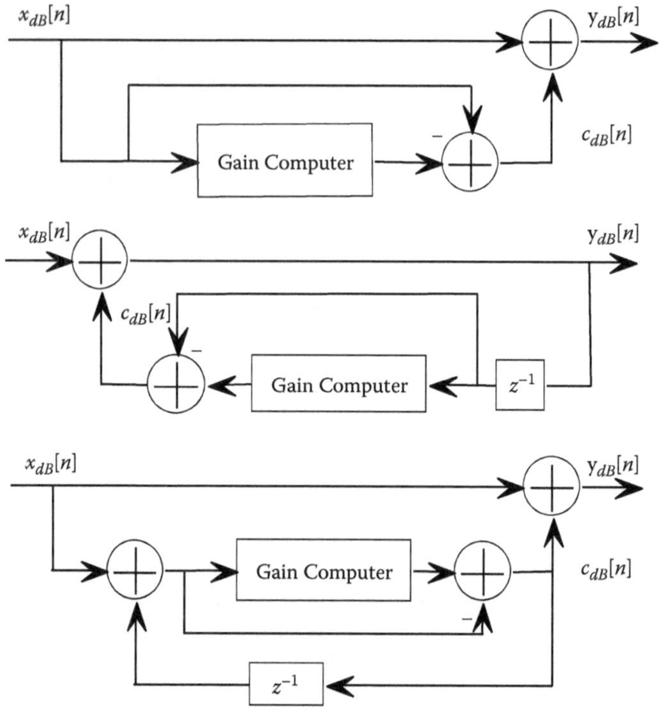

FIGURE 6.8
Static compressor block diagrams with linear/decibel conversion not depicted. Feedforward design on top, feedback design in the middle, and alternate feedback design on bottom.

the control signal. This is why feedback compressors are not capable of perfect limiting.

In contrast, the control signal of the feedforward compressor, for $x_L > T$, is

$$c_{dB}[n] = (1/R - 1)(x_G[n] - T) \tag{6.16}$$

Here, since the slope for a limiter approaches –1, implementing limiting is not a problem using a feedforward compressor. The feedforward compressor is also able to go smoothly into overcompression (with $r < 0$); the slope variable simply becomes smaller than –1.

An Alternate Digital Feedback Compressor

As an alternative to the feedback design depicted in Figure 6.8b, we can use the previous gain multiplier on the current input sample in order to estimate the current output sample, as shown in Figure 6.8c. Since the compressor's gain is likely to change only by small amounts from sample to sample, the estimation is a fairly good one. Since the sidechain is now fed by the input

OVERCOMPRESSION AND THE LOUDNESS WAR

Dynamic range compression is used at almost every stage of the audio production chain. It is applied to minimize artifacts in recording (such as variation in loudness as a vocalist moves towards or away from a microphone), to reduce masking, and to bring different tracks into a comparable loudness range. Compression is also applied in mastering to make the recording sound "loud," since a loud recording will be more noticeable than a quiet one and the listener will hear more of the full frequency range. This has resulted in a trend to more and more compression being applied, a "loudness war."

Broadcasting also has its loudness wars. Dynamic range compression is applied in broadcasting to prevent drastic level changes from song to song and to ensure compliance with standards regarding maximum broadcast levels. But competition between radio stations for listeners has resulted in a trend to very large amounts of compression being applied.

So a lot of recordings have been compressed to the point where dynamics are compromised, transients are squashed, clipping occurs, and there can be significant distortion throughout. The end result is that many people think, compared to what they could have been, a lot of modern recordings sound terrible. And broadcast compression only adds to the problem.

Who is to blame? There is a belief among many that "loud sells records." This may not be true, but believing it encourages people to participate in the loudness war. And different individuals may think that what they are doing is appropriate. Collectively, the musician who wants a loud recording, the record producer who wants a wall of sound, the engineers dealing with artifacts, the mastering engineers who prepare content for broadcast, and the broadcasters themselves are all acting as soldiers in the loudness war.

THE TIDE IS TURNING

The loudness war may have reached its peak shortly after the start of the new millenium. Audiologists became concerned that the prolonged loudness of new albums might cause hearing damage. Musicians began highlighting the sound quality issue, and in 2006, Bob Dylan said, "… these modern records, they're atrocious, they have sound all over them. There's no definition of nothing, no vocal, no nothing, just like static. Even these songs probably sounded ten times better in the studio" [36]. Also in 2006, a vice-president at a Sony Music subsidiary wrote an open letter decrying the loudness war, claiming that mastering engineers are being forced to make releases louder in order to get the attention of industry heads.

In 2008 Metallica released an album with tremendous compression, and hence clipping and lots of distortion. But a version without overuse of compression was included in downloadable content for a game, Guitar Hero III, and listeners all over noticed and complained about the difference. Again in 2008, Guns N' Roses producers (including the band's frontman Axl Rose) chose a version with minimal compression when offered three alternative mastered versions.

Recently, an annual Dynamic Range Day has been organized to raise awareness of the issue, and the nonprofit organization Turn Me Up! was created to promote recordings with more dynamic range.

The European Broadcasting Union addressed the broadcast loudness wars with EBU Recommendation R 128 and related documents that specify how loudness and loudness range can be measured in broadcast content, as well as recommending appropriate ranges for both.

Together, all these developments may go a long way toward establishing a truce in the loudness war.

signal, we could instead feed in an arbitrary signal in the sidechain, in order to achieve sidechaining operation (Chapter 12). A similar technique has been used in analog compressors such as the SSL Bus Compressor (by using a slave VCA that mirrors the main VCA's action).

Detector Placement

There are various choices for the placement of the detector circuit inside the compressor's circuitry, as depicted in Figure 6.9 for feedforward compressors. In [5, 33, 34], the suggested position for the detector is within the linear domain and before the log converter and gain computer. That is,

$$\begin{aligned} x_L[n] &= |x[n]| \\ x_G[n] &= 20\log_{10} y_L[n] \\ c_{dB}[n] &= y_G[n] - x_G[n] \end{aligned} \tag{6.17}$$

However, the detector circuit then works on the full dynamic range of the input signal, while the gain computer only starts to operate once the signal exceeds the threshold (the control signal will be zero for a signal below the threshold). The result is that we again experience a discontinuity in the release envelope when the input signal falls below the threshold. It also generates a lag in the attack trajectory since the detector needs some time to charge up to the threshold level even if the input signal attacks instantaneously.

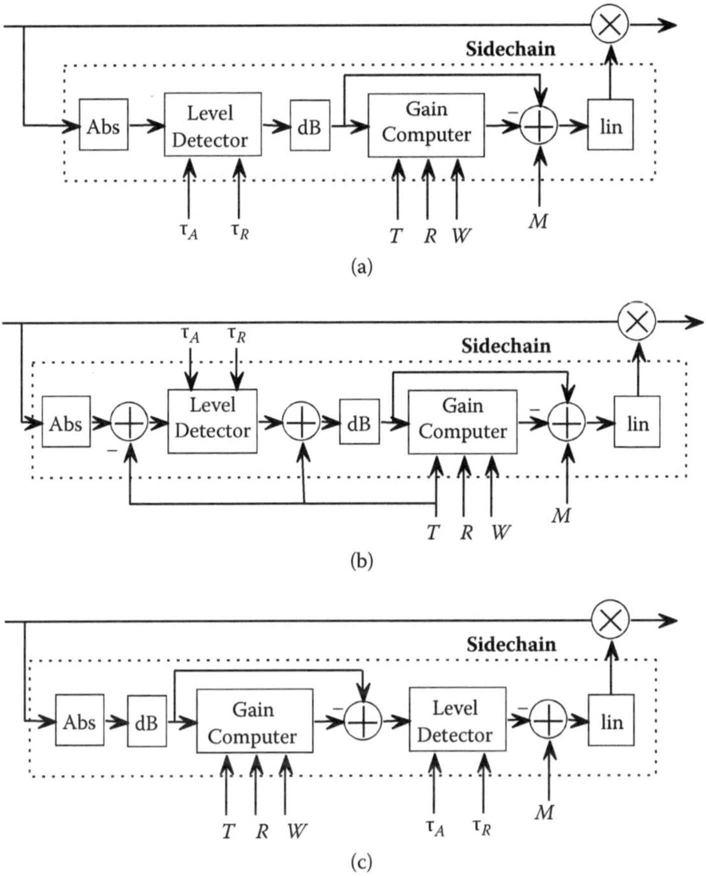

FIGURE 6.9
Block diagrams of the compressor configuration: (a) the return-to-zero detector, (b) the return-to-threshold detector, and (c) the log domain detector.

A way to overcome this, achieve a smooth release trajectory, and avoid the envelope discontinuity is by leaving the detector in the linear domain but bias it at the threshold level. That is, subtract the threshold from the signal before it enters the detector and add the threshold back in again after the signal has left it.

$$
\begin{aligned}
x_L[n] &= |x[n]| - 10^{T/20} \\
x_G[n] &= 20\log_{10}\left(y_L[n] + 10^{T/20}\right) \\
c_{dB}[n] &= y_G[n] - x_G[n]
\end{aligned}
\tag{6.18}
$$

This turns the return-to-zero detector into a return-to-threshold type, and the envelope will smoothly fade out once the signal falls below the threshold. However, this solution becomes problematic once we start using a soft knee characteristic. Since the threshold becomes a smooth transition instead of a hard boundary, we do not have a fixed value with which to bias the detector.

A similar approach is to place the detector in the linear domain but after the gain computer [37, 38]. In this case, the detector circuit works directly on the control signal.

$$\begin{aligned} x_G[n] &= 20\log_{10}|x[n]| \\ x_L[n] &= 10^{y_G[n]/20} \\ c[n] &= y_L[n] \end{aligned} \tag{6.19}$$

For each of Equations (6.17) to (6.19), since the release envelope discharges exponentially toward zero in the linear domain, this is equivalent to a linear discharge in the log (or decibel) domain. Although the release rate in terms of decibels per time is now constant, it also means that the release time will be longer for heavier and shorter for lighter compression. Unfortunately, this is not what the ear perceives as a smooth release trajectory, and thus the return-to-zero detector in the linear domain is mostly used by compressors where artifacts are generated on purpose [39]. Therefore, the preferred position for the detector is within the log domain and after the gain computer [30].

$$\begin{aligned} x_G[n] &= 20\log_{10}|x[n]| \\ x_L[n] &= x_G[n] - y_G[n] \\ c_{dB}[n] &= -y_L[n] \end{aligned} \tag{6.20}$$

Now, the detector directly smooths the control signal instead of the input signal. Since the control signal automatically returns back to zero when the compressor does not attenuate, we do not depend on a fixed threshold, and a smooth release envelope is guaranteed. The trajectory now behaves exponentially in the decibel domain, which means that the release time is independent of the actual amount of compression. This behavior seems smoother to the ear since the human sense of hearing is roughly logarithmic [27]. It is therefore used in most compressors that want to achieve smooth and subtle (artifact-free) compression characteristics for use with complicated signals (such as program material).

Code Example

The following C++ code fragment, adapted from the materials that accompany the book, implements a dynamic range compressor.

```
AudioSampleBuffer inputBuffer;  // Working buffer to analyse
                                // the input signal
int bufferSize;                 // Size of the input buffer
float samplerate;               // Sampling rate
float yL_prev;                  // Previous sample used for
                                // gain smoothing
float *x_g, *x_l, *y_g, *y_l;   // Buffers used in control
                                // voltage calculation
float *c;                       // Output control voltage
                                // used for compression

float threshold_;               // Compressor thresh. in dB
float ratio_;                   // Compression ratio
float tauAttack_, tauRelease_;  // Attack and release time
                                // constants
float makeUpGain_;              // Compressor make-up gain

inputBuffer.clear(0, 0, bufferSize);

// Mix down left-right to analyse the input
inputBuffer.addFrom(0, 0, buffer, 0, 0, bufferSize, 0.5);
inputBuffer.addFrom(0, 0, buffer, 1, 0, bufferSize, 0.5);

// Compression: calculates the control voltage
float alphaAttack = exp(-1/(0.001 * samplerate *
                                    tauAttack_));
float alphaRelease = exp(-1/(0.001 * samplerate *
                                     tauRelease_));

for (int i = 0 ; i < bufferSize ; ++i)
{
    // Level detection- estimate level using peak detector
    if (fabs(inputBuffer.getSampleData(0)[i]) < 0.000001)
        x_g[i] = -120;
    else
        x_g[i] = 20*log10(fabs(
                      inputBuffer.getSampleData(0)[i]));
    // Gain computer- static apply input/output curve
    if (x_g[i] >= threshold_)
        y_g[i] = threshold_ + (x_g[i]-threshold_) / ratio_;
    else
        y_g[i] = x_g[i];
    x_l[i] = x_g[i] - y_g[i];

    // Ballistics- smoothing of the gain
    if (x_l[0] > yL_prev)
        y_l[i] = alphaAttack * yL_prev +
                 (1 - alphaAttack ) * x_l[i] ;
```

```
    else
        y_l[i] = alphaRelease* yL_prev +
                 (1 - alphaRelease) * x_l[i] ;

    // Find control
    c[i] = pow(10.0, (makeUpGain_ - y_l[i]) / 20.0);
    yL_prev = y_l[i];
}

// Apply control voltage to the audio signal
for (int i = 0 ; i < bufferSize ; ++i)
{
    buffer.getSampleData(0)[i] *= c[i];
    buffer.getSampleData(1)[i] *= c[i];
}
```

This code first implements a level detector, converting the level of the input signal to decibels. It then applies the compression curve to find the required gain for the given signal level. Finally, it applies the calculated gain to the sample data in the buffer. This code assumes a stereo input, and the level detector uses the mix of the two channels.

Application

As the name implies, dynamic range compression reduces the dynamic range of a signal. It is used extensively in audio recording, noise reduction, production work, and live performance applications. But it does need to be used with care, since its overuse or use with nonideal parameter settings can introduce distortion and unforeseen side effects, reducing sound quality.

Compressors have a wide variety of applications. When recording onto magnetic tape, distortion can result for high signal levels. So compressors and limiters, with no or minimal makeup gain, are used to prevent sudden transient sounds causing the distortion, while still ensuring that the signal level is kept above the background noise. Compression is also used when editing and mixing tracks to correct for issues that arose in the recording process. For example, a singer may move toward and away from a microphone, so a small amount of compression could be applied to reduce the resultant volume changes. And once tracks have been recorded, a compressor provides a means to adjust the dynamic range of the track. In some cases, compression may be used as an alternative to equalization, as we shall see in Chapter 12.

A popular use of dynamic range compression is to increase the sustain of a musical instrument. By compressing a signal, the output level is made more constant, by suppressing the louder portions while amplifying the overall signal. For example, after a note is played, the envelope will decay toward silence. A compressor with appropriate settings will slow this decay, and hence preserve the instrument's sound. Alternatively, a transient modifier could be used [40], attenuating or boosting just the transient portions (as opposed to the sustain), which include the attack stage of a musical note.

Artifacts

There are a large number of artifacts associated with compressors. These are primarily to do with parameter settings that result in unwanted modification of the signal. To name just a few:

- Dropouts: "Holes," or periods of unwanted near silence, in the output signal that result from a strong attenuation immediately after a short, intense sound.
- Pumping: Perceived variation of signal level, as a result of reducing gain as a signal crosses the threshold and turning up as the signal dips below.
- Breathing: Similar to pumping, perceived variation of background noise level due to rapid gain changes in conjunction with high background noise.
- Modulation distortion: Distortion that is caused by the gain control changing too rapidly.
- Spectral ducking: Broadband gain reductions in the processed signal that occur as a result of a narrowband interfering signal.
- SNR reduction: Reduction in the signal-to-noise ratio (SNR) caused by boosting low-level (noise) signals or attenuating high-level sources.

Dropouts, pumping, and breathing are functions of the attack and release time changes and, to some extent, the threshold. Pumping and breathing, in particular, are quite well known and sometimes used intentionally. Sometimes, especially with dance music, the producer may want an audible change every time the compressor "kicks in." A short attack or release time can be used in order to achieve a quick change in the gain and achieve modulation of the overall signal level. This gives a "pumping" sound.

When the sound level drops below the threshold, the gain increases with a rate dependent on the release time. With appropriate choice of time constants, the signal level can remain reduced even though the input level is low. Thus, the noise can be made audible, giving the impression of breathing. A more sophisticated compressor may watch the input closely and adjust the gain when the input hits zero momentarily to reduce the "breathing" effect. Since breathing involves raising the noise floor, it could be considered a subset of SNR reduction. Spectral ducking is dealt with through sideband filtering or multiband compression, and is discussed in Chapter 12.

Generally, a compressor should leave the power spectrum unchanged. If our input is a pure sinusoid, with a sudden change in level, then the spectrum should be a single peak, with a tiny bit of harmonic distortion in just the window where the transition occurred.

Summary

Based on the analysis and design choices presented, we can now present a compressor configuration that serves the goals of ease of modification and avoidance of artifacts.

Feedforward compressors are preferred since they are more stable and predictable than the feedback ones, and high dynamic range problems do not occur with digital designs. The detector is placed in the log domain after the gain computer, since this generates a smooth envelope, has no attack lag, and allows for easy implementation of variable knee width. For the compressor to have smooth performance on a wide variety of signals, with minimal artifacts and minimal modification of timbral characteristics, the smooth, decoupled peak detector should be used. Alternately, the smooth, branching peak detector could be used in order to have more detailed knowledge of the effect of the time constants, although this may yield discontinuities in the slope of the gain curve when switching between attack and release phases.

The analysis in this chapter was limited to the design of standard compressors. Their uses and recommended parameter settings are discussed in detail in other texts [14, 15, 41, 42]. Variations and more advanced designs, such as sidechain filtering or multiband compressors, are discussed in Chapter 12.

Noise Gates and Expanders

The expander is a dynamic processor that attenuates the low-level portions of a signal and leaves the rest unaffected. A noise gate is expansion taken to the extreme, where it will heavily attenuate the input or eliminate it entirely, leaving only silence. The expander and noise gate, which act on low-level signals, are analogous to the compressor and limiter, which act on high-level signals.

Theory and Implementation

The expander can be viewed as a variable gain amplifier, where the gain is controlled by the level of the input signal and always set less than or equal to 1. When the signal level is high, the expander has unity gain. But when the signal drops below a predetermined level, gain will decrease, making the signal even lower. The basic structure of an expander is as a level-dependent,

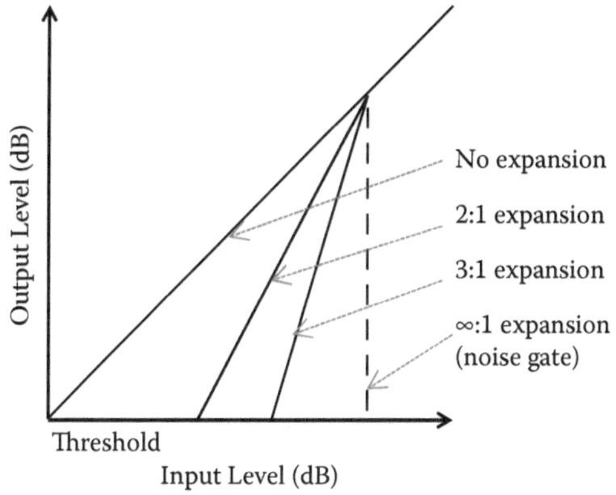

FIGURE 6.10
The expander reduces the signal level only when it drops below the threshold.

feedforward gain control, identical to the feedforward compressor block diagram (Figure 6.1a).

The input/output relationship is represented with a simple graph, such as the one in Figure 6.10. The input signal level is given in decibels by the horizontal axis, and the output level is given by the vertical axis. When the input/output curve has slope 1 (i.e., angled at 45°) and intersects the origin, the gain of the expander is 1 and the output level is identical to the input level. A change in the height of this curve corresponds to a change in the expander's gain. For the expander, part of the line will have slope greater than 1. The point where the slope of the line changes is the *threshold*, which is generally a user-adjustable parameter. When the input signal level is above the threshold nothing happens, and the output equals the input. But, a gain reduction results whenever the level drops or stays below the threshold. This gain reduction lowers the input level, thus expanding the dynamic range. For a typical expander, the signal levels are taken from an average level based on a root mean square (RMS) calculation, rather than from instantaneous measurements, since even a signal with high average level may produce low instantaneous measurements.

As with compression, the amount of expansion that is applied is usually expressed as a ratio between the change in input level (expressed in dB) and the corresponding change in output level. So with a 4:1 expansion ratio (with the input level below the threshold), a dip of 2 dB in the input will produce a drop of 8 dB in the output.

Since the level detection is based on a short time average, it takes some time for a change in the input level to be detected, which then triggers the change in the gain. As with the compressor, the ballistics are given by attack and release times, which may optionally be used in the level sensing or in smoothing the applied gain. The time required for the expander to restore the gain to 1 once the input level rises above the threshold is the *attack time*.

Likewise, the time taken for the expander to reduce its gain after the input drops below the threshold is the *release time*. The attack and release times give the expander a smoother change in the gain, rather than abrupt changes that may produce pops and other noise. Note that these are different from those in the compressor, where attack relates to the time to reduce the gain and release to the time to restore to the original levels. Figure 6.11 shows how the attack and release times in an expander affect an example input signal.

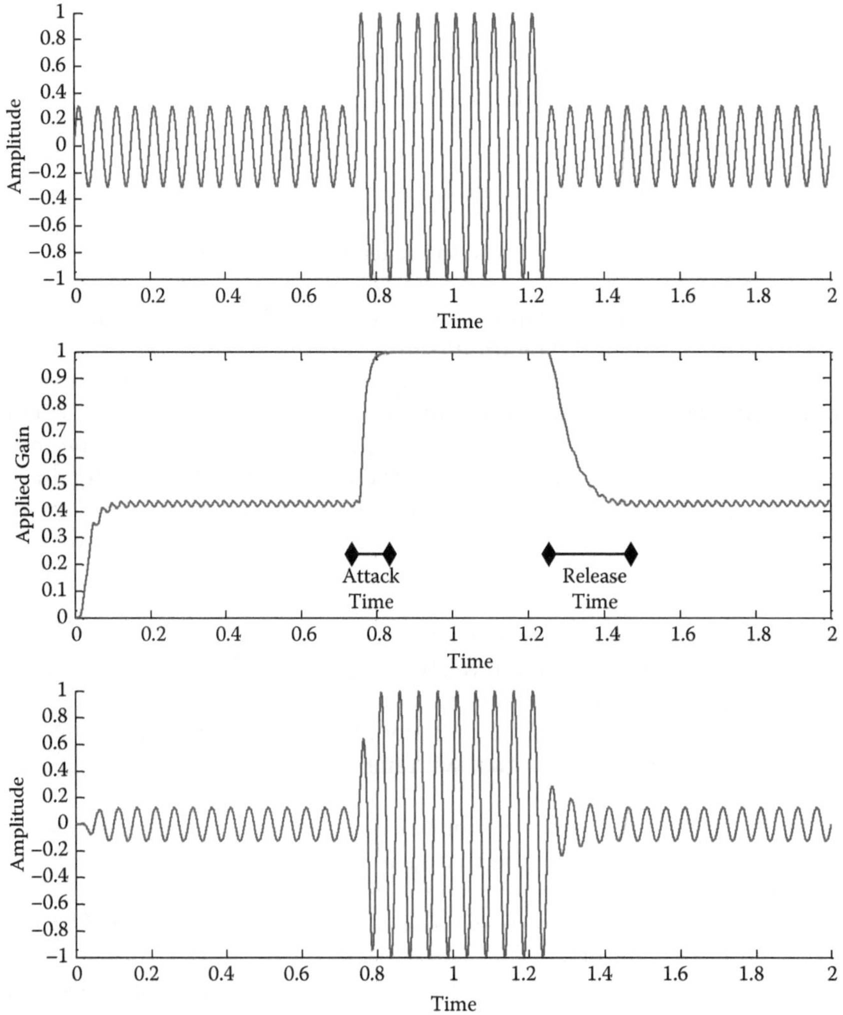

FIGURE 6.11
Effect of an expander. Only the middle portion of input is above the expander's threshold value. It takes time for the expander to increase gain when the input rises above the threshold. When input drops below the threshold, the expander slowly reduces gain.

If an expander is used with extreme settings where the input/output characteristic becomes almost vertical below the threshold, e.g., expansion ratio larger than 8:1, it is known as a *noise gate*. In this case, the signal may be very strongly attenuated or even completely cut. The noise gate will act as an on/off switch for an audio signal. When the signal has large amplitude, the switch is on and the input reappears at the output, but when it drops below the threshold, the switch is off and there is no output. As the name suggests, noise gates are used to reduce the level of noise in a signal.

A noise gate has five main parameters: threshold, attack, release, hold, and gain. Threshold and gain are measured in decibels, and attack, release, and hold are measured in seconds. The threshold is the level above which the signal will open the gate and below which it will not. The gain is the attenuation applied to the signal when the gate is closed. The attack and release parameters control how quickly the gate opens and closes. The attack is a time constant representing the speed at which the gate opens. The release is a time constant representing the speed at which the gate closes. The hold parameter defines the minimum time for which the gate must remain open. It prevents the gate from switching between states too quickly, which can cause modulation artifacts.

Applications

There are many audio applications of noise gates. For example, noise gates are used to remove breathing from vocal tracks, hum from distorted guitars, and bleed on drum tracks, particularly snare and kick drum tracks.

Consider a drum kit containing kick drum, snare, hi-hats, cymbals, and any number of tom-toms. An example microphone setup will include a kick drum microphone, a snare microphone (possibly two), a microphone for each tom-tom, and a set of stereo overheads to capture a natural mix of the entire kit. In some instances a hi-hat microphone will also be used. When mixing the recording, the overheads will be used as a starting point. The signals from the other microphones are mixed into this to provide emphasis on the main rhythmic components, that is, the kick, snare, and tom-toms. Processing is applied to these signals to obtain the desired sound. Compression is invariably used on kick drum recordings. A compressor raises the level of low-amplitude regions in the signal, relative to high-amplitude regions, which has the affect of amplifying the bleed. Noise gates are used to reduce (or remove) bleed from the signal before processing is applied.

Figure 6.12a shows an example kick drum recording containing bleed from secondary sources [43]. Figure 6.12b shows the amplitude envelope of the kick drum contained within the recording, and Figure 6.12c and d show the amplitude envelope of bleed contained within the signal. The large and small spikes up to 1.875 s in Figure 6.12c are snare hits, and the final 2 large spikes are tom-tom hits. Figure 6.12d has reduced limits on the y-axis. This figure shows the cymbal hit at 0 s, and hi-hat hits at 1.625 s. The amplitude

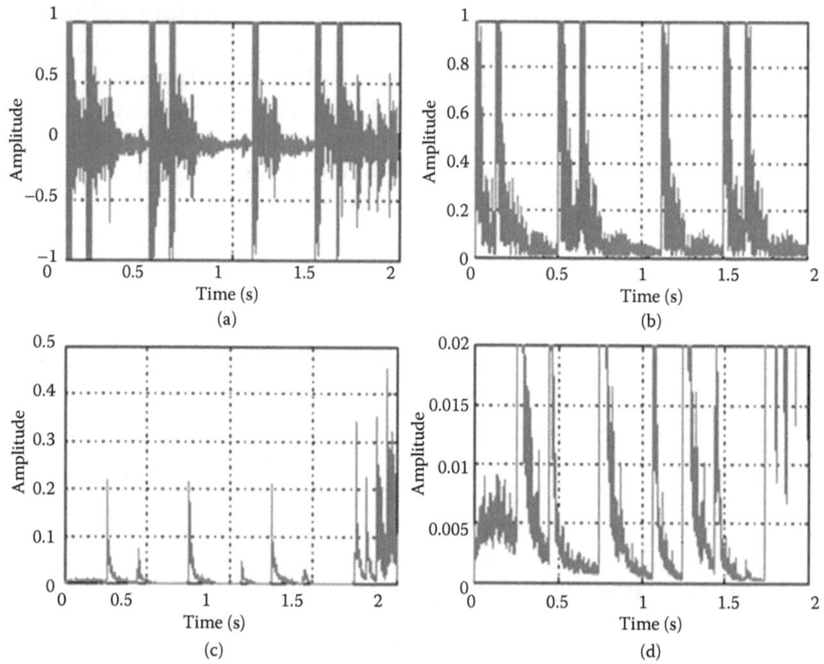

FIGURE 6.12
(a) A noisy signal that includes kick drum and bleed from other drum kit components. (b) The amplitude envelope of the kick drum contained within the noisy signal. (c) The amplitude envelope of the bleed contained within the noisy signal. (d) Same as (c), but with a zoomed-in *y*-axis to show cymbals and hi-hats in the bleed signal. (Reprinted from Terrell, M. J. et al., *EURASIP Journal on Advances in Signal Processing*, 1–9, 2010.)

of these portions of the bleed is very low and will have minimal effect on the gate settings. Components of the bleed signal that coincide with the kick drum cannot be removed by the gate, because the gate is opened by the kick drum. The snare hits coincide with the decay phase of the kick drum hits and so will have the biggest impact on the noise gate time constants. If the release time is short, the gate will be tightly closed before the snare hit, but the natural decay of the kick drum will be choked.

If the release time is long the gate will remain partially open, and the snare hit will be audible to some extent, but the kick drum hit will be allowed to decay more naturally. If the threshold is below the peak amplitude of any part of the bleed signal, then the bleed will open the gate and will be audible. It is necessary to strike a balance between reducing the level of bleed and minimizing distortion of the kick drum.

Expanders have applications in consumer electronics. They are often used to produce more extremes on recordings that have a limited dynamic range, such as vinyl or cassettes. An expander will make the dynamics much more dramatic during playback.

One of the most significant applications for expanders is noise reduction. They help reduce feedback and unwanted audio content, such as background sounds or bleed and interference from other sources. Noise gates are often used to eliminate noise or hiss that may otherwise be amplified and heard when an instrument is not being played, in which case the threshold should be set high enough such that the ambient noise falls below it, but not set so high that the instrument's sound and sustained notes are prematurely cut off.

Expanders can also be used in conjunction with compressors to reduce the effects of noise when transmitting a signal, audio or otherwise. A transmission channel typically has limited dynamic range capacity. If the signal is compressed before transmission, one can increase the average level of the signal with respect to the noise in the system, thus reducing the effect of the noisy channel. An expander is then used on the receiving end to return the transmitted signal back to its original dynamic range (though it does not undo or invert the compression [44]). This process of compressing and then expanding a signal is called *companding* and is an important component of the Dolby A noise reduction technique. Compressing the signal when recording and then expanding it on playback reduces the overall noise level.

Problems

1. Define the following parameters for a dynamic range compressor: *threshold, ratio, attack, release,* and *knee.*
2. Explain whether or not compressors and expanders have the following properties, and why:
    a. Linearity: $f(x + y) = f(x) + f(y)$ and $f(ax) = af(x)$.
    b. Shift or time invariance: If $f(x[n]) = y[n]$, then $f(x[n - k]) = y[n - k]$.
    c. Memoryless: f depends only on the current input $x[n]$ and not any previous inputs or outputs.
3. The diagrams in Figure 6.13 show two different compressor input/output characteristics.

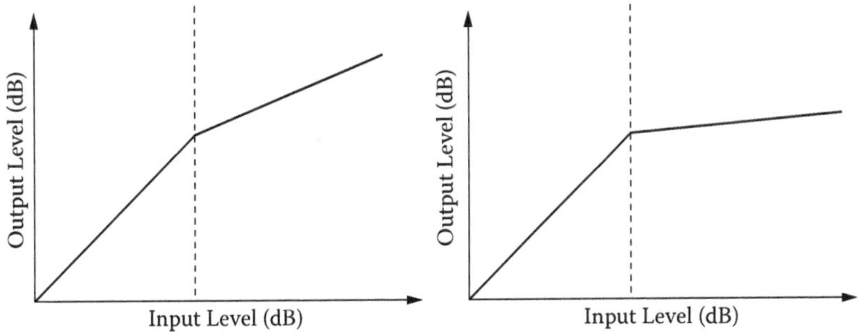

FIGURE 6.13
Possible compressor input/output curves.

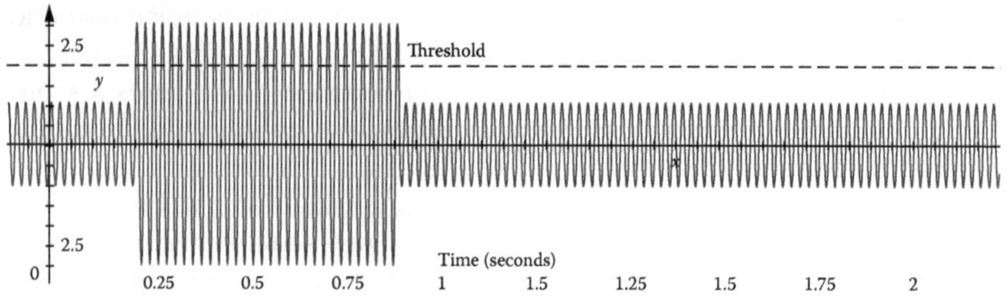

FIGURE 6.14
Example waveform.

a. Label the following quantities on each diagram: *threshold, ratio,* and *knee*; i.e., show what aspect of the diagram corresponds to each quantity.

b. Which curve more closely corresponds to a limiter? Why?

4. Define two side effects of compression, *pumping* and *breathing*. Explain the difference between them and how they can be addressed.

5. Consider the input signal depicted in Figure 6.14. Draw plots of the gain over time for both a compressor and an expander (assume a high ratio for both compressor and expander, and assume the hold time is zero on the expander), with the following two configurations. Exact numerical accuracy is not expected, but keep approximately the right scale in time and amplitude.

   a. Attack time = 20 ms, release time = 500 ms

   b. Attack time = 100 ms, release time = 100 ms

   c. For case (a), draw a plot of the *output* audio signal after the compressor is applied. In your diagram, label where *pumping* occurs and explain what can be done to reduce its effect.

7. Consider a dynamic range compressor with hard knee, threshold at –12 dB, and ratio of 3:1. What is the output signal level if the input signal level is –15, –12, or 3 dB?

7

Overdrive, Distortion, and Fuzz

Since the earliest days of the electric guitar, guitarists have been adding distortion to the sound of their instruments for expressive purposes. Distortion effects can create a wide palette of sounds ranging from smooth, singing tones with long sustain to harsh, grungy effects. Distortion can be introduced deliberately by the amplifier (especially in vacuum tube guitar amplifiers) or by a self-contained effect, and the particular choice of distortion effect is often part of a player's signature sound. An overview of many distortion-based effects, along with new implementations, is provided in [45].

This chapter covers overdrive, distortion, and fuzz effects, which are all based on the same principle of *nonlinearity*. Indeed, the three terms are sometimes used interchangeably. When a distinction is made, it is largely one of degree: *overdrive* is a nearly linear effect for low signal levels that becomes progressively more nonlinear at high levels, *distortion* operates mainly in a nonlinear region for all input signals, and *fuzz* is a completely nonlinear effect that creates more drastic changes to the input waveform, resulting in a harder or harsher sound.

Theory

Characteristic Curve

Most common audio effects are *linear* systems. In a linear system, if two inputs are added together and processed, the result is the same as processing each input individually and adding the results. And if an input is multiplied by a scalar value before processing, the result is the same as processing the input and then multiplying by that same scalar value. That is, for a linear audio effect, the following holds:

$$\begin{aligned} f\left(x_1[n]+x_2[n]\right) &= f\left(x_1[n]\right)+f\left(x_2[n]\right) \\ f\left(ax[n]\right) &= af\left(x[n]\right) \end{aligned} \tag{7.1}$$

Overdrive, distortion, and fuzz (hereafter collectively referred to as distortion) are always nonlinear effects for at least some input signals, meaning that Equation (7.1) does not hold.

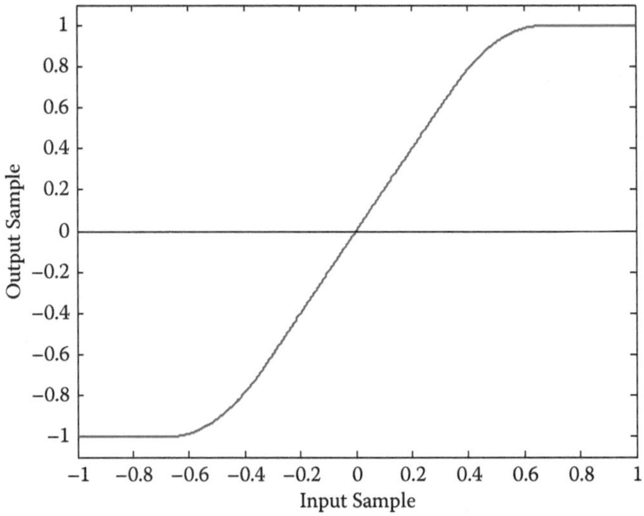

FIGURE 7.1
The characteristic input/output curve for a quadratic distortion.

Distortion effects can be largely described by a characteristic curve, a mathematical function relating the output sample $y[n]$ to the input sample $x[n]$. The following equation is one of many possible characteristic curves to produce a distortion effect [33]:

$$f(x)=\begin{cases} 2x & 0\le x<1/3 \\ 1-(2-3x)^2/3 & 1/3\le x<2/3 \\ 1 & 2/3\le x\le 1 \end{cases} \tag{7.2}$$

In this example, for input samples with magnitude less than 1/3, the effect operates in a linear region, but as the magnitude of x increases, it becomes progressively more nonlinear until *clipping* occurs above $x = 2/3$ and the output no longer grows in magnitude. A plot is shown in Figure 7.1. This particular equation is best classified as an *overdrive* effect since it contains a linear and a nonlinear region with a gradual transition between them. It is the nonlinear region that will give this effect its distinct sound.

The characteristic curve defines a *memoryless* effect: the current output sample $y[n]$ depends only on the current input sample $x[n]$ and not on any previous inputs or outputs. This is a reasonable approximation to how analog distortion circuits operate, though not an exact one, as we will see in the analog emulation subsection later in this chapter. Distortion is also a time-invariant effect in that the output samples depend only on the input samples and not the time at which they are processed.

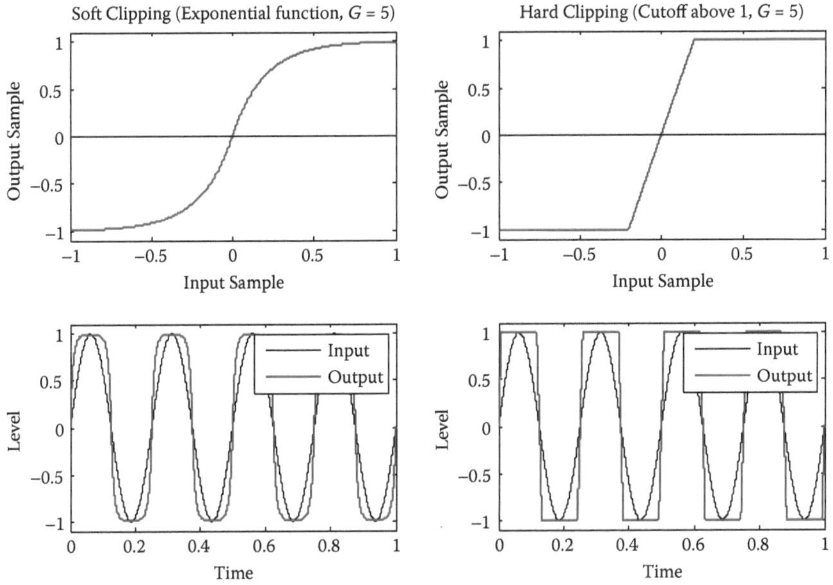

FIGURE 7.2
Comparison of hard and soft clipping.

Hard and Soft Clipping

Both digital and analog systems have limits to the magnitude of signal they can process. For analog systems, these limits are typically determined by the power supply voltages and architecture of each amplifier stage. In digital systems, the limits are usually determined by the number of bits in the analog-to-digital converter (ADC) and digital-to-analog converter (DAC). When a signal exceeds these limits, clipping occurs, meaning that a further increase in input does not produce any further increase in output. Clipping is an essential feature of distortion effects, and the way that an effect approaches its clipping point is a crucial part of its sound.

Distortion effects are often classified by whether they produce *hard clipping* or *soft clipping*. Figure 7.2 compares the two forms. Hard clipping is characterized by an abrupt transition between unclipped and clipped regions of the waveform, which produces sharp corners in the waveform. Soft clipping is characterized by a smooth approach to the clipping level, creating rounded corners at the peaks of the waveform. In general, soft clipping produces a smoother, warmer sound, whereas hard clipping produces a bright, harsh, or buzzy sound. Hard versus soft clipping is not a binary decision, and any given characteristic curve will fall on a continuum between the two.

The simplest, purest form of hard clipping simply caps the input signal above a certain magnitude threshold:

$$f(x)=\begin{cases}-1 & Gx\le -1\\ Gx & -1<Gx<1\\ 1 & Gx\ge 1\end{cases} \tag{7.3}$$

where G is an *input gain* applied to x before comparing to the threshold, explained in the next section. Digital systems produce this result when overloaded. Musicians generally find it to be an unpleasant, overly harsh sound. In the analog domain, many amplifiers based on transistors produce hard clipping, and hard clipping can also be created in an effect pedal through the use of silicon diodes.

The characteristic curve in Equation (7.2) produces a form of soft clipping since the transition from unclipped to clipped is gradual. The equation below [35] also produces soft clipping:

$$f(x)=\operatorname{sgn}(x)\left(1-e^{-|Gx|}\right) \tag{7.4}$$

In this equation, the output asymptotically approaches the clipping point as the input gets larger but never reaches it.* The amount of distortion added to the sound increases smoothly as the input level increases. Soft clipping occurs in analog vacuum tube amplifiers and certain effects pedals based on germanium diodes. It is not a natural occurrence in digital systems unless deliberately created by a suitable characteristic curve.

Input Gain

The term G in Equations (7.3) and (7.4) is a gain term applied to the input signal x before it passes through the nonlinear function. Because distortion is a nonlinear effect, the gain (or amplitude) of the input signal changes how the effect sounds. For nearly all practical characteristic curves, higher gain produces more distortion in the output. Notice that applying more gain to the input signal does not substantially affect the amplitude of the output, since the clipping level remains in the same place.

Figure 7.3 shows a sine wave subjected to soft clipping, Equation (7.4), with four different input gains. In the extreme case, the output approaches a square wave with amplitude equal to the clipping level. An extremely large input gain with a hard clipping effect would also produce an output approaching a square wave, showing that the differences between hard and soft clipping are less pronounced for very large gains.

* The expression $sgn(x)$ takes the value 1 for $x \ge 0$, –1 otherwise.

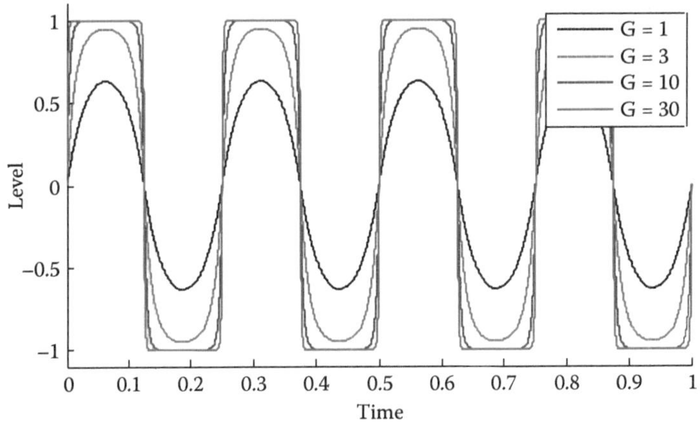

FIGURE 7.3
Soft clipping of a sine wave with four different input gains.

Symmetry and Rectification

The equations presented in the preceding sections were all *symmetrical* in that they applied the same nonlinear function to the positive and negative halves of the waveform. Real analog guitar amplifiers, especially those based on vacuum tubes, do not always behave this way. Instead, the clipping point might differ for positive and negative half-waves, or the curve for each half-wave could be entirely different. As we will see in the next section, symmetrical and asymmetrical characteristic curves produce different effects in the frequency domain, which are responsible for distinctive differences in sound.

Rectification is a special case of an asymmetrical function used in distortion effects. Rectification passes the positive half-wave unchanged but either omits or inverts the negative half-wave. It comes in two forms, shown in Figure 7.4. *Half-wave rectification* sets the negative half-wave to 0,

$$f_{half}(x) = \max(x, 0) \tag{7.5}$$

Full-wave rectification, equivalent to the absolute value function, inverts the negative half-wave:

$$f_{full}(x) = |x| \tag{7.6}$$

Rectification is often combined with another nonlinear transfer function in a distortion effect. It adds a strong *octave harmonic* (twice the fundamental

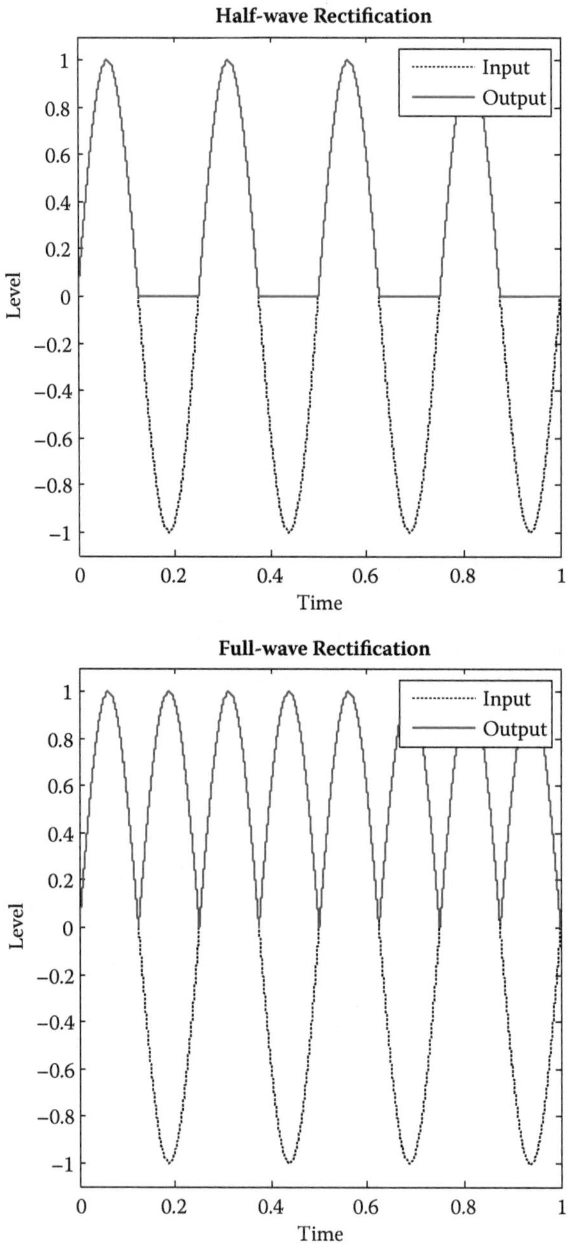

FIGURE 7.4
Half-wave and full-wave rectification.

frequency) to the output signal. The reason can be seen in Figure 7.4. In the full-wave rectifier, the period of the waveform is half the original input since the negative half-waves have been inverted. The half-wave rectifier is mathematically equivalent to the average of the input and its full-wave rectified version:

$$f_{half}(x) = \left(x + f_{full}(x)\right)/2 \tag{7.7}$$

For this reason, the half-wave rectifier contains both the original fundamental frequency and its octave harmonic.

Harmonic Distortion

The operation of a distortion effect is best understood as applying a nonlinear function to the input signal in the time domain. However, its characteristic sound comes from the artifacts the nonlinear function creates in the frequency domain. Linear effects have the property that while they may change the relative magnitudes and phases of frequency components in a signal, they cannot create new frequency components that did not exist in the original signal. By contrast, the nonlinear functions used in distortion effects produce new frequency components in the output according to two processes: *harmonic distortion* and *intermodulation distortion*.

Consider applying a distortion effect to a sine wave input with frequency f and sample rate f_s: $x[n] = \sin(2\pi f/f_s)$. A sine wave contains a single-frequency component at f (Figure 7.5, top). The output of the effect may have a different magnitude and phase at f, but it may also contain energy at every multiple of f: $2f$, $3f$, $4f$, etc. (Figure 7.5, bottom). These frequencies, which were not present in the input, are known as the harmonics of the fundamental frequency f, and the process that creates them is known as harmonic distortion. Every nonlinear function will introduce some amount of harmonic distortion. As a rough guideline, the more nonlinear the function, the greater the relative amplitude of the harmonics. Where multiple input frequencies are present, as in most real-world instrument signals, harmonics of each input frequency will appear in the output. In general, the magnitude of each harmonic decreases toward zero as frequency increases, but there is no frequency above which the magnitude of every harmonic is exactly zero. In other words, harmonic distortion will create *infinitely many* harmonic frequencies of the original input. This result can create problems with *aliasing* in digital implementations of distortion effects.

Detailed nonlinear analysis on the origins of harmonic distortion and its relation to specific characteristic curves is beyond the scope of this text, but in general, the more nonlinear the characteristic curve, the greater the magnitude of the harmonic distortion products that are introduced (Figure 7.6,

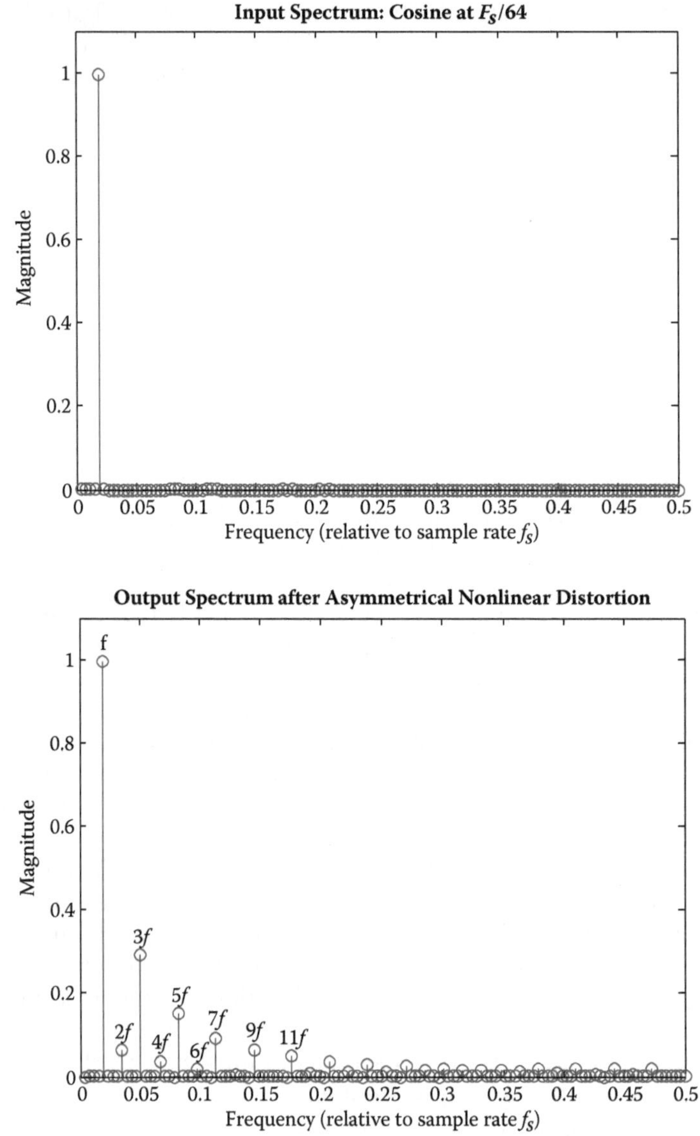

FIGURE 7.5
The spectrum of a single sine wave before (top) and after (bottom) asymmetric distortion has been applied.

top). Hard clipping also produces a different pattern of distortion products from soft clipping (Figure 7.6, bottom).

Another important relationship should be highlighted: *odd symmetrical* distortion functions produce only *odd* harmonics, and *even symmetrical* distortion functions produce only *even* harmonics, where *asymmetrical* functions

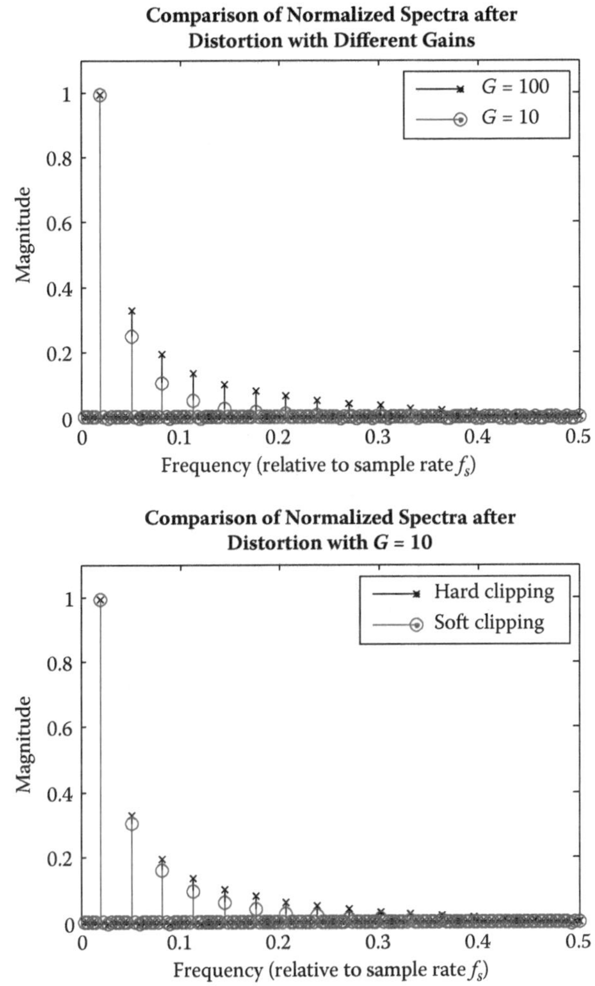

FIGURE 7.6
The output spectrum after distortion has been applied for sinusoidal input, comparing two values of distortion level for soft clipping (top) and comparing soft and hard clipping (bottom).

can produce both *even* and *odd* harmonics. Odd functions are those that obey the relationship $f(-x) = -f(x)$, known as *odd symmetry* in mathematical terminology. Similarly, even functions obey the relationship $f(-x) = f(x)$. For example, Equations (7.3) and (7.6) are both symmetrical by this definition. For a fundamental frequency f, the odd harmonics are the odd multiples of f: $3f$, $5f$, $7f$, etc. Similarly, the even harmonics are the even multiples of f: $2f$, $4f$, $6f$, etc. The octave harmonic created by rectification is an even harmonic: $2f$. Musicians often prefer the combination of both even and odd harmonics, and consequently asymmetrical functions are often preferred to symmetrical ones.

To see why an odd symmetrical function produces only odd harmonics, consider a sine wave input signal, $x(t) = \sin(\omega t)$. Recall that distortion effects are time invariant. So shifting the input signal by half a period (180°) is the same thing as inverting it, $x(t + \pi/\omega) = \sin(\omega t + \pi) = -\sin(\omega t) = -x(t)$.

As a consequence, for an odd function, adding the distorted outputs of the shifted and nonshifted sine waves will produce complete cancellation:

$$f\left(x(t+\pi/\omega)\right)+f\left(x(t)\right)=f\left(-x(t)\right)+f\left(x(t)\right)=-f\left(x(t)\right)+f\left(x(t)\right)=0 \quad (7.8)$$

We have said that the output of the nonlinear function contains infinitely many harmonically related sinusoids, so we can write it generically as

$$f\left(x(t)\right)=\sum_{k=0}^{\infty} a_k \sin\left(k\omega t+\phi_k\right) \quad (7.9)$$

where a_k are the magnitudes of each harmonic component and ϕ_k are the phases. Shifting the input by π/ω will shift the phase of every odd component ($k = 1, 3, 5, \ldots$) by π while leaving the even components ($k = 0, 2, 4, 6, \ldots$) unaltered:

$$\begin{aligned} f\left(x(t+\pi/\omega)\right) &= \sum_{k=0}^{\infty} a_k \sin\left(k\omega t+k\pi+\phi_k\right) \\ &= \sum_{k=0}^{\infty} a_k (-1)^k \sin\left(k\omega t+\phi_k\right) \end{aligned} \quad (7.10)$$

When the shifted and unshifted outputs, Equations (7.9) and (7.10), are added together, only the even harmonics remain in the expression,

$$f\left(x(t)\right)+f\left(x(t+\pi/\omega)\right)=\sum_{k=0}^{\infty} 2a_{2k} \sin\left(2k\omega t+\phi_{2k}\right) \quad (7.11)$$

However, Equation (7.8) showed that, for an odd function, adding these two outputs together cancels to 0, which means that the even harmonics must be equal to 0. Therefore, an odd symmetrical function can produce only odd harmonics of the original input frequency. A similar argument can be used to show that even symmetrical functions produce only even harmonics. Creating both even and odd harmonics requires that the positive and negative half-waves be treated asymmetrically.

Intermodulation Distortion

Harmonic distortion is a desirable property of overdrive, distortion, and fuzz effects. Another result, *intermodulation distortion*, is also a direct consequence of any nonlinear transfer function, but this result is generally undesirable in musical situations. Suppose the input signal contains two frequency components at f_1 and f_2:

$$x(t) = \sin(2\pi f_1 t) + \sin(2\pi f_2 t) \tag{7.12}$$

A general analysis of all nonlinear functions is beyond the scope of this text, but to see the mechanism behind intermodulation distortion, consider the simple nonlinear function $f(x) = x^2$:

$$f(x(t)) = \sin^2(2\pi f_1 t) + 2\sin(2\pi f_1 t)\sin(2\pi f_2 t) + \sin^2(2\pi f_2 t) \tag{7.13}$$

By trigonometric identity, the square terms produce an octave-doubling effect (twice the frequency):

$$\sin^2(2\pi f t) = \left[1 - \cos(2\pi(2f)t)\right]/2 \tag{7.14}$$

This property offers another way to understand the operation of the full-wave rectifier, which produces a similar (though not identical) output. However, it is the term in the middle, the product of two sines at different frequencies, that is responsible for the intermodulation distortion. Also by trigonometric identity:

$$\sin(2\pi f_1 t)\sin(2\pi f_2 t) = \left[\cos(2\pi(f_1 - f_2)t) - \cos(2\pi(f_1 + f_2)t)\right]/2 \tag{7.15}$$

The output will therefore contain *sum and difference frequencies* between the two frequency components at the input. Unless f_1 and f_2 are multiples of one another, these sum and difference frequencies will not be *harmonically related* to either one (that is, not a multiple of either f_1 or f_2). This in turn means that these new frequencies will sound discordant and often unpleasant. This intermodulation process happens with *every* pair of frequencies in the input signal, so the more complex the input, the greater the number and spread of intermodulation products. An example of intermodulation distortion is shown in Figure 7.7.

Sum and difference frequencies are also found in the *ring modulator* (Chapter 5), with similarly nonharmonic results. But in that case the frequency products are sums and differences with the *carrier* frequency and not between the frequencies of the input signal itself. Furthermore, in ring

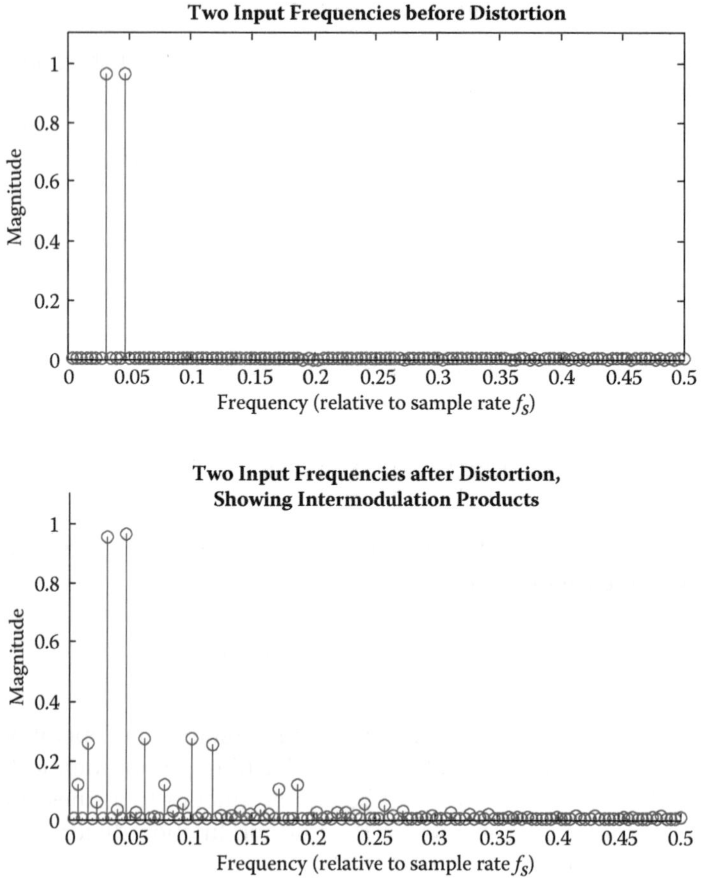

FIGURE 7.7
The spectrum of two sinusoids before (top) and after (bottom) distortion has been applied.

modulation, the original frequency is not present, while in intermodulation distortion it is still the most prominent.

Highly nonlinear characteristic curves such as those found in fuzz effects will have a higher amplitude of intermodulation products, just as they produce higher amplitudes of harmonic distortion. This is the reason single notes and "power chords" (combinations of octaves and perfect fifths) often work best with fuzz boxes: these inputs typically contain only harmonically related frequencies so all the intermodulation products remain harmonic. Unfortunately, we cannot choose only harmonic distortion products without intermodulation; the right type of distortion effect must be chosen for each musical application, which balances these two qualities.

Analog Emulation

Many guitarists hold the vacuum tube to be the ideal device for constructing amplifiers and distortion effects. Its soft, asymmetrical clipping creates sounds that have defined generations of blues, jazz, and rock musicians. Unfortunately, tube amplifiers are expensive, heavy, and noisy and require replacement parts every few years. Digital emulation of vacuum tube circuits has thus become an active and profitable area of development, and these emulation techniques can extend to other analog circuits as well, including diode- and transistor-based distortion effects.

Accurate emulation of even the simplest analog distortion effects rapidly becomes mathematically complex on account of the nonlinearity of each circuit element and the way the elements affect one another. Consider the *diode clipper* circuit in Figure 7.8. Each diode turns on when the voltage between its anode and cathode exceeds a fixed threshold voltage V_d. Once the diode turns on, it begins to conduct current and prevents the output voltage from rising much farther. Placing the diodes back-to-back in opposite directions therefore clips the output to approximately the range $[-V_d, V_d]$. However, real-world diodes do not exhibit perfectly sudden turn-on behavior, so there will be some degree of rounding of the waveform peaks before hard clipping sets in.

As this chapter has shown, hard and soft clipping can be easily simulated with *characteristic curves*, but there is a subtle aspect of this circuit that is not simulated. The characteristic curves implement a memoryless nonlinear system whose output depends only on the current input sample. While the diodes in Figure 7.8 by themselves might reasonably approximate a memoryless system, the capacitor C_1 and resistor R_1 behave quite differently. Specifically, these two components together form a low-pass filter with cutoff frequency $f_L = 1/(2\pi R_1 C_1) = 8$ kHz for the values given. But as the diodes turn on, they act for small signals like resistors whose resistance changes with the overall signal level [46]. As the diodes approach a completely on state, their resistance moves toward 0 and the cutoff frequency of the filter rises accordingly. Since this process depends on the signal level, the cutoff frequency of the filter will change dramatically over the course of a single waveform

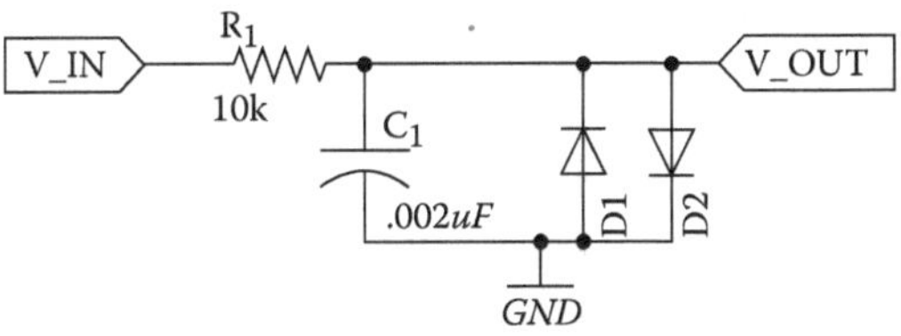

FIGURE 7.8
A diode clipper circuit.

period. But since the filter is not a memoryless system, it cannot be accounted for in the characteristic curve.

The mathematical techniques to solve this problem are beyond the scope of the book. Most of them involve iterative approximation methods. *Wave digital filters* [47] are one popular technique for handling interconnected analog circuit elements. Interested readers are referred to [48–50].

Implementation

Basic Implementation

In their basic form, overdrive, distortion, and fuzz are among the simplest effects to implement. Since the nonlinear characteristic curve is a memoryless effect (at least in the simpler cases), these effects can be calculated on a sample-by-sample basis by applying the nonlinear function to each input sample.

Aliasing and Oversampling

We have seen that the nonlinear functions used in overdrive, distortion, and fuzz create an infinite number of harmonics, frequency components that are integer multiples of an original frequency in the input signal. In the analog domain, this is not a problem: eventually, the frequency limits of the electronic devices or filters deliberately added to the effect attenuate the higher-frequency components to a level at which they are not heard. Even when they do appear in the output sound, the highest harmonics will not be perceived if they are above the range of human hearing.

In the digital domain, the unbounded series of harmonics creates a problem with aliasing. Harmonics that are above the *Nyquist frequency* will be aliased, appearing in the output as lower-frequency components (Figure 7.9a). The aliased components are no longer harmonically related to the original sound, nor can they be filtered out once they appear. Unless aliasing is avoided, the quality of digital distortion effects will suffer compared to their analog counterparts.

The best way to reduce aliasing in a distortion effect is to employ *oversampling*. Prior to applying the nonlinear function, the input signal is *upsampled* to several times the original sampling frequency. Oversampling by a factor of N can be accomplished by inserting $N - 1$ zeros between each input sample. This signal is then filtered to remove frequencies above the original Nyquist frequency (Figure 7.9b and c).

Once the signal has been upsampled, the nonlinear characteristic curve can be applied. This will still generate an infinite series of harmonic products, but

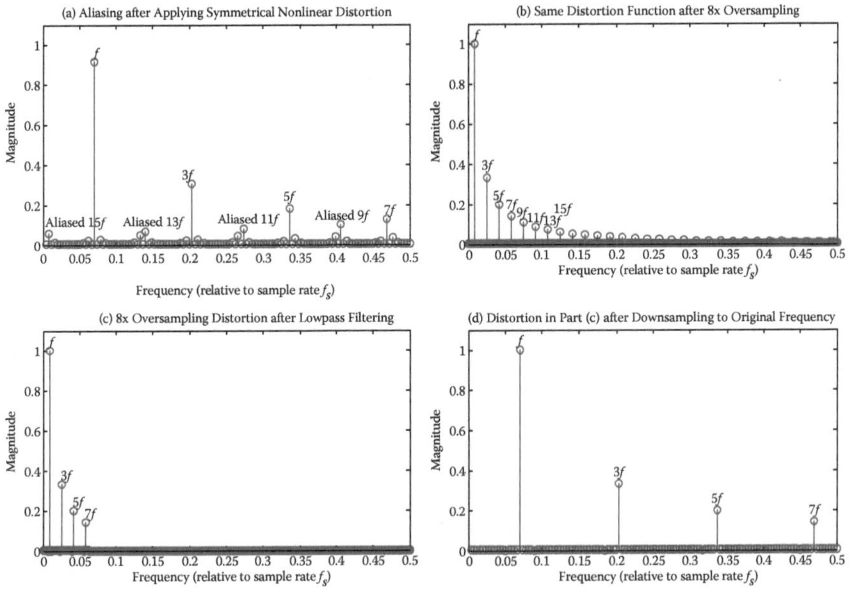

FIGURE 7.9
Output spectrum with aliasing due to distortion (a), and the output spectrum after oversampling (b), low-pass filtering (c), and downsampling (d).

now considerably more of them will fit within the new, higher Nyquist frequency. Furthermore, even though aliasing still occurs, the first aliased components are still in the higher-frequency regions above the original Nyquist frequency. Since the harmonic distortion components decrease in amplitude with increasing frequency, those components that are aliased back into the audible range will be greatly reduced in amplitude (Figure 7.9d).

After the nonlinear curve is applied, the signal is again filtered to remove frequencies above the original Nyquist frequency. The signal is then *downsampled* back to the original rate. Downsampling by a factor of N can be accomplished by choosing every Nth sample and discarding the rest.

Filtering

Even when aliasing is minimized, distortion effects can produce a large number of new frequency components extending all the way to the top of the human hearing range. In some cases, these high-frequency components create an undesirable harshness in the output. For this reason, some distortion effects incorporate a *low-pass filter* or *shelving filter* after the nonlinear function to reduce the magnitude of the high-frequency components. First-order filters are often used to create a gentle roll-off in the upper frequencies. The corner frequency of this filter or, in the case of the shelving filter, the gain may be a user-adjustable control.

Other distortion effects incorporate a low-pass filter *before* the nonlinear function. The purpose of this arrangement is to reduce the magnitude of high-frequency components in the input signal, which reduces their contribution to intermodulation distortion.

Common Parameters

The *characteristic curve* of a distortion effect is typically fixed by design. Most analog distortion effects have a particular circuit containing diodes, transistors, or tubes that determines the characteristic curve. Simple digital distortion effects generally follow analog effects in having a single curve; however, sophisticated multieffect units may let the user choose from a range of options to simulate different classic analog sounds.

The *input gain* (or just *gain*) is a user-adjustable parameter on most effects. This control changes the gain of the input signal before it passes through the nonlinear transfer function. Implementation is simply a matter of multiplying the input sample by a constant before putting it into the nonlinear function. A higher gain produces a more distorted sound.

Since a large input gain is usually required to produce a heavily distorted sound, the output of the nonlinear function might be much higher in level than the input. Thus, most distortion effects produce an output that is consistently near the *clipping level*. Therefore, it can be useful to incorporate a posteffect *volume* (or *output gain*) control that scales the level of the output to more closely match the input. This is accomplished by multiplying the output of the nonlinear function by a constant, which typically ranges from 0 (muted) to 1 (full volume). In a purely linear effect such as a filter or delay, the gain and volume controls would produce the same result, since it does not matter whether a scaling operation takes place before or after a linear effect. In the distortion effects, the two controls have different results, so it is useful to include them both in a practical effect.

Some effects also feature a *tone* control that affects the timbre or brightness of the output. This control can be implemented in several ways, but it typically involves a low-pass filter placed before or after the nonlinear transfer function. The control can affect the *cutoff frequency* of the filter or, if a low shelving filter is used, the *shelf gain*. Placing a low-pass filter before the nonlinear function can help reduce intermodulation distortion by eliminating high-frequency components from the input signal. Placing a low-pass filter after the nonlinear function will attenuate the resulting high-frequency distortion products.

Tube Sound Distortion

As discussed in earlier sections, guitarists often seek digital alternatives that recreate the sound of classic vacuum tube amplifiers. More accurate emulation of every component of a tube amplifier, including not just tubes but also transformers and speakers, is an active area of academic and industrial research [50, 51]. Emulation techniques are often mathematically complex, but the following choices in a basic distortion effect will help approach a tube-like sound:

1. Use a soft clipping characteristic curve that rounds the corners of the waveform as it approaches the clipping level.
2. Choose the curve to be at least mildly asymmetrical, which will produce even and odd harmonics. For example, the top and bottom half-waves in Equation (7.4) could use a different input gain.
3. Use oversampling to control nonharmonic products from aliasing. If the sound is still too harsh, consider adding a gentle low-pass filter before or after the nonlinear function.

Code Example

The following C++ code fragment implements several types of basic distortion effect.

```
int numSamples;          // How many audio samples to process
float *channelData;      // Array of samples, length numSamples
float inputGain;         // Input gain (linear), pre-distortion

float inputGainDecibels_; // Gain in dB, set by user
int distortionType_;      // Index of the type of distortion

// Calculate input gain once to save calculations
inputGain = powf(10.0f, inputGainDecibels_ / 20.0f);

for (int i = 0; i < numSamples; ++i) {
    const float in = channelData[i] * inputGain;
    float out;

    // Apply distortion based on type
    if(distortionType_ == kTypeHardClipping) {
        // Simple hard clipping
        float threshold = 1.0f;
        if(in > threshold)
            out = threshold;
        else if(in < -threshold)
            out = -threshold;
        else
            out = in;
    }
    else if(distortionType_ == kTypeSoftClipping) {
```

```
        // Soft clipping based on quadratic function
        float threshold1 = 1.0f/3.0f;
        float threshold2 = 2.0f/3.0f;
        if(in > threshold2)
            out = 1.0f;
        else if(in > threshold1)
            out = (3.0f - (2.0f - 3.0f*in) *
                          (2.0f - 3.0f*in))/3.0f;
        else if(in < -threshold2)
            out = -1.0f;
        else if(in < -threshold1)
            out = -(3.0f - (2.0f + 3.0f*in) *
                           (2.0f + 3.0f*in))/3.0f;
        else
            out = 2.0f* in;
    }
    else if(distortionType_ == kTypeSoftClippingExponential)
    {
        // Soft clipping based on exponential function
        if(in > 0)
            out = 1.0f - expf(-in);
        else
            out = -1.0f + expf(in);
    }
    else if(distortionType_ == kTypeFullWaveRectifier) {
        // Full-wave rectifier (absolute value)
        out = fabsf(in);
    }
    else if(distortionType_ == kTypeHalfWaveRectifier) {
        // Half-wave rectifier
        if(in > 0)
            out = in;
        else
            out = 0;
    }

    // Put output back in buffer
    channelData[i] = out;
}
```

The code first applies an input gain to the samples in the buffer. It then applies one of several characteristic curves based on the value of `distortionType_`. The curves follow the formulas given earlier in the chapter.

Applications

Expressivity and Spectral Content

Distortion is most commonly used with the electric guitar, though it is sometimes applied to other instruments, including the bass and even the voice. For some guitarists, the particular choice of distortion effect is as much a matter of personal identity as the choice of guitar. On the flip side, the designer seeking to recreate a particular player's distortion sound should remember that the tone ultimately depends not only on the distortion effect, but also on the amp, the guitar, and the manner of playing.

By adding harmonic distortion to the signal, the distortion effect creates a spectrally richer, "fatter" sound that can help an instrument achieve prominence in a mix. For example, a plucked guitar string may contain energy primarily in the bass or midrange frequencies, but adding distortion will create harmonics stretching all the way up the audio spectrum. Because of this extra spectral energy, distortion can be usefully paired with filter effects such as *wah-wah* and *equalization*, which boost some frequencies while attenuating others. For example, if a wah-wah pedal is placed after a distortion effect, the wah-wah effect can be much more pronounced than if using it on a clean guitar signal. Jimi Hendrix is said to have used the reverse arrangement, placing a Fuzz Face distortion pedal after his wah-wah pedal [52], such that the frequencies boosted by the wah-wah effect were particularly distorted.

Sustain

As with the compressor (Chapter 6), distortion effects can increase an instrument's apparent sustain. When a guitar string is plucked, the signal begins strongly but rapidly decays. However, when heavy distortion is used, the signal will be amplified to the point where clipping occurs (either hard or soft, depending on the type of distortion effect). Since the clipping point does not change over time, the output level will remain at or near this point until the original signal has decayed so much that, even with input gain applied, the amplified signal no longer reaches the clipping point. Figure 7.10 shows this process for a soft clipping distortion effect. Figure 7.10a shows the input, a gradually decaying tone. The output in Figure 7.10b stays near the clipping point and decays much more slowly, which creates the perception of longer sustain.

Comparison with Compression

Distortion and dynamic range compression both have the effect of attenuating or limiting the loudest signals. In fact, the nonlinear function in a

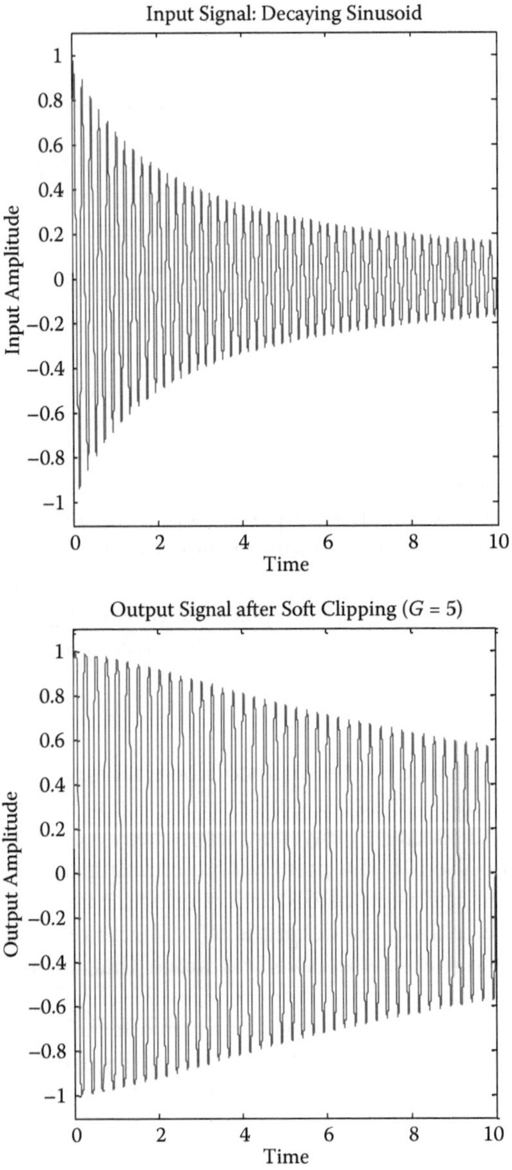

FIGURE 7.10
The effect of soft clipping on a decaying sinusoid.

distortion effect can be considered a nonlinear gain control where the gain depends on the level of the input signal. For example, we can calculate the gain for the hard clipping function in Equation (7.3):

$$gain(x) = f(x)/x = \begin{cases} -1/x & Gx \leq -1 \\ G & -1 < Gx < 1 \\ 1/x & Gx \geq 1 \end{cases} \tag{7.16}$$

We can see that the hard clipping function is linear with gain G when the level of the scaled input signal is less than 1, and that the gain progressively decreases as the input level increases. This is identical to the behavior of the *limiter* (compressor with a very high or infinite ratio). Why then do distortion effects produce audible harmonic distortion when compressors and limiters generally do not?

The difference between distortion, compression, and limiting has to do with the design of the *level detector.* In the compressor and limiter, the gain is smoothed, and for root mean square (RMS) level detectors, the signal level is determined by the local average level of the input signal and not by the instantaneous sample value. If the *attack time* and *decay time* parameters in a limiter were both set to 0 (instantaneous response) and a peak detector was used, the result would be similar to the distortion effect.

Problems

1. Define the terms *overdrive, distortion,* and *fuzz* (in the context of audio effects). How are they similar, and how are they different?
2. a. Using equations, demonstrate the concept of intermodulation distortion for modulation with two sine waves. What are the sidebands that result? Hint: You may use the following formula, cos(A + B) = cos(A)cos(B) – sin(A)sin(B).

   b. Why is intermodulation distortion unpleasing to hear, and why is it particularly problematic for distortion, overdrive, and fuzz (compared to other audio effects)?
3. Signal-to-noise ratio (SNR) can be defined as 10 $\log_{10}(P_I/P_N)$, where P_I is the input signal power and P_N is the noise (difference between input and output) power. Calculate the SNR of hard clipping for a square wave input. You can assume that the square wave has some amplitude A, and the signal is clipped at some threshold T.
4. Draw plots of hard clipping and soft clipping of a sine wave input. Which kind of clipping do vacuum tubes generally produce? Which kind do digital systems (by default) produce? Why?

5. Draw and explain the difference between half-wave rectification and full-wave rectification. Explain the musical use of rectification (either version) and what it does to the sound.
6. Which of the following distortion functions have even symmetry, $f(-x) = f(x)$, which have odd symmetry, $f(-x) = -f(x)$, and which are asymmetric?

$$f(x) = \begin{cases} -1 & Gx \le -1 \\ Gx & -1 < Gx < 1 \\ 1 & Gx \ge 1 \end{cases}$$

$$f(x) = \text{sgn}(x)\left(1 - e^{-|Gx|}\right)$$

$$f(x) = \max(x, 0)$$

$$f(x) = |x|$$

7. Show that even functions will produce only even harmonics. A similar approach can be taken to the one used in Equations (7.8) to (7.11) to show that odd functions produce only odd harmonics.
8. Explain why aliasing can be a problem in digital distortion implementations, and what can be done to minimize its effects.
9. A distortion effect produces odd harmonics of a 2 kHz input. Assuming a sampling frequency $f_s = 44.1$ kHz, what is the first harmonic to alias back to below $f_s/2$, and at what frequency? You may wish to refer back to the discussion of aliasing in Chapter 1.

8

The Phase Vocoder

The term *phase vocoder* is used to describe a group of sound analysis–synthesis techniques where the processing of the signal is performed in the *frequency domain*. Most audio effects, including delays, filters, compression, and distortion, are implemented directly on the incoming signal in the time domain. By contrast, phase vocoder effects use frequency and phase information calculated from *Fourier transforms* (Chapter 1) to implement a variety of audio effects, including time stretching, pitch shifting, robotization, and whisperization.

The basic phase vocoder operation involves segmenting the incoming signal into discrete blocks, converting each block to the frequency domain, performing amplitude and phase modification of specific frequency components, and finally converting each block back to the time domain to obtain the final output [53, 54]. There is now a widely recognized standard implementation [55, 56], which is well documented, and for which the term *phase vocoder* is most commonly used. The specific effect that is produced depends on the type of processing done on the frequency domain signal.

A detailed introduction to Fourier transform theory can be found in several excellent texts [3, 4], and this chapter cannot substitute for a complete digital signal processing course. Instead, it will provide an overview of how Fourier transforms are used to create the overall phase vocoder structure, with a focus on practical implementation strategies and specific audio effects that make use of the phase vocoder. Further details on phase vocoder effects can be found in [2].

Phase Vocoder Theory

Overview

The phase vocoder is based on the *short-time Fourier transform* (STFT). What sets the STFT apart from other Fourier transform techniques is that it deliberately operates only a small time segment of the input signal, giving a snapshot of the frequency content of the signal at a particular moment in time. By dividing the signal into a series of discrete frames of samples and performing the STFT on each frame, we get a picture of how the frequency content of the signal evolves over time. By modifying the frequency content in each

AUTO-TUNE

From 1976 through 1989, Dr. Andy Hildebrand worked for the oil industry, interpreting seismic data. By sending sound waves into the ground, he could detect the reflections and map potential drill sites. Dr. Hildebrand studied music composition at Rice University and then developed audio processing tools based on his knowledge in seismic data analysis. He was a leading developer of a variety of plug-ins, including MDT (Multiband Dynamics Tool), JVP (Jupiter Voice Processor), and SST (Spectral Shaping Tool). At a dinner party, a guest challenged him to invent a tool that would help her sing in tune. Based on the phase vocoder, Hildebrand's Antares Audio Technologies released Auto-Tune in late 1996.

Auto-Tune was intended to correct or disguise off-key vocals. It moves the pitch of a note to the nearest true semitone (the nearest musical interval in traditional, equal temperament Western tonal music), thus allowing the vocal parts to be tuned. The original Auto-Tune had a speed parameter which could be set between 0 and 400 milliseconds, and determined how quickly the note moved to the target pitch. Engineers soon realized that by setting this "attack time" very short, Auto-Tune could be used as an effect to distort vocals, and make it sound as if the voice leaps from note to note in discrete steps. It gives the voice an artificial, synthesiser like sound that can be appealing or irritating depending on taste. This unusual effect was the trademark sound of Cher's 1998 hit song, "Believe."

As with many audio effects, engineers and performers found a creative use, quite different from the intended use. As Hildebrand said, "I never figured anyone in their right mind would want to do that" [57]. Yet Auto-Tune and competing pitch correction technologies are now widely applied (in amateur and professional recordings, and across many genres) for both intended and unusual, artistic uses.

frame, many new effects are possible that are not easily implemented in the time domain.

Figure 8.1 shows a diagram of the phase vocoder process. The following steps are common to every phase vocoder effect. Each step is discussed in detail in a subsequent section.

1. Given an input signal of arbitrary length, choose a *frame* of N consecutive samples. The value N is known as the *frame size* or *window size.*
2. Multiply the signal by a *window function* of length N. The window function is defined to have a nonzero value for N consecutive samples and a value of zero everywhere else. By multiplying the input

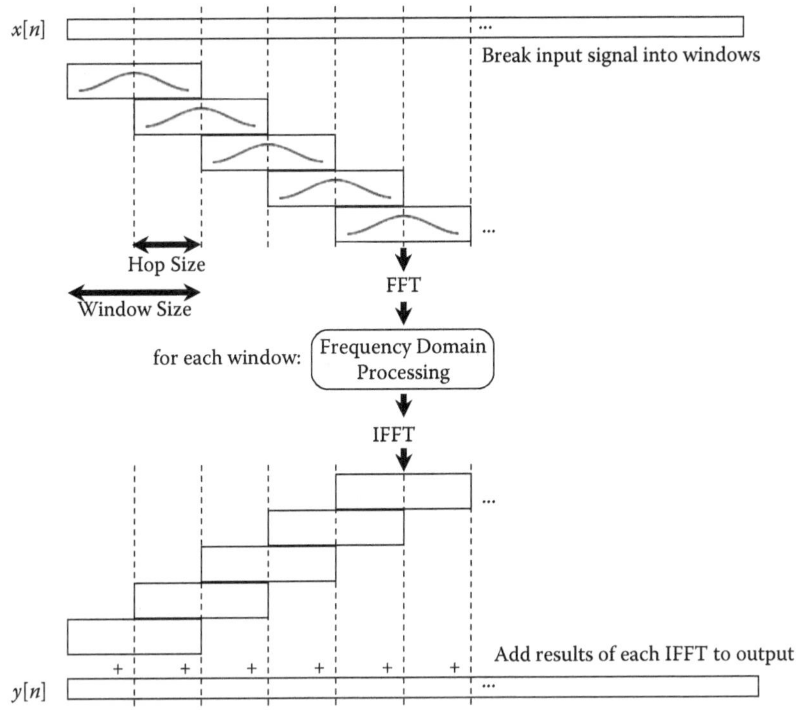

FIGURE 8.1
Overview of the overlap-add process for phase vocoder effects.

signal and the window function, only the N samples in the frame will remain; the rest will be set to zero.

3. After the signal has been *windowed*, apply a *fast Fourier transform* (FFT). Since the windowed signal contains N points, an FFT of size $M \geq N$ must be used. Typically the window size and FFT size are identical; however, in some cases shorter windows can be used with larger FFTs. In practice, the FFT size M is almost always a power of 2 for reasons of computational efficiency. The combination of window function and FFT constitutes the short-time Fourier transform.
4. The output of the FFT will be a collection of M frequency domain *bins* containing *magnitude* and *phase* information for each frequency. Each phase vocoder effect will apply a different type of processing in this step, as discussed below in the "Phase Vocoder Effects" section.
5. Apply the *inverse fast Fourier transform* (IFFT) to the output of step 4. This will once again produce M samples in the time domain.
6. Add the M samples from step 5 to the *output buffer*, which holds the output signal from the effect.

7. Move on to the next frame: move forward H samples in the input signal and return to step 1. The output in step 6 will also move forward H samples. The value H is called the *hop size*. The hop size is sometimes equal to the window size but is frequently a fraction of it (e.g., $H = N/2$ or $H = N/4$).

This process is known as *overlap-add*; it works by analyzing a set of overlapping frames within the input signal, and the output of each frame after processing, properly aligned in time, is added to form the output signal. The following sections discuss each aspect of the overlap-add process.

Windowing

It is important to note that the phase vocoder does not analyze the frequency content of the entire signal at once. Instead, the STFT analyzes only the frequency content present in a particular frame located at a specific time within the signal. A window function of length N will contain N nonzero samples starting from $n = 0$, with a value of 0 at all other samples. The simplest type is the *rectangular* window:

$$w_{rect}[n] = \begin{cases} 1 & 0 \le n < N \\ 0 & |n| \ge N \end{cases} \tag{8.1}$$

Many types of windows are possible. Other common variants are the *Bartlett* (triangular) window, the *Hann* window, and the *Hamming* window (Figure 8.2):

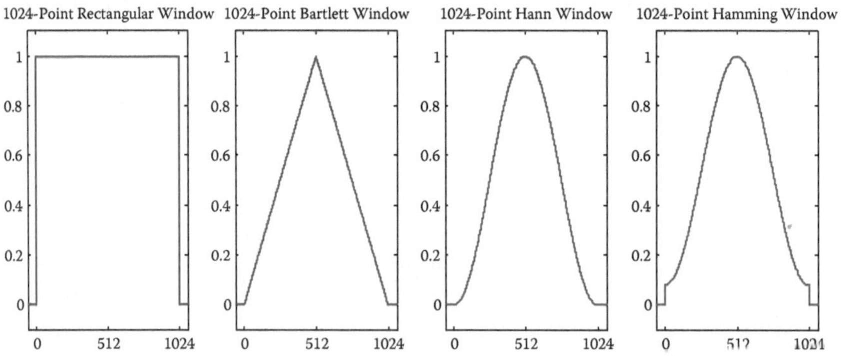

FIGURE 8.2
Four popular window functions.

$$w_{bart}[n] = \begin{cases} 1 - \left| \dfrac{2n}{N-1} - 1 \right| & 0 \le n < N \\ 0 & |n| \ge N \end{cases}$$

$$w_{hann}[n] = \begin{cases} \left[1 - \cos\left(\dfrac{2\pi n}{N-1} \right) \right] \Big/ 2 & 0 \le n < N \\ 0 & |n| \ge N \end{cases} \tag{8.2}$$

$$w_{hamm}[n] = \begin{cases} 0.54 - 0.46\cos\left(\dfrac{2\pi n}{N-1} \right) & 0 \le n < N \\ 0 & |n| \ge N \end{cases}$$

Intuitively, the motivation for choosing different types of windows relates to smoothing the edges of the windowed signal. As Figure 8.3 shows, the rectangular window cuts off abruptly at the start and end, and these discontinuities will create undesirable effects known as *sidelobes* in the frequency domain, where energy at one frequency will bleed into other frequency bins. The triangular, Hann, and Hamming windows produce more gradual transitions at the edges, which reduce the sidelobe amplitude. However, they do so at the cost of reducing the precision with which any given frequency component can be identified. In signal processing, the trade-off is described as *main lobe width* versus *sidelobe height*; a more complete discussion can be

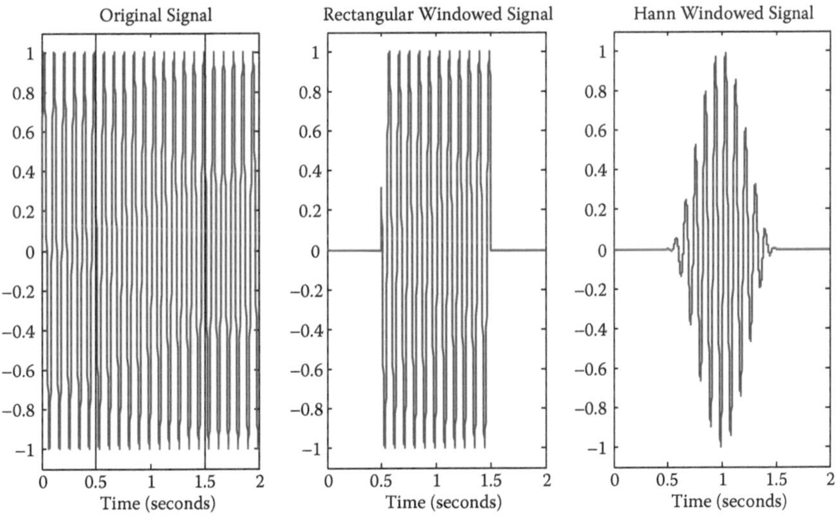

FIGURE 8.3
The effect of a rectangular window and a Hann window applied to a signal.

found in [2]. Though there is no single best solution for all cases; in phase vocoder audio effects Hann and Hamming windows are frequently used.

To apply a window function, the input signal is multiplied by the window. The window function can be offset in time to isolate different regions of the input signal:

$$x_{window}[m,n] = x[n]w[n-m] \tag{8.3}$$

where m is the offset of the window. The samples from m to $m + N - 1$ will be isolated by the window function, with all other samples set to zero.

Analysis: Fast Fourier Transform

The FFT is an algorithm for calculating the *discrete Fourier transform* (DFT) of a signal. In turn, the DFT takes M time domain points as input and produces M regularly spaced frequency domain bins as output. Converting from the time domain to the frequency domain in this way is known as the *analysis* step of the phase vocoder (in contrast to the *synthesis* step going from frequency to time domain). It is important that the size M of the FFT be at least as large as the length of the input signal. Since real-world audio signals can be of arbitrary length, this illustrates the importance of the window function in isolating only a small number of points for the FFT.

We can represent the combination of window and FFT (together, the STFT) as follows:

$$X[m,k] = \sum_{n=-\infty}^{\infty} x[n]h[m-n]e^{-j2\pi nk/M} \tag{8.4}$$

where n and k represent the short-time frame start and frequency bins, respectively. Here k ranges from 0 to $M - 1$, representing evenly spaced frequency bins between 0 and 2π.

Interpreting Frequency Domain Data

Audio signals are always real numbers, but the values of the frequency bins are complex, containing a real and an imaginary component, $x + jy$. Both components are crucial to making sense of the frequency data, but their meaning is easier to understand in *polar* (or *magnitude phase*) representation, $Ae^{j\phi}$. We can convert the polar representation and the *Cartesian* real-imaginary form,

$$\begin{aligned} &x + jy = Ae^{j\varphi} \rightarrow \\ &\quad A = |x + jy| = \sqrt{x^2 + y^2}\,; \phi = \arg(x + jy) = \operatorname{atan2}(y, x) \end{aligned} \tag{8.5}$$

where atan2 is a version of the arctangent function, available in most programming languages, which produces values in the range (–π, π] depending on the quadrant of x and y (see Chapter 1). So, the time frequency bins in Equation (8.4) can be written as

$$X[m,k] = |X[m,k]|e^{j\phi[m,k]} \tag{8.6}$$

One important use of phase information is to improve the resolution of frequency detection. Recall that the FFT produces only a fixed number of frequency bins, but signals may contain frequencies that fall between the bin frequencies. The following section shows how comparing phase from two consecutive frames can be used to recover exact frequencies between the bins.

Target Phase, Phase Deviation, and Instantaneous Frequency

For frequency bin k, a target phase, ϕ_t, can be calculated using the bin frequency and the unwrapped bin phase of the previous hop. This target phase is the sum of the previous unwrapped phase and the expected phase increment. The expected increment is the frequency of the sinusoid multiplied by the hop size. So we have

$$\phi_t[n,k] = \phi[n-1,k] + \omega_k h \tag{8.7}$$

where ω_k is the frequency of bin k and h is the hop size. This target phase represents the perfect case of a steady-state sinusoid fitting exactly into a frequency bin, i.e., no spectral leakage. Since this is almost never the case, we have some phase deviation ϕ_d, as shown in Figure 8.4 and given by

$$\phi_d[n,k] = \phi[n,k] - \phi_t[n,k] \tag{8.8}$$

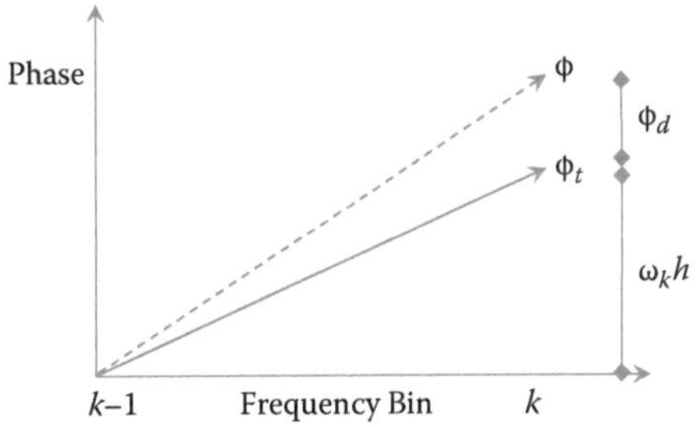

FIGURE 8.4
Relationship between actual phase and target phase. The instantaneous frequency is represented by the gradient of the dashed line, and the bin frequency is the gradient of the solid line.

The corresponding value in the range $(-\pi{:}\pi]$, known as the principal argument, of this deviation phase is then used to calculate the unwrapped phase increment per hop, $\Delta\phi_h$:

$$\Delta\phi_h[n,k] = \omega_k h + \arg\phi_d[n,k] \tag{8.9}$$

The instantaneous frequency, f_i, can then be calculated:

$$f_i[n,k] = \frac{\Delta\phi_h[n,k]}{2\pi h}\cdot f_s \tag{8.10}$$

where f_s is the sample frequency. This instantaneous frequency can then be viewed as a more accurate frequency measurement than the frequency resolution offered by the filterbank or STFT.

Synthesis: Inverse Fast Fourier Transform

The specific processing done in the frequency domain depends on the particular phase vocoder effect. Once this processing is complete, however, all phase vocoder effects will convert the signal back to the time domain using the inverse fast Fourier transform (IFFT):

$$x[m] = \frac{1}{M}\sum_{k=0}^{M-1}\left|X[m,k]\right|e^{j(2\pi km/M+\phi[m,k])} \tag{8.11}$$

This process is known as *synthesis* or *reconstruction*. It produces M points in the time domain, which can be added to the output buffer. Depending on the type of frequency domain processing performed, it is possible that the output frame may not have smooth edges even if a Hamming window (or similar) was used for analysis. Occasionally then, applying a second window before adding the result to the output buffer will help reduce audible artifacts.

Overlap-Add

The purpose of the phase vocoder process is to analyze the frequency content of each short frame, modify it, and reconstruct it in the time domain. The manner in which the frames advance from one to the next is important to the proper operation of the phase vocoder. Once a frame has been analyzed, processed, and synthesized, the effect should advance by the *hop size*. Suppose the hop size is given by H. Then if the window in frame i previously began at sample m, the window in frame $i + 1$ will begin at sample $m + H$. The hop size is always less than or equal to the window size; if it were greater than the window size, there would be a gap between successive windows. Smaller hop sizes (more overlap) will often produce better-quality output in many phase vocoder effects; however, they require more computation.

Hop sizes of one-half, one-fourth, or one-eighth the window size are common. A useful guideline for choosing hop size is the *constant overlap-add* (COLA) *criterion* [2]. Suppose that in the steps listed above for the phase vocoder theory overview, no processing at all is done in the frequency domain (step 4), and instead, the FFT is immediately followed by the inverse FFT. For windows and hop sizes meeting the COLA criterion, the output signal at the end of the overlap-add process would be identical to the input signal, with no distortion or modulation introduced by the windowing process. Essentially, this requires that the window functions, when overlapped, add to a constant value, as depicted in Figure 8.5. Rectangular windows meet the COLA criterion for a hop size equal to the window size; Bartlett, Hann, and Hamming windows require a hop size of at most half the window size. Integer divisions of this maximum hop size are also possible: for example, a hop size of one-eight the window size will meet the COLA criterion for all four windows.

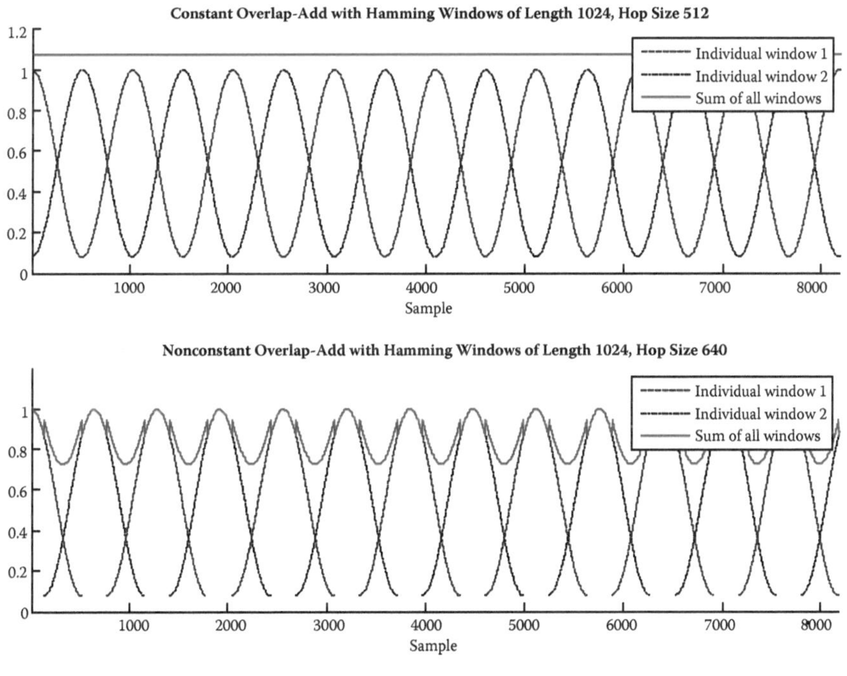

FIGURE 8.5
The constant overlap-add criterion requires that the window functions, when overlapped, add to a constant value. It holds in the top plot, but not the bottom plot.

To summarize, it is important to choose a window and hop size such that the windowing process itself does not introduce unnecessary artifacts into the output. The exact choice of window type, length, and hop size depends in large part on the specific effect, several of which are discussed below.

Filterbank Analysis Variant

Implementation of the phase vocoder is also possible using a filterbank approach. This leads to a computationally more expensive implementation, but it can be shown to be theoretically equivalent, and it is often straightforward to consider the phase vocoder as a filterbank.

Returning to the STFT equation, Equation (8.4), it is clear that

$$X[n,\omega] = h[n] * x[n]e^{-j\omega n} \tag{8.12}$$

where ω is now used to represent $2\pi k/N$.

This can be seen as a demodulation of the signal components at frequency ω down to baseband, followed by a low-pass filtering of the signal using the filter $h[n]$. This is known as the complex baseband filterbank implementation, and is illustrated in Figure 8.6, top.

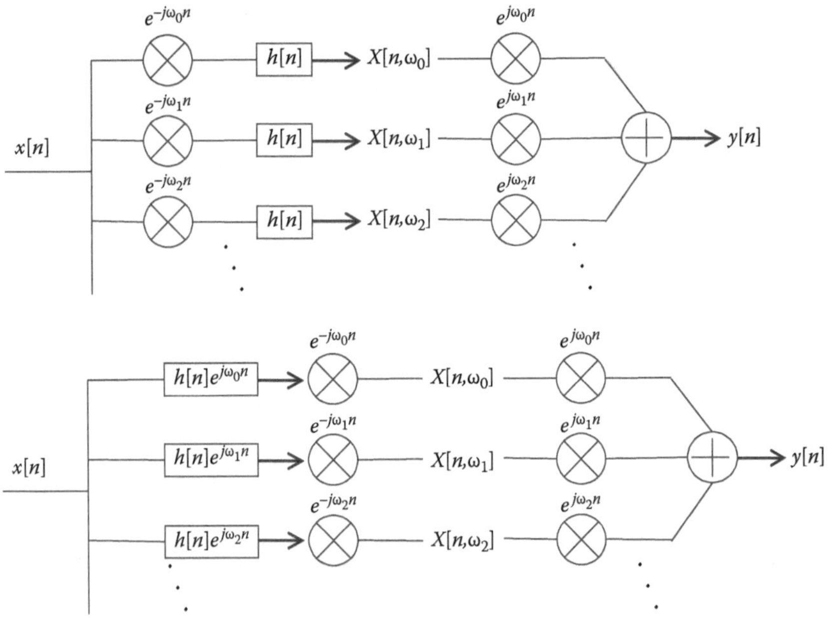

FIGURE 8.6
The complex baseband filterbank implementation (top) where $h[n]$ is a low-pass filter, and the complex band-pass implementation (bottom). The filters for the first three bins only are shown.

If the variables are switched in Equation (8.4) such that $m \to n - m$, we obtain

$$X[n,\omega] = e^{-j\omega n}\sum_{m} x[n-m]h[m]e^{j\omega m} = e^{-j\omega n}\left[x[m]*\left(h[n]e^{j\omega m}\right)\right] \qquad (8.13)$$

Now we can view the filter as being band-pass at the frequency ω. After filtering, the result is then demodulated back down to baseband. This implementation is known as the complex band-pass implementation. It is illustrated in Figure 8.6, bottom.

For the signal to be reconstructed from the magnitude and phase values of $X(n, w)$, each baseband signal must be modulated back to the frequency ω.

$$y_k[n] = e^{jw_k n}X(n,w_k) = \left|X(n,w_k)\right|e^{j\left[w_k n + \phi(n,w_k)\right]} \qquad (8.14)$$

The signal $y[n]$ is reconstructed by summing these terms for each frequency bin.

Oscillator Bank Reconstruction Variant

Since we can assume that the time domain signal $x[n]$ is real, frequency bins that are symmetric about the Nyquist frequency will be conjugate pairs.

$$X[n,k] = X^*[n, N-k] \qquad (8.15)$$

These two signals may then be summed to simplify the analysis. This also results in a more meaningful interpretation:

$$\begin{aligned}\hat{y}_k(n) &= \left|X(n,k)\right|\left[e^{j\phi(n,k)} + e^{-j\phi(n,k)}\right]\left[e^{jw_k n} + e^{-jw_k n}\right] \\ &= 2\left|X(n,k)\right|\cos\left(w_k n + \phi_k(n,w_k)\right)\end{aligned} \qquad (8.16)$$

Oscillator bank reconstruction is clearly computationally expensive. Despite this, it is generally a musically intuitive way of viewing the synthesis stage, especially for musicians. Using an IFFT overlap and add approach is much more efficient. The STFT represents a downsampled version of the filterbank outputs. This is possible due to the filtering step band-limiting the channel signals.

Phase Vocoder Effects

The phase vocoder and its underlying theory have a wide range of applications. In the fields of machine listening and music informatics, these include signal content analysis, pitch detection, and steady-state/transient separation. In the domain of audio effects, important applications include *time scaling* and *pitch shifting*. Normally, when an audio file is played at a higher sample rate than it was recorded at, faster playback rate and higher pitch go together. The phase vocoder allows playback speed and pitch to be varied independently of one another. Other common phase vocoder effects include robotization and whisperization voice effects.

Robotization

The *robotization* effect is most commonly used on voice signals. It applies a constant pitch to the signal while preserving the vocal formants that determine vowel and consonant sounds, resulting in a robot-like monotone voice that is nonetheless very intelligible.

Within the context of the overlap-add phase vocoder procedure described in the "Analysis: Fast Fourier Transform" section, the robotization effect itself is very simple. Following the FFT at each frame, the phase of every frequency bin is set to zero, while the magnitude is left unchanged. Setting the phase to zero is equivalent to making each frequency bin a real number (imaginary component set to 0). Suppose the value of frequency bin k is $a_k + jb_k$. Then the output value following robotization will be

$$\sqrt{a_k^2 + b_k^2}\,.$$

This procedure should be repeated identically for each bin of each frame. By preserving the magnitude, the overall shape of the spectrum remains the same, preserving the vocal formants. But by regularizing the phase information, each frequency component will effectively restart from zero phase on each hop rather than connecting smoothly from one hop to the next. This causes a constant audible pitch that depends on the *hop size*. In general, the pitch of the robot voice can be determined by

$$f_{robot} = f_s / H \tag{8.17}$$

where f_s is the sample rate and H is the hop size in samples. The sound of the robotization effect also depends on the *window size*. In general, moderately sized windows (roughly 256 to 1024 samples) produce the most striking effect. Very small windows reduce the clarity of the output, where longer windows attenuate the robot-like quality by passing through more of the signal's original pitch. Intuitively, we can understand this by noting that phase information is used to resolve small frequency differences between bins. If there are a large number of bins, each pitch will be closely determined even without phase information, but if fewer bins are used, then regularizing the phase will better obscure the original frequencies.

Note that for both robotization and whisperization, the *constant overlap-add criterion* for choosing window and hop size is not an important consideration, since both use deliberate artifacts of the phase vocoder analysis and resynthesis process to achieve their signature sounds.

Robotization Code Example

The following C++ code fragment is adapted from the materials that accompany this book. This example implements robotization using the phase vocoder. Details of calculating the FFT and inverse FFT are not included here, as the goal is to show the overall architecture.

```
int inwritepos;          // Write pointer for input buffer
int outwritepos;         // Write pointer for output
                         // (overlap-add) buffer
int outreadpos;          // Read pointer for output buffer
int inputBufferLength;   // Length of input buffer (samples)
int outputBufferLength;  // Length of output buffer (samples)
int sampsincefft;        // Counter of how many samples have
                         // elapsed since last FFT
float *windowBuffer;     // Buffer that holds the
                         // (pre-calculated) window function
int windowBufferLength;  // Length of the window function
float *fftTimeDomain;    // Buffer that holds time-domain
                         // samples for the FFT calculation
float *fftFrequencyDomain; // Buffer that holds frequency-
                           // domain samples from FFT
float fftScaleFactor;    // Scaling factor to normalize
                         // output level; depends on
                         // window/hop sizes

int fftTransformSize_;   // Size of the FFT calculation (in
                         // samples); normally equals
                         // window size but could be longer
int hopSize_;            // Hop size parameter (in samples)

for (int i = 0; i < numSamples; ++i)
{
    const float in = channelData[i];

    // Store the next buffered sample in the output. Do this
    // first before anything changes the output buffer-- we
    // will have at least one FFT size worth of data
    // stored and ready to go. Set the result to 0 when
    // finished in preparation for the next overlap/add.
    channelData[i] = outputBufferData[outreadpos];
    outputBufferData[outreadpos] = 0.0;
    if(++outreadpos >= outputBufferLength)
        outreadpos = 0;
```

```
// Store the current sample in the input buffer,
// incrementing the write pointer. Also increment how
// many samples we've stored since the last transform.
// If it reaches the hop size, perform an FFT and any
// frequency-domain processing.
inputBufferData[inwritepos] = in;
if (++inwritepos >= inputBufferLength)
    inwritepos = 0;
if (++sampsincefft >= hopSize_)
{
    sampsincefft = 0;

    // Find the index of the starting sample in the
    // buffer. When the buffer length is equal to the
    // transform size, this will be the current write
    // position but this code is more general for larger
    // buffers.
    int inputBufferStartPosition = (inwritepos +
              inputBufferLength - fftTransformSize_) %
              inputBufferLength;

    // Window the buffer and copy it into the FFT input
    int inputBufferIndex = inputBufferStartPosition;
    for(int fftBufferIndex = 0;
        fftBufferIndex < fftTransformSize_;
        fftBufferIndex++)
    {
        // Set real part to windowed signal; imaginary
        // part to 0.
        fftTimeDomain[fftBufferIndex][1] = 0.0;

        // Safety check, in case window isn't ready:
        if(fftBufferIndex >= windowBufferLength)
            fftTimeDomain[fftBufferIndex][0] = 0.0;
        else
            fftTimeDomain[fftBufferIndex][0] =
                    windowBuffer[fftBufferIndex]
                    * inputBufferData[inputBufferIndex];
        inputBufferIndex++;
        if(inputBufferIndex >= inputBufferLength)
            inputBufferIndex = 0;
    }

    // Perform the FFT on the windowed data.
    // Result will be in fftFrequencyDomain
    fftw_execute(fftForwardPlan_);

    // *** PHASE VOCODER PROCESSING GOES HERE ***
    // This is the place where frequency-domain
    // calculations are made on the transformed signal.
```

```
// Put the result back into fftFrequencyDomain
// before transforming back.
// ******************************************

for(int bin = 0; bin < fftTransformSize_; bin++)
{
    float amplitude=sqrt(
       (fftFrequencyDomain[bin][0] *
       fftFrequencyDomain[bin][0]) +
       (fftFrequencyDomain[bin][1] *
       fftFrequencyDomain[bin][1]));

    // Set the phase of each bin to 0. phase = 0
    // means the signal is entirely positive-real,
    // but the overall amplitude is the same
    fftFrequencyDomain[bin][0] = amplitude;
    fftFrequencyDomain[bin][1] = 0.0;
}

// Perform the inverse FFT to get back to the time
// domain. Result wll be in fftTimeDomain. If we've
// done it right (kept the frequency domain
// symmetric), the time domain result should be
// real allowing us to ignore the imaginary part.
fftw_execute(fftBackwardPlan_);

// Add the result to the output buffer, starting at
// the current write position (Output buffer will
// have been zeroed after reading the last time
// around). Output needs to be scaled by the
// transform size to get back to original amplitude:
// this is a property of how fftw is implemented.
// Scaling will also need to be adjusted based on
// hop size to get the same output level (smaller
// hop size produces more overlap so higher level)
int outputBufferIndex = outwritepos;
for(int fftBufferIndex = 0;
    fftBufferIndex < fftTransformSize_;
    fftBufferIndex++)
{
    outputBufferData[outputBufferIndex] +=
          fftTimeDomain[fftBufferIndex][0] *
                          ftScaleFactor;
    if(++outputBufferIndex >= outputBufferLength)
        outputBufferIndex = 0;
}

// Advance the write position within the buffer by
// the hop size
```

```
        outwritepos = (outwritepos + hopSize_) %
                      outputBufferLength;
    }
}
```

Most of the code is devoted to the mechanics of the overlap-add phase vocoder process, including accumulating enough samples to fill a window, applying the window function, and transforming it to the frequency domain. The specific robotization code goes through each frequency bin and sets the phase to 0. The remainder of the code performs an inverse FFT and adds the result to the output buffer, with the multiplier `fftScaleFactor` (dependent on the combination of window size and hop size) needed for the input and output levels to match. The function `fftw_execute()` performs the FFT or IFFT using the `fftw` library. Other FFT libraries could be used with minor changes to the code.

This code fragment does not include the initialization, which includes several important steps, such as calculating the window, calculating `fftScaleFactor`, setting initial values for the read and write pointers, and preparing the FFT library.

Whisperization

The *whisperization* effect, like robotization, is also most commonly used on voice signals. It maintains the vocal formants while completely eliminating any sense of pitch. The resulting effect sounds similar to a person whispering: the contents of speech remain clear, while any sense of voicing is lost.

Whisperization is implemented similarly to robotization, but instead of setting the phase of each frequency bin to zero at every frame, the phase is set to a random value in the range $\phi = [0, 2\pi)$. Assuming the original contents of bin k can be written $a_k + i^*b_k$ and ϕ_k holds the random phase value for bin k, the output is

$$\sqrt{a_k^2 + b_k^2}\left(\cos\psi_k + j\sin\psi_k\right) \tag{8.18}$$

Notice that a different random value is used for each frequency bin, each frame. As with robotization, the magnitude of each bin is preserved, which maintains the overall shape of the spectrum. But scrambling the phase erases any sense of periodicity from one frame to the next.

The most important parameter determining the whisperization effect is window size. In this case, shorter windows (e.g., 64 to 256 samples) are typically most effective at eliminating any pitch content. If the window is too short, the effect becomes unintelligible, but for longer windows, the original pitch of the signal remains apparent. Hop size is a less important parameter that can be adjusted experimentally, though generally it should be no longer than the window length or other artifacts will result.

Whisperization Code Example

To adapt the previous robotization code example to instead perform whisperization, the basic overlap-add structure stays the same and we only need to change the lines following the FFT calculation.

```
for(int bin = 0; bin <= fftTransformSize_ / 2; bin++)
{
    float amplitude=sqrt(
        (fftFrequencyDomain[bin][0] *
        fftFrequencyDomain[bin][0]) +
        (fftFrequencyDomain[bin][1] *
        fftFrequencyDomain[bin][1]));

    // This is how we could exactly reconstruct the signal:
    // float phase = atan2(fftFrequencyDomain[bin][1],
    //                     fftFrequencyDomain[bin][0]);

    // But instead, this is how we scramble the phase:
    float phase = 2.0 * M_PI * (float)rand() /
                               (float)RAND_MAX;

    fftFrequencyDomain[bin][0] = amplitude * cos(phase);
    fftFrequencyDomain[bin][1] = amplitude * sin(phase);

    // FFTs of real signals are conjugate-symmetric. We need
    // to maintain that symmetry to produce a real output,
    // even as we randomize the phase.
    if(bin > 0 && bin < fftTransformSize_ / 2) {
        fftFrequencyDomain[fftTransformSize_ - bin][0] =
              amplitude * cos(phase);
        fftFrequencyDomain[fftTransformSize_ - bin][1] =
              -amplitude * sin(phase);
    }
}
```

This code calculates the amplitude and phase of each bin based on the real and imaginary components. However, instead of using the phase of the original signal, the phase is replaced with a random number between 0 and 2π. Amplitude and phase are converted back to real and imaginary values using `sin` and `cos`.

Another change between robotization and whisperization code occurs in the first line of the `for()` loop. Notice that in this example, the loop goes through only the first half of the bins. This is because the FFT of a real-valued signal is always *conjugate-symmetric*: $F(k) = F(N - k)^*$, where k is the bin and N is the total transform size. If we want the output to remain as a real signal, we need to maintain conjugate symmetry even as we randomize the phase. The code inside the last `if()` statement fills in the second half of the frequency bins using the complex conjugates of the first half.

Time Scaling

The phase vocoder allows a signal to be rescaled in time without any change in pitch. To perform time scaling, the basic idea is to take advantage of the basic relationship between time, frequency, and phase, $\phi = \omega t$. Looking at this equation, we can see that frequency can be preserved, and time can be varied, at a cost of the original analysis phase being lost. Despite this loss of phase preservation, results are surprisingly good for many phase vocoder applications, especially when a short analysis hop size, such as one-eighth of the window length, is used.

When time scaling using the phase vocoder, the analysis stage (steps 1–3 in the "Overview" section) is performed identically to any other phase vocoder application. The synthesis stage (steps 5–7) is then varied to facilitate time compression and expansion. The analysis and synthesis hop sizes are no longer equal.

If R is the stretching ratio (e.g., for 20% expansion, R equals 1.2) applied to the signal, the synthesis hop size, h_s, is related to the analysis hop size, h_a, by h_s and is Rh_a.

Recall that the phase vocoder analysis offers a method for calculation of the instantaneous frequency using phase information. This instantaneous frequency is proportional to the phase increment over a single analysis hop. This phase increment is the parameter that is used in this time-scaling application. If we consider a single-frequency bin k, representing a sinusoidal track over time, the phase and amplitude increment per sample within hop n are given by

$$\begin{aligned}\Delta\phi_i(n,k) &= \frac{\omega_k h_a + \arg\left[\phi_d(n,k)\right]}{h_a}\\ \Delta A_i(n,k) &= \frac{A_i(n,k) - A_i(n-1,k)}{h_a}\end{aligned} \tag{8.19}$$

where h_a is the analysis hop size. Refer to Equations (8.7) to (8.9) for explanation of the terms.

Time-Scaling Resynthesis

These values may now be used in the resynthesis stage. For the same sinusoidal track, the phase is calculated at each sample, m, using

$$\theta(m,k) = \theta(m-1,k) + \Delta\phi_i(n,k) \tag{8.20}$$

In this case, θ is used to denote synthesis phase. The synthesis phase is then incremented by the same amount as was calculated in the analysis, for the number of samples in the synthesis hop size. This leads to a difference in phase by the end of the hop (recall the phase deviation mentioned earlier), as long as the synthesis hop size differs from that of the analysis hop size, which is a definition of time scaling. In the case of amplitude, the analysis increment cannot be used in the same way, because the same cumulative errors applied to amplitude would lead to severe artifacts compared to phase.

The amplitude increment is calculated instead using the synthesis hop size, to maintain identical analysis and synthesis amplitudes at both the beginning and the end of the hop.

$$\Delta A_{is}(n,k) = \frac{A_i(n,k) - A_i(n-1,k)}{h_s} \tag{8.21}$$

The amplitude can then be calculated for the duration of the synthesis hop size using

$$A_k(m,k) = A_k(m-1,k) + \Delta A_{ks}(n,k) \tag{8.22}$$

These sinusoidal components are then summed to synthesize the time-scaled audio:

$$y(x) = \sum_{k=0}^{N/2} A(m,k)\cos\left(\theta(m,k)\right) \tag{8.23}$$

Clear problems arise from time scaling using a spectral method such as this, discussed in the phase vocoder artifacts subsection. Also, by definition, time scaling cannot be a real-time audio effect except for a limited period of time. If the output is compressed in time compared to the input (i.e., plays faster), then at some point the effect would become *noncausal* since the output would depend on future input samples. On the other hand, if the output is stretched in time (plays slower), the difference in time between input and output will steadily accumulate and an ever-increasing amount of memory will be needed to buffer the audio waiting to play. However, the converse case of pitch shifting without time scaling, discussed in the following section, is a common real-time audio effect.

Pitch Shifting

There are several ways to shift the pitch of a signal without changing its speed using the phase vocoder. One of the most straightforward approaches uses the time-scaling algorithm presented in the previous section. Suppose we apply a time stretch factor of R; then every block of N input samples will produce $R \cdot N$ output samples after time scaling. If we then changed the sample rate to play R times faster, then the output would have the same speed as the input but with a pitch R times higher.

In practice, we don't actually change the sample rate at the output, but we achieve a similar effect using interpolation to fit $R \cdot N$ samples in the space of N. If $x[n]$, $0 < n < R \cdot N - 1$, represents the output of a single frame of the phase vocoder, then we can calculate the pitch-shifted output using linear interpolation:

$$y[n] = \left(1 + \lfloor Rn \rfloor - Rn\right) x\left[\lfloor Rn \rfloor\right] + \left(Rn - \lfloor Rn \rfloor\right) x\left[\lfloor Rn \rfloor + 1\right] \tag{8.24}$$

This interpolation is performed for each frame of the phase vocoder output. With time scaling, the synthesis hop size was $R*h$ samples, but in the pitch shifting, each of the interpolated buffers advances by the analysis hop size h, ensuring that input and output signals remain at the same speed despite the pitch shift.

To summarize, raising the pitch of the output requires first stretching the signal in time ($R > 1$), then compressing the longer output buffer with interpolation to fit in the original length. Lowering the pitch requires compressing the signal in time, producing fewer output samples that are then stretched with interpolation to fit the original length.

Code Example

The following C++ code fragment uses much of the same phase vocoder structure as the robotization and whisperization effects, but instead performs real-time pitch shifting. Some initial code that is identical to the robotization example has been omitted.

```
float *windowBuffer;        // Buffer that holds the analysis
                            // window function
int windowBufferLength;     // Length of the analysis window
float *synthWindowBuffer;   // Buffer that holds the synthesis
                            // window function
int synthesisWindowLength;  // Length of the synthesis window

float *resampledOutput;     // Buffer holding resampled
                            // (interpolated) output from FFT
float **lastPhase;          // Previous phase values for each
                            // bin and channel
float **psi;                // Adjusted phase values for each
                            // bin and channel

double pitchRatio_;       // Ratio of output/input frequency
int analysisHopSize_;     // Hop size for input (in samples)
int synthesisHopSize_;    // Hop size for output (in samples)
                          // Synthesis / analysis size should
                          // match pitchRatio_
```

```
// [...]
// Up until this point, the code is the same as the
// robotization example earlier in the chapter. This code
// executes the pitch shift for one (overlapped) FFT window:
// [...]

fftw_execute(fftForwardPlan_);

for (int i = 0; i < fftTransformSize_; i++) {
    // Convert the bin into magnitude-phase representation
    double magnitude = sqrt(
        (fftFrequencyDomain[bin][0] *
        fftFrequencyDomain[bin][0]) +
        (fftFrequencyDomain[bin][1] *
        fftFrequencyDomain[bin][1]));

    double phase = atan2(fftFrequencyDomain[i][1],
                         fftFrequencyDomain[i][0]);

    // Calculate frequency for this bin
    double frequency = 2.0 * M_PI * (double)i /
                                    fftTransformSize_;

    // Increment the phase based on frequency and hop sizes
    double deltaPhi = (frequency * analysisHopSize_) +
                    princArg(phase - lastPhase[i][channel] -
                            (frequency * analysisHopSize_));
    lastPhase[i][channel] = phase;
    psi[i][channel] = princArg(psi[i][channel] +
                            deltaPhi * synthesisHopSize_);

    // Convert back to real-imaginary form
    fftFrequencyDomain[i][0] = magnitude *
                               cos(psi[i][channel]);
    fftFrequencyDomain[i][1] = magnitude *
                               sin(psi[i][channel]);
}

// Perform the inverse FFT
fftw_execute(fftBackwardPlan_);

// Resample output using linear interpolation to stretch it
double outputLength = floor(fftTransformSize_ /
                            pitchRatio_);

for(int i = 0; i < outputLength; i++) {
    x = i * fftTransformSize_ / outputLength;
```

```
    ix = floor(x);
    dx = x - (double)ix;
    resampleOutput[i] = fftTimeDomain[ix]*(1.0 - dx) +
                        fftTimeDomain[(ix+1)%fftTransformSize_]*dx;
}

// Add the result to the output buffer, starting at the
// current write position
int outputBufferIndex = outwritepos;

for(int fftBufferIndex = 0; fftBufferIndex < outputLength;
    fftBufferIndex++) {
    if (fftBufferIndex > synthesisWindowLength)
        outputBufferData[outputBufferIndex] += 0;
    else
        outputBufferData[outputBufferIndex] +=
                resampleOutput[fftBufferIndex] *
                fftScaleFactor *
                synthesisWindowBuffer[fftBufferIndex];
    if(++outputBufferIndex >= outputBufferLength)
        outputBufferIndex = 0;
}

// Advance the write position within the buffer by the hop
// size (Use the original hop size since we have resampled
// the output back to the expected length)
outwritepos = (outwritepos + analysisHopSize_) %
              outputBufferLength_;
```

In this example, `princArg()` implements the principal argument function (*princ*). After performing the FFT, each bin is converted to magnitude phase representation. At that point, the phase is updated based on Equation (8.19) so the windows can be overlapped at a different synthesis hop size. Normally, making analysis and synthesis hop sizes different would result in a time stretch. However, the output of the inverse FFT is resampled and then overlapped at the original (analysis) hop size. This results in a pitch shift without changing the timing of the signal.

Phase Vocoder Artifacts

Amplitude estimation is not easily achieved with linear interpolation, especially when using a long synthesis window. Consider the idea of a piano piece being played more slowly: the attacks would have much the same temporal envelope, but steady-state and decay regions would be longer before the start of the next note, although the decay rate would be the same. Linear interpolation implies that all regions of the envelope stretched equally.

Also, problems arise in phase relationships, as the phase error is cumulative. If phase coherence is lost at transients (note attacks), transient smearing occurs that softens the attacks and loses the natural sound of these regions. Loss of phase coherence across harmonic partials of the same note can lead to loss of natural-sounding steady-state regions.

Finally, a "phasiness" is introduced, which adds a reverb-like quality to the sound. One reason for this phasiness is the loss of coherence of phase within the same sinusoidal component. If the phase is not maintained across all components that correspond to a windowed sinusoid, although frequency is maintained, severe amplitude distortions can occur. This produces a robot-like effect when applied to signals such as voice.

Further problems arise when chirp-like signals are applied to phase vocoders. When the signal crosses over to the next frequency bin, it takes the phase of the new frequency track, leading to discontinuities. This is the kind of problem that can be solved by using higher-level peak picking and sinusoidal tracking.

Problems

1. Write pseudocode to perform a short-time Fourier transform on a sampled signal. You can call another function to perform the FFT.
2. Consider the block diagram of the phase vocoder given by Figure 8.1. If a Hamming window of 1024 samples is used, what is the maximum hop size that will allow perfect reconstruction of the signal? Why?
3. Suppose the sampling frequency is 32.768 kHz and the FFT size is 1024 points. What is the width of one frequency bin (i.e., how far apart in frequency are two adjacent bins)?
4. We can perfectly reconstruct any signal under the right conditions, but the FFT has limited frequency resolution. Suppose the input is a sine wave that doesn't exactly align with any bin frequency. Explain how phase information can be used to determine the exact frequency.
5. Explain the operation of the robotization effect, and explain what parameter determines the frequency of the robot voice.
6. Explain the operation of the whisperization effect. What is the restriction on the window length, and why is it necessary?
7. Explain the steps involved in a pitch-shifter effect (changing pitch without changing speed).

9

Spatial Audio

Previously, we described a digital audio signal as a discrete series of values, sampled uniformly in time. But the listener has two ears and hears the sound differently in each ear depending on the location of the source. Stereo audio files encode two signals, or *channels*, for listening over headphones or loudspeakers, so that sources can be localized. Furthermore, spatial audio reproduction systems will often use a large number of loudspeakers, recreating an entire sound scene, thus requiring more channels.

For reproduction of spatial audio via multiple loudspeakers, we should first consider how we localize sound sources. Consider a listener hearing the same content coming from two different locations, and at different times and levels. Under the right conditions, this will be perceived as a single sound source, but emanating from a location between the two original locations. This fundamental aspect of sound perception is a key element in many spatial audio rendering techniques.

In this chapter, we describe some of the main techniques used to spatialize audio signals. We concentrate on the placement of sound sources using level difference (*panorama*) and time difference (*precedence*), and variations and advances on these approaches. We also discuss some advanced multichannel spatial audio reproduction methods, such as *ambisonics* and *wave field synthesis*. Finally, it should be noted that spatial audio continues to be a very active research area. New approaches, such as directional audio coding [58], are gaining popularity and may offer some advantages over the methods mentioned here.

Theory

Panorama

Suppose we have two loudspeakers in different locations. Then the apparent position of a source can be changed just by giving the same source signal to both loudspeakers, but at different relative levels. When a camera is rotated to depict a panorama, or wide-angle view, this is known as *panning*. Panning in audio is derived from this and describes the use of level adjustment to move a virtual sound source. During mixing, this panning is often

THE BEGINNING OF STEREO

The sound reproduction systems for the early 'talkie' movies often had only a single loudspeaker. Because of this, the actors all sounded like they were in the same place, regardless of their position on screen.

In 1931, the electronics and sound engineer Alan Blumlein and his wife Doreen went to see a movie where this monaural sound reproduction occured. According to Doreen, as they were leaving the cinema, Alan said to her, "Do you realize the sound only comes from one person?" And she replied, "Oh does it?" "Yes," he said, "and I've got a way to make it follow the person" [59].

The genesis of these ideas is uncertain (though it might have been while watching the movie), but he described them to Isaac Shoenberg, managing director at EMI and Alan's mentor, in the late summer of 1931. Blumlein detailed his stereo technology in the British patent "Improvements in and relating to Sound-transmission, Sound-recording and Sound-reproducing systems," which was accepted June 14, 1933.

accomplished separately for each sound source, giving a panorama of virtual source positions in the space spanned by the loudspeakers.

Consider a standard stereo layout. The listener is placed in a central position as depicted in Figure 9.1. In this figure, there is a 60° angle between loudspeakers, which is typical, but not a requirement. φ is the angle of the apparent source position, known as the *azimuth* angle, and θ is the angle (in this case, 30°) formed by each loudspeaker with the frontal direction. $\mathbf{p}$ defines the unit length vector pointing toward the source, and $\mathbf{l}_1$ and $\mathbf{l}_2$ are the unit vectors in the directions of the two loudspeakers.

The unit vectors $\mathbf{p}$, $\mathbf{l}_1$, and $\mathbf{l}_2$ can be written in terms of the angles φ and θ,

$$\begin{aligned} p_1 &= \cos\phi,\ p_2 = \sin\phi \\ l_{11} &= \cos\theta,\ l_{12} = \sin\theta \\ l_{21} &= \cos\theta,\ l_{22} = -\sin\theta \end{aligned} \tag{9.1}$$

and the unit vectors in the loudspeaker directions can be defined as a matrix:

$$\mathbf{L} = \begin{bmatrix} \mathbf{l}_1 \\ \mathbf{l}_2 \end{bmatrix} = \begin{bmatrix} \cos\theta & \sin\theta \\ \cos\theta & -\sin\theta \end{bmatrix} \tag{9.2}$$

Importantly, the vector pointing toward the source can be constructed by applying gains, g_1 and g_2, to the vectors pointing to the loudspeakers.

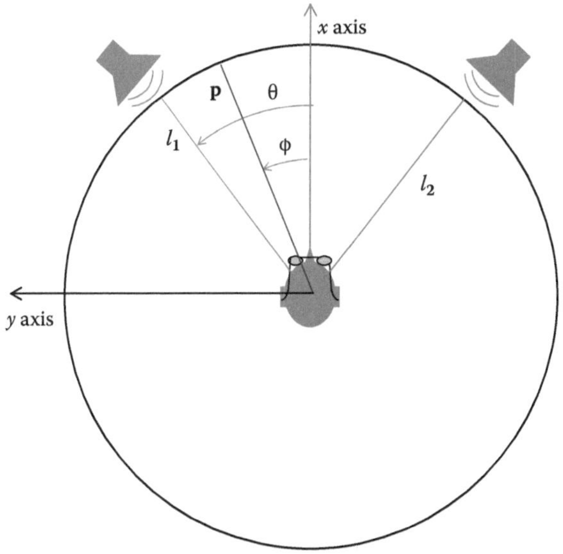

FIGURE 9.1
Listener and loudspeakers configuration for placing a sound source using level difference.

$$\mathbf{p} = \begin{bmatrix} p_1 & p_2 \end{bmatrix} = \mathbf{gL} \tag{9.3}$$

So we can invert this to find $\mathbf{g} = \mathbf{pL}^{-1}$:

$$\begin{aligned}\begin{bmatrix} g_1 & g_2 \end{bmatrix} &= \frac{1}{l_{11}l_{22} - l_{21}l_{12}} \begin{bmatrix} p_1 & p_2 \end{bmatrix} \begin{bmatrix} l_{22} & -l_{12} \\ -l_{21} & l_{11} \end{bmatrix} \\ &= \frac{1}{-2\cos\theta\sin\theta} \begin{bmatrix} \cos\phi & \sin\phi \end{bmatrix} \begin{bmatrix} -\sin\theta & -\sin\theta \\ -\cos\theta & \cos\theta \end{bmatrix} \\ &= \begin{bmatrix} \dfrac{\cos\phi\sin\theta + \sin\phi\cos\theta}{2\cos\theta\sin\theta} & \dfrac{\cos\phi\sin\theta - \sin\phi\cos\theta}{2\cos\theta\sin\theta} \end{bmatrix}\end{aligned} \tag{9.4}$$

However, as is, these gains may change the power of the signal, causing the signal level to change depending on the direction of the source. So the gains must be scaled:

$$\mathbf{g}_{scaled} = \frac{\mathbf{g}}{\sqrt{g_1^2 + g_2^2}} \tag{9.5}$$

Thus, we can find the gains that need to be applied for a given azimuth angle for the source. This also gives a simple relationship for the azimuth angle in terms of the gains, known as the *tangent law*:

$$\frac{g_1 - g_2}{g_1 + g_2} = \frac{2\sin\phi\cos\theta}{2\cos\phi\sin\theta} = \frac{\tan\phi}{\tan\theta} \rightarrow$$
$$\tan\phi = \frac{g_1 - g_2}{g_1 + g_2}\tan\theta \qquad (9.6)$$

This has been found to yield accurate perceived direction in listening tests under anechoic conditions. A similar law is often used, known as the *sine law* or *Blumlein law*.

$$\sin\phi = \frac{g_1 - g_2}{g_1 + g_2}\sin\theta \qquad (9.7)$$

Figure 9.2 depicts the gain and power for constant power panning as a function of the azimuth angle φ. Here total power is constant, but total gain varies as a function of azimuth angle, reaching its maximum when the source is positioned equidistant from both loudspeakers.

Figure 9.3 shows the perceived azimuth angle as a function of the level difference between the applied gains, using the tangent law, for a typical loudspeaker placement.

If θ is 45°, then stereo panning can be put in a more compact form using a simple rotation matrix. From (9.4) and (9.5), it can be seen that

$$\mathbf{g} = \mathbf{g}^{scaled} = \begin{bmatrix} \cos\phi & \sin\phi \\ -\sin\phi & \cos\phi \end{bmatrix} \begin{bmatrix} 1/\sqrt{2} \\ 1/\sqrt{2} \end{bmatrix} \qquad (9.8)$$

Note that this approach is much preferred over cross-fade panning, where the apparent position of the sound source is shifted by linearly interpolating the amplitude between the two extremes of hard left and hard right. This method produces a "hole" in the middle due to the reduced power when not scaling.

Precedence

The precedence effect is a well-known phenomenon that plays a large part in our perception of source location.

In a standard stereo loudspeaker layout, the perceived azimuth angle of a monophonic source that is fed to both loudspeakers can be changed by having a small time difference between the two channels. Figure 9.4 shows

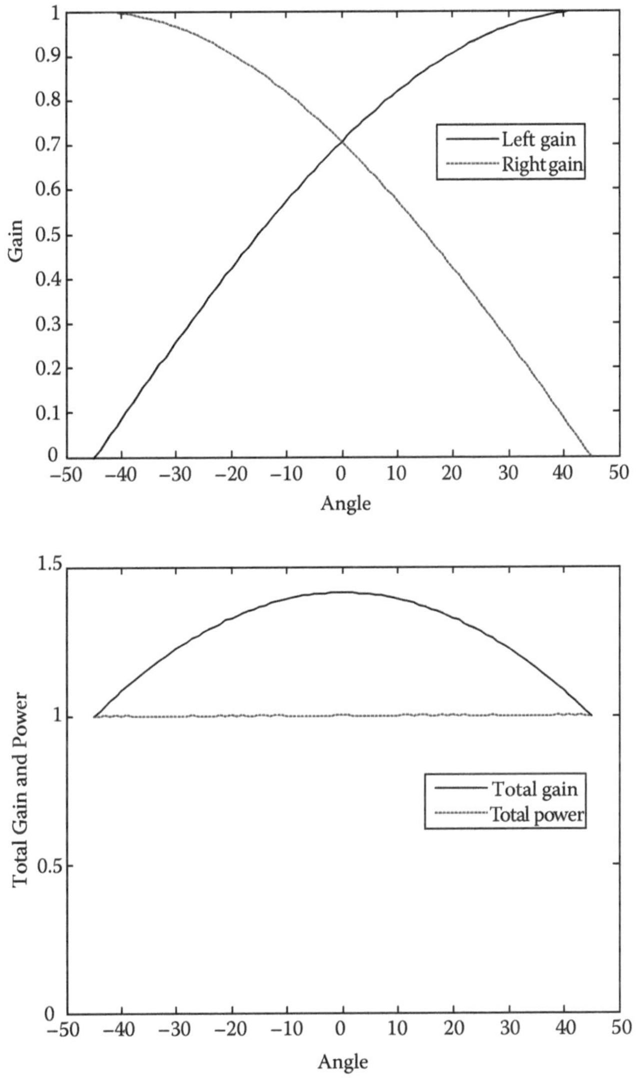

FIGURE 9.2
Constant power panning for two channels. On the top is the gain for each channel, and on the bottom is the total power and total gain.

the qualitative dependency of the apparent azimuth on the relative delay between channels. If the time difference between the signals fed to the two loudspeakers is below the echo threshold, the listener will perceive a single auditory event. This threshold can vary widely depending on the signal, but ranges from about 5 to 40 ms. When this time difference is below about 1 ms (so much lower than the echo threshold), the source angle can be perceived

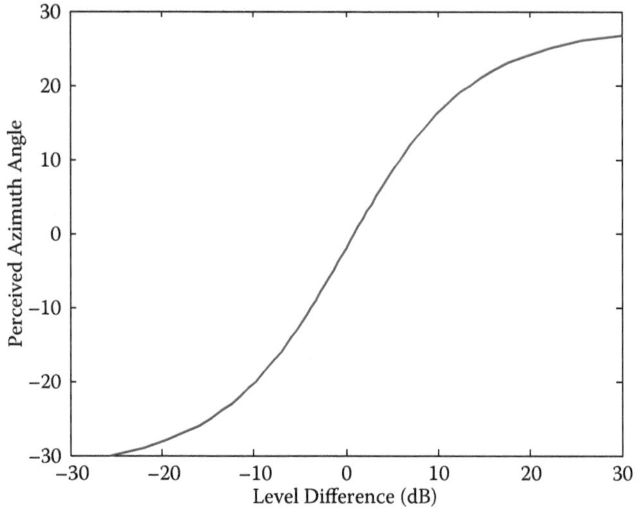

FIGURE 9.3
Perceived azimuth angle as a function of level difference.

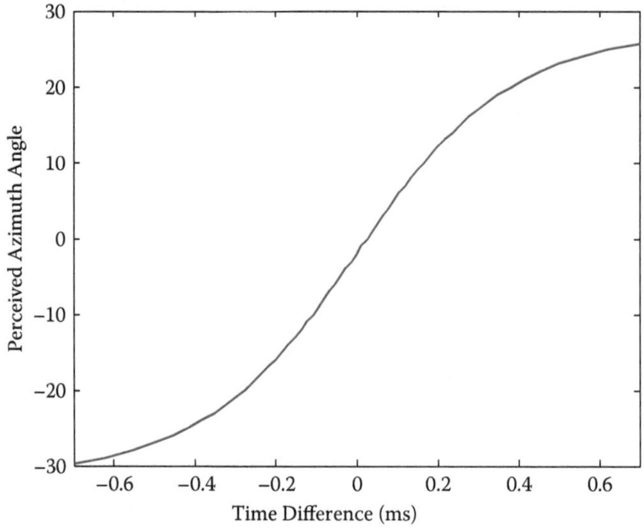

FIGURE 9.4
Perceived azimuth angle as a function of time difference.

as being between the two loudspeakers. In between 1 ms and the echo threshold, the sound appears to come just from whichever loudspeaker has the least delay. More generally, the fact that for appropriate choice of delay we perceive the two sounds as a single entity coming from the location of the first to arrive is known as the precedence effect.

This effect has several implications. In a stereo loudspeaker layout, if the listener is far enough away from the central position, he or she will perceive the source as being located at the closest loudspeaker, and this apparent position does not change even if the other channel is significantly louder.

Subjective testing has shown that an almost equivalent relationship can exist between the effect of time difference and the effect of level difference on perceived azimuth angle [60]. However, the actual relationship can depend on the characteristics of the sounds that are played, the exact placement of the loudspeakers, and the listener [61].

Vector Base Amplitude Panning

Vector base amplitude panning (VBAP) is an extension of stereo panning to arbitrary placement of loudspeakers in three dimensions [62]. A unit vector,

$$\mathbf{l}_n = \begin{bmatrix} l_{n1} \\ l_{n2} \\ l_{n3} \end{bmatrix} \tag{9.9}$$

points from the listening position toward loudspeaker n. Thus, unit vectors $\mathbf{l}_n$, $\mathbf{l}_m$, and $\mathbf{l}_k$ give the directions of loudspeakers n, m, and k. Then $\mathbf{p}$ gives a panning direction for a virtual source in terms of gains g_n, g_m, and g_k applied to the unit vectors in the directions of each loudspeaker.

$$\mathbf{p} = \begin{bmatrix} p_n \\ p_m \\ p_k \end{bmatrix} = \begin{bmatrix} \mathbf{l}_n & \mathbf{l}_m & \mathbf{l}_k \end{bmatrix} \begin{bmatrix} g_n \\ g_m \\ g_k \end{bmatrix} = \begin{bmatrix} l_{n,x} & l_{m,x} & l_{k,x} \\ l_{n,y} & l_{m,y} & l_{k,y} \\ l_{n,z} & l_{m,z} & l_{k,z} \end{bmatrix} \begin{bmatrix} g_n \\ g_m \\ g_k \end{bmatrix} = \begin{bmatrix} l_{n,x}g_n + l_{m,x}g_m + l_{k,x}g_k \\ l_{n,y}g_n + l_{m,y}g_m + l_{k,y}g_k \\ l_{n,z}g_n + l_{m,z}g_m + l_{k,z}g_k \end{bmatrix} \tag{9.10}$$

This can now be solved to find the gains that need to be applied to each loudspeaker in order to place the source in a given position.

$$\mathbf{g} = \begin{bmatrix} g_n \\ g_m \\ g_k \end{bmatrix} = \begin{bmatrix} l_{n,x} & l_{m,x} & l_{k,x} \\ l_{n,y} & l_{m,y} & l_{k,y} \\ l_{n,z} & l_{m,z} & l_{k,z} \end{bmatrix}^{-1} \begin{bmatrix} p_x \\ p_y \\ p_z \end{bmatrix} \tag{9.11}$$

And finally, the applied gain should be normalized so that

$$\sqrt{g_n^{\,2} + g_m^{\,2} + g_k^{\,2}} = 1 \tag{9.12}$$

Ambisonics

Ambisonics comprises methods for both spatial audio recording and reproduction. By encoding and decoding sound signals for a number of channels, a two- or three-dimensional sound field can be captured and rendered. However, sound sources that were not recorded using ambisonics techniques can still be given virtual positions using ambisonic reproduction [63].

Ambisonics can be used for full three-dimensional sound reproduction. However, we will focus on the two-dimensional case and follow the approach taken in [64]. We consider an incoming reference wave and attempt to create an outgoing wave that provides a faithful representation of the original using a finite number of loudspeakers. Although we refer to incoming and outgoing waves for the original plane wave and the attempt at recreating it, both waves are converging on the center of the listening area. These terms are used because the original reference plane wave is incoming on the loudspeakers but the recreation attempt is outgoing from the speakers.

We will assume that both the incoming reference sound and outgoing sound from the loudspeakers are plane wave, which is roughly valid if the listener is far from the source and the loudspeakers. Note, though, that these assumptions are not general requirements for ambisonics [65].

Now assume that we have the configuration shown in Figure 9.5. The x-axis points toward the front of the room and the y-axis to the left of the room (this is typical in representing ambisonics). The listener is at a radial distance r at an angle φ, represented by the vector $\mathbf{r}$, and a plane wave comes from an angle ψ with respect to the x-axis.

So the plane wave is given by $P_\psi e^{j\mathbf{k}\cdot\mathbf{r}}$. P_ψ is the pressure of the plane wave and $\mathbf{k}$ represents a wave at an angle ψ and with wave number $k = 2\pi f$, where f is the frequency (in acoustics, signals are often represented by wave number,

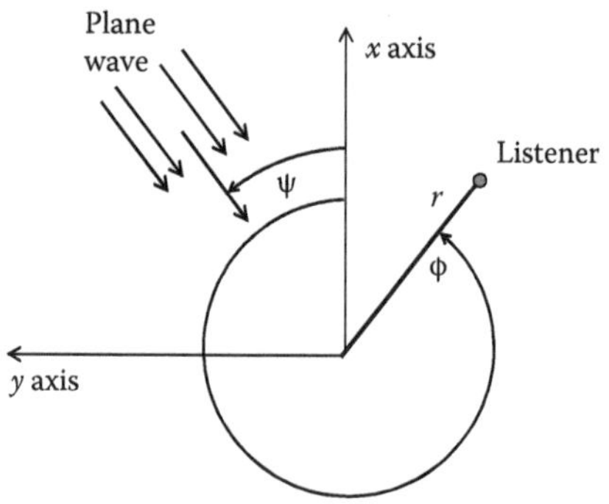

FIGURE 9.5
Standard depiction of the coordinate system in two-dimensional ambisonics.

which gives the number of wavelengths per 2π units of distance). The plane wave arriving at the listener may be expressed as

$$S_\psi = P_\psi e^{jkr\cos(\phi-\psi)} \tag{9.13}$$

Ambisonics attempts to reproduce this plane wave in the center of the listening area. If this wave can be expressed with a series expansion, then it should be possible to reproduce the wave if one were able to add an infinite number of signals or channels to represent each term in the series. And the lower terms in the series can be used to give an approximation to that wave and to drive a system of loudspeakers. This is the essence of ambisonics.

From wave propagation theory [66, 67], a plane wave can be expanded as a series of cosines and cylindrical Bessel functions,

$$S_\psi = P_\psi J_0(kr) + P_\psi \sum_{m=1}^{\infty} 2i^m J_m(kr)\left[\cos(m\psi)\cos(m\phi) + \sin(m\psi)\cos(m\phi)\right] \tag{9.14}$$

The subscript ψ is used to denote a quantity with respect to the original plane wave, and the subscript n is used to denote a quantity with respect to the nth speaker.

An ambisonic loudspeaker array should consist of N loudspeakers, each at the same distance from the center point in a regular polygonal array, as shown in Figure 9.6. If each loudspeaker produces plane wave output, then the output of the nth speaker will be given by

$$S_n = P_n J_0(kr) + P_n \sum_{m=1}^{\infty} 2i^m J_m(kr)\left[\cos(m\psi)\cos(m\phi_n) + \sin(m\psi)\cos(m\phi_n)\right] \tag{9.15}$$

where φ_n is the angle of the nth speaker. And summing this over the N loudspeakers gives the total reproduced wave:

$$S_n = \sum_{n=1}^{N} P_n J_0(kr) + \sum_{m=1}^{\infty} 2i^m J_m(kr)\left[\sum_{n=1}^{N} P_n \cos(m\phi_n)\cos(m\phi) + \sum_{n=1}^{N} P_n \sin(m\phi_n)\sin(m\phi)\right] \tag{9.16}$$

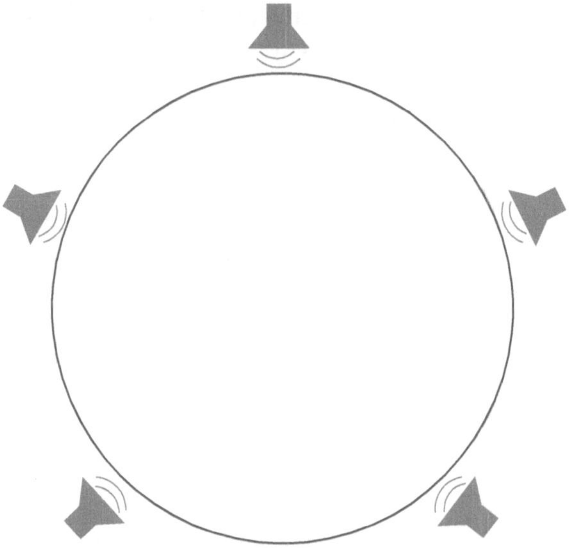

FIGURE 9.6
A typical ambisonics layout. Five loudspeakers arranged in a regular layout, suitable for second-order two-dimensional ambisonics.

This reproduced plane wave must match the original plane wave, (9.14). So,

$$P_\psi = \sum_{n=1}^{N} P_n$$

$$P_\psi \cos(m\psi) = \sum_{n=1}^{N} P_n \cos(m\phi_n) \tag{9.17}$$

$$P_\psi \sin(m\psi) = \sum_{n=1}^{N} P_n \sin(m\phi_n)$$

Equation (9.17) represents a set of criteria, known as *matching conditions*, that must be met in order for the original plane wave to match the reproduced plane wave. Each value m gives the mth-order spherical harmonic that needs to be matched. Since we truncate the series, the higher spherical harmonics will not be reproduced.

For two-dimensional ambisonics, $2m + 1$ channels are needed to reproduce the signal, where m is the order of the system. If a three-dimensional case were to be considered, the number of channels would be $(m + 1)^2$ [64]. Thus, it is clear that three-dimensional ambisonics requires many more loudspeakers (and more complex math).

For a zeroth-order match to a plane wave, only the lowest order in (9.17) will need to be matched, i.e., $m = 0$. This would match just the pressure of the waves, so that the original and reproduced plane waves would have the same amplitude. The first part of Equation (9.17) gives the pressure of the plane wave, denoted by W in ambisonic notation.

This first-order match, $m = 1$, provides the velocity of the plane wave. That is, the velocities of the original and reproduced plane waves will be identical, and hence, both waves will be in the same direction. We can rewrite Equation (9.17) for just zeroth- and first-order terms,

$$\begin{aligned} W &\equiv P_\psi = \sum_{n=1}^{N} P_n \\ X &\equiv P_\psi \cos\psi = \sum_{n=1}^{N} P_n \cos\phi_n \\ Y &\equiv P_\psi \sin\psi = \sum_{n=1}^{N} P_n \sin\phi_n \end{aligned} \tag{9.18}$$

At this point the feed or gain applied to the nth loudspeaker, P_n, will need to be considered. There are multiple approaches, so we will use one similar to that provided in Michael Gerzon's original work [64, 68]. The feed for a first-order N loudspeaker ambisonic system is

$$P_n = (W + 2X\cos\phi_n + 2Y\sin\phi_n)/N \tag{9.19}$$

which will satisfy Equation (9.17). As an example, let's suppose we have four loudspeakers, placed at 0, 90, 180, and 270°. So (9.19) gives

$$\begin{aligned} P_1 &= (W + 2X)/4 \\ P_2 &= (W + 2Y)/4 \\ P_3 &= (W - 2X)/4 \\ P_4 &= (W - 2Y)/4 \end{aligned} \tag{9.20}$$

We can see that the matching conditions of Equation (9.17) hold.

$$
\begin{aligned}
&\sum_{n=1}^{N} P_n = W \\
&\sum_{n=1}^{N} P_n \cos\phi_n = (W+2X)/4-(W-2X)/4 = X \\
&\sum_{n=1}^{N} P_n \sin\phi_n = (W+2Y)/4-(W-2Y)/4 = Y
\end{aligned}
\tag{9.21}
$$

We can now plug Equation (9.18) into Equation (9.20) to arrive at the gain applied to each loudspeaker in order to render a plane wave source arriving from an angle ψ:

$$
\begin{aligned}
P_1 &= P_\psi(1+2\cos\psi)/4 \\
P_2 &= P_\psi(1+2\sin\psi)/4 \\
P_3 &= P_\psi(1-2\cos\psi)/4 \\
P_4 &= P_\psi(1-2\sin\psi)/4
\end{aligned}
\tag{9.22}
$$

By matching up to second order, we obtain two additional terms, $U = P_\psi \cos(2\psi)$ and $V = P_\psi \sin(2\psi)$. A second-order system is composed of the five signals W, X, Y, U, and V. These terms are then added to the feeds such that the above matching conditions still hold.

$$
P_n = \left(W + 2X\cos\phi_n + 2Y\sin\phi_n + 2U\cos(2\phi_n) + 2V\sin(2\phi_n)\right)/N \tag{9.23}
$$

If a system were to contain those five signals with enough loudspeakers, a second-order approximation of the plane wave would be reproduced in the center of the listening area.

Although ambisonics places a minimum requirement on the number of channels for a given order reproduction, it does not explicitly place a requirement on the number of loudspeakers. However, the matching conditions of Equation (9.17) suggest that the number of loudspeakers be at least as many as the number of channels. For instance, if four loudspeakers are used with second-order ambisonics, then not all the channels will be used, in which case it makes sense to use just a lower-order reproduction.

Recall also that ambisonics typically requires that the angles between the loudspeakers must be equal. We can relax this constraint by adding parameters in front of the channels in Equations (9.19) and (9.23) for the second-order case. The parameters are then determined for a particular layout by solving the system of equations given by (9.17).

Three-dimensional ambisonics is a straightforward extension of the two-dimensional case, for use with three-dimensional loudspeaker setups. But now all the math and derivations become more challenging. Directions are expressed using either an angle/elevation representation or Cartesian coordinates, related by

$$\begin{aligned} x &= \cos\alpha\cos\varepsilon \\ y &= \sin\alpha\cos\varepsilon \\ z &= \sin\varepsilon \end{aligned} \tag{9.24}$$

where α corresponds to the azimuth angle and ε to the elevation angle.

Wave Field Synthesis

Wave field synthesis (WFS) is another spatial audio reproduction method, used to create a virtual acoustic environment. It uses a large number of individually driven speakers to produce an approximation to the wave fronts produced by sound sources. The wave fronts that it produces are perceived as originating from virtual sources. Unlike some other spatial audio techniques such as stereo or surround sound, the localization of virtual sources in wave field synthesis is not dependent on the listener's position.

Fundamental to understanding of wave field synthesis is Huygens' principle. This states that any wave front can be represented as a superposition of elementary spherical waves. So we can attempt to simulate the wave fronts from a finite number of these elementary waves. To implement this, a large number of loudspeakers are controlled by software that, for each loudspeaker, plays a processed version of the source sound at the same time that the wave front passes through the loudspeaker location.

The math behind WFS (and to some extent, behind ambisonics) is based on the Kirchhoff-Helmholtz integral, which states that when the sound pressure and velocity are known on the entire surface of a volume, then the sound pressure is completely determined within that volume. So we can position a large number of loudspeakers on that surface to approximately reconstruct the sound field. As with ambisonics, we'll focus on the two-dimensional space. In this case, we will consider a horizontal line of loudspeakers used to synthesize a wave field on the horizontal plane beyond that line.

Now look at this in more detail. If a wave emitted by a point source P_S with a frequency f is considered at any time t, all the points on the wave front can be taken as point sources for the production of a new set of waves with the same frequency and phase. The pressure amplitude of these secondary sources is proportional to the pressure due to the original source at these points. This principle of wave diffraction was discovered by Huygens in 1690 and is depicted in Figure 9.7.

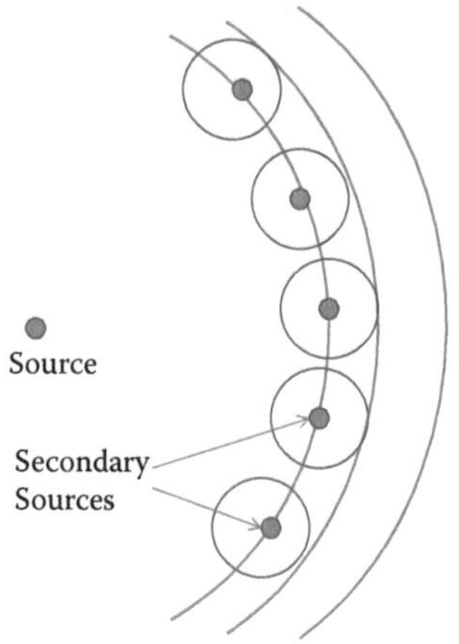

FIGURE 9.7
Illustration of Huygens' principle.

Wave field synthesis is a direct application of this concept. Each loudspeaker in a loudspeaker array acts as a source of a secondary wave, and the whole system will recreate the sound field generated by sounds positioned behind the array. The challenge then is to determine the driving signals applied to each loudspeaker due to the original sources, their locations, and the locations of the loudspeakers.

Consider a source-free volume V enclosed by a surface S. The Kirchhoff–Helmholtz integral gives the Fourier transform of the sound pressure at a listening position L inside V,

$$P(\mathbf{r},\omega) = \frac{1}{4\pi}\int_S \left[P(\mathbf{r}_S,\omega)\frac{\partial}{\partial n}\left(\frac{e^{-j\omega|\mathbf{r}-\mathbf{r}_S|/c}}{|\mathbf{r}-\mathbf{r}_S|}\right) - \frac{\partial P(\mathbf{r}_S,\omega)}{\partial n}\frac{e^{-j\omega|\mathbf{r}-\mathbf{r}_S|/c}}{|\mathbf{r}-\mathbf{r}_S|}\right] dS \qquad (9.25)$$

ω is the angular frequency of the wave, c is the speed of sound, $\mathbf{r}$ defines the position of the listening point inside V, and $P(\mathbf{r}_S, \omega)$ is the Fourier transform of the pressure distribution on S.

This integral is incredibly complicated, and it is not necessary to delve into its derivation or fine details here. But it implies that by setting the correct pressure distribution $P(\mathbf{r}_S, \omega)$ and its gradient on a surface S, a sound field in the volume enclosed within this surface can be created. In our case, we have a finite set of loudspeakers, so we can set the pressure at discrete locations and transform the integral into a summation.

The pressure field produced at a distance d from a source with a spectrum $S(\omega)$ is

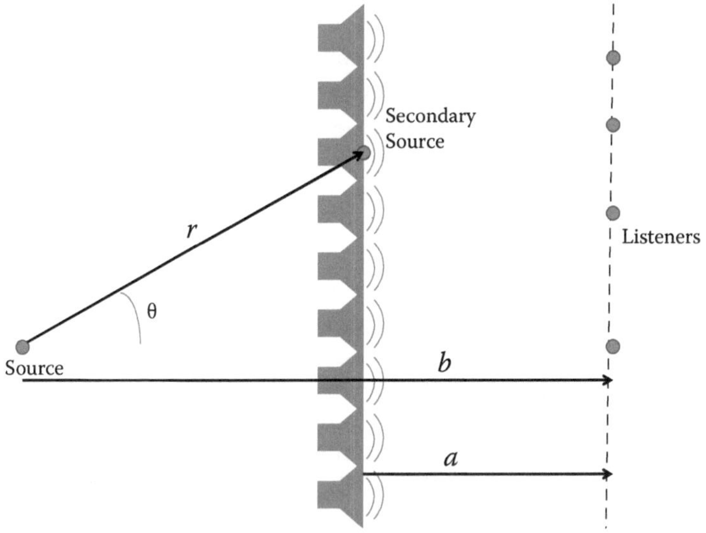

FIGURE 9.8
Geometry for the calculation of the driving functions, given a virtual source behind a line of loudspeakers.

$$P(d,\omega) = S(\omega)\frac{e^{-j\omega d/c}}{d} \tag{9.26}$$

So we know the sound field that should be produced by a virtual source. Now consider the setup shown in Figure 9.8. We won't go into the steps here, but we can find a driving function that determines the signal to send to each loudspeaker [69]. The driving functions for the loudspeakers are derived from the synthesized sound field produced by the notional sources.

$$Q_n(\mathbf{r},\omega) = S(\omega)\cos\theta_n\sqrt{\frac{j\omega}{2\pi c}}\sqrt{\frac{a}{b}}\frac{e^{-j\omega r/c}}{\sqrt{r}} \tag{9.27}$$

This driving function $Q_n(\mathbf{r}, \omega)$ is the sound pressure at the nth loudspeaker due to the virtual source. Each loudspeaker is fed with a filtered version of the source signal.

The driving function's terms can be interpreted as follows:

- e^{-jkr} describes the delay due to sound traveling from the virtual source location to the nth loudspeaker.
- The amplitude factor $1/\sqrt{r}$ is the dispersion factor for a cylindrical wave.

- The factor $\sqrt{a/b}\cos\theta_n$ is an attenuation based on the distances between the virtual source, the loudspeaker array, and the listener position. It does not change much within the listening area.
- $\sqrt{j\omega/(2\pi c)}$ gives high-pass filtering of the signal. Essentially, for high frequencies, the line of loudspeakers corresponds to fewer samples per period, and so this filter ensures equal weighting regardless of frequency.

So, given the distance from a virtual source to the loudspeaker array, the distance from the loudspeaker array to the listener position, and the number of and distance between loudspeakers, we have all the necessary information to synthesize a wave field for the line of listener positions.

Note that the driving function is given in the frequency domain. So most implementations will split the signal into overlapping segments (overlap of 50%) and form the columns of a matrix with the N-point discrete Fourier transforms of these segments. This is repeated for as many loudspeakers as there are on the array. These matrices are then transformed into the time domain with an inverse Fourier transform.

The Head-Related Transfer Function

When spatializing sound for listening on headphones, a quite different approach is taken. Wave field synthesis, ambisonics, and VBAP all treat the listener as a single point. But of course, we use both ears and other cues to determine the location of sound sources. A listener is able to determine the distance, elevation, and azimuth (horizontal) angle of sound sources by comparing the sounds received at each ear. Before entering the ear canal, a sound is modified by, among other things, the acoustics of the room and the shape of the listener's body, head, and outer ear.

There are two primary cues for azimuth, the interaural level difference (ILD) and interaural time difference (ITD). They relate to the different signal levels and delays received by each ear due to a source arriving from a given location. Many of these differences, especially level differences, are due to *head shadowing*. This describes sound traveling either through or around the head in order to arrive at an ear. The head provides filtering and significant attenuation of the source signal.

ILD and ITD are what we exploit for panorama and precedence. At low frequencies below about 1.6 kHz, the auditory system analyzes the interaural time shifts between the signal's fine structure. But at high frequencies, the interlevel difference (ILD) is used, along with the timing between the envelopes of the signals [70]. The maximum naturally occurring ITD is about 0.65 ms [71], and the maximum ILD is about 20 dB, and both can be estimated based on the shape of the human head. For sources at the side, both ILD and

ITD are at their maximum. And for sources directly in front or behind the listener, they are near zero.

However, the ILD and ITD do not provide much information about the sound source elevation. This information is given mostly by the filtering done by the head, body, and outer ear before sounds reach the inner ear. This effect is referred to as the head-related transfer function (HRTF), though of course it relates to much more than just the shape of the head.

An HRTF is a transfer function that characterizes how sound from a particular point in space is received by the ear. A pair of HRTFs, one for each ear, can be used to synthesize binaural sound. HRTFs are very useful for accurate localization of sounds, especially those not coming from just the horizontal plane. HRTFs for left and right ear give the filtering of a sound source (represented here in the time domain) $x[n]$ before it is perceived by the ears as $x_L[n]$ and $x_R[n]$, respectively. The HRTF may be found by measuring a head-related impulse response (HRIR).

ITD Model

The physicist Lord Rayleigh (1842–1919) was perhaps the first to explain the ITD [72], in his description of sound localization known as *duplex theory*. Assume the listener's head is completely spherical (this is a ludicrous assumption, but a common starting point for modeling binaural sound), with radius a. A sound source is located far from the listener, at an angle θ, and so the sound is approximately a plane wave. This is depicted in Figure 9.9.

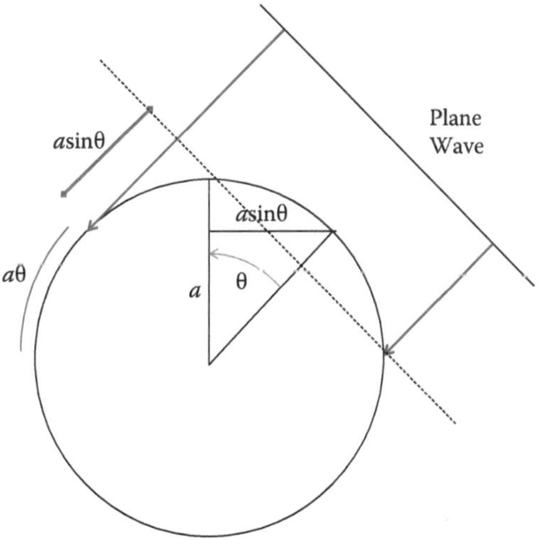

FIGURE 9.9
A sound wave from a distant source acts like a plane wave and approaches a spherical head of radius a from a direction specified by the azimuth angle θ.

Unless $\theta = 0$, the sound will arrive at one ear first. In the figure, this is the right ear. The sound must first travel an additional distance $a\sin\theta$ to reach the left-hand side of the head, and then a distance $a\theta$ to reach the left ear. From this, we have the following estimate of the interaural time difference:

$$ITD = a(\theta + \sin\theta)/c \tag{9.28}$$

From Equation (9.28), the maximum ITD occurs when the sound arrives from one side, along the line that intersects both ears, and is given by $a(\pi/2 + 1)/c$. This is approximately 0.65 ms for a typical human head, which agrees with the measured ITD maximum mentioned above. As with the interchannel time difference that can be exploited in a stereo loudspeaker setup, we can use this effect to change the perceived azimuth angle of a source when listening over either loudspeakers or headphones.

Equation (9.29) provides an implementation of the ITD, where the azimuth is offset to the positions of the ears [73]. It introduces two azimuth-dependent delays, one for each ear:

$$\begin{gathered} T_d(\theta) = \begin{cases} a(1-\cos\theta)/c & |\theta| < \pi/2 \\ a(|\theta| + 1 - \pi/2)/c & \pi/2 < |\theta| < \pi \end{cases} \\ ITD = T_{d,L}(\theta + \pi/2) - T_{d,R}(\theta - \pi/2) = a(\theta + \sin\theta)/c \end{gathered} \tag{9.29}$$

This simple model generates a sound that moves smoothly from the left ear to the right ear as the azimuth goes from –90° to +90°. But it is not effective in creating the impression that the sound came from outside the head, or in assisting with front/back discrimination. Furthermore, though the ITD cue suggests that the source is displaced, the energy at the two ears is the same, and thus the ILD cue indicates that the source is in the center. So the listener may sometimes get the impression of two sounds, one displaced and one at the center of the head. This problem can be addressed by adding head shadow, as discussed next.

ILD Model

Based on Lord Rayleigh's duplex theory, the magnitude response for sound at a frequency ω and azimuth angle θ can be approximated by a simple transfer function [74, 75],

$$H(\omega,\theta) = \frac{\alpha(\theta)\omega + \beta}{\omega + \beta} \tag{9.30}$$

where $\alpha(\theta) = 1 + \cos\theta$ and $\beta = 2c/a$.

This transfer function will give high-frequency attenuation for azimuth angle $\theta = \pi$ and will boost the high-frequency content when $\theta = 0$, as is expected for head shadowing. As in Equation (9.29), if we again offset the azimuth to the ear positions, we get the following model for the ILD:

$$\begin{aligned} H_L(\omega,\theta) &= \frac{\alpha(\theta+\pi/2)\omega+\beta}{\omega+\beta} \\ H_R(\omega,\theta) &= \frac{\alpha(\theta-\pi/2)\omega+\beta}{\omega+\beta} \end{aligned} \tag{9.31}$$

where $\alpha(\theta) = 1 + \cos\theta$ and $\beta = 2c/a$.

As with the ITD model, the ILD model does not provide good front/back discrimination or externalization. However, as the azimuth angle is changed, it can give a smooth perceived motion of the virtual sound source.

At high frequencies, this transfer function will not produce a significant delay between the response for left and right ears. The ITD and ILD models need to be combined so that both time and level information are giving the same spatial cues.

The Spherical Head

By cascading the ITD and the ILD, as in Figure 9.10, we obtain a spherical head model of the HRTF.

The HRTF that we have developed here deals only with the azimuth angle. It could be extended to incorporate both azimuth and elevation angles. However, the elevation cues are much harder to notice and pick up on than the azimuth cues. One reason for this is that the HRTF parameters often need to be fine-tuned to a particular user's ears.

Monaural Pinna Model

The pinnae are the ridges on the outer part of the ear. The way that they reflect incoming sound depends on the angle of the source, and so they provide significant information used for sound localization. Pinna reflections are used in the perception of elevation. And notably, the way that sound reflects off the ridges on the pinnae is used to help distinguish whether a sound source is arriving from in front or in back of the listener. Sounds from behind the listener will have very few of these reflections. So without this information (as when listening over headphones without binaural processing) sound will usually appear to have come from behind the listener, or even from inside his head.

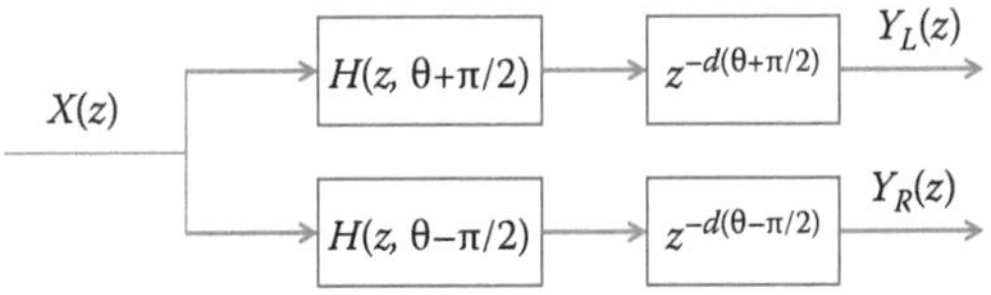

FIGURE 9.10
HRTF modeling ITD and ILD as a filter based on the input signal and azimuth angle.

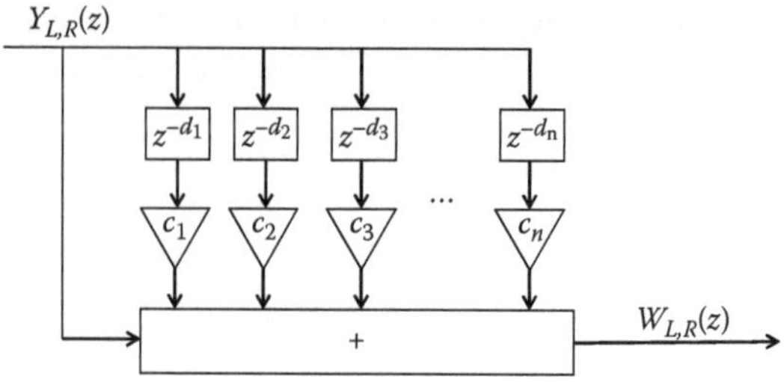

FIGURE 9.11
The pinna echoes implemented as an FIR filter.

The pinnae are also involved in resolving the cone of confusion [70], virtual source locations that all produce the same ITD and ILD values.

Simulation of the pinna reflections can be achieved by tapping a delay line. The pinna reflections are short echoes that result in notches in the spectrum whose positions depend on the elevation angle. A typical simulation of pinna reflections is shown in Figure 9.11. This can be applied independently to the left and right signals, $Y_L(z)$ and $Y_R(z)$, that result from filtering the source.

The gains and time delays are a function of azimuth and elevation. This dependence is nontrivial and may vary from person to person. However, even a simple model helps provide more effective spatialization of the sound.

Implementation

Joint Panorama and Precedence

As mentioned, sound sources can be placed in an apparent location using two factors: delay and amplitude. A delay of 1 ms is enough to give the impression of coming almost completely from one side. A difference in amplitude of 30 dB or more between two equally spaced speakers will have a similar effect.

A simple block diagram that provides control of both panorama and precedence is shown in Figure 9.12. The range of gains and delay values should be set to cover the values in Figures 9.3 and 9.4.

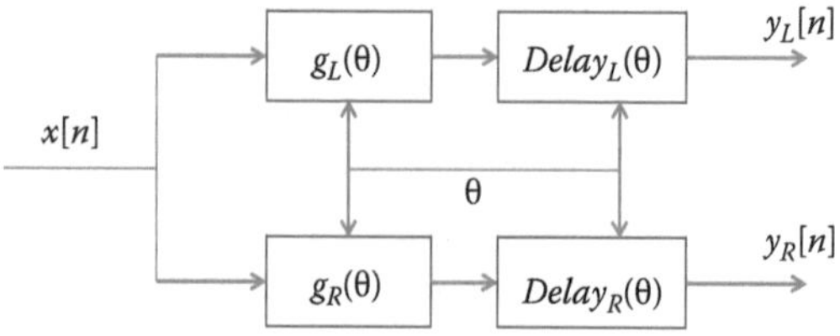

FIGURE 9.12
Joint control of panorama and precedence.

Ambisonics and Its Relationship to VBAP

One popular first-order three-dimensional ambisonics encoding format is known as B-Format. It uses the following channels:

$$\begin{aligned} W &\equiv P_{\alpha,\varepsilon}/\sqrt{2} \\ X &\equiv P_{\psi}\cos\alpha\cos\varepsilon \\ Y &\equiv P_{\psi}\sin\alpha\cos\varepsilon \\ Z &\equiv P_{\psi}\sin\varepsilon \end{aligned} \tag{9.32}$$

The loudspeakers are arranged on the surface of a virtual sphere, and the gains applied to each loudspeaker are found by using a linear combination of these four channels, where each gain depends on the angle of the line between that loudspeaker and the center of the sphere. A popular decoding function is

$$P_n = \left(W/\sqrt{2} + X\cos\alpha_n\cos\varepsilon_n + Y\sin\alpha_n\cos\varepsilon_n + Z\sin\varepsilon_n\right)/N \tag{9.33}$$

Note that this format is written slightly differently from the one we presented for two-dimensional ambisonics, since B-Format has a root 2 term in Equation (9.32).

In other approaches to decoding ambisonics, spatial equalization is applied to the signals to account for the differences in the methods we use for localizing high- and low-frequency sound. Further refinements take into account the distance from the listener to the loudspeakers and to the virtual source location.

Ambisonics can be viewed as an amplitude panning method in which the source signal is applied to all the loudspeakers. For first-order ambisonics, the gains are set as [76]:

$$g_i = (1 + 2\cos\alpha_i)/N \tag{9.34}$$

where g_i is the gain of the ith speaker, N is the number of loudspeakers, and α is the angle between loudspeaker and panning direction. The sound signal is generated by all loudspeakers, which may result in spatial artifacts.

Second-order ambisonics applies the gain factors

$$g_i = (1 + 2\cos\alpha_i + 2\cos 2\alpha_i)/N \tag{9.35}$$

to a similar loudspeaker system. The source signal is still produced by all loudspeakers, but now the gains are significantly less for loudspeakers far from the source direction. This creates fewer artifacts, and higher-order designs offer further improvement. However, we still have constraints on loudspeaker positions and requirements for minimum number of loudspeakers that are not needed for some other amplitude panning techniques, such as VBAP.

Implementation of WFS

Though wave field synthesis has incredibly high potential, it has so far been mostly limited to custom installations. This is at least partly due to the high cost. A very large number of loudspeakers is needed, and hence most WFS implementations are more costly than other spatial audio alternatives.

With most WFS implementations, one of the most perceptible differences between the intended and rendered sound field is error in the reproduction of ambience due to the reduction of the sound field to two dimensions. Furthermore, since WFS attempts to simulate the acoustic characteristics of a recording space, the actual acoustics of the reproduction area must be suppressed. This is often achieved either by minimizing room reflections or by limiting playback to the near field where the direct sound dominates.

There are also undesirable spatial distortions due to spatial aliasing. That is, the discretization to a finite number of loudspeakers results in an inability to effectively render narrow frequency bands. Their frequency depends on the angle of the virtual source and on the angle of the listener to the loudspeaker arrangement.

Since the reproduced wave front is a composite of elementary waves, a sharp pressure change can occur at the last loudspeaker in the array. This is known as the *truncation effect* [69, 77]. It is essentially spectral leakage, but occurring in the spatial domain, and can be viewed as a rectangular window function applied to an infinite array of speakers.

HRTF Calculation

The most common method used to estimate an HRTF from a given source location is to measure the HRIR, $h[n]$. This is done by generating an impulse at the source location and then measuring the received signal at the ear. The HRTF $H(z)$ is then the Fourier transform of the HRIR. Alternatively, HRTFs can also be calculated in the frequency domain using a sine wave whose frequency increases over time, otherwise known as a chirp signal [78].

HRTFs are complicated functions of both spatial location and frequency of the source. But for distances greater than 1 m from the head, the HRTF magnitude is roughly inversely proportional to distance. So at least in most cases, the dependence on distance can be estimated, and it is for this far-field case that the HRTF, $H(f, \theta, \varphi)$, has most often been measured.

An anechoic chamber (Chapter 11) is often used to measure HRTFs, in order to prevent reverberation from causing inaccuracies in the measured response. The HRTFs are measured with varying azimuth and elevation angles, and thus HRTFs at angles that were not measured can be estimated by interpolating between nearby measurements. But even with small increments in the direction of arrival for measured HRTFs, these interpolated values can contain significant errors.

Applications

Transparent Amplification

For a live performance, it is often desirable to place the virtual sound sources all in front of the listener, so that they are perceived as coming from the sound stage. Furthermore, it is important that the time at which the sound is heard agrees with the time it would take for the sound to travel to the listener from the performer seen creating the sound on stage. However, if loudspeakers are placed near the back of the venue and if no delay is applied, they won't be aligned with the front speakers or with the performance. And if only the front loudspeakers are used, listeners near the back of the venue would hear the performance at reduced levels, and without much stereo width. So the audience would not be provided with a well-balanced sound.

One solution, known as *transparent amplification*, is to delay the signal sent to the rear loudspeakers. Ideally, it could be made to match the delay introduced by sound traveling from the front loudspeakers to the rear. However, as long as the delay is at least this long, the precedence effect will help ensure that the perceived location of the sound source is near the front speakers, which are placed close to the stage. So for a room of length L, the delay should be set to $D = L/c$ seconds, where c is the speed of sound.

Surround Sound

Constant power stereo panning can be extended easily to the case of an arbitrary number of loudspeaker channels. This is fundamental to surround sound systems, which aim to reproduce spatial audio to an audience, especially in front of the listeners. In Figure 9.13, angles are given to the right (R), center (C), left (L), surround left (LS), and surround right (RS) channels in a possible surround sound system. Note that most specifications for surround sound will allow some flexibility in the placement of the loudspeakers.

The gain of the two loudspeakers that are on either side of the desired source angle is the same as for the case of two-channel stereo panning, and all other gains are set to zero. Figure 9.14 shows the channel gains, total gain, and total power for five-channel surround sound, using a constant power panning law.

The most common surround sound system is known as 5.1. The "point one" is due to the addition of a subwoofer, which delivers the low-frequency

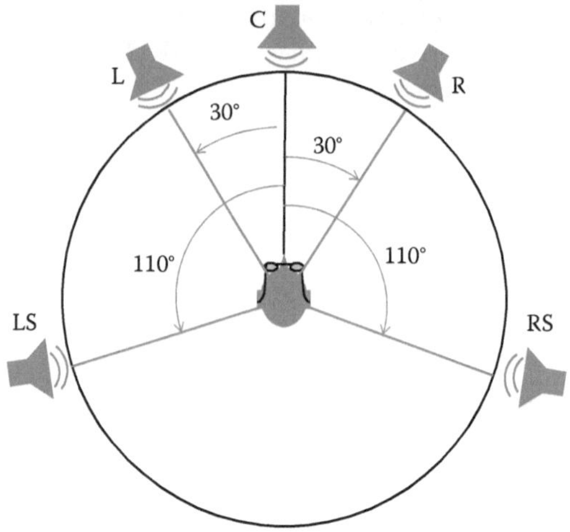

FIGURE 9.13
A five-channel surround sound system.

content. The location of this subwoofer is not considered important, since we do not perform much localization of (very) low frequencies.

Sound Reproduction Using HRTFs

Similar to convolutional reverb (Chapter 11), convolution of a sound signal with the HRIRs for each ear will produce the sound that would have been heard by a listener due to the source being played at the appropriate angle and distance. Using this approach, HRIRs have been employed to create virtual surround sound. When played over headphones, recordings that have been convolved with an HRTF will be perceived as if they comprise sounds coming from various locations around the listener, rather than directly into the ears without any binaural cues. The perceived localization accuracy from this approach will depend on how well the used HRTF matches the characteristics of the listener's actual HRTF.

Some consumer products that are intended to reproduce spatial sound when listened to over headphones will use HRTFs. Variations on HRTF processing are also sometimes used to give the appearance of surround sound playback from computer loudspeakers.

Using an overlap and add method (Chapter 8), it is possible to create the illusion of a moving, rotating sound source about the listener's head. The procedure consists of performing HRTF processing on a small segment of the audio, and then overlap-adding this segment together with another at a slightly different azimuth or elevation angle. The overlap-add does not attempt to perform any processing on the input, as one might do in the case of most phase vocoder applications. It simply attempts to smooth different frames of output.

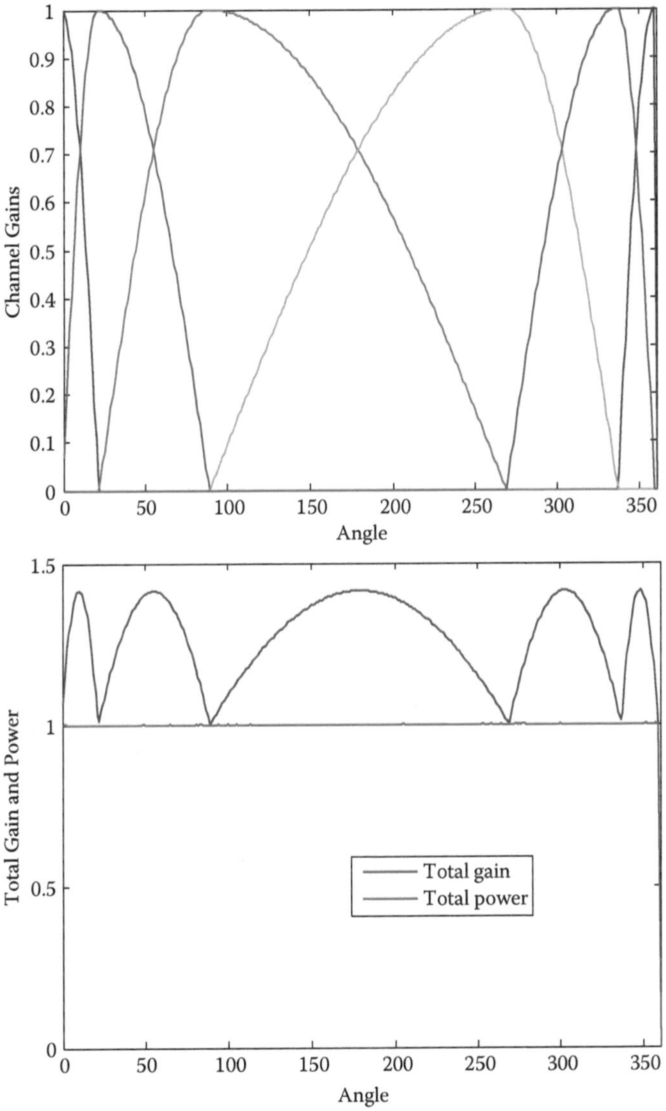

FIGURE 9.14
Constant power panning for five channels: channel gains (top) and total gain and total power (bottom).

Problems

1. Using the formula for ITD, estimate the ITD for a spherical head of radius 8.5 cm, a source in the far field arriving from an angle of 45°, and where the speed of sound is assumed to be 340 m/s.
2. Consider a set of loudspeakers that could be positioned at arbitrary angles on the perimeter of a circle. Given these conditions, explain how ambisonics, stereo panning, multichannel surround sound, vector-based amplitude panning, and wave field synthesis could be used for positioning sources. Comment on the number of loudspeakers, their positions, and the possible positions of sources in each case.
3. Which of the spatial audio techniques that we have discussed, and under which conditions, can represent a source at a given azimuth angle, at a given elevation angle, or with a given depth?
4. Assume loudspeakers are at 45° from the frontal position, and a virtual source is placed at a 30° angle. Estimate the gain applied to each loudspeaker for stereo panning using both the tangent law and the sine law.
5. Consider two-dimensional first-order ambisonics with only three loudspeakers at the angles 0, 120, and 240°. What would be the driving equations for each loudspeaker? Derive the gain applied to each loudspeaker, given a plane wave source at an angle ψ.
6. Assume four loudspeakers, placed at angles $\theta = 45, 135, 225,$ and 315° (so they are equidistant, each 90° apart). Sketch/generate figures for amplitude as a function of virtual azimuth angle under first-order and second-order two-dimensional ambisonics.
7. Compare and contrast ambisonics, wave field synthesis, and vector-based panning. What do they have in common, and what are the advantages and disadvantages of each one?

10

The Doppler Effect

The Doppler effect, named after Austrian mathematician and physicist Christian Andreas Doppler (1803–1853), is the apparent change in frequency of a wave that is perceived due to either motion of the source or motion of the observer.

A Familiar Example

The best way to describe this effect is with a familiar example. Most people have heard an ambulance go by. The pitch of the siren first becomes higher, then lower. This change of pitch as the vehicle moves toward the listener and then moves away is basically the Doppler effect in action. The perceived change of pitch is due to a shift in the frequency of the sound wave.

As the ambulance moves toward the listener, as shown in Figure 10.1a, the sound waves from its siren appear condensed, relative to the listener. Thus, intervals between the waves are reduced, which results in an increase in frequency or pitch. Then once the ambulance has passed and is now moving away from the listener, as in Figure 10.1b, the sound waves are stretched relative to the listener, causing a decrease in the siren's pitch. The change in pitch

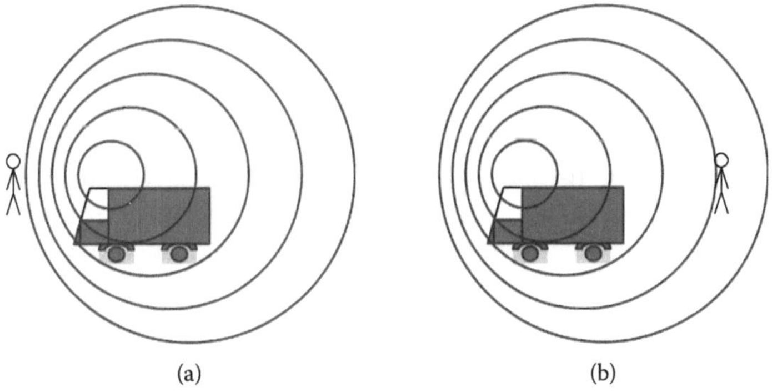

FIGURE 10.1
An ambulance siren produces the Doppler effect. A higher pitch is perceived when the ambulance moves toward the listener (a), and a lower pitch is perceived when the ambulance moves away from the listener (b).

of the siren allows one to determine whether the ambulance is approaching nearer or speeding away.

Consider a stationary sound source that is producing a constant frequency f_0. The wave fronts emanating from this source propagate in all directions away from the source at the speed of sound c. The distance between wave fronts with the same phase is the wavelength. Without movement of the source, this wavelength remains constant. So all stationary listeners will hear the frequency of the source.

Now suppose this sound source is moving toward the listener. The wave fronts are still created with the same frequency f_0. But because the source is moving, the wave fronts will be compressed in front of the moving source and will be spread farther apart behind the source. Thus, if the source moves toward the listener, he or she will hear a higher frequency, $f > f_0$, and a listener placed behind the moving source will hear a lower frequency, $f' < f_0$.

BREAKING THE SOUND BARRIER

Consider a source moving at the speed of sound (Mach 1). The sounds it produces will travel at the same speed as the source, so that in front of the source, each new wavefront is compressed to occur at the same point. A listener placed in front of the source will not detect anything until the source arrives. All the wavefronts add together, creating a wall of pressure. This shock wave will not be perceived as a pitch but as a "thump" as the pressure front passes the listener.

Pilots who have flown at Mach 1 have described a noticeable "barrier" that must be penetrated before achieving supersonic speeds. Traveling within the pressure front results in a bouncy, turbulent flight.

Now consider a sound source moving at supersonic speed, i.e., faster than the speed of sound. In this case, the source will be in advance of the wavefront. So a stationary listener will hear the sound after the source has passed by. The shock wave forms a Mach cone, which is a conical pressure front with the plane at the tip. This cone creates the sonic boom shock wave as a supersonic aircraft passes by. This shock wave travels at the speed of sound, and since it is the combination of all the wavefronts, the listener will hear a quite intense sound. However, supersonic aircraft actually produce two sonic booms in quick succession. One boom comes from the aircraft's nose and the other one from its tail, resulting in a double thump.

The speed of sound varies with temperature and humidity, but not directly with pressure. In air at sea level, it is about 343 m/s. But in water, the speed of sound is far quicker (about 1,484 m/s), since molecules in water are more compressed than in air and sound is produced by the vibrations of the substance. So the sound barrier can be broken at different speeds depending on air conditions, but is far more difficult to break underwater.

Derivation of the Doppler Effect

Simple Derivation of the Basic Doppler Effect

We first start with a simple derivation of the Doppler effect, where we ignore the fact that source and listener velocities may be changing over time. Suppose the listener moves toward the source with velocity v_{ls} and the source moves toward the listener with velocity v_{sl} (these can be negative for source/listener moving away from listener/source). Consider a sound emitted by the source with a frequency f_s. The period is then $T_s = 1/f_s$. Assume that initially the source is at position 0 and the listener is at position x.

At time t_1, the sound produced by the source at time 0 has now traveled to a position $c \cdot t_1$. The listener is at position $x - v_{ls}t_1$. So the sound has reached the listener when these are equal, that is, at time $t_1 = x/(c + v_{ls})$.

At time t_2, the sound produced by the source at time T_s has now traveled to a position $v_{sl}T_s + c(t_2 - T_s)$. The listener is at $x - v_{ls}t_2$. So the sound has reached the listener when $v_{sl} \cdot T_s + c(t_2 - T_s) = x - v_{ls}t_2$, that is, at time $t_2 = (x - v_{sl} \cdot T_s + c \cdot T_s)/(c + v_{ls})$.

Thus, the Doppler shifted period is $T_l = t_2 - t_1 = T_s(c - v_{sl})/(c + v_{ls})$. The Doppler shifted frequency is just one over this Doppler shifted period, and hence we have the one-dimensional Doppler formula:

$$\frac{f_l}{f_s} = \frac{c + v_{ls}}{c - v_{sl}} \tag{10.1}$$

For movement in three dimensions, we simply consider vector velocities and their scalar components along the line between source and listener.

The scalar velocity v_{sl} of a source in the direction from the source to the listener is given by

$$v_{sl} = \overline{v}_s \cdot \hat{x}_{sl} = \overline{v}_s \cdot \overline{x}_{sl} / \|\overline{x}_{sl}\| \tag{10.2}$$

And similarly, the scalar velocity v_{ls} of a listener in the direction from the source to the listener is given by

$$v_{ls} = \overline{v}_l \cdot \hat{x}_{ls} = \overline{v}_l \cdot \overline{x}_{ls} / \|\overline{x}_{ls}\| \tag{10.3}$$

We use the scalar projection since it prevents us from having to use the vector velocities, and as we shall see, it correctly provides the sign of the velocity.

These values are then plugged directly into Equation (10.1), giving

$$\frac{f_l}{f_s} = \frac{c + \overline{v}_l \cdot \overline{x}_{ls} / \|\overline{x}_{ls}\|}{c - \overline{v}_s \cdot \overline{x}_{sl} / \|\overline{x}_{sl}\|} \tag{10.4}$$

FIGURE 10.2
A moving source emits a sound at time τ, which is heard by a moving listener at time t.

General Derivation of the Doppler Effect

Now let's consider the general case, without approximations. A sound is emitted from a source at time τ and heard by the listener at time t. Both source and listener are moving, with position x_l and velocity v_l for the listener and position x_s and velocity v_s for the listener. This is depicted in Figure 10.2.

Consider a single-frequency component, expressed as a complex exponential. At time t, the listener hears the sound $e^{j\omega_s\tau}$, where $\omega_s = 2\pi f_s$, produced at some previous time τ, so

$$\left\|\overline{x}_l(t) - \overline{x}_s(\tau)\right\| = c(t-\tau) \tag{10.5}$$

That is, the distance between the two positions is the time it takes sound to travel between them multiplied by the speed of sound. Note that τ is dependent on time, since a small change in t must come from the sound being produced at a different time τ. Now let's consider the time derivative of this:

$$\frac{\partial\left\|\overline{x}_l(t) - \overline{x}_s(\tau)\right\|}{\partial t} = c\left(1 - \frac{\partial\tau}{\partial t}\right) \tag{10.6}$$

When the sound is emitted at time τ, the frequency component $e^{j\omega_s\tau}$ has instantaneous phase $\varphi = \omega_s\tau$ and instantaneous angular frequency $\omega_s = \partial\phi/\partial\tau$. We need to find the new instantaneous angular frequency when this sound is heard by the listener, $\omega_s = \partial\phi/\partial\tau$. So,

$$\frac{\partial\tau}{\partial t} = \frac{\partial\tau}{\partial\phi}\frac{\partial\phi}{\partial t} = \frac{\omega_l(t)}{\omega_s} \tag{10.7}$$

Now we use a well-known property from vector algebra. The derivative of the magnitude of a vector is the dot product of the unit length direction vector and the vector velocity (i.e., the derivative of each component of the vector):

$$\begin{aligned}\frac{\partial\|v\|}{\partial t} &= \frac{\partial\sqrt{v_x^2+v_y^2+v_z^2}}{\partial t} \\ &= \left(v_x^2+v_y^2+v_z^2\right)^{-1/2}\left(v_x\frac{\partial v_x}{\partial t}+v_y\frac{\partial v_y}{\partial t}+v_z\frac{\partial v_z}{\partial t}\right)=\frac{v}{\|v\|}\cdot\dot{v}\end{aligned} \tag{10.8}$$

So,

$$c\left(1-\frac{\omega_l(t)}{\omega_s}\right)=\frac{\left[\bar{x}_l(t)-\bar{x}_s(\tau)\right]\cdot\dfrac{\partial(\bar{x}_l(t)-\bar{x}_s(\tau))}{\partial t}}{\|\bar{x}_l(t)-\bar{x}_s(\tau)\|} \tag{10.9}$$

The derivative term on the right-hand side of this equation is

$$\frac{\partial(\bar{x}_l(t)-\bar{x}_s(\tau))}{\partial t}=\bar{v}_l(t)-\bar{v}_s(\tau)\frac{\partial\tau}{\partial t}=\bar{v}_l(t)-\bar{v}_s(\tau)\frac{\omega_l(t)}{\omega_s} \tag{10.10}$$

So,

$$\begin{aligned}c\left(1-\frac{\omega_l(t)}{\omega_s}\right)&=\frac{\left[\bar{v}_l(t)-\omega_l(t)\bar{v}_s(\tau)/\omega_s\right]\cdot\left[\bar{x}_l(t)-\bar{x}_s(\tau)\right]}{\|\bar{x}_l(t)-\bar{x}_s(\tau)\|} \\ &=\frac{\bar{v}_l(t)\cdot\left[\bar{x}_l(t)-\bar{x}_s(\tau)\right]}{\|\bar{x}_l(t)-\bar{x}_s(\tau)\|}-\frac{\omega_l(t)}{\omega_s}\frac{\bar{v}_s(\tau)\cdot\left[\bar{x}_l(t)-\bar{x}_s(\tau)\right]}{\|\bar{x}_l(t)-\bar{x}_s(\tau)\|}\end{aligned} \tag{10.11}$$

And by rearranging terms,

$$\frac{\omega_l(t)}{\omega_s}=\frac{c-\bar{v}_l(t)\cdot\left[\bar{x}_l(t)-\bar{x}_s(\tau)\right]/\|\bar{x}_l(t)-\bar{x}_s(\tau)\|}{c-\bar{v}_s(\tau)\cdot\left[\bar{x}_l(t)-\bar{x}_s(\tau)\right]/\|\bar{x}_l(t)-\bar{x}_s(\tau)\|} \tag{10.12}$$

This then is the full Doppler effect, explaining the change in frequency of a moving source as perceived by a moving listener. We can integrate this to get the instantaneous phase of the sound heard by the listener:

$$\phi_l(t)=\int_0^t \omega_l(t')dt'+\phi_l(0) \tag{10.13}$$

So if there is time dependence in ω_l, then $e^{j\omega_s\tau}$ does not give rise to $e^{j\omega_l\tau}$, but rather, it gives rise to $e^{j\phi_l\tau}$.

This derivation of the Doppler is most closely related to the ones in [67] and [79]. But these derivations are restricted to a stationary listener, and assume the source moves with constant velocity. It is also similar, at least in notation, to Julius Smith's vector formulation [1, 80], but this is not derived and assumes that the times the sound is emitted by the source and received by the listener are equal. Related derivations are also provided in [81, 82].

Simplifications and Approximations

If the listener is stationary, $\overline{v}_l(t) = 0$ and Equation (10.12) reduces to

$$\frac{\omega_l}{\omega_s} = \frac{c}{c - \overline{v}_s(\tau) \cdot \overline{x}_l - \overline{x}_s(\tau) / \left\| \overline{x}_l - \overline{x}_s(\tau) \right\|} \tag{10.14}$$

Whereas if the source is stationary, $\overline{v}_s(\tau) = 0$ and the Doppler effect reduces to

$$\frac{\omega_l(t)}{\omega_s} = \frac{c - \overline{v}_l(t) \cdot \left[\overline{x}_l(t) - \overline{x}_s \right] / \left\| \overline{x}_l(t) - \overline{x}_s \right\|}{c} \tag{10.15}$$

If we assume that the *velocities are much less than c*, then the distance between source and listener is large compared to the distance a source or listener moves during the time it takes for sound to travel from source to listener. So, we assume the velocities and positions are roughly constant over the time period from t to τ,

$$\frac{\omega_l}{\omega_s} \approx \frac{c - \overline{v}_l \cdot \left[\overline{x}_l - \overline{x}_s \right] / \left\| \overline{x}_l - \overline{x}_s \right\|}{c - \overline{v}_s \cdot \left[\overline{x}_l - \overline{x}_s \right] / \left\| \overline{x}_l - \overline{x}_s \right\|} = \frac{c + v_{ls}}{c - v_{sl}} \tag{10.16}$$

where all distances and velocities are taken at the same time. This is the simple version of the vector Doppler formula.

And if the motion of both source and listener is in one dimension (they are traveling along a line), then the position and velocity vectors become scalars. Thus,

$$\frac{\omega_l}{\omega_s} = \frac{c - v_l(t) \operatorname{sgn}\left[x_l(t) - x_s(\tau) \right]}{c - v_s(\tau) \operatorname{sgn}\left[x_l(t) - x_s(\tau) \right]} \tag{10.17}$$

which is also equivalent to the plane wave case.

Implementation

It is well known that a time-varying delay line results in a frequency shift. We have seen in Chapter 2 that time-varying delay is often used, for example, to provide *vibrato* and *chorus* effects. We therefore expect a time-varying delay line to be capable of precise Doppler simulation.

The implementation of the Doppler shift can be achieved by directly applying the movement of sources and listeners in a natural environment. The air between the source and listener can be represented as a delay line. A write pointer can be used to represent the source, and a read pointer represents the listener. If both source and listener are stationary, the listener simply receives the source with a delay. The distance between source and listener is represented by the distance on the delay line between the two pointers, and the speed of sound equates to incrementing the pointers from one sample to the next at each time step. If either listener or source is moving, a Doppler shift is observed by the listener, according to the Doppler equation. For now, let us consider the simplified Doppler equation, given in Equations (10.1) and (10.16).

Changing the read pointer increment from 1 sample to $1 + v_{ls}/c$ samples (thereby requiring interpolated reads) corresponds to listener motion away from the source at speed v_{ls}. Similarly, changing the write pointer increment from 1 to $1 + v_{ls}/c$ corresponds to source motion toward the listener at speed v_{ls}. But when changing the increment of the write pointer, we use *interpolating writes* into the buffer, also known as *deinterpolation.* A review of time-varying, interpolating, delay line reads and writes, together with a method using a single shared pointer, is given in [83].

Time-Varying Delay Line Reads

If $x[n]$ denotes input to time-varying delay, the output can be written as $y[n] = x[n - d(n)]$, where $d(n)$ denotes the time-varying delay in samples, at sample n. But the delay is typically not an integer multiple of the sampling interval. So $x[n - d(n)]$ may be approximated using *band-limited interpolation* or other techniques for implementation of *fractional delay,* as discussed in Chapter 2.

Let's analyze the frequency shift caused by a time-varying delay by setting a continuous time signal $x(t)$ to a complex sinusoid at frequency ω_s:

$$x(t) = e^{j\omega_s t} \tag{10.18}$$

The output is now

$$y(t) = x\big(t - D(t)\big) = e^{j\omega_s(t-D(t))} \tag{10.19}$$

The exponent gives the instantaneous phase of this signal,

$$\theta(t) = \omega_s\left(t - D(t)\right) \tag{10.20}$$

where $D(t)$ is the time-varying delay in seconds. As mentioned in the derivation of the Doppler effect, the instantaneous frequency is just the derivative of the instantaneous phase,

$$\omega_l = \omega_s\left(1 - dD(t)/dt\right) \tag{10.21}$$

where ω_l denotes the output frequency. The time derivative of the delay, $dD(t)/dt$, represents the *delay growth rate*, or the *relative frequency downshift*:

$$dD(t)/dt = \frac{\omega_s - \omega_l}{\omega_s} \tag{10.22}$$

which can be rewritten as

$$\frac{\omega_l}{\omega_s} = \frac{f_l}{f_s} = 1 - dD(t)/dt \tag{10.23}$$

So from Equation (10.1), if the source is stationary and we have a moving listener, we have

$$dD(t)/dt = -v_{ls}/c \tag{10.24}$$

That is, the delay growth rate should be set to the normalized speed of the listener *away* from the source. Simulating source motion is also possible, but the relation between delay change and desired frequency shift is more complex. From Equations (10.1) and (10.22),

$$dD(t)/dt = -\frac{v_{ls}/c + v_{sl}/c}{1 - v_{sl}/c} = -\frac{v_{ls} + v_{sl}}{c - v_{sl}} \tag{10.25}$$

A simplified approach is possible using multiple write pointers to move the delay input instead of its output.

Multiple Write Pointers

If multiple write pointers are located with a fixed spacing between them, then they represent a set of stationary sources. But for moving sources, where

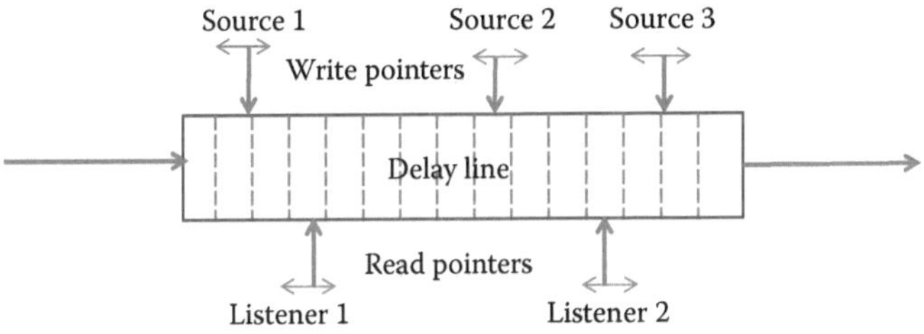

FIGURE 10.3
A delay line with multiple read and write pointers, corresponding to multiple sources and listeners.

each source produces its own Doppler effect, the write pointers will move independently of each other. Each write pointer will write a different signal, and a unique filter can be applied to that signal. This source-dependent filter can be used to implement the filtering incurred along the propagation path from each source to a single listener.

When a circular buffer is used, the write pointer that is writing farthest ahead in time will *overwrite* memory, instead of summing into it. The write pointers may cross each other without causing issues, since all but this first pointer will just sum into the shared delay line.

So, a single delay line can simulate any number of moving sources and a single listener, or a single source and any number of moving listeners. But is this still the case if we have both moving sources and moving listeners (as depicted in Figure 10.3)? The different listeners will not perceive the same Doppler shift for each moving source. So the movement of the read pointer will not accurately represent the movement of multiple sources, and we need either a delay line for every moving source or a delay line for every moving listener. In fact, for M moving sources and N moving listeners, our Doppler simulation approach will require min(M, N) delay lines [80].

Code Example

The time-varying delay line was described in Chapter 2. Here, we provide C/C++ pseudocode, based on [1], for a time-varying delay line used in simulating the Doppler effect. Note that the code below features an interpolated read, but not an interpolated write, which can be implemented in the same manner.

```
// Variables whose values are set externally:
float *delayData;    // Our own circular buffer of samples
int delayBufLength; // Length of our delay buffer in samples
int writePointer;    // Write location in the delay buffer
float readPointer;   // Read location in the delay buffer
```

```
// User-adjustable effect parameters:
float delta_;       // Derivative of delay time

// Set the delay in (fractional) number of samples, by
// calculating the read pointer relative to the write
// pointer
void setDelay(float delayLength)
{
    readPointer = (float)writePointer - delayLength;
    while(readPointer < 0)
        readPointer += (float)delayBufLength;
}

// Process a group of samples in channelData, putting the
// output in the same buffer where the input came from
void process(float *channelData, int numSamples)
{
    for (int i = 0; i < numSamples; ++i)
    {
        const float in = channelData[i];
        float out = 0.0;

        int sampleBefore = floor(readPointer);
        int sampleAfter = (sampleBefore + 1) %
                          delayBufLength;
        float fractionalOffset = readPointer -
                          (float)sampleBefore;

        // Calculate the output using linear interpolation
        // between samples before and after
        float out = (1.0 - fractionalOffset) *
                    delayData[sampleBefore] +
                    fractionalOffset *
                    delayData[sampleAfter];

        // Store the current sample in the delay buffer
        delayData[writePointer] = in;

        // Increment the pointers. Write pointer is an
        // integer so will always wrap around strictly to 0;
        // read pointer is fractional so may wrap around to
        // a fractional value
        if(++writePointer >= delayBufLength)
            writePointer = 0;
        readPointer += 1.0 - delta_;
        if(readPointer >= delayBufLength)
            readPointer -= (float)delayBufLength;
```

```
        // Store output in buffer, replacing the input
        channelData[i] = out;
    }
}
```

Delta (Δ) is the growth parameter, corresponding to the derivative of the time-varying delay, i.e., $dD(t)/dt = \Delta$. When $\Delta = 0$, we have a fixed delay line and there is no relative movement between source and listener. But when $\Delta > 0$, the delay grows by Δ samples per sample, which we may also interpret as seconds per second. By Equation (10.24), we can see that $\Delta = -v_{ls}/c$ will simulate a listener traveling toward the source at speed v_{ls}.

DOPPLER, LESLIE, AND HAMMOND

Donald Leslie (1913–2004) bought a Hammond organ in 1937, as a substitute for a pipe organ. But at home in a small room, it could not reproduce the grand sound of an organ. Since the pipe organ has different locations for each pipe, he designed a moving loudspeaker.

The Leslie speaker uses an electric motor to move an acoustic horn in a circle around a loudspeaker. Thus, we have a moving sound source and a stationary listener, as shown in Figure 10.4.

It exploits the Doppler effect to produce frequency modulation. The classic Leslie speaker has a crossover that divides the low and high frequencies. It consists of a fixed treble unit with spinning horns, a fixed woofer, and a spinning rotor. Both the horns (actually, one horn and a dummy used as a counterbalance) and a bass sound baffle rotate, thus creating vibrato due to the changing velocity in the direction of the listener, and tremolo due to the changing distance. The rotating elements can move at varied speeds, or be stopped completely. Furthermore, the system is partially enclosed and uses a rotating speaker port. So the listener hears multiple reflections at different Doppler shifts to produce a chorus-like effect.

The Leslie speaker has been widely used in popular music, especially when the Hammond B-3 organ was played out through a Leslie speaker. This combination can be heard on many classic and progressive rock songs, including hits by Boston, Santana, Steppenwolf, Deep Purple, and The Doors. And the Leslie speaker has also found extensive use in modifying guitar and vocal sounds.

Ironically, Donald Leslie had originally tried to license his loudspeaker to the Hammond company, and even gave the Hammond company a special demonstration. But at the time, Laurens Hammond (founder of the Hammond organ company) did not like the concept at all.

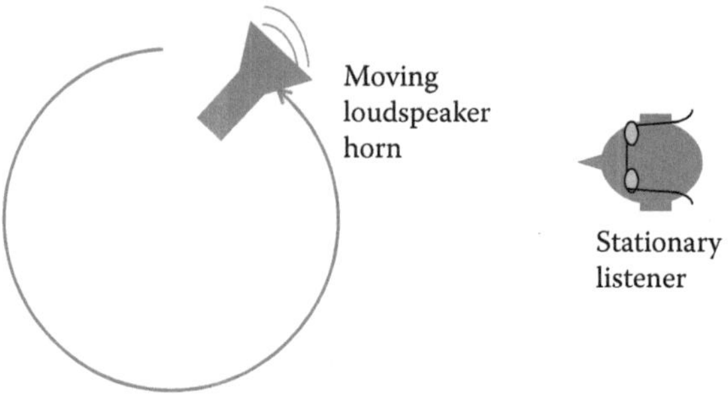

FIGURE 10.4
A moving loudspeaker and stationary listener, as in a Leslie speaker.

Note that when the read and write pointers are driven directly from a model of sound propagation in a natural environment, they are always separated by predictable minimum and maximum delay intervals [1]. This implies it should not be necessary to worry about the read pointer passing the write pointers, or vice versa (though good programming practice suggests that an implementation should always check if this happens).

Applications

The Doppler effect is used in sound design and composition in order to achieve realistic simulation of moving sound sources, and is one of the main characteristics of the Leslie speaker.

The Doppler effect is used heavily in a lot of game and film special effects, to give a sense of realism or even hyperrealism. Moving sources often have an exaggerated frequency shift to ensure that the listener picks up on auditory cues and focuses attention on the moving source.

SWINGING MICROPHONES AND SLASHING LIGHTSABERS

Sound designers for film and games often use creative methods to generate the appropriate sound from existing sources, rather than through signal processing techniques designed to synthesise or process audio. One well-known technique for generating the Doppler effect is to swing a microphone back and forth in front of a sound source. This was used in the original Star Wars to generate the original lightsaber sound. As described by Ben Burtt, the sound designer: "… once we had established this tone of the lightsaber of course you had to get the sense of the lightsaber moving because characters would carry it around, they would whip it through the air, they would thrust and slash at each other in fights, and to achieve this addtional sense of movement I played the sound over a speaker in a room.

"Just the humming sound, the humming and the buzzing combined as an endless sound, and then I took another microphone and waved it in the air next to that speaker so that it would come close to the speaker and go away and you could whip it by. And what happens when you do that by recording with a moving microphone is you get a Doppler's shift, you get a pitch shift in the sound and therefore you can produce a very authentic facsimilie of a moving sound. And therefore give the lightsaber a sense of movement…" [84].

Problems

1. From the formulae

$$\frac{\omega_l}{\omega_s} \approx \frac{c + v_{ls}}{c - v_{sl}}, \; v_{ls} = \overline{v}_l \cdot \hat{x}_{ls}, \; v_{sl} = \overline{v}_s \cdot \hat{x}_{sl},$$

show that the relative change in frequency is given by

$$\frac{\omega_l - \omega_s}{\omega_s} = \frac{(\overline{v}_l - \overline{v}_s) \cdot \hat{x}_{ls}}{c + \overline{v}_s \cdot \hat{x}_{ls}}.$$

2. Find an expression for the Doppler effect for a source moving in a straight line at constant velocity through a stationary listener located at 0. At time 0, the source is at the same location as the listener.
3. Find an expression for the Doppler effect for a source and listener moving on x-axis with constant velocities. At time 0, both the source and listener are at 0.

4. a. Assume the listener is fixed at 0, and the source moves with constant acceleration away from the listener. Find an expression for the Doppler effect.
   b. Assume this source is emitting a single frequency, $e^{j\omega_s\tau}$, at any time τ. What frequency component(s) does the listener receive at time t?
5. Assume a source is moving with constant angular velocity on a circle (or sphere) of radius r_s, and the listener is fixed at $(r_l, 0)$. Find an expression for the Doppler effect.
6. Suppose a source moves in a straight line toward the listener at constant speed $2c$. Show that for each frequency f emitted by the source, the apparent sound heard by the listener has frequency $-f$. In relation to the original sound produced by the source, what does the listener hear?
7. Find an expression for the Doppler effect for a source moving in a straight line on the x-axis past the listener. Specifically, assume the sound source velocity is (10, 0), the listener position is (0, 2), the initial source position is (–10, 0), the speed of sound is 340 m/s, and the frequency emitted by the sound source is 1000 Hz. What frequency is heard by the listener?
8. Simulating Doppler typically involves time-varying delay lines. What sort of artifacts and issues might arise? You may wish to refer to the discussion of delay lines in previous chapters.

11

Reverberation

Reverberation (*reverb*) is one of the most often used effects in audio production. In this chapter, we will look at the causes, the main characteristics, and the measures of reverb. We then focus on how to simulate reverb. First we describe algorithmic approaches to generating reverb, focusing on two classic designs. Then we look at a popular technique for generating a room impulse response, the image source method. Next, we describe convolutional reverb, which adds reverb to a signal by convolving that signal with a room impulse response, either recorded or simulated (such as from using the image source method). The chapter concludes by looking at implementation details and applications.

Theory

In a room, or any acoustic environment, there is a direct path from any sound source to a listener, but sound waves also take longer paths by reflecting off the walls, ceiling, or objects, before they arrive at the listener, as shown in Figure 11.1. These reflected sound waves travel a longer distance than the direct sound and are partly absorbed by the surfaces, so they take longer to arrive and are weaker than the direct sound. These sound waves can also reflect off of multiple surfaces before they arrive at the listener. These delayed and attenuated copies of the original sound are what we call reverberation, and it is essential to the perception of spaciousness in the sounds.

Reverberation is more than just a series of echoes. An echo is the result of a distinct, delayed version of a sound, as could be heard with a delay of at least 40 ms. With reverberation from a typical room, there are many, many reflections, and the early reflections arrive on a much shorter time scale. So these reflections are not perceived as distinct from the sound source. Instead, we perceive the effect of the combination of all the reflections.

Reverberation is also more than a simple delay device with feedback. With reverb the rate at which the reflections arrive will change over time, as opposed to just simulating reflections that have a fixed time interval between them. In reverberation, there is a set of reflections that occur shortly after the direct sound. These *early reflections* are related to the position of the source and listener in the room, as well as the room's shape, size, and material

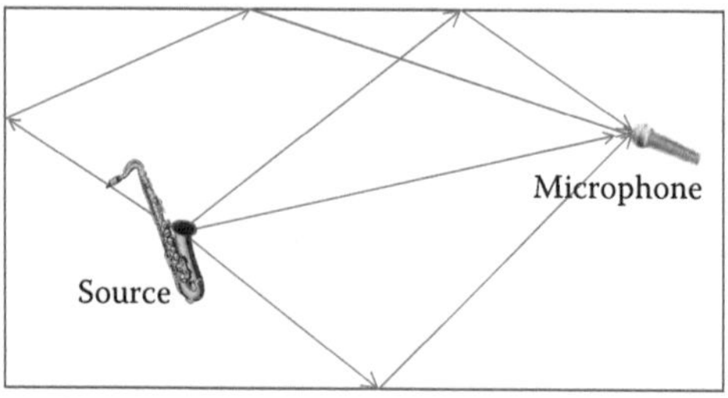

FIGURE 11.1
Reverb is the result of sound waves traveling many different paths from a source to a listener.

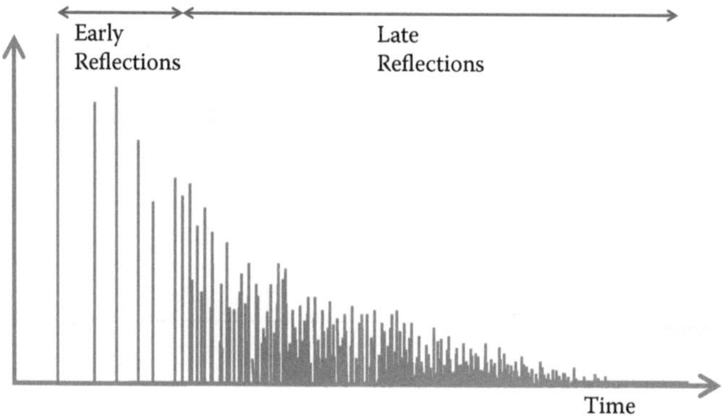

FIGURE 11.2
Impulse response of a room.

composition. The later reflections arrive much more frequently, appear more randomly, usually decay exponentially, and are difficult to directly relate to the physical characteristics of the room. These *late reflections* give rise to *diffuse reverberation.* An example impulse response for a room is depicted in Figure 11.2. Each vertical line marks when the original sound is repeated, and the height of each of these lines is the amplitude of the sound at that time.

A measure that is often used to characterize the reverb in an acoustic space is the *reverberation time,* often denoted RT_{60}. This is the time that it takes for sound pressure level or intensity to decay by 60 dB, i.e., 1/1,000,000th of its original intensity, or 1/1000th of its original amplitude (see Chapter 1). A long reverberation time implies that the reflections remain strong for a long time before their energy is absorbed. The reverberation time is associated with room size. Small rooms tend to have reverb times on the order of hundreds of milliseconds, though this can vary greatly depending on the acoustic treatment and other factors. Larger rooms will usually have longer reverberation times since, on average, the sound waves will travel a larger distance between reflections. Concert halls typically have reverberation times around

1.5 to 2 s. Cathedrals and other highly reverberant environments may have reverb times of more than 3 s.

It is possible to construct a large room with short reverberation time, and vice versa. The reverberation time is dictated primarily by the size of the room and the surfaces in the room. The surfaces determine how much energy is lost or absorbed each time the sound is reflected. Highly reflective materials, such as a concrete or tile floor, will result in a long reverb time. Absorptive materials, such as curtains, cushions, or heavy carpet, will reduce the reverberation time. People and their clothing absorb a lot of sound. This explains why a room may sound "bigger" during a sound check prior to a performance, but smaller and more intimate once the audience has arrived. The absorptivity of most materials usually varies with frequency, which is one reason the reverb time is dependent on the spectral content of the source signal (formal measurement of reverb time is performed using an impulse or turning off a noise generator). The air in the room will also attenuate the sound waves, reducing the reverberation time. This attenuation is a function of temperature and humidity and is most significant for high frequencies. Because of this, many audio effect implementations of reverb will include some form of low-pass filtering, as will be discussed later in this chapter.

Another important measure of reverberation is the *echo density*, defined as the frequency of peaks (number of echoes per second) at a certain time t during the impulse response. The more tightly packed together the reflections are, the higher the echo density. If the echo density is larger than 20–30 echoes per second, the ear no longer hears the echoes as separate events, but fuses them into a sensation of continuous decay. In other words, the early reflections become a late reverberation.

Sabine and Norris–Eyring Equations

The *mean free path* of a room gives the average distance a sound wave will travel before it hits a surface. Assuming a rectangular box room, this is given by $4V/S$, where V is the volume and S is the surface area of the room. Dividing this by the speed of sound c, the mean time τ until a sound source hits a wall is $\tau = 4V/(cS)$. So the mean number of reflections over a time t is

$$n(t) = t/\tau = t\frac{cS}{4V} \tag{11.1}$$

At each reflection off a surface S_i, α_i is the proportion of the energy absorbed. So $1 - \alpha_i$ is the proportion of the energy that is reflected back into the room. Now assume all surfaces have the same absorption coefficient, α. So after n reflections, the sound has been reduced by a factor $(1 - \alpha)^n$. Thus, after a time t, the sound energy has been reduced to

$$E(t) = (1-\alpha)^{tcA/(4V)}E(0) \tag{11.2}$$

Taking the log base (1 – α) of both sides, we have

$$\log_{(1-\alpha)}\left(E(t)/E(0)\right) = tcS/(4V) \tag{11.3}$$

Now recall that $\log_A(x) = \ln(x)/\ln(A)$. So, putting the time t on one side,

$$t = \frac{4V\log_{(1-\alpha)}\left(E(t)/E(0)\right)}{cS} = \frac{4V\ln\left(E(t)/E(0)\right)}{cS\ln(1-\alpha)} \tag{11.4}$$

Recall that the reverberation time, RT_{60}, is the time for the sound energy to decrease by 60 dB. Thus,

$$RT_{60} = \frac{4V\ln(10^{-6})}{cS\ln(1-\alpha)} \approx \frac{-0.161V}{S\ln(1-\alpha)} \tag{11.5}$$

This is known as the Norris–Eyring formula. However, it has several approximations. The most important is that it assumes a single absorption coefficient, α. A more accurate form of Equation (11.5) is

$$RT_{60} = \frac{-0.161V}{S\ln\left(1-\frac{1}{S}\sum_i S_i\alpha_i\right)} \tag{11.6}$$

Alternatively, it can be simplified even further. For small α, ln(1 – α) ~ –α. So Equation (11.5) becomes

$$RT_{60} \approx \frac{0.161V}{S\alpha} \tag{11.7}$$

This is the Sabine equation, which was first found empirically by Wallace Clement Sabine in the late 1890s.

The absorption coefficient of a material ranges from 0 to 1 and indicates the proportion of sound that is not reflected by (so either absorbed by or transmitted through) the surface. A thick, smooth painted concrete ceiling would have an absorption coefficient very close to 0. Analogous to a mirror reflecting light, almost all sound would be reflected with very little attenuation. Conversely, a large, fully open window would have an absorption coefficient of 1, since any sound reaching it would pass straight through and not be reflected, in which case Sabine's formula would be a very poor approximation, since it could still generate significant reverberation time.

As mentioned, absorption, and hence the reverberation time, is a function of frequency. Usually, less sound energy is absorbed in the lower-frequency ranges, resulting in longer reverb times at lower frequencies. Nor do the equations above take into account room shape or losses from the sound traveling through the air, which is important in larger spaces. More detailed discussion of the reverbation time formulae (with differing interpretations) is available in [85, 86].

Direct and Reverberant Sound Fields

The reverberation due to sound reflection off surfaces is extremely important. Reverberation keeps sound energy contained within a room, raising the sound pressure level and distributing the sound throughout. Outside in the open, there are far less reflective surfaces, and hence much of the sound energy is lost.

For music, reverberation helps ensure that one hears all the instruments, even though they may be at different distances from the listeners. Also, many acoustic instruments will not radiate all frequencies equally in all directions. For example, without reverberation the sound of a violin may change considerably as the listener moves with respect to the violin. The reverberation in the room helps to diffuse the energy a sound wave makes so that it can appear more uniform when it reaches the listener. But when the reverberation time becomes very large, it can affect speech intelligibility and make it difficult to follow intricate music.

A distinction is often made between the direct and reverberant sound fields in a room. The sound heard by a listener will be a combination of the direct sound and the early and late reflections due to reverberation. When the sound pressure due to the direct sound is greater than that due to the reflections, the listener is in the *direct field*. Otherwise, the listener is in the *reverberant field*.

The *critical distance* is defined as the distance away from a source at which the sound pressure levels of the direct and reverberant sound fields are equal. This distance depends on the shape, size, and absorption of the space, as well as the characteristics of the sound source. A highly reverberant room generates a short critical distance, and a nonreverberant or anechoic room generates a longer critical distance.

For an omnidirectional source, the critical distance may be approximately given by the following [87]:

$$d_c \sim \sqrt{\frac{V}{100\pi RT_{60}}} \sim 0.141\sqrt{S\alpha} \tag{11.8}$$

where critical distance d_c is measured in meters, volume V is measured in m^3, and reverberation time RT_{60} is measured in seconds. More accurate approximations are also available [88].

THE AVANT-GARDE ANECHOIC CHAMBER

An acoustic anechoic chamber is a room designed to be free of reverberation (hence non-echoing or echo-free). The walls, ceiling, and floor are usually lined with a sound absorbent material to minimize reflections and insulate the room from exterior sources of noise. All sound energy will travel away from the source with almost none reflected back. Thus, a listener within an anechoic chamber will hear only the direct sound, with no reverberation.

Anechoic chambers effectively simulate quiet open-spaces of infinite dimension. Thus, they are used to conduct acoustics experiments in "free field" conditions. They are often used to measure the radiation pattern of a microphone or of a noise source, or the transfer function of a loudspeaker.

An anechoic chamber is very quiet, with noise levels typically close to the threshold of hearing in the 10–20 dBA range (the quietest anechoic chamber has a decibel level of –9.4 dBA, well below hearing). Without the usual sound cues, people find the experience of being in an anechoic chamber very disorienting and often lose their balance. They also sometimes detect sounds they would not normally perceive, such as the beating of their own hearts.

One of the earliest anechoic chambers was designed and built by Leo Beranek and Harvey Sleeper in 1943. Their design is the one upon which most modern anechoic chambers are based. In a lecture titled "Indeterminacy," the avant-garde composer John Cage described his experience when he visited Beranek's chamber: "In that silent room, I heard two sounds, one high and one low. Afterward I asked the engineer in charge why, if the room was so silent, I had heard two sounds .... He said, 'The high one was your nervous system in operation. The low one was your blood in circulation'" [89].

After that visit, he composed his famous work entitled 4'33", consisting solely of silence and intended to encourage the audience to focus on the ambient sounds in the listening environment.

In his 1961 book *Silence,* Cage expanded on the implications of his experience in the anechoic chamber. "Try as we might to make silence, we cannot .... Until I die there will be sounds. And they will continue following my death. One need not fear about the future of music" [90].

Implementation

Algorithmic Reverb

Early digital reverberators that tried to emulate a room's reverberation primarily consisted of two types of infinite impulse response (IIR) filters, allpass and comb filters, to produce a gradually decaying series of reflections.

Schroeder's Reverberator

Perhaps the first important artificial reverberation was devised by Manfred Schroeder of Bell Telephone Laboratories in 1961. Early Schroeder reverberators [91, 92] consisted of three main components: comb filters, allpass filters, and a mixing matrix. The first two are still used in many algorithmic reverbs of today, but the mixing matrix, designed for multichannel listening, is either not used or is replaced with more sophisticated spatialization methods.

Figure 11.3 is a block diagram of the Schroeder reverberator. This design does not create the increasing arrival rate of reflections, and modern algorithmic approaches are more realistic. Nevertheless, it provides an important basic framework for more advanced approaches.

There is a parallel bank of four feedback comb filters. The comb filter shown in Equation (11.9) is a special case of an IIR digital filter, because there is feedback from the delayed output to the input. The comb filter effectively simulates a single-room mode. It represents sound reflecting between two parallel walls and produces a series of echoes. The echoes are exponentially decaying and uniformly spaced in time. The advantage is that the decay time can be used to define the gain of the feedback loop.

The comb filters are connected in parallel. The comb filters have an irregular magnitude response and can be considered a simulation of four specific echo sequences. The delay lengths in these comb filters may be used to adjust the illusion of room size, although if they are shortened, there should be more of them in parallel according to Schroeder. They also serve to reduce the spectral anomalies. Each comb filter has different parameters in order to attenuate frequencies that pass through the other comb filters. By controlling

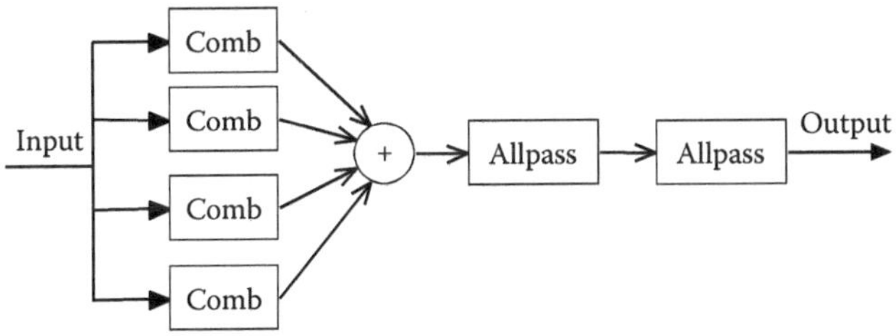

FIGURE 11.3
Schroeder's reverberator.

the delay time, which is also called loop time, of each filter, the sound waves will become reverberated.

The time domain and z domain form of Schroeder's comb filter is given by

$$y[n] = x[n-d] + gy[n-d]$$
$$H_{Comb}(z) = z^{-d} / \left(1 - gz^{-d}\right) \tag{11.9}$$

where d is a delay in samples and g is the filter's feedback coefficient. The block diagram is shown in Figure 11.4a. The parallel comb-filter bank is intended to give an appropriate fluctuation in the reverberator frequency response. A feedback comb filter can simulate a pair of parallel walls, so one could choose the delay line length in each comb filter to be the number of samples it takes for a wave to propagate from one wall to the opposite wall and back. Schroeder based his approach on trying to get the same number of impulse response peaks per second as would be found in a typical room.

The comb-filter delay line lengths can be more or less arbitrary, as long as enough of them are used in parallel (with mutually prime delay line lengths) to achieve a perceptually adequate fluctuation density in the frequency response magnitude. In Schroeder's paper, four such delays are chosen between 30 and 45 ms, and the corresponding feedback coefficients g_i are set to give the desired overall decay time.

One problem with a single comb filter is that the distances between adjacent echoes are decided by a single delay parameter. Thus, the output of a comb filter has very distinct periodicity, producing a metallic sound, sometimes known as flutter echoes. This rapid echo is often found in the acoustics of long narrow spaces with parallel walls. To counteract this, Schroeder's main design connects two allpass filters in series.

The allpass filter is given below in (11.10), and a block diagram is depicted in Figure 11.4b.

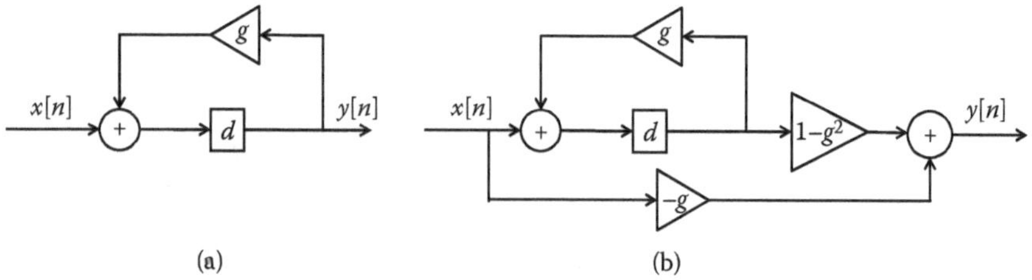

FIGURE 11.4
(a) Schroeder's comb filter. (b) A Schroeder allpass section. A typical value for g is 0.7.

$$y[n] = -gx[n] + x[n-d] + gy[n-d]$$
$$H_{AP}(z) = \frac{z^{-d} - g}{1 - gz^{-d}} \tag{11.10}$$

The allpass filters provide "colorless" high-density echoes in the late impulse response of the reverberator. Essentially, these filters transform each input sample from the previous stage into an entire infinite impulse response, which results in a higher echo density. For this reason, Schroeder allpass sections are sometimes called *impulse diffusers*. Unlike the comb filters, these allpass filters give the same gain at every frequency. But though they do not provide an accurate physical model of diffuse reflections, they succeed in expanding the single reflections into many reflections, which produces a similar qualitative result.

Schroeder recognized the need to separate the coloration of reverberation (changing the frequency content) from its duration and density aspects. In Schroeder's original work, and in much work that followed, allpass filters are arranged in series, as shown in Figure 11.3, thus maintaining the uniform magnitude response. Since all of the filters are linear and time invariant, the series allpass chain can go either before or after the parallel comb-filter bank.

Schroeder suggests a progression of allpass delay line lengths close to the following:

$$d_i \sim 100\ \mathrm{m}/3^i, \quad i = 0,\ 1,\ 2,\ 3,\ 4 \tag{11.11}$$

The delay line lengths d_i are typically mutually prime and spanning successive orders of magnitude. The 100 ms value was chosen so that when $g = 0.708$ in Equation (11.10), the time to decay 60 dB (T_{60}) would be 2 s. Thus, for $i = 0$, $T_{60} \sim 2$, and each successive allpass has an impulse response duration that is about a third of the previous one. Using five series allpass sections in this way yields an impulse response echo density of about 810 per second, which is close to the desired thousand per second.

A system using one of these reverberators simply adds its output, suitably scaled, to the reverberator input sample at the current time.

Moorer's Reverberator

The next important advance in algorithmic reverberators is attributable to James Moorer in 1979 [93]. Moorer's reverberator is the combination of a finite impulse response (FIR) filter that simulates the early impulse response activity of the room in cascade with a bank of low-pass and comb filters. The FIR filter coefficients were based on the simulation of a concert hall.

Although comb filters can be used for modeling the decaying impulse response, as in Schroeder's reverberator, they do not simulate the tendency

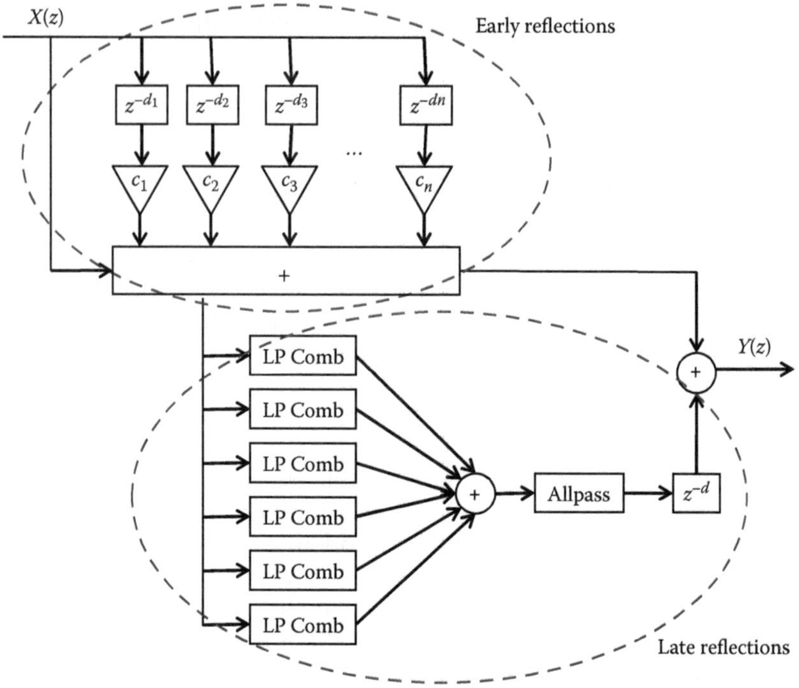

FIGURE 11.5
Moorer's reverberator used an FIR filter to simulate the early reflections and parallel comb filters with low-pass filtering to simulate the late reflections.

of the reverb to be attenuated at high frequencies, corresponding to absorption by the air and walls. To solve this problem, Moorer embedded a low-pass filter in the feedback loop of each comb filter. Now reverberation time is a function of frequency. This helps simulate a more natural-sounding reverberation, avoiding the unnatural metallic sound that can be observed without the presence of the filter. A simple form of low-pass filter was sufficient to get satisfactory results. An allpass filter then followed the low-pass comb filters, in order to increase the reflection intensity.

Moorer's reverberator is depicted in Figure 11.5. The top block takes care of early reflections, and the bottom block, consisting of six parallel comb filters with different delay lengths, takes care of late reflections.

Generating Reverberation with the Image Source Method

Background

The reverberation heard when a source is recorded in a room is characterized by the *room impulse response* (RIR), which gives the impulse response corresponding to a sound source and a listener in a room.

The *image source model* is a popular method for generating simulated room impulse responses. Once an RIR is available, reverberation can be applied to an audio signal by convolving it with the RIR. This approach generates a sound that appears as if the source signal had been recorded by a microphone in the room. The technique gives a relatively simple way to generate a number of RIRs with differing characteristics, such as their reverberation times.

The Image Source Model

The image source method was originally presented for rectangular enclosures in a seminal paper by Allen and Berkley from 1979 [94]. To explain this method, we will first show how the individual echoes that together produce reverberation can be visualized as virtual sources. Then we will find a unit impulse response for each echo with the proper time delay given the listener position. After this, we calculate the magnitude of each echo's unit impulse response. So we have then combined the times and magnitudes of each echo to generate the room impulse response. A discrete time implementation of the impulse response can be achieved with an FIR filter.

Modeling Reflections as Virtual Sources

Figure 11.6 shows a rectangular room (often referred to as a shoebox) on the left. Within it are a sound source and a microphone. We are trying to calculate the impulse response at the location of the microphone. The direct sound path is the line between the source and the microphone. The sound is also reflected off a wall before arriving at the microphone. The listener perceives this echo as coming from a location past that wall. So we create a mirror image of the room and place it on the other side of the wall. The mirror image of the source, known as a *virtual source*, resides in this virtual room at the location from which we perceive this reflected sound to be located.

The solid lines in Figure 11.6 are the actual path taken by the sound wave, and the dotted line is the perceived path. We treat the virtual sources as if

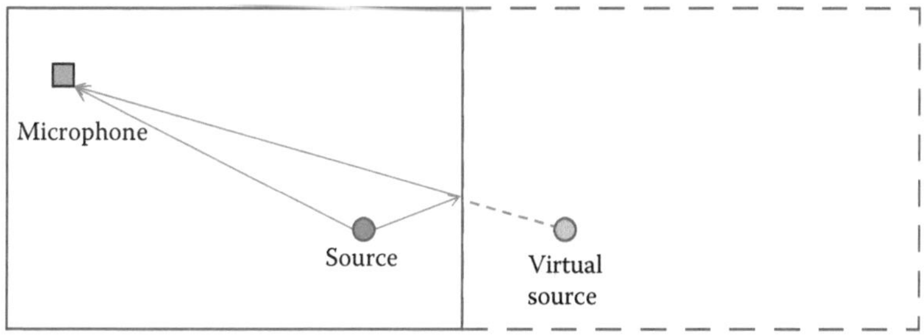

FIGURE 11.6
A room with a source sound and microphone, and its mirror image containing a virtual source.

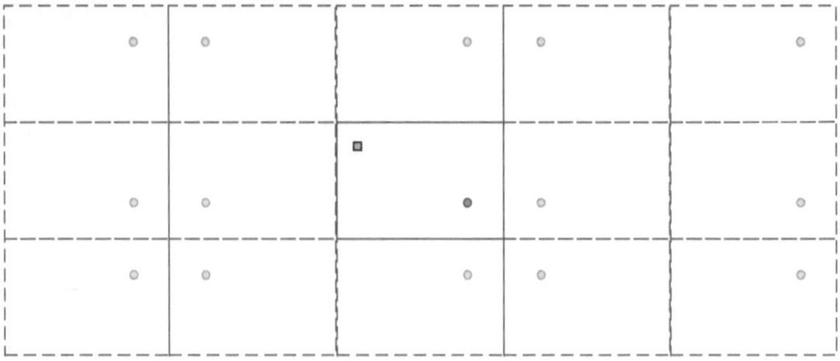

FIGURE 11.7
A room with multiple mirror images in two dimensions, corresponding to reflections of the sound source off of the walls.

they were individual sound sources and ignore each virtual source's echo. This process is repeated by making mirror images of the room's mirror image, each with another virtual source. We can extend this to two dimensions, as in Figure 11.7, or three dimensions.

Locating the Virtual Sources

Let us first consider virtual sources along just one dimension. We set the origin to be the position of the microphone, and x_r is the length of the room along the x-axis. The ith virtual source is located at x_i. If $i = 0$, then the virtual source is actually the real sound source. If i is negative, then the virtual source is located on the negative x-axis. The distance between the microphone and the ith virtual sound source along the x-axis is given by

$$x_i = \begin{cases} (i+1)x_r - x_0 & i \text{ odd} \\ ix_r + x_0 & i \text{ even} \end{cases} \tag{11.12}$$

Similarly, we can find the positions of virtual sources along the y- and z-axes:

$$y_j = \begin{cases} (j+1)y_r - y_0 & j \text{ odd} \\ jy_r + y_0 & j \text{ even} \end{cases} \tag{11.13}$$

$$z_k = \begin{cases} (k+1)z_r - z_0 & k \text{ odd} \\ kz_r + z_0 & k \text{ even} \end{cases} \tag{11.14}$$

The three-dimensional distance from the microphone to a virtual source is then given by

$$d_{ijk} = \sqrt{x_i^{\,2} + y_j^{\,2} + z_k^{\,2}} \tag{11.15}$$

The Impulse Response for a Virtual Source

We now define the following delta function:

$$\delta_{ijk} = \begin{cases} 1 & d_{ijk} = tc \\ 0 & \text{otherwise} \end{cases} \tag{11.16}$$

where t is the time, d_{ijk} is the distance to a virtual source, and c is the speed of sound. So $d_{i,j,k}/c$ is the effective time delay of each echo. Equation (11.16) gives the unit impulse response for a virtual source, with unity magnitude when the sound from that virtual source reaches the microphone.

Now note that magnitude is inversely proportional to the distance it travels to get from the source to the microphone.

$$m_{ijk} \propto 1/d_{ijk} \tag{11.17}$$

Also, magnitude is affected by the number of reflections that the sound wave makes before arriving at the microphone. Assuming that all walls have the same absorption coefficients, we can take the coefficient α and raise it to the exponent $n = |i|+|j|+|k|$, which represents the total number of reflections the sound has made.

$$\alpha_{ijk} = \alpha^{|i|+|j|+|k|} \tag{11.18}$$

This can be extended to the case where each wall could have a different reflection coefficient. Let $\alpha_{x=0}$ be the reflection coefficient for the wall perpendicular to the x-axis that is closest to the origin, and let $\alpha_{x=xr}$ be the reflection coefficient for the wall opposite that, use similar notation for the walls opposite the y- and z-axes. The reflection coefficients for all the reflections made are given by the following equation:

$$\begin{aligned}
\alpha_{x_i} &= \begin{cases} \alpha_{x=0}{}^{|(i-1)/2|}\alpha_{x=x_r}{}^{|(i+1)/2|} & i \text{ odd} \\ \alpha_{x=0}{}^{|i/2|}\alpha_{x=x_r}{}^{|i/2|} & i \text{ even} \end{cases} \\
\alpha_{y_j} &= \begin{cases} \alpha_{y=0}{}^{|(j-1)/2|}\alpha_{y=y_r}{}^{|(j+1)/2|} & i \text{ odd} \\ \alpha_{y=0}{}^{|j/2|}\alpha_{y=y_r}{}^{|j/2|} & i \text{ even} \end{cases} \\
\alpha_{z_k} &= \begin{cases} \alpha_{z=0}{}^{|(k-1)/2|}\alpha_{z=z_r}{}^{|(k+1)/2|} & i \text{ odd} \\ \alpha_{z=0}{}^{|k/2|}\alpha_{z=z_r}{}^{|k/2|} & i \text{ even} \end{cases}
\end{aligned} \tag{11.19}$$

To find the total reflection coefficient of a virtual source with the indices *i*, *j*, and *k*, we multiply these components together:

$$\alpha_{ijk} = \alpha_{x_i} \alpha_{y_j} \alpha_{z_k} \quad (11.20)$$

Now we can generate the impulse response by multiplying the delta function from Equation (11.16) with the magnitude of each echo, magnitude m_{ijk}, and the reflection coefficient α_{ijk}, and then summing over all three indices. This can be thought of as the summation of all the sounds arriving from all the virtual sources.

$$h(t) = \sum_{i=-n}^{n} \sum_{j=-n}^{n} \sum_{k=-n}^{n} \delta_{ijk} m_{ijk} \alpha_{ijk} \quad (11.21)$$

In Figure 11.8, a circle is shown, with the microphone at its center and with its edge touching the nearest wall. The portion of the impulse response that comes from virtual sources within this circle represents a truncated room impulse response. When extended into three dimensions, Figure 11.8 would form a partitioned cuboid, and the truncated RIR would come from virtual sources within a sphere.

This approach makes several assumptions that are known to be inaccurate. It ignores any attenuation of the sound that may result from traveling through the air. Furthermore, it assumes that no change in phase takes place upon reflection, and that the reflection coefficients are independent of angle and frequency.

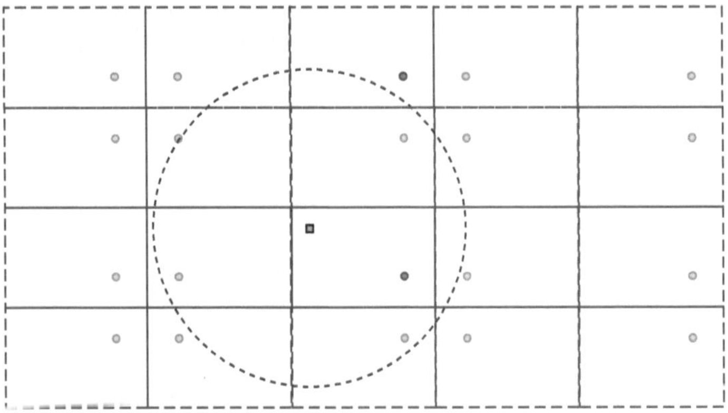

FIGURE 11.8
Image source representation, with a circle drawn to indicate virtual sources used for early reflections.

Many image source model variants and extensions based on this standard technique have been proposed in the literature. For instance, [95] extended the method to calculation of late reflections, as well as speeding up computation, and [96] proposed an improvement where each virtual source is given using fractional delays.

Convolutional Reverb

Convolution and Fast Convolution

Convolution is an important mathematical technique for combining two signals. By convolving a signal with a room impulse response, we can create the reverberated signal as it would be heard in a room. Given an input signal *s*, the filtered output *r* is the result of the convolution of *s* by the finite impulse response $h[0], \ldots, h[n-1]$:

$$r[n] = (s * h)[n] = \sum_{k=0}^{N-1} s[n-k]h[k] \tag{11.22}$$

However, though convolution is very useful, it is excessively computationally expensive. For realistic simulation of a natural environment, the required impulse response can last more than 2 s. For processing one sample with convolutional reverb, addition and accumulation operations must be performed on the entire length of the impulse response. Thus, assuming a 44.1 kHz sampling frequency and an impulse response of just 1 s, roughly $2*10^9$ adds and multiplies are required each second. Fast convolution provides a means to address this complexity issue.

The fast convolution uses the well-known convolution theorem: performing multiplication in the Fourier domain is equivalent to performing convolution in the time domain (and vice versa).

$$\begin{aligned} r &= s * h \leftrightarrow R = S \cdot H \\ &\rightarrow r = F^{-1}\{F(s) \cdot F(h)\} \end{aligned} \tag{11.23}$$

That is, rather than convolving two signals together directly, one can compute their Fourier transforms, multiply them together, and then take the inverse Fourier transform. This may seem like more steps, but the fast Fourier transform (FFT) can be used, which offers vast efficiency savings over convolution operations. Whereas convolving two signals of length N requires N^2 operations, the FFT requires on the order of $N \log(N)$ operations. Again, assuming a sampling frequency of 44.1 kHz and an impulse response of 1 s, only about 10^6 operations are needed each second if this fast convolution is used.

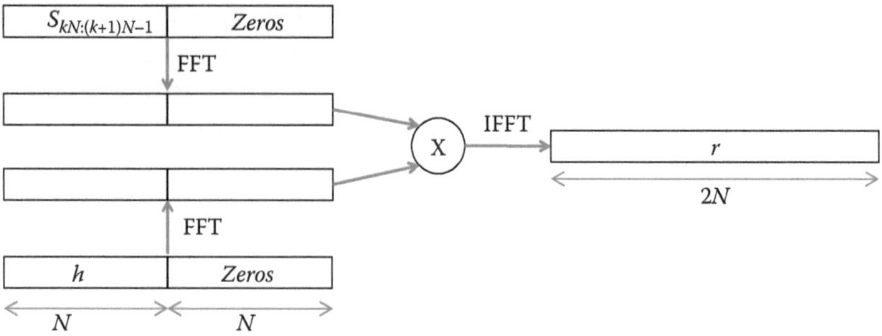

FIGURE 11.9
One block convolution, as implemented in block-based convolutional reverb. The kth block is convolved with the impulse response h of length N.

Block-Based Convolution

There are at least two main approaches to performing fast convolution on a real-time signal: the overlap and add method and the overlap and save method. They both rely on cutting the input signal into blocks. Here, we will describe the overlap and add method, which is slightly simpler to understand, and is discussed in more detail in Chapter 8. The input signal s is cut into blocks of length N. The kth block $s_{kN:(k+1)N-1} = s[kN], \ldots, s[(k+1)N-1]$ is convolved with the impulse response h of length N, as shown in Figure 11.9.

This convolution is performed by zero padding the input signal block of length N in order to realize a $2N$ long Fourier transform. As a result, the fast convolution of one block with h produces a filtered signal r of length two blocks. The second of these blocks is summed with the next first resulting block to create a complete filtered response, as shown in Figure 11.10. To further improve performance, the Fourier transform of h can be precomputed and reused until h is changed.

From the definition of convolution and a change of variables,

$$u = l - j \rightarrow r[kN+l] = \sum_{j=0}^{N-1} s[kN+l-j]h[j] = \sum_{u=l-N+1}^{l} s[kN+u]h[l-u] \quad (11.24)$$

This summation can be separated into positive and negative terms for u:

$$r[kN+l] = \sum_{u=0}^{l} s[kN+u]h[l-u] + \sum_{u=l-N+1}^{-1} s[kN+u]h[l-u] \quad (11.25)$$

which, again from the definition of convolution, becomes

$$r[kN+l] = s_{kN:kN+l} * h + s_{kN+l-N+1:kN-1} * h \quad (11.26)$$

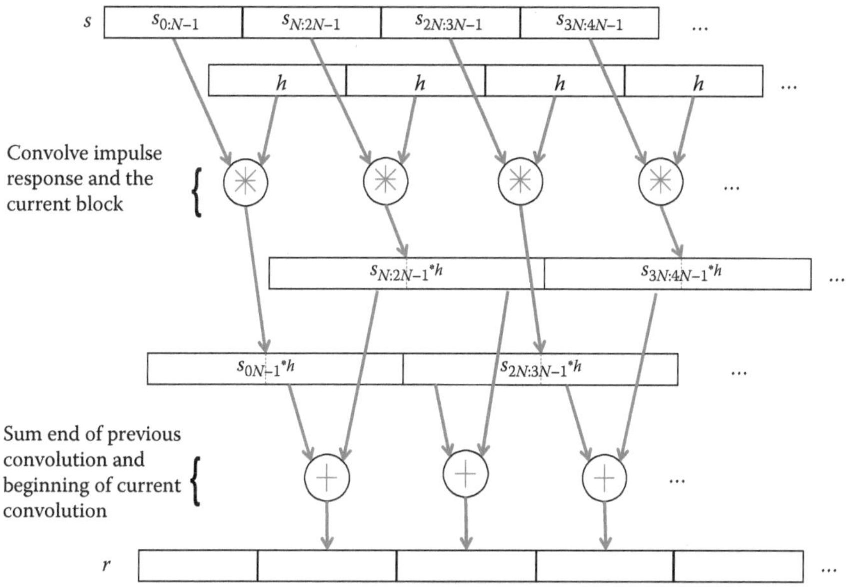

FIGURE 11.10
Partitioned convolution for real-time artificial reverberation.

Thus, we obtain

$$r_{kN:(k+1)N-1} = \left(s_{(k-1)N:kN-1} * h\right)_{N:2N-1} + \left(s_{kN:(k+1)N-1} * h\right)_{0:N-1} \tag{11.27}$$

That is, the kth output block is obtained by adding together the tail of the convolution of the $(k-1)$th block and h and the head of the convolution of the kth block and h. This is shown for the first few blocks in Figure 11.10.

Note that the kth output block will be ready at the earliest at time $(k + 1)N$. This minimum delay of one block size can be problematic. For instance, if the impulse response lasts 1 s, a device that uses this overlap and add fast convolution method will have at least 1 s of delay. Also, blocks are convolved with the full impulse response, which can be quite computational.

Physical Meaning

The partitioned convolution has a simple physical interpretation. Suppose h is a room impulse response and that convolutional reverb is applied to the input signal. Assuming a source produces a sound frame at time t, the direct path brings this frame to the listener. The other paths have reflections from the walls and ceiling, resulting in modified versions of the original frame with different attenuation and delay. The delays depend on the length of the path, including the number of reflections.

If sounds are produced continuously, then at any point in time a listener will hear the direct sound and delayed and transformed versions of previous sounds. The partitioned convolution is just an expression of this phenomenon. That is, at any point in time the sum is made over the length of the filter h plus the length of the last block. Since input blocks are convolved with h, we effectively obtain a delayed and transformed version of sounds that were emitted in the past.

Other Approaches

As mentioned, one issue with the partitioned convolution is the partition size. Since it is based on convolving with the whole impulse response, there is still a lot of processing and latency. Gardner [97] developed a solution to the high delay issue that uses the same idea as fast convolution. Since the input signal is partitioned into blocks, the impulse response can also be partitioned. Block convolution is then performed on the appropriate combination of input blocks and filter blocks and summed in order to produce the desired output. This efficient approach relies on a fast convolution that is performed many times, but on smaller blocks.

Today, many of the fastest convolutional reverbs are improvements on this approach. Another technique used to speed up calculation and maintain low latency is to use a low-latency partitioned convolutional reverb for the early reflections, and then an algorithmic reverb for the late reflections, in which case an FIR filter is typically used to generate the early reflections, and then IIR filters may be applied to create the diffuse reverberation. Low-pass filters may also be used to account for air absorption.

More advanced algorithms can be developed to model specific room sizes, whether for generating a room impulse response or for designing an algorithmic reverb. Ray tracing techniques can also be used to derive the reverberation for a given room geometry, source, and listener location.

Applications

Why Use Reverb?

We usually inhabit the reverberant field with many sources of reverberation already around us. Yet it is still useful to add reverb to recordings. We often listen to music in environments with very little or poor reverb. A dry signal may sound unnatural, so the addition of reverb to recordings is used to compensate for the fact that we cannot always listen to music in well-designed acoustic environments. The reverberation in a car may not adequately recreate the majestic sound of a symphony orchestra. And when listening over headphones, there is no reverberation added to the music.

ACOUSTIC REVERBERATORS

Many recording studios have used special rooms known as reverberation chambers to add reverb to a performance. Elevator shafts and stairwells (as in New York City's Avatar Recording Studio) work well as highly reverberant rooms. The reverb can also be controlled by adding absorptive materials such as curtains and rugs.

Spring reverbs are found in many guitar amplifiers and have been used in Hammond organs. The audio signal is coupled to one end of the spring by a transducer that creates waves traveling through the spring. At the far end of the spring, another transducer converts the motion of the string into an electrical signal, which is then added to the original sound. When a wave arrives at an end of the spring, part of the wave's energy is reflected. However, these reflections have different delays and attenuations from what would be found in a natural acoustic environment, and there may be some interaction between the waves in a spring; thus, this results in a slightly unusual (though not unpleasant) reverb sound.

Often several springs with different lengths and tensions are enclosed in a metal box, known as the reverb pan, and used together. This avoids uniform behavior and creates a more realistic, pseudorandom series of echoes. In most reverb units though, the spring lengths and tensions are fixed in the design process and not left to the user to control.

The plate reverb is similar to a spring reverb, but instead of springs, the transducers are attached at several locations on a metal plate. These transducers send vibrations through the plate, and reflections are produced whenever a wave reaches the plate's edge. The location of the transducers and the damping of the plate can be adjusted to control the reverb. However, plate reverbs are expensive and bulky and, hence, not widely used.

Water tank reverberators have also been used. Here, the audio signal is modulated with an ultrasonic signal and transmitted through a tank of water. The output is then demodulated, resulting in the reverberant output sound. Other reverberators include pipes with microphones placed at various points.

These acoustic and analogue reverberators can be interesting to create and use, but they lack the simplicity and ease of use of digital reverberators. Ultimately, the choice of implementation is a matter of taste.

Stereo Reverb

Another important aspect of reverb is the correlation of the signals that reach the listener's ears. In order for a listener to perceive the spaciousness of a large room, the sounds at each ear should be slightly offset. This is one reason concert halls have such high ceilings. With a low ceiling, the first reflections to reach the listener usually are reflections from the ceiling, and they reach both ears at the same time. But if the ceiling is high, the first reflections come from the walls of the concert hall. And since the walls are generally different distances away from a listener, the sound arriving at each ear is different. Ensuring some slight differences in the reverberation applied to left and right channels is important for stereo reverb design.

Gated Reverb

A gated reverb is created by truncating the impulse response of a reverberator, thus changing the IIR filters to FIR. The amount of time before the response is cut off is known as the *gate time,* as labeled in Figure 11.11. Some reverberation implementations provide for a more gradual decay of the sound, rather than a sharp cutoff that produces abrupt silence. Gated reverbs are often used on percussive instruments.

Reverse Reverb

Rather than generating reflections that become quieter and gradually fade away, the impulse response can be reversed. This will generate reflections that get louder over time, and then abruptly cut off. This sounds a bit like slapback delay because it ends suddenly, but analogous to the difference between echo and reverb, it has more complicated and less uniform behavior than slapback delay.

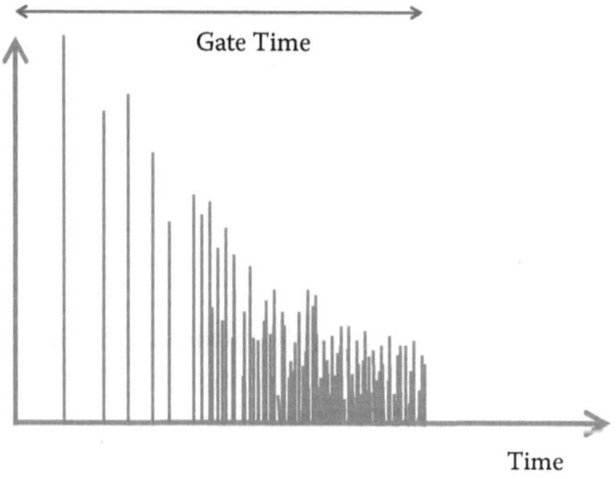

FIGURE 11.11
Impulse response of a gated reverb.

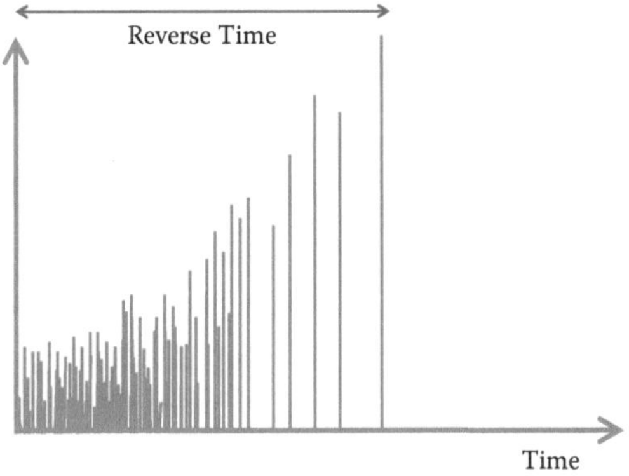

FIGURE 11.12
Impulse response for reverse reverb.

The length of time it takes for the reflections to build up is known as the *reverse time*, or the gate time, since it works like a gated reverb that has been reversed in time. Figure 11.12 depicts a possible reverse reverb impulse response.

An interesting, related technique is to reverse the signal, apply the reverb, and reverse again.

Common Parameters

The available parameters to control a reverberator can vary widely. The following parameters apply mainly to algorithmic reverb. For convolutional reverb, the choice of the room impulse response is of primary importance, and a commercial audio effect will often come with a wide range of precomputed room impulse responses that can then be fine-tuned to fit the needs of the user. Alternatively, some convolutional reverbs will allow the user to specify the room size, in which case the image source method or a similar approach is used to generate the impulse response.

Reverb time: This is also known as the decay time, or the reverb decay, and usually represents the reverberation time as described in the beginning of this chapter. It indicates how long the reverb can be heard after the input stops, usually for a 1 kHz input. The actual measure of what can be heard can vary among manufacturers. This parameter is typically in terms of milliseconds, which can be thought of as something like the reverb time.

Long reverb times applied to tracks often work well in a sparse mix where there are few sources, but they can produce clutter when there are lots of sources. Short but distinct reverbs can be applied to each source in a busy ensemble mix so that each one will have a unique ambience and they won't mask each other in the final mix.

Diffusion/density: This parameter is usually related to the echo density, also discussed at the beginning of the chapter. A highly diffuse reverb will sound smooth but can also result in noticeable filtering of the signal, or coloration. Low diffusion values often sound nice on vocals, but may result in reverb with a coarse or grainy sound reverberation.

Note that some commercial reverbs will have both a diffusion and a density parameter, in which case diffusion is often specific to just the early reflections, whereas density refers to just the late reflections.

Direct-to-reverberant ratio: This is essentially the dry/wet mix parameter, as found on many other effects. It determines how much of the original sound is used. That is, if the reverb is simulating an acoustic environment, it determines to what extent the source travels direct to the listener, without reflecting off of any surfaces.

Predelay: The predelay is usually defined as the amount of time before the first reflection in the impulse response, i.e., the time until the first reverberations are heard.

More advanced reverberation units may allow the user to set a second predelay for the amount of time before the first late reflection, as shown in Figure 11.13. Of course, for simulation of a realistic environment, the predelay for the early reflections should always be less than the predelay for the late reflections.

Filtering/room damping: Typically, high-frequency content in the reflections will be attenuated more than low-frequency content, due to both absorption of sound while traveling through the air and absorption when reflecting off surfaces. Thus, most reverberators will provide some form of filtering to simulate this damping of high frequencies. This is often in the form of a single-frequency value that defines the cutoff frequency of a low-pass filter. Reverb designs that

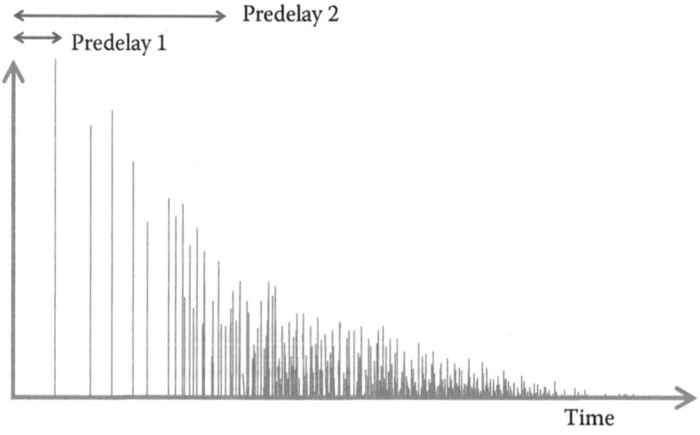

FIGURE 11.13
A room impulse response with the predelay parameters labeled.

give more control to the user may also specify a crossover point for both low and high shelving filters along with the gain for each shelf.

Having minimal attenuation of the high-frequency content may give a bright, airy sound to the reverb, and is often used on vocals. Strong attenuation of this content is more typical of emulation of classic reverberators, since they often couldn't reproduce the high frequencies.

Gate time: This parameter applies to gated reverbs. The gate time is just the amount of time, usually in milliseconds, for which the reverb is allowed to sound. This may also refer to the duration of a reverse reverb.

Gate decay time: Some gated reverberators will also provide a decay time, which controls the behavior of the gate as it is closed. A short gate decay time means that the reverb will attenuate rapidly, as is the case with the gated reverb depicted in Figure 11.11. A long decay time implies that the reverb will gradually fade away.

Gate threshold: Instead of applying gated reverb to an entire signal, the gating of the reverb can be made level dependent. Typically, the gate on a reverb will be kept open (the impulse response is not truncated) when signals are above the threshold. But if the signal level drops below the threshold, the gate closes and the reverb is truncated. If the signal level rises back above the threshold, the gate will then reopen.

Problems

1. Explain why impulse responses are useful for modeling the properties of an acoustic space. How is an impulse measured with a static sound source and a static mono microphone?
2. a. Sketch an impulse response plot for a typical room. Label the early and late reflections.
   b. How would the plot in part (a) be changed for a larger room, and for the same size room with higher reflectivity off all surfaces?
3. Define the main difference between *echo* and *reverberation*.
4. Why are FIR filters often used to generate early reflections and IIR filters used to generate late reflections?
5. Show that Schroeder's allpass section has the required properties of an allpass filter. That is, show that the magnitude response is always equal to 1.
6. Give the impulse response of a single Schroeder comb filter.
7. Explain the function of a gated reverb compared to a standard reverb. What is the effect of the gate time control?
8. Explain the difference between convolutional and algorithmic reverb. What are the advantages and disadvantages of each?

9. Use both Sabine's formula and the Norris–Eyring formula to estimate the reverberation time RT_{60} for a room with floor area 12 × 10 m and 5 m high ceilings. The floor is carpeted ($\alpha = 0.15$), the ceiling is acoustic tiles ($\alpha = 0.6$), and the walls are covered with thick drapes ($\alpha = 0.5$). Now estimate reverberation time for the same room but without drapes and all surfaces made of brick ($\alpha = 0.03$).

12

Audio Production

In this chapter, we take a look at how audio effects are used in production. We first look at the main devices that host the audio effects that we have covered and that are used in recording, editing, and mixing audio. We then proceed to a discussion of how the effects can be used with these devices, and how they can be ordered or modified to create new effects or achieve various production goals.

It is important to start with a few basic concepts. A *multitrack recorder* is a device that can record several tracks of audio simultaneously. The term *track* originates from when recordings were made on tape, and the track referred to the discrete area on the tape where a sequence of audio events was preserved. So multitrack audio is the collection of different audio signals that, when combined, constitute the intended sound; e.g., guitar and vocals can be separate tracks recorded by a singer-songwriter. In contrast, a *mixer* is a device that can process one or more tracks of audio before they are combined.

Most multitrack recording devices will also provide mixing functionality, and vice versa. So various tracks, such as instrument and microphone signals, come into the mixer, where the levels and other attributes are modified. Then the output can be sent to a sound reinforcement system for a live performance, or to a multitrack recorder for recording either the processed tracks or a single, processed, and combined output track.

The devices for mixing and recording multitrack audio are divided into two main categories: *mixing consoles* (typically dedicated physical devices) and *digital audio workstations* (DAWs; typically computers with specialized hardware and software). However, with the growth in functionality and versatility, including the rise of sophisticated control surfaces for DAWs and networking capabilities in mixing consoles, there is now a gray area between the two. Nevertheless, we will provide a formal description of mixing consoles, which tend to follow a standard structure, and then extend the discussion to DAWs, while highlighting some of the more important distinctions. For a more detailed discussion of mixing consoles and their structure, we encourage the reader to read [15].

We begin with a discussion of some of the core components often seen on DAWs and mixing consoles.

The Mixing Console

A mixing console (also known as audio mixer, sound desk, or mixing desk) may be defined as an electronic device for routing, combining, and changing the characteristics of audio signals. Depending on the type of mixer, the mixing console can mix analog or digital signals, or both. The modified signals (either discrete digital values or continuous time voltages) are summed to create the output signals.

Mixing consoles are used in many applications, including sound reinforcement systems, public address systems, studio recording, broadcasting, and (television, film, and game) postproduction. For example, one application would be to combine multiple microphone signals such that they could be heard simultaneously through one set of loudspeakers.

The mixing console offers four main functionalities: summing, processing, routing, and metering. When summing, various audio signals are combined, and channels are summed to stereo (or surround, or other multichannel formats) via the mix bus. For processing, consoles often have on-board equalizers and sometimes dynamics processors. And to enable the use of effects, processors, and grouping, mixers offer routing functionality via auxiliary sends, insert points, and routing matrices. The various channels and buses may be monitored and metered, to indicate clipping and to show estimates of signal levels and other useful aspects of the signals. Many audio mixers can also provide phantom power as required by some microphones, read and write console automation, create test tones, and add external effects.

When used for mixing live performance, the output signal produced by the sound desk will usually be sent to an amplifier. However, the mixing console could also have a built-in amplifier, or be directly connected to powered loudspeakers (i.e., the loudspeakers themselves have built-in amplifiers).

The mixing console also has two distinct sections, the channel section and master section.

The Channel Section

In a multitrack recorder, each input signal to the mixer resides on a track. Each channel is then fed from one of these tracks. The *channel section* in a mixing console is a collection of channels organized in physical strips. Each channel corresponds to a track on the multitrack recorder. Most channels support monaural (usually referred to as just mono) input, though some consoles will have several types of channels (mono, stereo, channels with different equalizers (EQs)).

The channels will have dedicated *channel strips* on the console, where the user can manipulate and route the signals. Figure 12.1 shows a simple channel strip, as might be found on a basic multitrack recorder. The audio signal

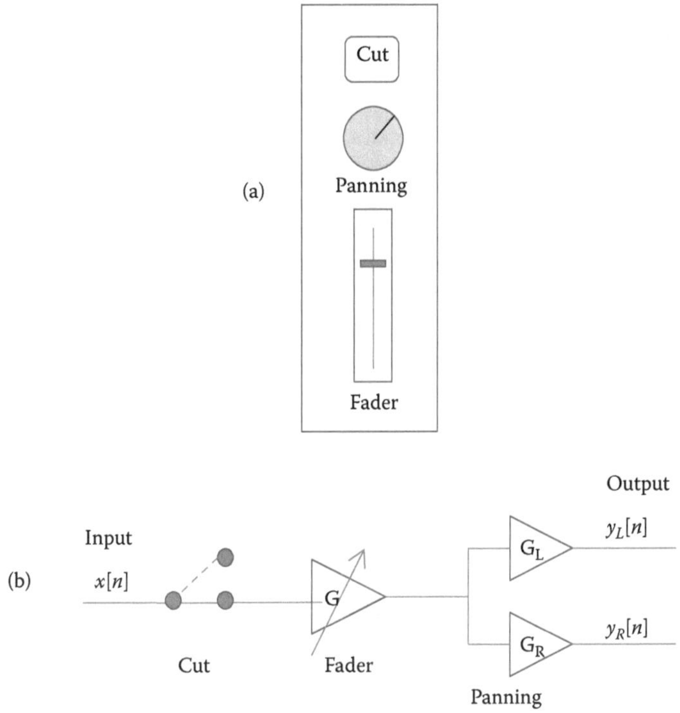

FIGURE 12.1
(a) A simple channel strip having only a cut control, a panning knob, and a level fader. (b) The corresponding signal flow diagram.

travels through a *cut switch*, *pan pot*, and *fader*. The pan pot takes a monaural signal as input and produces a stereo output signal. Note that the layout of controls on the interface need not be the same as the ordering in the signal flow.

The channel strip will often have a lot more than just this basic functionality, and will often have several sections:

- Input socket, for connecting an input jack that provides the audio signal.
- Microphone preamplifier, that provides a gain to increase the amplitude of an input microphone signal.
- Cut or mute switch, used as a gate to allow or prevent the signal from reaching the output. Similarly, a solo switch is often available, which will mute all other channels.
- Faders, or sliding volume controls, to manually adjust the level of the output signal.
- Equalization, typically parametric and tone controls.

- Dynamics processing (e.g., noise gates and dynamic range compressors).
- Panning controls, for positioning the output in the stereo field.
- Metering, including clipping indicators and level or volume meters.
- Routing, including direct outs, aux sends, and subgroup assignments, which will be discussed later.

A more functional channel strip is shown in Figure 12.2. This also shows the types of audio effects that are most commonly seen on a channel strip in a mixing console: gains and faders, simple filters (especially parametric equalizers), and dynamic range compressors.

The line gain is a simple amplifier that boosts or attenuates the signal level before the signal enters the channel. This is used to prevent clipping as well as to get each channel into a reasonable working range. It sets the 0 dB point for the channel, used for further operations that depend on relative signal levels. The line gain control is used to boost or attenuate the level of the

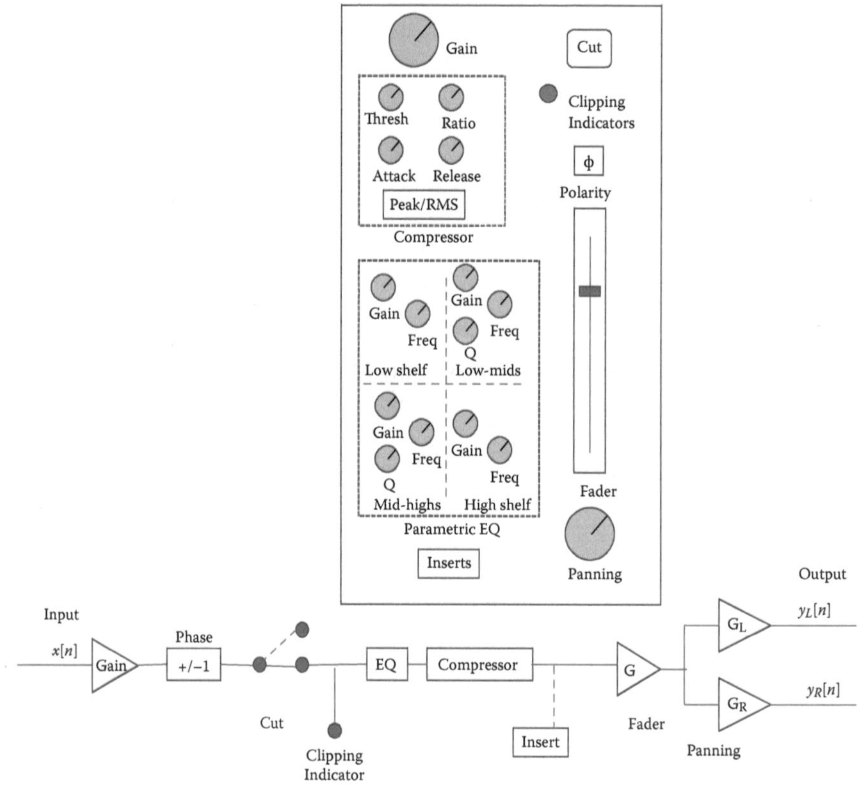

FIGURE 12.2
A channel strip and associated block diagram, with additional controls such as dynamics (a compressor) and frequency (a parametric equalizer) processing.

signal before it enters the channel path. It lets us optimize the level of the incoming signal. It can also be deliberately used to add distortion.

Audio equipment will often *invert* a signal (positive values become negative, and vice versa). This is particularly problematic when a signal is summed with another, possibly modified, version of itself. Polarity inversion will result in the two signals canceling each other out. This inversion can also occur naturally, such as when two microphone signals from inside and outside a kick drum are combined. When a track is recorded with inverted sign, a polarity invert or switch may be used to correct the inversion by simply flipping the sign of the signal.

The clipping indicators do not affect or process the signal, but instead act as a simple meter or alert system. They show when the signal level has overshot a threshold.

Processors will typically be provided for each channel, from basic tone controls to a filter section and dynamics section. Dynamic range compression and channel equalization are two of the most common on-board processors. These controls affect the equalization of the signal by separately attenuating or boosting a range of frequencies. Many mixing consoles have a parametric equalizer on each channel. A simple parametric EQ is included in Figure 12.2.

Note also that the sequence of processing depicted on the channel strip isn't necessarily the sequence in which the processing is actually performed. For instance, the fader may actually be applied before filtering and dynamics processing, even though it appears toward the end of the channel strip for ease of use and interface design.

The Master Section

The *master section* provides global functionality and central control over the console. It includes master auxiliary sends, effect returns, control room level, etc. The master control section almost always includes various fader or level controls, such as auxiliary bus and return level controls, and master and subgroup faders. This section may also include solo monitoring, muting, a stage talk-back microphone control, and an output matrix mixer. On smaller mixing consoles the master controls are often placed on the right of the mixing board and the inputs are found on the left. In larger mixers, the master controls are typically placed in the center with the inputs on both sides.

Metering and Monitoring

The audio level meters are not considered a separate section since they are often merged into the input and master sections. There are usually volume unit (VU) or peak meters that show the levels for each channel and for the master outputs, often in pairs to indicate left and right stereo channel levels. More recently, there has also been a movement toward meters that show more perceptually relevant loudness levels. Clipping indicators are also often provided to show whether the console levels exceed maximum allowable levels.

Since sound is perceived on a logarithmic scale, mixing console displays and control interfaces are almost always given level values in decibels. The professional nominal level is often given as +4 dBu, where dBu is referenced to 0.775 V root mean square (RMS). The consumer grade level is –10 dBV, where dBV is referenced to 1 V RMS. Thus, 0 dB on the mixing console will typically correspond to either +4 dBu or –10 dBV of electrical signal at the output.

When *monitoring* capabilities are provided within the channel strips, this is known as an in-line configuration, and is common to smaller consoles. But many mixers have at least one additional output, besides the main mix. In split configuration, a separate monitoring section is available to provide a mix heard by the engineer. Mixers may have other outputs as well, including either individual bus outputs or auxiliary outputs. For example, these outputs can be used to provide different mixes to on-stage monitor loudspeakers.

Basic Mixing Console

A basic mixing console will have several channels, each outputting a stereo signal. These stereo signals are then summed to the mix bus. Figure 12.3 depicts such a console. The channel strips could be as simple as the one in Figure 12.1 or more complex than the one depicted in Figure 12.2.

Signal Flow and Routing

As mentioned previously, the mixing console typically includes *summing*, *processing*, *routing*, and *metering* functionality. In this section, we focus on the routing. That is, we will be concerned with the signal flow and how signals may be routed or grouped in order to enable external processing and the creation of submixes.

In Figure 12.3 we depict the most basic aspect of routing, where all channels are routed to a summing amplifier. This may be sufficient in the simple situation where no additional mixes are needed and there is no option to perform any processing beyond the default processing in the channel and master sections.

But in most consoles, there is a bewildering number of ways in which signal flow can be modified, for example:

- A processor may be added to the signal flow using an insertion point.
- An effect may be added to the signal flow using an auxiliary send.

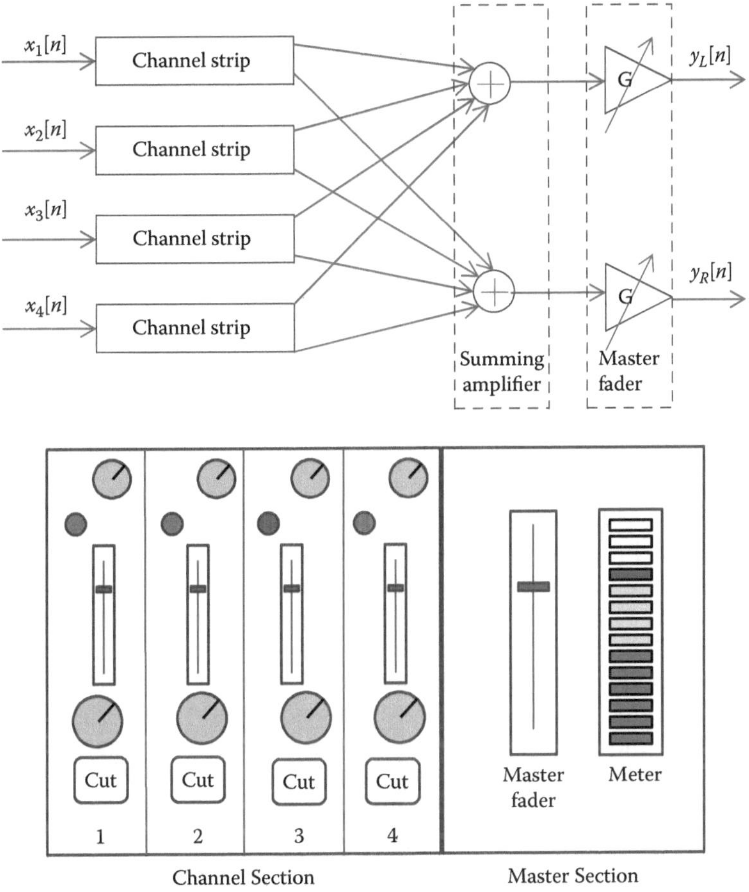

FIGURE 12.3
Signal flow diagram and user interface for a simple mixing console with four channels and a master section.

- Signals may be grouped together so that a single control can be used on all signals within the group.
- Signals may be routed to a common signal path, known as a bus, to be sent to a new destination.

Inserts for Processors, Auxiliary Sends for Effects

One common point of confusion is the difference between *inserts* and *auxiliary sends*. To understand this difference, we begin with an important distinction between the two types of devices used to treat audio signals. Generally, one refers to audio effects as techniques, usually based on signal processing, to modify audio signals. But for the practical aspects of mixing, a different

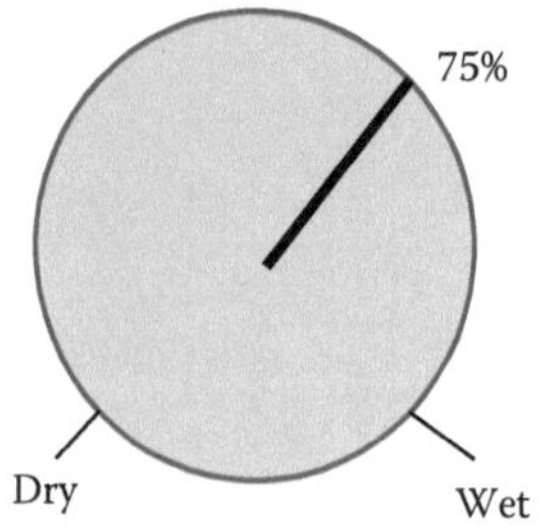

FIGURE 12.4
An implementation of a dry/wet mix.

definition is used to distinguish *effects* and *processors*. Effects are usually intended to be added to the original sound, whereas processors are usually intended to replace the input with the processed version at output. Effects typically use delay lines and almost always have a dry/wet knob, as in Figure 12.4, where a fully dry version is the original sound and a fully wet version is the affected sound. Processors, like EQ, gates, compressors, and panners, produce a modified version of the signal and rarely come with a dry/wet mix.

As shown in Figure 12.5, the standard method for connecting effects is using an auxiliary send, whereas processors are normally connected using an insertion point. Having said that, the distinction is often blurred. For instance, it is often possible to add a processed signal to the original, as if it were an effect, and it is possible to connect them in different ways (connecting an effect with an insertion point, for instance).

Insertion points, depicted in Figure 12.6, are used to add an external device into the signal path. They break the signal path, sending the signal to an external device and replacing the original with the externally processed signal. If an insert send is not connected to an external device, it can also be used to simply obtain a copy of the signal.

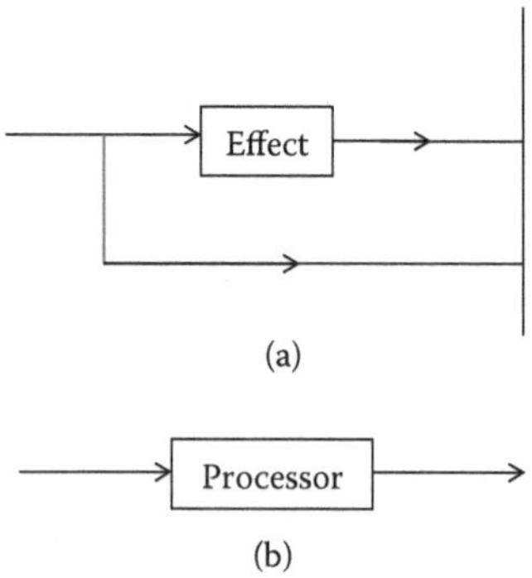

FIGURE 12.5
Standard method to connect an effect (a) and a processor (b).

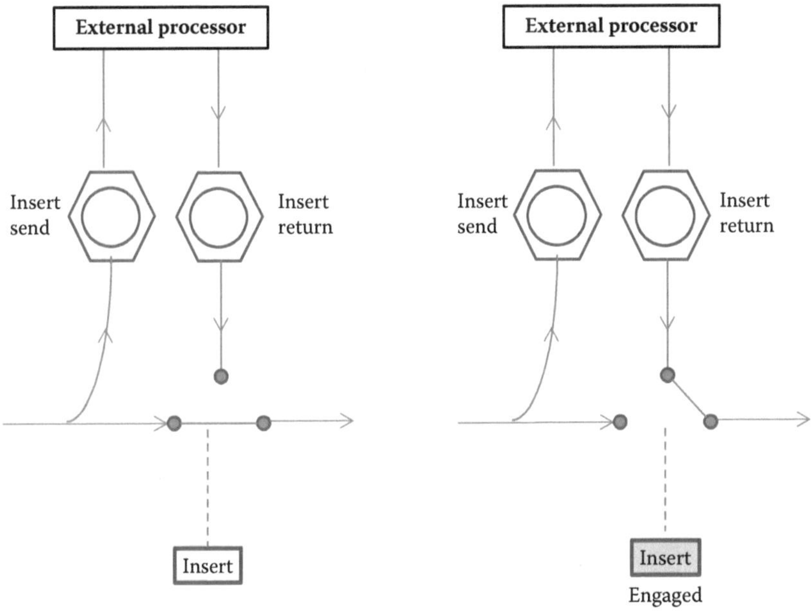

FIGURE 12.6
Signal flow for insertion points.

An auxiliary send (or just aux send) creates a copy of the signal in the channel path that is then routed to an internal auxiliary bus. As shown in Figure 12.7, the auxiliary send splits the incoming signal, and one path is sent to an auxiliary bus, which can be sent to other effects or devices. Typically, each channel strip on a sophisticated console will have a set of aux send-related controls, such as level and pan controls, and an on/off switch. As opposed to insert sends, where only one channel is sent to an external unit, each channel can be sent to the same auxiliary bus. Thus, aux sends allow effects to be shared between channels.

Since the aux sends are used for effects (reverb, delay), where the output is typically mixed with the original, we would expect the signal to be returned. Thus, there are also *aux returns,* also known as FX returns, which are usually in the master section. However, in most cases there are unused channels, so the output of effects is often brought back into channels instead of using returns.

Subgroup and Grouping

The signals on selected channels may be combined on a bus as a submix, or just summed to create the main mix [98]. Grouping of all the drum channels is very common. So the tracks representing many microphones around a drum kit can feed channels, which are then grouped into a bus, creating

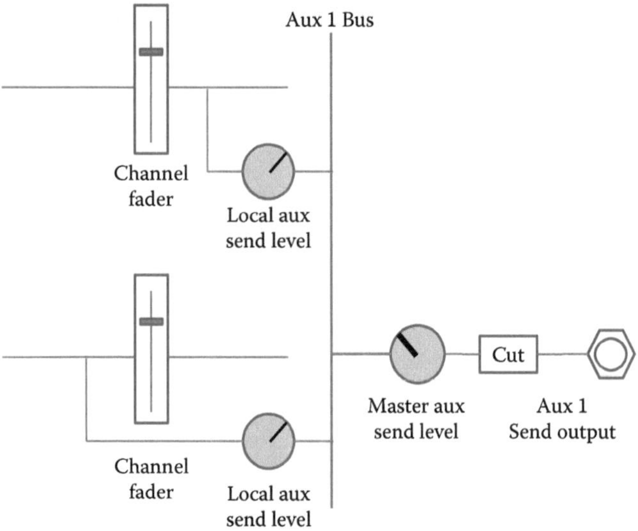

FIGURE 12.7
Signal flow for auxiliary sends.

a submix, and the level of all the drum signals can be controlled by a single fader.

Grouping is a very common procedure in mixing. While a drum group will often represent a dozen or more individual tracks, groups could consist of just two tracks, e.g., the microphone and amplifier for a guitar.

Channels are assigned to different groups using routing matrices, depicted in Figure 12.8. Each channel strip may have a routing matrix, which is usually presented on the interface either as a button for each group bus or with a button for each pair of groups. A routing matrix assignment switch may also be provided and used to determine whether the original channel signal is used to feed the mix bus.

Note that this is quite different from *control grouping*. Control grouping is a form of automation that simply allows a control to operate in an identical

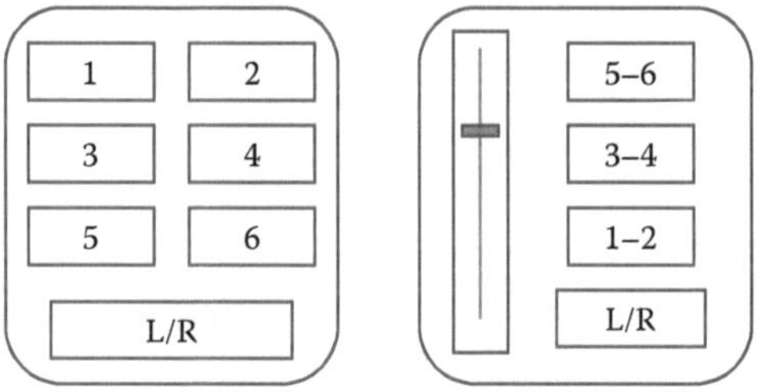

FIGURE 12.8
Routing matrices.

manner on a group of tracks [15]. So it does not actually process the signals collectively, nor does it change the signal path. Rather, the same processing is applied simultaneously to each signal in the group.

Digital versus Analog

One of the most important classifications of mixing consoles is whether they operate on digital or analog signals. This dictates the signal processing approaches and implementations, and is known to affect the resultant sound. Many recording engineers and artists have expressed a strong preference for the analog sound, but digital mixing consoles have more features and provide more versatility than analog consoles. Digital circuitry is also more resistant to interference. In addition, digital consoles often include a more extensive range of effects and processors, and may be expandable via third-party software.

Whether analog or digital systems are preferred for mixing and recording audio is highly dependent on the quality and design choices of the systems under review. Arguments for analog audio systems include minimal latency and the absence of fundamental errors common in digital systems, such as quantization noise and aliasing. Those in favor of digital approaches often point out the high levels of theoretical performance, including low noise and distortion levels, and highly linear behavior in the audible band.

Latency

Digital mixers have an inherent amount of latency or propagation delay, usually ranging from 1.5 to 10 ms. Every analog-to-digital conversion, digital sample rate conversion, and digital-to-analog conversion within a digital device will result in some delay. Hence, audio inserts to external analog processors may almost double the usual delay. And more delay can be caused by format conversions and normal digital signal processing operations.

The amount of latency in a digital mixer can vary widely depending on the routing and the amount and type of signal processing (for instance, infinite impulse response (IIR) versus finite impulse response (FIR) filters) that is performed. And comb filtering can result when a signal is given as input to two parallel paths with differing delays that are later combined.

This small amount of delay is not a serious issue in most situations, but can still cause problems. For instance, when in-ear monitoring is performed, the performer hears his or her voice acoustically in his or her head and may hear a delayed, electronically amplified version in his or her ears. This can be disorienting and annoying. Furthermore, all the delays in the chain will sum together, making latency more perceptible. Thus, some digital mixers will have built-in techniques for latency correction and avoidance in order to avoid such problems.

Digital User Interface Design

Digital mixing consoles often allow for presets, stored configurations, offline editing of the mix, advanced automation, and undo operations. They can also exploit digital interface design techniques to reduce the physical space requirements. Some digital mixers may allow the faders to be used as controls for other inputs or other effects. With most digital mixers, one can also make reassignments so that groupings of related inputs can appear near each other on the interface. However, the design choices needed to present these powerful features in a compact space can present a confusing interface to the operator.

Sound Quality

Microphone signals are often much weaker than what is needed for processing and routing in a mixing console. So both analog and digital systems use analog *microphone preamplifiers* to boost the signal. This circuit affects the timbre of the sound and can be the cause of much of the perceived difference in sound quality between consoles. In a digital mixer, an analog-to-digital converter will occur after the (analog) microphone preamplifier. Ideally, the quantization and sampling of the converter are carefully designed in order to avoid clipping or overloading, while also producing a highly precise and accurate digital representation of the signal over the whole linear dynamic range. Clipping and requantization need to be avoided, or at least minimized, in any further digital signal processing.

Analog mixers, too, must also avoid overload at the microphone preamplifier or at the mix buses. However, analog mixers achieve this with a gradual degradation, rather than the all or nothing approach that is often taken in digital design. Background hiss is also a problem in analog systems, but gain management is used to minimize its audibility. And low-level gating is used to avoid addition of further noise from inactive subgroups that may have been left in a mix.

In digital systems, the bandwidth is typically limited by the sample rate used, and the signal-to-noise ratio is limited by the bit depth of the quantization process. In contrast, bandwidth of an analog system is restricted by the physical capabilities of the analog circuits and recording medium. In an analog system, natural noise sources such as thermal noise and imperfections in the recording medium will lower the signal-to-noise ratio.

Those who favor digital consoles often claim that the analog sound is more a product of analog inaccuracies than anything else. This may be true, especially since for high-level signals that overload the system, analog devices usually produce a fairly smooth limiting behavior.

Do You Need to Decide?

Many aspects of system design combine to affect the perceived sound quality, which makes the question of analog versus digital systems difficult to decide. There have been few controlled listening tests, and no conclusive answer can yet be reached. High-performance systems of both types can be built to match most constraints, but it is often more cost-effective to achieve a given level of signal quality with a digital system, except when the requirements are minimal. The distinction is also blurred by digital systems that aim at analog-like behavior.

Engineers and producers will often mix and match analog and digital techniques when making a recording. The mixing style and approach has a bigger influence over the recording than the specific choice of audio console, though it is sometimes said that the digital mixer encourages more editing of the content. However, the difference between analog and digital is only one hardware sound quality issue. Microphones and especially loudspeakers may be considered the bottlenecks in the sound recording, production, and playback process. They both have significant distortion levels and do not easily produce a flat frequency response. In terms of being able to accurately reproduce the sound of a performance, they have a much greater influence over sound quality than the choice of mixer.

PLAYING THE MIXING DESK

King Tubby (1941–1989) was a Jamaican electronics and sound engineer, and his innovative studio work is often cited as one of the most significant steps in the evolution of a mixing engineer from a purely technical role to a very creative one [6].

In the 1950s and 1960s, he established himself as an engineer for the emerging sound system scene, and he built sound system amplifiers as well as his own radio transmitter. While producing versions of songs for local DJs, Tubby discovered that the various tracks could be radically reworked through the settings on the mixer and primitive early effects units. He turned his small recording studio into his own compositional tool.

Tubby would overdub the multitracks after passing them through his custom mixing desk, accentuating the drum and bass parts, while reducing other tracks to short snippets. He would splice sounds, shift the emphasis, and add delay-based effects until the original content could hardly be identified.

King Tubby would also rapidly manipulate a tunable high-pass filter, in order to create an impressive narrow sweep of the source until it became inaudible high-frequency content. In effect, he was able to "play" the mixing desk like a musical instrument, and in his creative overdubbing of vocals, he became one of the founders of the "dub music" genre.

Software Mixers

Mixing and editing of audio tracks can be performed on screen, using computer software and appropriate recording and playback hardware. This software-based mixing is an essential part of a digital audio workstation (see below). Space requirements are reduced since the large control surface of the traditional mixing console is not utilized. In a software studio, either there is no physical mixer or there is a small device, possibly touchscreen, with a minimal set of faders.

Digital Audio Workstations

A *digital audio workstation* (DAW) is a term that describes a computer equipped with a high-end sound card and a software suite for working with audio signals. Digital audio workstations can range from a simple two-channel audio editor to a complete, professional recording studio suite. DAWs usually provide specialized software to record, edit, mix, and play back multitrack audio content. They have the ability to freely manipulate recorded sounds, akin to how a word processor is used to create, edit, and save text. Although almost any home computer with multitrack and editing software can function as an audio workstation, the DAW is typically a more powerful system with high-quality external analog-to-digital (ADC) and digital-to-analog (DAC) conversion hardware, as well as extensive audio software. ProTools, Logic Pro, Ableton Live, Cubase, Nuendo, Reaper, and Reason are all popular DAW software platforms.

A common sound card can suffice for many audio applications, but a professional DAC is generally an external and sometimes rack-mounted unit and produces wider dynamic range with less noise or jitter.

DAWs can be classified into two categories:

1. *Integrated DAWs* evolved from the traditional mixer and consist of one device comprising a mixing console, control surface, and digital interface. Integrated DAWs were more popular when computational power and memory on personal computers were insufficient for many audio production tasks. However, they are still preferred in some markets and combine the benefits of the robust, physical console with the versatility of a graphical user interface. They have also found new appeal given the recent rise of touchscreens and embedded devices.
2. *Computer-based DAWs* consist of three components: a computer, an ADC–DAC, and digital audio editor software, such as that depicted in Figure 12.9. The computer hosts the sound card and software and provides processing power and memory for audio editing. The sound card provides an audio interface, converts analog audio signals into

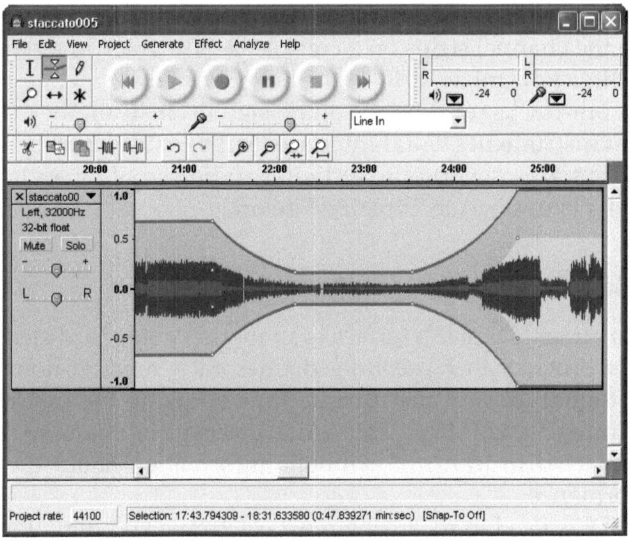

FIGURE 12.9
A screenshot of Audacity, a popular open-source DAW.

digital form, and may also assist in processing audio. The software controls the hardware components and provides a user interface to allow for audio recording, editing, and playback.

Common Functionality of Computer-Based DAWs

DAWs are often based around the same concepts as mixing consoles, but with some important distinctions. Most DAWs have a standard layout that includes transport controls (play, pause, rewind, record, etc.), track controls, a waveform display, and a mixer. In multitrack DAWs, each track will have some built-in controls, such as overall level and stereo position adjustment for each waveform in a track. And of course, plug-ins can be placed on the tracks in order to apply the various effects that have been discussed in previous chapters.

Almost all DAWs will also feature automation, often achieved by manipulating *envelope points*. Here, the user can mark up multiple points on a waveform. By adjusting the positions of these markers, the user can shape the sound, or adjust parameters for processing the sound over time, e.g., applying a time-varying panning position.

Unlike the mixing console, in a software mixer there is generally no separation between the multitracks and the mixer. Instead, the multitrack is represented as a sequence window, also known as arrangement, edit, or project window. It sees tracks and audio regions. So we no longer have channels, and instead we just have tracks and mixer strips. These mixer strips operate similarly to the channel strips on a console. A new track in a sequence window results in a new mixer strip in the mixer window.

However, our tracks need not be audio signals. Instead, they could represent Musical Instrument Digital Interface (MIDI) data, which behave like an audio track but are converted to a digital audio signal by a virtual instrument only at a later stage, as explained below.

MIDI and Sequencers

Musical Instrument Digital Interface is an industry standard electronic communications protocol that precisely defines each musical note performed on or by a digital musical instrument, thus allowing the instruments and computers to exchange data. The MIDI protocol is not used to transmit audio, but instead to transmit symbolic information about the notes in a music performance.

Today, MIDI is used in recording most electronic and digital music. MIDI is also used to control hardware, including live performance equipment, such as effects pedals and stage lighting. MIDI also is the basis of simple ringtones and the music in many games.

One important device for audio production that relies heavily on MIDI information is the *sequencer*. This is a software program for the creation and composition of electronic music. With a MIDI sequencer, one can record and edit a musical performance without requiring audio input. The performance is recorded as a series of events and is often played on a keyboard instrument.

The MIDI sequencer records events related to the performance, such as what note was played at what time, or how hard a key was pressed, but does not record the actual audio. This MIDI data are played back into software or into a MIDI instrument. So, a performer can select a particular instrument for a musical piece, but later choose another one without needing to create a new performance. In fact, the performer can use a single device to record multiple parts, and then modify attributes of each part to give the illusion of a performance by an entire orchestra.

Some music sequencers are intended to be an instrument for live performances, as well as or rather than a tool for composing and arranging. These are often used by DJs for live mixing of tracks.

Although the term *sequencer* is used mainly in reference to software, many hardware synthesizers and almost all music workstations include a built-in MIDI sequencer. Drum machines, for instance, usually will have a built-in sequencer, and there are stand-alone hardware MIDI sequencers. Furthermore, many sequencers can show the musical score in a piano roll notation, and some also provide traditional musical notation features. Most modern sequencers now have the ability to record audio and feature audio editing and processing capabilities as well, and some well-known DAWs have evolved from MIDI sequencers. Consequently, the terms *music sequencer* and *digital audio workstation* are sometimes used loosely and interchangeably.

Audio Effect Ordering

Over the past few chapters, we've covered the audio effects that are most often used. So now it is time to see how these effects can be used together to edit a signal in order to achieve a desired result. One essential factor to consider is the order in which the effects are placed. However, the first rule of effect ordering is, *there is no rule to audio effect ordering*. That is, even when trying to improve the technical aspects of the mix (as opposed to creative choices), there are justifications for almost any placement of the effects. Having said that, we will look at a variety of options and see if we can establish some guidelines.

First, you need to consider your concerns. Are you starting with a noisy signal, or are you worried about the noise introduced by the effects? What is each effect intended to do, and what sort of input signal does each effect expect? Do some effects counteract other effects? And of course, what is your goal in manipulating the sound, regardless of the effects and the placement that you might choose in order to achieve this result?

Noise Gates

If the audio effects are producing significant noise (or amplifying existing noise), then a noise gate could be placed toward the end of the audio effects chain. Placing the noise gate after those other effects ensures that the noise is not heard when the signal should be silent. The exception to this is if the effects applied to a signal involve reverberation or a delay line effect, in which case having a noise gate at the end of the effect chain may eliminate the ends of slowly decaying sounds. If instead a gate is applied before a delay or before reverberation, then even if it abruptly cuts off the sound, sustain produced by the delay line effect will partly disguise this. Delay-based effects help ensure that the sound will decay naturally rather than having a sudden silence.

Compressors and Noise Gates

Noise gates can be applied to give a relatively clean signal, on which various effects can act. So the noise gate would appear first in the change. Figure 12.10 presents an audio signal with some low-level noise on top, and the same signal after a dynamic range compressor has been applied on bottom. In the top waveform, a noise gate can be applied to remove most of

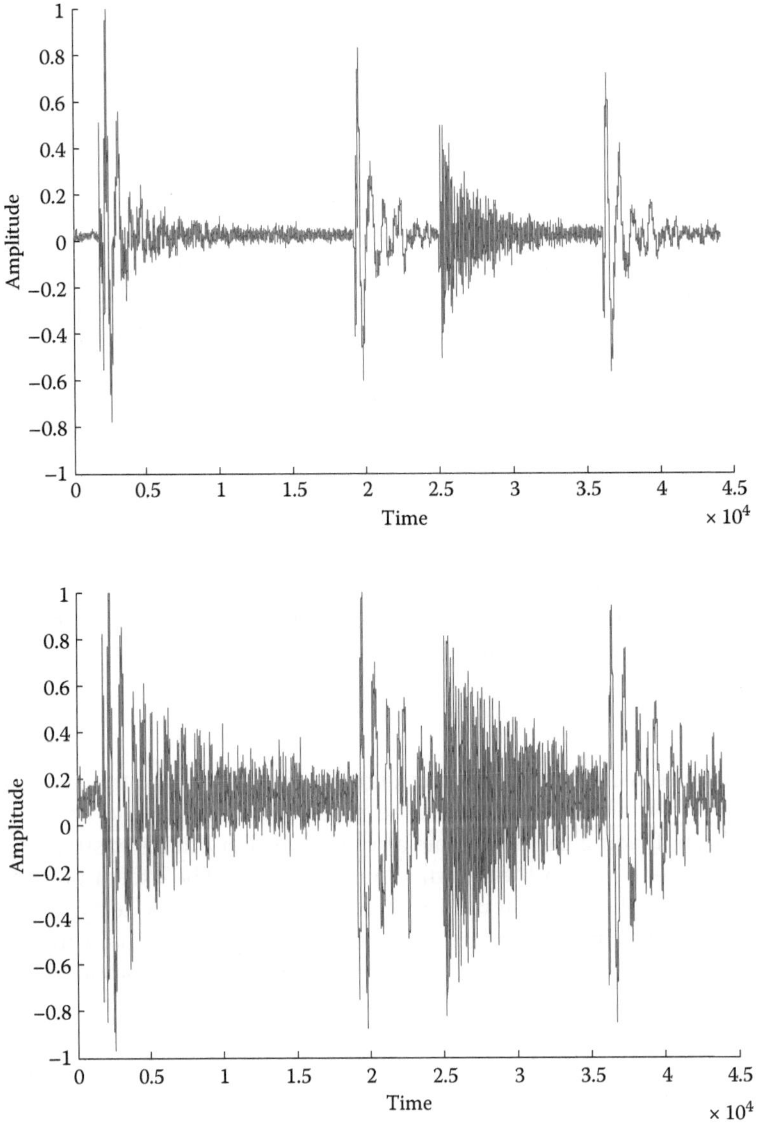

FIGURE 12.10
A gate can be applied to reduce the low-level background noise in the top waveform, whereas this noise is more difficult to gate in the compressed waveform depicted at bottom.

the noise because it can be distinguished from the high-amplitude signal. However, the compressed signal has a smaller dynamic range than the original. Compression results in the noise being boosted, until it is comparable in level to the wanted signal, making it very difficult to establish the threshold for the noise gate. Hence, compression is often applied after noise gating. Keep in mind, though, that the noise gate is not noise reduction, and there may still be unwanted noise when the source is active and the gate is not in operation.

If gates are not applied, another option is to put compression first in the chain. This is appropriate if the compressor will be combined with other effects that may introduce noise and artifacts. When the compressor is active (reducing output peak dynamic range) and output level is increased by the compressor's makeup gain, the noise will be amplified along with the instrument's sound. Other audio effects can introduce more noise into the system. If the compressor is placed after those effects, it may amplify that noise as well.

Care must be taken, however, to consider all the editing, mixing, and mastering that is done. Though the compressor has a makeup gain, additional gain may be applied at any point, or even in a later mastering stage. It may be that the gain applied during compression is small in comparison to later gain stages.

Compression and EQ

Whether to put compression before equalization, or vice versa, is a rather tricky question. There is no universal answer for this, partly because compression can serve different purposes. Transients are generally broadband and high level, so both EQ and compression will act on these together.

Suppose there is a single instrument signal with a highly resonant filter sweep. On some notes, the level may become very large when a note's fundamental frequency is very close to the resonant frequency. So a compressor can be used to reduce this. But you may also want to apply an equalizer to boost some broad mid-frequency range. In this case, one could put the compressor first to attenuate the high transient peaks and then apply equalization on a well-behaved signal.

But now suppose that the resonance is not serious, but a much more significant boost is required on the midrange frequencies. In which case the compressor may be placed after the equalizer, since the equalization may be causing unnaturally high levels. With a high threshold on the compressor, a midrange boost can still be achieved while at the same time avoiding the most problematic level issues.

Another reason to place an equalizer before a dynamic range compressor is to make the compression more sensitive to frequency content. This approach can also be achieved, with subtle differences, using multiband compression or a sidechain filter on a single-band compressor.

Reverb and Flanger

Effect ordering can be quite challenging when reverberation is applied. Suppose both reverberation and flanging, which can be quite a dramatic effect, are to be applied on a signal. Should the flanger be placed before or after reverberation?

Keep in mind that the flanger is driven by a low-frequency oscillator. If the flanger is placed before a reverberator, the reflections due to reverberation will break up the low-frequency, periodic nature of the flanger, resulting in a more diffuse sound. The flanger will sound more subtle, like a reverb with shimmer. But if the reverberation is applied before flanging, the late reflections will all be flanged, producing the flanger's characteristic "whooshy" effect.

Reverb and Vibrato

With vibrato but without reverb, what we hear resembles the direct sound of the instrument. However, we are used to hearing instruments from a distance, and in a room that provides reverberation. In other words, normal listening includes the direct sound coming from the instrument added to the sound that is reflected off walls, floor, and ceiling. When no vibrato is used, this reverberation makes relatively little difference. The frequencies of all the reflections are the same, so they all add up to make a relatively simple spectrum. By contrast, when playing with vibrato, the delayed sounds may have different frequencies and that difference changes with time. This gives rise to complex interference effects, producing a richer, livelier sound than a note played without vibrato.

Delay Line Effects

Delay line effects (and here we include reverb) are very often placed near the end of an effect chain, to give a natural-sounding decay. So the real questions become when to break this rule, and how to order multiple delay line effects placed in series.

Consider again the flanger, but this time used with a delay block. If the flanger is placed before a delay with feedback, then the delay effect will produce delayed repeats of the flanging sweep and each repeat will be, in effect, an image of the same section of the flanger sweep. These "flanging echoes" may overlap, especially for sustained sounds. The result will be to overlay a flanger sweep with several more sweeps, decaying in level, but starting at different times depending on the delay time setting. The flanging effect may become less prominent, but the sound will become more complex and interesting. However, unlike applying reverb after flanging, due to the sparsity of delays, some impression of flange sweep or movement should remain.

Putting the flanger last in the effect chain will impart the flanger's sweeping sound onto the original signal and every other effect that was applied.

Chorus is sometimes applied before a reverb effect, to add depth and richness to the signal. This often works well on more ethereal sounds, or pianos. Chorus can also be placed prior to delay or echo, to heighten the impression of distance and space.

Let's return to flanger before delay. A small amount of reverb could be added after a delay (and after other possible effects), because then each discrete delay would be transformed into a diffuse set of decaying delays over a short duration, rather than just a repetition of the signal. This makes the delay line effects seem more natural and increases the sense of space.

Distortion

Distortion will often be placed at the beginning of the effect chain so that any later effects will apply to the new harmonics that were introduced by the distortion. For example, a flanger applied to a distorted signal can sound quite dramatic, because it produces a sweep on a rich set of harmonics.

Because distortion often applies a high gain and also introduces harmonics of background sounds, the effect can introduce unwanted noise. So noise gates are often applied in conjunction with distortion. These may be placed directly after the distortion block (or after any filtering applied to the distortion).

An example ordering based on some of the above justifications is shown in Figure 12.11. In this case, the ordering was made with the goal of minimizing the accumulation of noise due to the signal processing in each effect.

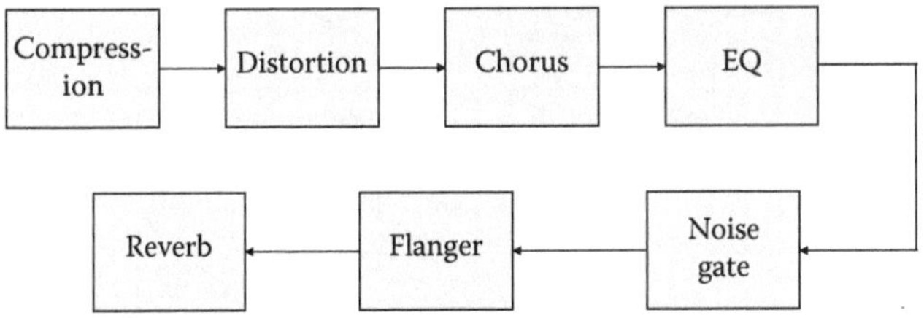

FIGURE 12.11
Just one approach to audio effect ordering, where noise from other effects is gated toward the end of the chain, but delay effects have a natural, ungated behavior.

Order Summary

Here, we list some of the suggestions for effect ordering.

- Distortion and other nonlinear effects should come right at the front of the signal chain so that any following effects blocks can work on the new harmonics introduced by the distortion.
- Gates come before compressors, so that the makeup gain in compression does not boost significant noise.
- Delay or reverb at the end of the chain creates a natural-sounding signal decay.

Combinations of Audio Effects

Many of the effects that have been described can be combined. In fact, common, advanced implementations will often present a single effect that has combined the functionality of multiple effects. In this section, we will take a look at some more ways that effects can be combined together.

Parallel Effects and Parallel Compression

So far we have been talking about series connection, but it is also possible to put effect blocks in parallel, as shown in Figure 12.12. For example, if distortion and reverberation were put in parallel, the output would be a mix of two distinctly separate effects: a distorted direct sound and clean reflections.

Running audio effects in parallel actually occurs whenever there is a wet mix, which involves adding the original signal back in with the modified signal, in which case we place an audio effect in parallel with an empty

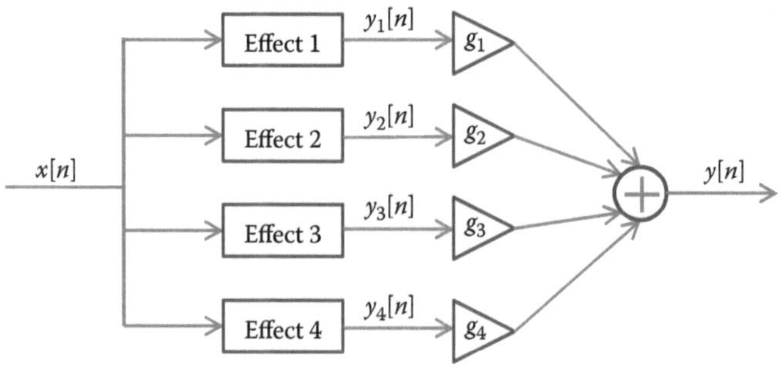

FIGURE 12.12
Parallel combination of audio effects.

effect that just passes the signal without modification. Recall the distinction between effects and processors (as mentioned, this is awkward terminology); processors replace the input with the processed version, but effects add the modified version to the original sound. So simply by adding a dry/wet mix, a processor can be made to act as an effect. This is the case with *parallel compression*. Consider a dynamic range compressor with extreme settings (high ratio, short attack, and release). By adding this output to the input, we have an interesting result. When the signal level is below the threshold, the sum is twice the original, resulting in a 6 dB increase. If the input signal level is far above the threshold, then most of the signal will be compressed. So the summed output is almost entirely due to the input signal on the direct (unprocessed) path, and there is almost no level change. Thus, simply by putting compression in parallel with the direct path, the compressor, without a makeup gain, will apply a boost to the quiet parts of a signal while leaving the loud parts relatively unaffected. This is a form of *upward compression*.

Putting a reverb and a delay, or just multiple reverbs, in parallel is also widely used since it gives the impression of rich acoustics. Complex sounds can also be introduced by putting an audio effect in the feedback loop of another, or by feeding the output signals from audio effects acting in parallel back into the inputs of the other, parallel effects.

Sidechaining

As mentioned in Chapter 6, the sidechain refers to a path within an audio effect other than the main path that produces the output. In effects (as opposed to processors), it often refers to the signal path that generates the affected signal to be added to the original. *Sidechaining* involves feeding an additional signal into an audio effect, where the effect is applied to some other signal. Although frequently used on compressors, gates, limiters, and expanders, it can also be found on vocoders, synthesizers, and other effects. It allows one to modify one signal depending on the characteristics of another signal. For instance, it can be used to prevent multiple sources in the same frequency range from clashing in a mix. As an example of this, the instrumental tracks in a multitrack music recording can be put into a bus, which then feeds the sidechain of a dynamic range compressor that has a large makeup gain. With this sidechain compression, the vocal level can be raised whenever the sum of the background tracks becomes particularly loud.

Ducking

In some cases, it is useful to have a signal's level controlled by a different signal so that when one signal level is high, the other signal is attenuated, as in Figure 12.13. This is known as *ducking* or *cross-limiting*, where one signal ducks under the other one, and is a form of sidechain compression. Ordinarily,

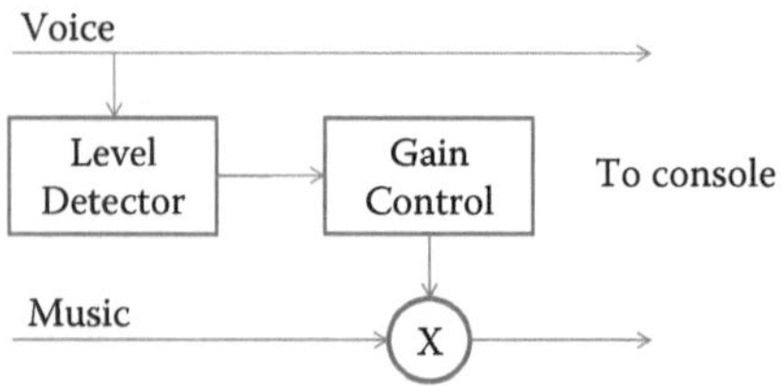

FIGURE 12.13
A ducker or cross-limiting setup.

dynamic range compression will reduce the gain based on the volume of the signal going through it. But a ducker reduces the gain based on a different signal. The most common application would be a radio or podcast DJ. If music is playing, when the DJ talks into the microphone, the level of the music will drop in order to ensure speech intelligibility. So the microphone signal is the input to the sidechain, but the control acts on the music signal. A ducker may also be used to emphasize certain elements in a mix. Hitting the kick drum could lower the other tracks, increasing its presence. Ducking is also often used in dance music to achieve a characteristic "pumping" sound, as discussed in Chapter 6. Though pumping may be seen in general as an artifact of compression, it can also be a means by which the rest of the mix reacts to the presence of a particular source.

De-Esser

The compressor forms the basis for another audio effect, the de-esser. A de-esser is used for reducing sibilant sounds in speech and singing, such as "s," "sh," and "ch." These sibilants often have highly exaggerated high-frequency response in recordings. Instead of monitoring the overall level of the input signal, it is possible to monitor and modify only a certain frequency range. This is what a de-esser does to attenuate the "ess" sounds.

There are two common forms of de-esser, as shown in Figure 12.14. The split-band de-esser is essentially a form of multiband compressor, where compression is applied only to the frequency range that produces the problematic sibilance. In the broadband de-esser, a broadband compressor is applied that uses an estimate of the signal level based on a filtered version of the input signal. That is, the sidechain of the compressor applies a filter to boost the frequency range where sibilance occurs. This filtered signal is used to trigger the compressor, but the gain reduction still applies to the original signal.

Sidechain Compression for Mastering

Compressing a mixdown, as is often done in the mastering stage of audio production, is different from compressing a single track because every instrument in the mix will get compressed the same amount. In practice,

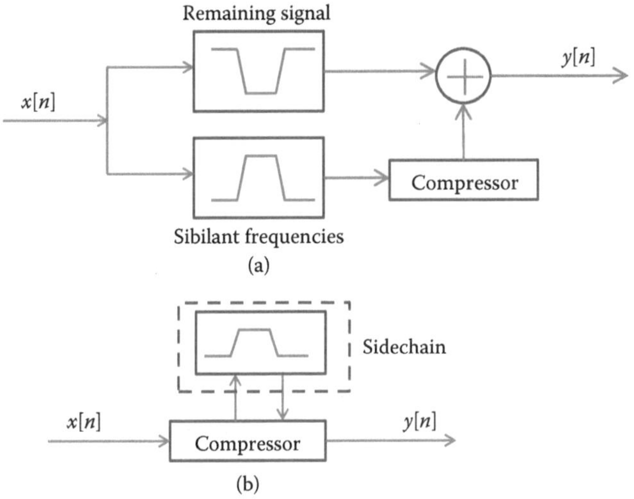

FIGURE 12.14
Split-band (a) and broadband (b) de-essing.

this often means that the bass instruments cause the whole mix to get over-compressed, which makes it sound like the bass instruments are "punching out" the other instruments. This can be compensated for by feeding the side-chain of a compressor with a filtered signal. Similar to the de-esser, high-pass filtering can be applied in order to minimize the compression due to low-frequency content.

Multiband Compression

Multiband compression is a versatile and popular tool that combines a filter-bank and a dynamic range compressor. As with loudspeaker crossover, discussed in Chapter 3, low-pass, band-pass, and high-pass filters are first used to separate the input signal into several frequency bands. Each band is then passed to a dynamic range compressor, which can be controlled independently of the other compressors. These parallel paths are then summed together to produce the output signal. A block diagram of a multiband compressor is shown in Figure 12.15.

Multiband compression is a particularly useful effect when mastering. For instance, the mixdown of a multitrack session may include an overly loud kick drum as well as vocals with wide dynamic range. If a normal, single-band compressor is applied, it may be triggered by both the offending kick drum and the wanted vocals. By applying multiband compression, we can ensure that loud low-frequency components, such as from the kick drum, result in dynamic range compression only over the low frequencies. Multiband compressors are also often used in broadcast, and the particular

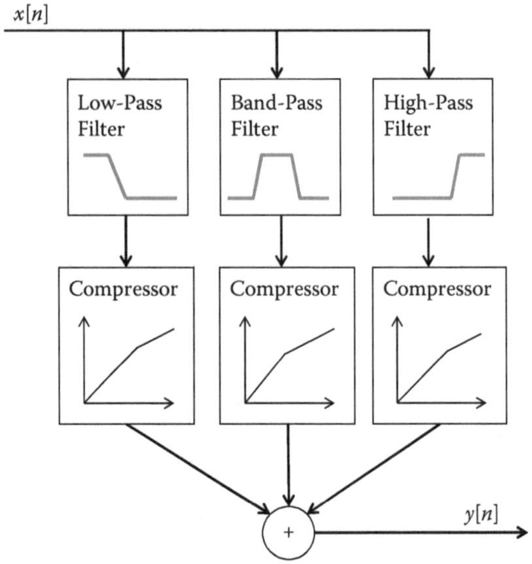

FIGURE 12.15
A multiband dynamic range compressor, with three frequency bands.

implementation and settings used can often give a radio station a characteristic sound. Multiband compression can also be used as an alternative to sidechain compression, often with better results, and is highly effective as a de-esser.

However, the dynamic range compressor is a nonlinear effect with a large set of standard parameters that interact in complicated ways. The multiband implementation greatly increases the complexity of the effect. The number of adjustable parameters is usually on the order of the number of bands multiplied by the number of parameters in a single-band compressor. Thus, great care should be taken in using the effect. It is often considered good practice to start with the compressors on each band configured with identical settings, and then selectively make small adjustments to address known issues or achieve predefined goals.

Dynamic Equalization

In dynamic equalization, the frequency response of an equalizer depends on signal level. So, for instance, a notch filter could be applied such that the amount of attenuation at the center frequency of the notch increases as the signal level increases. The equalizer is no longer a linear filter, and the transfer function $H(\omega)$ must now include level dependence, $H(\omega,L)$. Simplified versions of such functions are known as *describing functions*, with output dependent on both frequency and amplitude. However, level dependence in a dynamic equalizer is usually based on some estimation of the signal envelope, and would include time constants such as usually found in a dynamic range compressor.

Dynamic equalizers are closely related to multiband compressors and can be used to address many of the same audio production tasks. In multiband compression, different input/output level curves are applied for different input frequencies, whereas in dynamic equalizers different frequency response curves are applied for different input levels. Thus, in both cases, the output signal level is a function of input level and input frequency. This relationship between the two effects, as well as the overall framework in which they fit, is described in [99].

Dynamic equalization is not a widely used effect, though there are a few commercial implementations, and some analog equalizers and digital emulations of analog equalizers implicitly have dependence on signal level.

Combining LFOs with Other Effects

Many of the effects that we have encountered are driven by low-frequency oscillators, such as phasing and chorus. The low-frequency oscillator (LFO) can also be used with other effects to create interesting combinations. For example, stereo panning can be modulated via an LFO, or even by the envelope of the sound being processed. This latter option needs an effects unit that includes an envelope follower. Filter sweeps, similar to those found in synthesizers, that follow the input signal level can be created. Another option is to use the envelope of the input signal to control a gain placed before a reverberator. This technique, known as reverb ducking, can be used to increase the reverb during quiet sections, but emphasize the direct sound when the signal level is high. It is a useful tool for applying reverb when dealing with a dense mix.

Another tool that can be used is the sample and hold LFO, which can be seen in many classic analog synthesizers. The source has a variable frequency like any LFO, but it generates a random series of steps rather than a periodic signal. So rather than creating a continuous filter sweep, it will produce regular steps at random frequencies, which can produce interesting electronic sounds when used to control filter frequencies. Other creative techniques include using the sample and hold waveform to trigger an autopan so that the sound will jump to random positions, or to use the input envelope follower to control the stereo positioning, so that a source's stereo position is a function of its loudness.

The outcome is possibly unstable, and generally less predictable, when complicated feedback loops are used. For example, pitch shifters can include both delay and feedback options. So if a pitch shift is used with a feedback delay, each repeat produced by the delay will be frequency shifted farther than the preceding one, until it becomes inaudible.

Discussion

In this chapter, we have provided a taste of how the audio effects are used, both in terms of their application within audio devices such as mixing consoles and digital audio workstations, and in terms of how they are ordered and combined in the editing and mixing of audio devices. Audio production (and audio mixing in particular) is, of course, a vast field combining many technical and creative challenges. Even an understanding of the theory of audio effects, along with the skills to create them, does not give someone the knowledge required to effectively use them. For this, both critical listening skills and in-depth understanding of production and perception are necessary.

However, there are conceptual approaches that can be of great assistance. David Gibson [42] suggests that the challenges in mixing audio can be conceptualized by positioning each audio track on four axes: the volume, spatial position, frequency contour, and depth placement of the track. This visual approach can be used to assist in applying effects to tracks so as to organize the tracks along the axes and avoid conflicts in a mix. Others take a more bottom-up approach [14, 15], beginning with an understanding of the tools at one's disposal (including those described in previous chapters) and how these tools may be used to address mixing goals.

A note of caution should be made here. Although talented, experienced engineers have provided their own guidance and wisdom regarding approaches to mixing, best practices have, for the most part, not been formally established. Most of the rules that can be found in the literature have not been subject to formal study and evaluation. In [100, 101], Pestana found that many of the assumptions often made by practicing engineers or researchers regarding recommended approaches for audio production were unfounded, or did not agree with the actual approaches that were taken. This suggests that formal study of the best practices in and psychoacoustics of audio production is ripe for further investigation.

Problems

1. Where are the compressor and noise gate usually placed in the effects chain, and why?
2. In Figure 12.7, what operations are performed on Aux 1? Is this mono or stereo?
3. Compare and contrast dynamic EQ and multiband compression.
4. Draw a block diagram of a de-esser. Explain how it works and its relationship to a compressor.

5. Draw a block diagram of a ducker. Explain how it works and its relationship to a compressor.
6. What sort of effects or processing might be applied in the mastering stage during postproduction, and which ones might be applied in mixing but rarely in mastering? Which effects might rarely be used in live sound?
7. What audio effects, or combinations of audio effects, might you use and why to deal with the following problems? You may wish to refer to effects discussed in other chapters.
   a. A singer is slightly out of tune and off-pitch.
   b. There is an intermittent loud low-frequency noise in the background.
   c. A 35 s piece of music needs to fit into a 30 s TV advertisement and catch the listener's attention.
   d. An electronic, synthesized sound needs to be mixed with other tracks that were all recorded in a large venue.

13

Building Audio Effect Plug-Ins

The preceding chapters have presented the theory and implementation of the major types of audio effects, examining the mathematical principles behind each effect. This chapter describes how to put these principles into practice by creating an audio plug-in. Plug-ins are the most common way of implementing audio effects in software. A typical plug-in is a self-contained block of code that is compiled to run on a particular processor and operating system, but which can be used within many different audio software environments. This chapter will examine the process of creating plug-ins using the Jules' Utility Class Extensions (JUCE) programming framework, which can be used to create plug-ins for many different software platforms. The latest information for this chapter, as well as example code for several plug-ins, can be found on the website for this textbook.

Plug-In Basics

Audio plug-ins are designed to be self-contained effects that can be used within many different digital audio workstations (DAWs). To ensure compatibility across different DAWs, several industry standard plug-in formats have been developed. These include Steinberg's Virtual Studio Technology (VST) format, widely supported in nearly all professional audio software; Apple's AudioUnit format, supported on most Mac programs; and the Real-Time AudioSuite (RTAS) and newer Avid Audio Extension (AAX) formats by Digidesign/Avid. Each format provides similar functionality, typically including ways of passing audio into and out of the plug-in, negotiating sample rates and number of channels, and querying and setting user-adjustable parameters for the effect.

Programming Language

Most audio plug-ins are written in the C or C++ languages. The code will be compiled to run on a specific processor and operating system. However, the same code can typically be compiled to run on any hardware and operating system, as long as the code does not use any OS-specific functionality.

This book is not intended as an introduction to C or C++. Examples in the remainder of this chapter will be presented in C++ with the assumption that the reader has a basic familiarity (though not necessarily significant expertise) with the language. Excellent introductions to C++ programming can be found in many sources, including [102–104]. An audio-focused introduction to C++ is included in [105], which also goes into detail on many aspects of audio programming not covered in this text. A further reference for C++ audio effect programming can be found in [106].

Plug-In Properties

The essential task of an audio plug-in is to receive an input audio signal, apply an effect to it, and produce an output audio signal. In some cases, including virtual instrument or synthesizer plug-ins, no audio input is used, and the output may be produced in response to Musical Instrument Digital Interface (MIDI) messages. However, the effects in this book all assume an input and an output.

Important properties of a plug-in include the *number of channels* it supports and the allowable *sample rates*. Many effects can operate with different numbers of channels (for example, on mono or stereo inputs), but others will require specific channel configurations (for example, a ping-pong delay would need at least two output channels, but it could take one or two inputs). Some effects may have restrictions on the sample rates they support, though it is useful wherever possible to write plug-ins that operate at any sample rate. Plug-ins will also define one or more user-adjustable *parameters* that can be changed either through a standard interface provided by the DAW or by a custom graphical user interface (GUI) created by the plug-in author.

The JUCE Framework

The example code for this book uses the JUCE environment, created by Julian Storer, which provides a cross-platform, multiformat method for building audio plug-ins. JUCE projects are written in C++, and the JUCE libraries allow the same code to be compiled into VST, AudioUnit, RTAS, or AAX plug-ins. JUCE also provides a cross-platform set of GUI controls and a very large library of useful C++ classes. JUCE is free for use in open-source projects. Documentation and download links can be found on its website: http://www.juce.com.

Theory of Operation

JUCE audio plug-ins are divided into two components: a *processor* that handles the audio calculations and an *editor* or GUI that lets the user interact with the plug-in. The processor provides several functions: a *callback function* that the DAW calls every time it needs a new block of audio samples, methods for getting and setting effect parameters, and initialization and cleanup routines. The editor provides graphical controls for the user to see and change the parameters. Most DAWs will provide a generic editor when the plug-in does not define its own.

Callback Function

The most important task for an audio plug-in is receiving and processing audio samples. How does the plug-in know how many samples to process, and when to process them? If the effect is operating in real time, it is clearly impossible to wait for the entire audio signal to arrive before applying the effect. Instead, audio needs to be processed in small *blocks* or *buffers* of samples as it comes in. To receive blocks of samples, plug-ins implement a callback function, a function that the DAW calls every time it has new audio to process. Thus, it is always the DAW, and *not* the plug-in, which determines how many audio samples to process and when. The advantage of this arrangement is that the plug-in author never needs to be concerned with where the audio samples come from, when they should arrive, or where they go after the effect has been applied. The author simply needs to write a callback function that processes as many samples as requested by the DAW.

When the DAW runs the callback function, it will provide several pieces of information. These include the *buffer size* (how many audio samples to process), the *sample rate*, the *number of input and output channels*, and a *buffer* (region of memory) containing the input audio. The host will also provide a buffer in which the audio output should be stored. In JUCE (as in many plug-in formats), the plug-in is expected to put its output in the same buffer where the input samples were found.

When the callback function finishes, it simply returns control to the DAW, which decides what should happen to the processed samples. The callback function will be called again when there are more samples to process. The buffer size used by the DAW partly determines the overall *latency* (delay) from input to output; smaller buffer sizes produce a low delay but increase the risk of *underruns* (gaps) if the computer cannot respond quickly enough. A typical conservative buffer size would be 512 samples; a high-performance buffer size might be as small as 32 samples. At a 44.1 kHz sample rate, a buffer size of 32 means that the callback function would run over 1300 times per second.

Managing Parameters

Nearly every audio effect will have one or more user-adjustable parameters. For example, a parametric equalizer plug-in might let the user change the center frequency, the gain, and the Q of the filter. Most plug-ins provide a user interface to allow the user to adjust parameters. Every operating system and plug-in format provides different routines for managing a GUI, but there

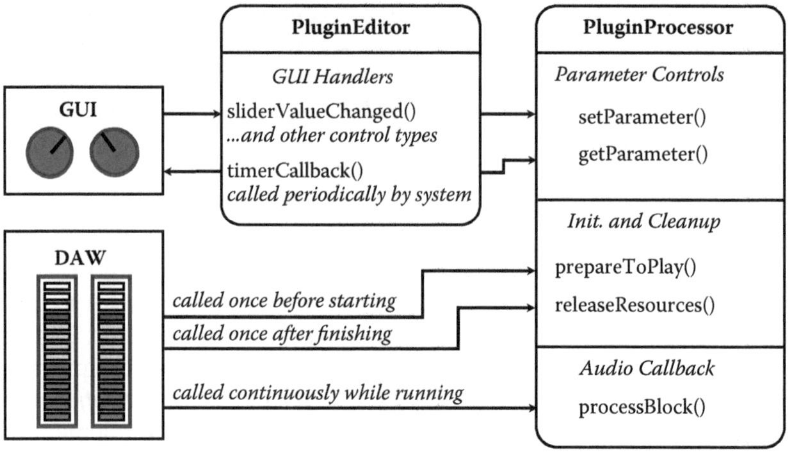

FIGURE 13.1
Basic components of a JUCE audio plug-in and their relationship to the DAW.

are several common requirements. In particular, the plug-in must provide a set of functions for the user to see or change the parameters, and there must be a way for the callback function to discover the current parameter values.

JUCE provides several methods (C++ object functions) related to managing parameters, described in detail in the example in the next section. The most important of these methods are `getParameter()` and `setParameter()` within the audio processor object (see Figure 13.1). When the DAW calls `getParameter()`, it provides a single argument indicating the index of the parameter it wants to query. The plug-in is expected to return the value of this parameter as a floating-point number (C++ type `float`). It is up to the plug-in to define what the indices mean (for example, a parametric equalizer might have frequency as parameter 0, gain as parameter 1, and Q as parameter 2). With `setParameter()`, the host provides an index of the parameter to set and a floating-point value to which it should be set. The plug-in stores this information so the audio callback function can access it later.

In JUCE, the plug-in keeps track of its current parameters by using *instance variables*, variables declared inside a C++ class that are accessible to any of its methods. When the DAW calls `getParameter()`, the current value of the relevant instance variable is returned; when it calls `setParameter()`, the value of the instance variable is changed. The callback function, `processBlock()`, accesses the values of these variables to discover the current parameter settings.

Initialization and Cleanup

Before a plug-in can process audio, certain initialization tasks must be performed. For example, in a delay plug-in, memory for delay buffers might need to be allocated; for an equalizer plug-in, filter coefficients might need to be calculated and internal variables holding previous samples might need to be initialized to 0. For plug-ins with low-frequency oscillators, the phase of the oscillator may need to be initialized.

Every plug-in format will provide a method for initializing the plug-in. In JUCE, basic initialization can be performed in the *constructor* of the audio processor object, which runs once when the plug-in is first loaded. JUCE also provides a method called `prepareToPlay()` that runs immediately before audio processing begins. By allocating resources just before the audio starts, the plug-in uses resources only while actively running.

All resources that are allocated by the plug-in will eventually need to be released. JUCE provides a method called `releaseResources()` that runs immediately after the host stops processing audio. This method should be used to free any resources allocated in `prepareToPlay()`. It is safe to assume that the audio callback function will never run after a call to `releaseResources()`. Similarly, the counterpart to the C++ constructor is the *destructor*, which runs once when the user removes the plug-in from the host environment. Anything that is allocated in the constructor should be freed in the destructor.

Preserving State

Each time the DAW calls the plug-in's callback function, it will provide only a small block of input samples to be processed. The plug-in often depends on previous state information to know how to process these samples. For example, phases of oscillators, pointers within circular buffers, and previous values of input and output samples may be needed to calculate the output. It is up to the plug-in to save any state that it needs during the callback function.

To understand the importance of managing state, consider a simple effect where the current output is equal to the sum of the last two inputs: $y[n] = x[n] + x[n-1]$. Suppose that the host requests 512 samples beginning at sample N. It will therefore supply a buffer containing 512 input samples $x[N]$ to $x[N+511]$ and require 512 output samples $y[N]$ to $y[N+511]$.

At first glance, it may seem as if the callback function has enough information to calculate the output without any reference to what has happened previously. But what about calculating $y[N]$, the very first sample in the buffer? We have $y[N] = x[N] + x[N-1]$, but $x[N-1]$ was supplied last time the callback was run, and that value is no longer available. The plug-in must therefore use a separate instance variable to remember what has come earlier. Here, a single `float` for each channel would be needed to remember the previous sample. The float should be declared inside the class, so its value is preserved across calls to the callback function.

The following example shows the implementation of a delay plug-in in JUCE, including the management of parameters and preservation of state between callbacks.

Example: Building a Delay Effect in JUCE

This section will describe the implementation of a simple plug-in in the JUCE environment. We will take as an example a delay with feedback (Chapter 2), with user-adjustable controls for delay time, feedback level, and wet/dry mix. The complete code for this effect can be found in the materials that accompany the book, along with example code for several other effects.

Required Software

To build the plug-ins that come with the book, the following software is required.

1. The JUCE (Jules' Utility Class Extensions) C++ library by Julian Storer. JUCE runs on nearly every platform, including Mac, Windows, and Linux, and can be downloaded free from http://www.juce.com.
2. A C++ compiler: Visual Studio on Windows, Xcode on Mac OS X, or g++ on Linux. They are all generally available as free downloads, sometimes after a registration process.
3. On the Mac, two other pieces: Xcode Audio Tools, which can be installed from within Xcode, and the Core Audio Utility Classes, which can be found on Apple's website. Platform-specific setup instructions often change over time; please consult the companion website for this book to find the most recent instructions.
4. To build VST plug-ins, VST SDK (version 2.4). This can be obtained free from Steinberg (http://www.steinberg.net) after creating a developer account. VST SDK is required on Windows, but is optional on Mac where AudioUnits can be created instead. Whether you use VST or AudioUnits, your program in JUCE will be written identically.
5. A suitable DAW or other host environment in which to test the plug-ins. On the Mac, Xcode Audio Tools provides the AU Lab program, which is a simple, lightweight way of testing AudioUnit plug-ins. Several other cross-platform options are available, including Audacity and Reaper.

Creating a New Plug-In in JUCE

In JUCE, new projects are created using a program called *Introjucer.* Introjucer needs to be compiled on your system before anything further can take place. Within the main JUCE folder, Introjucer project files for each of the major development environments (Visual Studio, Xcode, etc.) can be found. Open the project in your development environment and build it. It should compile without errors if JUCE was correctly installed.

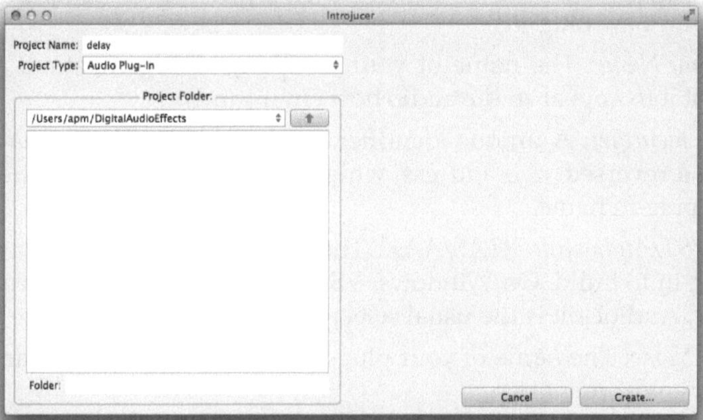

FIGURE 13.2
Creating a new audio plug-in in Introjucer.

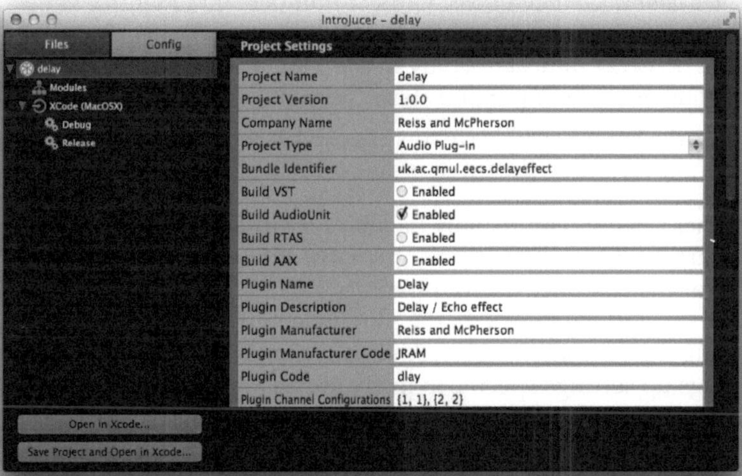

FIGURE 13.3
Introjucer settings for audio plug-in. List at left shows a single build target for Xcode.

Run Introjucer once it finishes compiling, and select *New Project* from the *File* menu. Enter a project name and set the *Project Type* to *Audio Plug-In* (see Figure 13.2). Click *Create* to make the JUCE project for your new plug-in. From this point, you will get a window where you can edit the details of the plug-in (Figure 13.3). Several fields are important:

Project Version: The version number of your plug-in (the default value is fine for new plug-ins).

Company Name: The name of your company or organization, as you want it to appear in the audio host environment.

Bundle Identifier: A unique identifier for the plug-in. The format looks like a reversed web address, which identifies the organization and the plug-in name.

Built VST/AudioUnit/RTAS/AAX: These boxes select which format of plug-in to build. On Windows, VST is the most common format; on Mac, AudioUnit is the usual selection.

Plugin Name: The name of your plug-in as you want it to appear in the host environment.

Plugin Description: A short description of your plug-in.

Plugin Manufacturer: Company name, similar to *Company Name* above.

Plugin Manufacturer Code: A four-letter code identifying your company or organization. Use a single code consistently across all the plug-ins you develop.

Plugin Channel Configurations: Pairs of numbers that identify valid configurations of input channels and output channels. For example, `{1,1}, {2,2}` indicates a plug-in that can take mono input and mono output, or stereo input and stereo output.

Silence: Most effects can leave this checked, but if your plug-in produces sound even when the input is silent, uncheck this box.

The other settings can usually be left at their defaults. The next step is to make a target for your specific compiler. By default, Introjucer should create a target for the compiler on your platform. If not, or if you want to make an additional target, right-click on the plug-in icon (Figure 13.4).

Selecting the compiler target from the list on the left-hand side of the window brings up settings specific to the platform. Most of these options can be left at their default values. It is important, though, to correctly set the *Local JUCE Folder* to the location where you have installed JUCE. If you are building a VST plug-in, setting the *VST Folder* is also important.

When you have finished entering all the details, click *Save Project and Open in Xcode* (on Mac) or *Save Project and Open in Visual Studio* (on Windows). This should bring up the project within your compiler, where it can be built using the same procedure you normally use to compile projects. On the Mac, building the project will automatically copy the resulting plug-in to the system plug-ins directory (`~/Library/Audio/Plug-Ins/Components/`), where it will be found by audio software, including AU Lab. In Windows, your DAW may need to be manually set to look for your plug-in. In most cases, restarting the audio host program (AU Lab, Audacity, etc.) is necessary every time the plug-in is recompiled.

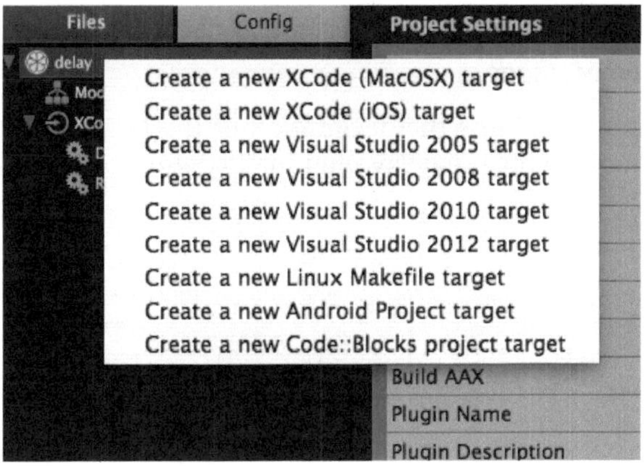

FIGURE 13.4
Right-clicking on the plug-in icon produces a menu for generating additional build targets.

Opening Example Plug-Ins

This book comes with several example audio plug-ins that can be opened in the compiler of your choice. Within each plug-in directory, look in the `Builds` directory for a version specific to your compiler. If you do not find one, open the .jucer file in the Introjucer and create a new target for your platform. Following the instructions in the previous section, you should be able to compile the plug-in and get it running in your audio host environment.

File Overview

JUCE plug-ins contain four source files by default:

PluginProcessor.h: The header file for PluginProcessor.cpp; defines the C++ object whose code is filled out in PluginProcessor.cpp. Includes declaration of methods and instance variables.

PluginProcessor.cpp: The main file where the audio processing is done.

PluginEditor.h: The header file for PluginEditor.cpp, containing the definition of the C++ object for the editor.

PluginEditor.cpp: Contains the code for the graphical user interface for the plug-in.

In your own projects, for more complex effects, you might find occasion to add extra source files to the project. But most effects can be implemented in just these four. We will examine each file in turn. Not all lines of each file are included in this text, so please refer to the accompanying materials for the complete source.

PluginProcessor.h

Declaration and Methods

PluginProcessor.h contains the declaration of the `DelayAudioProcessor` class, which implements the delay plug-in. Its definition begins here:

```
class DelayAudioProcessor  : public AudioProcessor
{
public:
    //==============================================
    DelayAudioProcessor();
    ~DelayAudioProcessor();
```

In your own effects, you may want to change the name of the class to reflect what your plug-in does. Be sure to change the name consistently across all four source files. This block of code also shows the first two methods of the `DelayAudioProcessor` class: `DelayAudioProcessor()` and `~DelayAudioProcessor()`. These are the constructor and destructor, respectively. They run when the plug-in is loaded and unloaded by the DAW. The following lines declare a collection of other methods that are standard to every JUCE plug-in:

```
//=======================================================
//=======================================================
void prepareToPlay (double sampleRate,
                    int samplesPerBlock);
void releaseResources();
void reset();
void processBlock (AudioSampleBuffer& buffer,
                   MidiBuffer& midiMessages);

//=======================================================
AudioProcessorEditor* createEditor();
bool hasEditor() const;

//=======================================================
const String getName() const;

      int getNumParameters();

      float getParameter (int index);
      void setParameter (int index, float newValue);

      const String getParameterName (int index);
      const String getParameterText (int index);

const String getInputChannelName (int channelIndex) const;
const String getOutputChannelName (int channelIndex) const;
```

```
bool isInputChannelStereoPair (int index) const;
bool isOutputChannelStereoPair (int index) const;

bool silenceInProducesSilenceOut() const;
double getTailLengthSeconds() const;
bool acceptsMidi() const;
bool producesMidi() const;

//==============================================================
int getNumPrograms();
int getCurrentProgram();
void setCurrentProgram (int index);
const String getProgramName (int index);
void changeProgramName (int index, const String& newName);

//==============================================================
void getStateInformation (MemoryBlock& destData);
void setStateInformation (const void* data,
                          int sizeInBytes);
```

The contents of these methods will be found in PluginProcessor.cpp. These lines should not be modified; however, it is common to add your own methods in more complex plug-ins. Additional methods can be declared either below these standard methods or, if the methods will be called only internally by the object itself, below the `private:` line later in the file.

Variables

Following the methods is a declaration of *instance variables* for the class:

```
    //==============================================================

    // these are used to persist the UI's size - the values are
    // stored along with the filter's other parameters, and the
    // UI component will update them when it gets resized.
    int lastUIWidth_, lastUIHeight_;

    enum Parameters
    {
        kDelayLengthParam = 0,
        kDryMixParam,
        kWetMixParam,
        kFeedbackParam,
        kNumParameters
    };
```

```
    // Adjustable parameters:
    float delayLength_; // Length of delay line in seconds
    float dryMix_;      // Mix level of original signal (0-1)
    float wetMix_;      // Mix level of delayed signal (0-1)
    float feedback_;    // Feedback level (0-just less than 1)

private:
    // Circular buffer variables for implementing delay
    AudioSampleBuffer delayBuffer_;
    int delayBufferLength_;
    int delayReadPosition_, delayWritePosition_;

    //==========================================================
    JUCE_DECLARE_NON_COPYABLE_WITH_LEAK_DETECTOR(
        DelayAudioProcessor);
};
```

By declaring the variables here rather than in a particular method, the variables can be accessed from any method within the object. The variables declared below the `private:` line are accessible only within the `DelayAudioProcessor` class; the others are accessible to any object (`public`). Here, these variables are declared `public` because the `DelayAudioProcessorEditor` class needs to access them. The functions of the variables are as follows:

1. `lastUIWidth_` and `lastUIHeight_` are used by JUCE to remember the size of the graphical interface between times the plug-in was loaded.
2. The `enum` statement declares a group of constant values in sequential order. For example, `kDelayLengthParam` has a value of 0, `kDryMixParam` has a value of 1, and so forth. These define the indices of parameters that control the plug-in. Your plug-in may change this list, but always keep `kNumParameters` at the end so the code in PluginProcessor.cpp knows the number of valid parameters.
3. `delayLength_`, `dryMix_`, `wetMix_`, and `feedback_` hold the current values of each parameter. The convention of putting an underscore at the end of the variable name helps distinguish instance variables from local variables declared in particular methods. For clarity it is helpful to maintain this convention when declaring new instance variables in your plug-in.
4. `delayBuffer_`, `delayBufferLength_`, `delayReadPosition_`, and `delayWritePosition_` are internal state variables used by the delay code. They are declared `private` because only the `DelayAudioProcessor` class needs access to them. Their uses are explained in the section on PluginProcessor.cpp. Your plug-ins will likely declare a different list of state variables here.

The final line of the class is a macro used internally by JUCE, and should not be changed (except to update the name of the class if you change that). Notice that the initial values of the variables have not been declared here. This will be done in PluginProcessor.cpp.

PluginProcessor.cpp

Of the four files in the plug-in, PluginProcessor.cpp is the one that handles the most important parts of the audio processing. The file implements the methods and uses the instance variables declared in PluginProcessor.h. The two most important elements of this file are the audio callback function `processBlock()` and a collection of methods for getting and setting parameters. The complete file can be found in the accompanying materials to this book. Rather than proceeding line by line, let us begin by examining the audio callback function.

Audio Callback

```
void DelayAudioProcessor::processBlock (AudioSampleBuffer&
                               buffer, MidiBuffer& midiMessages)
{
    // Helpful information about this block of samples:
        // How many input channels for our effect?
    const int numInputChannels = getNumInputChannels();
        // How many output channels for our effect?
    const int numOutputChannels = getNumOutputChannels();
        // How many samples in the buffer for this block?
    const int numSamples = buffer.getNumSamples();

        // dpr = delay read pointer; dpw = delay write pointer
    int channel, dpr, dpw;

    // Go through each channel of audio that's passed in. In
    // this example we apply identical effects to each channel,
    // regardless of how many input channels there are. For
    // some effects, like a stereo chorus or panner, you might
    // do something different for each channel.

    for (channel = 0; channel < numInputChannels; ++channel)
    {
        // channelData is an array of length numSamples which
        // contains the audio for one channel
        float* channelData = buffer.getSampleData(channel);

        // delayData is the circular buffer for implementing
        // delay on this channel
```

```
        float* delayData = delayBuffer_.getSampleData(
                           jmin (channel,
                           delayBuffer_.getNumChannels() - 1));

        // Make a temporary copy of any state variables
        // declared in PluginProcessor.h which need to be
        // maintained between calls to processBlock(). Each
        // channel needs to be processed identically which
        // means that the activity of processing one channel
        // can't affect the state variable for the next channel

        dpr = delayReadPosition_;
        dpw = delayWritePosition_;

        for (int i = 0; i < numSamples; ++i)
        {
            const float in = channelData[i];
            float out = 0.0;

            // In this example, the output is the input plus
            // the contents of the delay buffer (weighted by
            // delayMix). The last term implements a tremolo
            // (variable amplitude) on the whole thing.

            out = (dryMix_ * in + wetMix_ * delayData[dpr]);

            // Store the current information in the delay
            // buffer. delayData[dpr] is the delay sample we
            // just read, i.e. what came out of the buffer.
            // delayData[dpw] is what we write to the buffer,
            // i.e. what goes in

            delayData[dpw] = in + (delayData[dpr] * feedback_);

            if (++dpr >= delayBufferLength_)
                dpr = 0;
            if (++dpw >= delayBufferLength_)
                dpw = 0;

            // Store the output in the buffer, replacing input
            channelData[i] = out;
        }
    }

    // Having made a local copy of the state variables for each
    // channel, now transfer the result back to the main state
    // variable so they will be preserved for the next call of
    // processBlock()

    delayReadPosition_ = dpr;
    delayWritePosition_ = dpw;
```

```
    // In case we have more outputs than inputs, we'll clear
    // any output channels that didn't contain input data,
    // (because these aren't guaranteed to be empty - they may
    // contain garbage).
    for (int i = numInputChannels; i < numOutputChannels; ++i)
    {
        buffer.clear (i, 0, buffer.getNumSamples());
    }
}
```

The first line of this block specifies the name of the method, which is prefaced by `DelayAudioProcessor::` to indicate that this method is part of the `DelayAudioProcessor` class. The method takes two arguments, `buffer` and `midiMessages`, which hold the audio and MIDI input information, respectively. In this example we will ignore the MIDI messages, but they might be used in a synthesizer plug-in. Since the method is declared `void`, it does not return a value. `processBlock()` is the callback function that will be run by the DAW every time there are new audio samples to process.

The first three lines of the method establish some basic properties of the environment. JUCE provides standard functions for retrieving the number of input channels, the number of output channels, and the sample rate (`getSampleRate()`), though the latter is not used here. The input argument `buffer` is an object of type `AudioSampleBuffer`, which holds information about the number and content of input samples.

Given a number of input channels and number of requested samples, the basic procedure is to iterate through every sample of every channel and apply the effect to each sample. The method contains two nested `for()` loops, first iterating over the channels, then iterating over the samples within each channel. For each channel, the code first converts the JUCE `AudioSampleBuffer` class to a standard C array:

```
// channelData is an array of length numSamples which
// contains the audio for one channel
float* channelData = buffer.getSampleData(channel);

// delayData is the circular buffer for implementing
// delay on this channel
float* delayData = delayBuffer_.getSampleData(
                   jmin (channel,
                   delayBuffer_.getNumChannels() - 1));
```

At this point, the array `channelData` holds the input audio samples for one channel and `delayData` holds the contents of the delay buffer. The core audio processing then takes place inside the inner `for` loop:

```
            const float in = channelData[i];
            float out = 0.0;
```

The above lines store the current input sample in the local variable `in` and declare a variable `out` that will hold the result.

```
out = (dryMix_ * in + wetMix_ * delayData[dpr]);
```

This applies the basic delay equation from Chapter 2, calculating the output in terms of the sum of the input and the output of the delay buffer. Each term is weighted by a parameter (`dryMix_` and `wetMix_`, respectively). `dpr` is the *read pointer* into the delay buffer that keeps track of the next sample to read out. Next, the content of the delay buffer is updated:

```
delayData[dpw] = in + (delayData[dpr] * feedback_);
```

`dpw` is the *write pointer* into the delay buffer. The content of the buffer is updated as the sum of the input and the feedback from the output, as detailed in Chapter 2. Finally, the position of the read and write pointers is advanced, wrapping around at the end to form a *circular buffer*:

```
if (++dpr >= delayBufferLength_)
    dpr = 0;
if (++dpw >= delayBufferLength_)
    dpw = 0;
```

`delayBufferLength_` is an instance variable that has its value set elsewhere to indicate the size of the delay buffer in samples.

In addition to updating the read and write pointers for each sample, two other questions must be addressed: First, how are the read and write pointers initially set? Second, how are their values maintained at the end of the callback? Initialization will be considered later, but the question of maintaining values across callbacks is crucial to making the effect work. The callback will process only a small buffer of samples at a time, and the pointers cannot be allowed to reset with each call. To remember the values across callbacks, the instance variables `delayReadPosition_` and `delayWritePosition_` are used. Since they are declared in PluginProcessor.h, their values will persist beyond the end of the callback.

It might seem reasonable to use `delayReadPosition_` and `delayWritePosition_` directly in place of `dpr` and `dpw` in `processBlock()`. However, consider the operation of a stereo effect, where each channel is processed in turn. We do not want the left channel to change the pointer locations for the right channel. `dpr` and `dpw` are therefore introduced as local copies of `delayReadPosition_` and `delayWritePosition_`:

```
dpr = delayReadPosition_;
dpw = delayWritePosition_;
```

At the end of the callback, their values are written back to the instance variables:

```
        delayReadPosition_ = dpr;
        delayWritePosition_ = dpw;
```

This plug-in applies the same effect to all channels; in other cases, such as a stereo flanger or chorus where the channels are handled differently, the outer `for()` loop iterating over the channels might be handled differently, and in some situations, separate instance variables for each channel may be required to remember the state between callbacks.

Initialization

Before the audio callback can run, all parameters and instance variables need to be initialized with usable values. Initialization in JUCE plug-ins takes place in two functions: in the constructor `DelayAudioProcessor()`, which runs once when the plug-in is loaded, and in `prepareToPlay()`, which runs each time the audio is started, just before the first call to `processBlock()`. Here is the constructor:

```
DelayAudioProcessor::DelayAudioProcessor() : delayBuffer_ (2, 1)
{
    // Set default values:
    delayLength_ = 0.5;
    dryMix_ = 1.0;
    wetMix_ = 0.5;
    feedback_ = 0.75;
    delayBufferLength_ = 1;

    // Start the circular buffer pointers at the beginning
    delayReadPosition_ = 0;
    delayWritePosition_ = 0;

    lastUIWidth_ = 370;
    lastUIHeight_ = 140;
}
```

In the first line, the colon following the method name starts the *initialization list*, a way of initializing variables and objects in C++. The `delayBuffer_` object, used to hold the internal delay buffer, is initialized to have two channels with one sample per channel. Its size will be updated later, when more is known about the audio sample rate. Within the constructor, all other variables declared in PluginProcessor.h are given initial values. Some of these, including `delayReadPosition_` and `delayWritePosition_`, will be updated before audio begins playing. If a variable is not initialized, its value will be undefined and its behavior will be unpredictable.

The second round of initialization takes place in `prepareToPlay()`, at which point the audio sample rate and system buffer size are known:

```
void DelayAudioProcessor::prepareToPlay (double sampleRate,
                                         int samplesPerBlock)
{
    // Allocate and zero the delay buffer (size will depend on
    // current sample rate) Sanity check the result so we don't
    // end up with any zero-length calculations
    delayBufferLength_ = (int)(2.0*sampleRate);
    if(delayBufferLength_ < 1)
        delayBufferLength_ = 1;
    delayBuffer_.setSize(2, delayBufferLength_);
    delayBuffer_.clear();

    // This method gives us the sample rate. Use this to figure
    // out what the delay position offset should be (since it
    // is specified in seconds, and we need to convert it to a
    // number of samples)
    delayReadPosition_ = (int)(delayWritePosition_ -
                              (delayLength_ * getSampleRate())
                              + delayBufferLength_) %
                              delayBufferLength_;
}
```

This effect allows a maximum delay of 2 s. The necessary buffer size for a 2 s delay depends on the sample rate, so here `delayBuffer_` and `delayBufferLength_` are updated to the correct size. The actual length of delay depends on the difference between the read and write pointers, so `delayReadPosition_` is given an initial offset with respect to `delayWritePosition_` to achieve the delay specified by `delayLength_`. This calculation features *modulo arithmetic* needed to manage the circular buffer, described further in Chapter 2.

Managing Parameters

While the effect is running, the user may change the value of the parameters. PluginProcessor.cpp implements a number of methods related to parameter management, details of which can be found in the JUCE documentation. We will highlight the most important ones here. First, `getNumParameters()` reports how many parameters the plug-in supports:

```
int DelayAudioProcessor::getNumParameters()
{
    return kNumParameters;
}
```

As long as the `enum` statement in PluginProcessor.h is correctly handled, this code should never need to be updated. Next, `getParameter()` returns the value of a parameter given its index:

```
float DelayAudioProcessor::getParameter (int index)
{
    // This method will be called by the host, probably on the
    // audio thread, so it's absolutely time-critical. Don't
    // use critical sections or anything UI-related, or
    // anything at all that may block in any way!
    switch (index)
    {
        case kDryMixParam:      return dryMix_;
        case kWetMixParam:      return wetMix_;
        case kFeedbackParam:    return feedback_;
        case kDelayLengthParam:return delayLength_;
        default:                return 0.0f;
    }
}
```

Generally speaking, it is sufficient to return the current value of the relevant instance variable in this method. As the comments in the code indicate, nothing time-consuming or GUI-related should take place in this method. Finally, `getParameterName()` provides a human-readable string describing each parameter:

```
const String DelayAudioProcessor::getParameterName (int index)
{
    switch (index)
    {
        case kDryMixParam:      return "dry mix";
        case kWetMixParam:      return "wet mix";
        case kFeedbackParam:    return "feedback";
        case kDelayLengthParam:return "delay";
        default:                break;
    }

    return String::empty;
}
```

A complementary method allows external objects, including the GUI, to set the parameters.

```
void DelayAudioProcessor::setParameter (int index, float newValue)
{
    // This method will be called by the host, probably on the
    // audio thread, so it's absolutely time-critical. Don't
    // use critical sections or anything UI-related, or
    // anything at all that may block in any way!
    switch (index)
    {
```

```
        case kDryMixParam:
            dryMix_ = newValue;
            break;
        case kWetMixParam:
            wetMix_ = newValue;
            break;
        case kFeedbackParam:
            feedback_ = newValue;
            break;
        case kDelayLengthParam:
            delayLength_ = newValue;
            delayReadPosition_ = (int)(delayWritePosition_ -
                     delayLength_ * getSampleRate()) +
                     delayBufferLength_) % delayBufferLength_;
            break;
        default:
            break;
    }
}
```

The arguments to this method define which parameter to set and the new value it should take. In many cases, where the parameter is used directly by `processBlock()`, it will suffice to set the instance variable to the new value here as seen in the first three parameters.

In some cases, changing a parameter affects other aspects of the internal state of the plug-in. In the case of changing the delay length, `processBlock()` does not make direct use of the `delayLength_` variable, but rather derives its delay from the difference between read and write pointers. Therefore, when the delay is changed, the read pointer is updated relative to the write pointer to achieve the new delay. Notice that it is important that the read pointer moves while the write pointer stays fixed; this avoids discontinuities being written into the delay buffer.

It is possible for `setParameter()` to be called at the same time `processBlock()` is running. In certain cases, including recalculating filter coefficients or reallocating buffers, changing a parameter might temporarily interfere with operations in `processBlock()` and could even cause a crash. This issue of thread safety is addressed at the end of the chapter.

Another pair of methods, `getStateInformation()` and `setStateInformation()`, allow the settings of a plug-in to be stored and retrieved across sessions. Further information can be found in the JUCE documentation, or your effects can simply adapt the example code to your own set of parameters.

Cleanup

It is important that the plug-in release all the resources it has allocated when it is finished. There are two cleanup methods in JUCE plug-ins:

releaseResources() and the destructor ~DelayAudioProcessor(). These are complementary to the two initialization methods. releaseResources() runs each time audio processing finishes, and it should be used to free any resources allocated in prepareToPlay(). In this particular example, no memory was allocated in prepareToPlay() and the delayBuffer_ object will be released in the destructor, so releaseResources() is empty:

```
void DelayAudioProcessor::releaseResources()
{
    // When playback stops, you can use this as an opportunity
    // to free up any spare memory, etc.

    // The delay buffer will stay in memory until the effect is
    // unloaded.
}
```

The destructor runs once when the plug-in is removed by the host environment. Anything allocated in the constructor should be released here. C++ objects such as delayBuffer_, which have their own constructors, will be released automatically; hence, this method is also empty in the example. However, if your effect contains any new or malloc() statements in the constructor, they must be balanced here by a delete or free() statement.

```
DelayAudioProcessor::~DelayAudioProcessor()
{
}
```

PluginEditor.h

PluginEditor.h contains the declaration of the DelayAudioProcessorEditor class, which creates a graphical user interface for the plug-in:

```
class DelayAudioProcessorEditor  : public AudioProcessorEditor,
                                   public SliderListener,
                                   public Timer
{
public:
    DelayAudioProcessorEditor (DelayAudioProcessor*
                               ownerFilter);
    ~DelayAudioProcessorEditor();

    //==============================================================
    // This is just a standard Juce paint method...
    void timerCallback();
    void paint (Graphics& g);
    void resized();
    void sliderValueChanged (Slider*);
```

```
private:
    Label delayLengthLabel_, feedbackLabel_, dryMixLabel_,
          wetMixLabel_;
    Slider delayLengthSlider_, feedbackSlider_, drymixSlider_,
           wetMixSlider_;

    ScopedPointer<ResizableCornerComponent> resizer_;
    ComponentBoundsConstrainer resizeLimits_;

    DelayAudioProcessor* getProcessor() const
    {
        return static_cast <DelayAudioProcessor*>
                             (getAudioProcessor());
    }
};
```

The first line declares the class name. Following the colon is a list of classes that `DelayAudioProcessorEditor` inherits from. A complete discussion of inheritance can be found in any C++ text, and in most cases your own plug-ins do not need to change this list. However, it is worth highlighting the `SliderListener` class. `DelayAudioProcessorEditor` contains JUCE `Slider` controls, and whenever these change value, they send a message to the object that created them. Including `SliderListener` in the list of parent classes is necessary for these messages to be received. If your plug-in editor uses other types of controls, additional parent classes may be needed. For example, using `ComboBox` controls may require the inclusion of `ComboBox::Listener` in the parent class list; this can be seen in the accompanying example code for phase vocoder effects.

The next lines declare the methods of `DelayAudioProcessorEditor`, beginning with the constructor and destructor. As with `DelayAudioProcessor`, these will be run once when the plug-in is loaded and removed by the host environment. The other methods are standard to JUCE and usually do not need to be changed. However, if additional types of controls are used, new methods may need to be declared here (e.g., `comboBoxChanged()` when `ComboBox` controls are used). The JUCE documentation contains a complete list of controls and the methods they require.

Following the `private:` line is a list of instance variables for this class. The `Label` and `Slider` types define text labels and user-adjustable sliders, respectively. Notice that each of the four parameters in PluginProcessor.h has both a text label (to identify it to the user) and a slider (to let the user adjust it). We will see in PluginEditor.cpp how adjusting the sliders results in updates to the parameters.

The remainder of the file is standard for all JUCE plug-ins and does not need to be changed, with the caveat that if you change the name of the `DelayAudioProcessor` class, it should be updated accordingly here.

PluginEditor.cpp

PluginEditor.cpp implements the user interface whose methods and variables are declared in PluginEditor.h. The interface this file creates can be seen in Figure 13.5. The activities of PluginEditor.cpp can be divided into four categories: initialization, managing parameters, handling resizing, and cleanup. We will consider each in turn.

Initialization

Initialization in PluginEditor.cpp takes place in the constructor, and is often more elaborate that the initialization in PluginProcessor.cpp. The initialization needs to define the meaning and ranges of all the on-screen controls. Note that as an alternative to manually writing the code for the interface, the Introjucer offers a tool for creating GUI layouts graphically that automatically generates code equivalent to the example below.

```
DelayAudioProcessorEditor::DelayAudioProcessorEditor
(DelayAudioProcessor* ownerFilter)
    : AudioProcessorEditor (ownerFilter),
      delayLengthLabel_("", "Delay (sec):"),
      feedbackLabel_("", "Feedback:"),
      dryMixLabel_("", "Dry Mix Level:"),
      wetMixLabel_("", "Delayed Mix Level:")
{

    // Set up the sliders
    addAndMakeVisible (&delayLengthSlider_);
    delayLengthSlider_.setSliderStyle (Slider::Rotary);
    delayLengthSlider_.addListener (this);
    delayLengthSlider_.setRange (0.01, 2.0, 0.01);
```

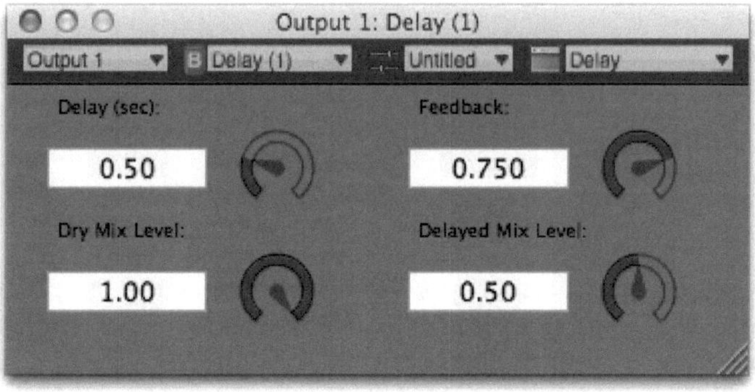

FIGURE 13.5
Editor (user interface) for example delay plug-in.

```
    addAndMakeVisible (&feedbackSlider_);
    feedbackSlider_.setSliderStyle (Slider::Rotary);
    feedbackSlider_.addListener (this);
    feedbackSlider_.setRange (0.0, 0.995, 0.005);

    addAndMakeVisible (&dryMixSlider_);
    dryMixSlider_.setSliderStyle (Slider::Rotary);
    dryMixSlider_.addListener (this);
    dryMixSlider_.setRange (0.0, 1.0, 0.01);

    addAndMakeVisible (&wetMixSlider_);
    wetMixSlider_.setSliderStyle (Slider::Rotary);
    wetMixSlider_.addListener (this);
    wetMixSlider_.setRange (0.0, 1.0, 0.01);

    delayLengthLabel_.attachToComponent(&delayLengthSlider_,
                                         false);
    delayLengthLabel_.setFont(Font (11.0f));

    feedbackLabel_.attachToComponent(&feedbackSlider_, false);
    feedbackLabel_.setFont(Font (11.0f));

    dryMixLabel_.attachToComponent(&dryMixSlider_, false);
    dryMixLabel_.setFont(Font (11.0f));

    wetMixLabel_.attachToComponent(&wetMixSlider_, false);
    wetMixLabel_.setFont(Font (11.0f));

    // add the triangular resizer component for the
    // bottom-right of the UI
    addAndMakeVisible(resizer_ =
       new ResizableCornerComponent (this, &resizeLimits_));
    resizeLimits_.setSizeLimits(370, 140, 500, 300);

    // set our component's initial size to be the last one that
    // was stored in the filter's settings
    setSize(ownerFilter->lastUIWidth_,
            ownerFilter->lastUIHeight_);

    startTimer(50);
}
```

Similar to PluginProcessor.cpp, each method name is preceded by `DelayAudioProcessorEditor::` to make clear that it implements a method declared in PluginEditor.h. Also like PluginProcessor.cpp, an initialization list follows the declaration of the constructor. Here, this list is used to initialize the parent class `AudioProcessorEditor` defined by JUCE and the values displayed in the four text labels (delayLengthLabel_, feedbackLabel_, dryMixLabel_, and wetMixLabel_). Your plug-ins will not need to change the AudioProcessorEditor line, but depending on the parameters your plug-in uses, the number and value of labels may change.

Within the constructor, the first task is to initialize the four sliders that control each parameter. Each slider contains four lines of initialization, for example:

```
addAndMakeVisible (&feedbackSlider_);
feedbackSlider_.setSliderStyle (Slider::Rotary);
feedbackSlider_.addListener (this);
feedbackSlider_.setRange (0.0, 0.995, 0.005);
```

The first line adds the slider to the editor. The second causes the slider to display a rotary (rather than linear) control. The third line tells the slider to notify the editor whenever its value changes; the value this is a C++ keyword meaning the current object (here, DelayAudioProcessorEditor). The final line sets the minimum, maximum, and granularity of the slider's range. In this case, the slider is allowed to range from 0.0 to 0.995 in increments of 0.005. Notice that this is the feedback control, so its value is limited to strictly less than 1 to avoid instability. Your plug-ins will most likely declare different ranges and granularities for each control.

The next task of the constructor is to attach the text labels to each slider:

```
feedbackLabel_.attachToComponent(&feedbackSlider_, false);
feedbackLabel_.setFont(Font (11.0f));
```

The label text itself was set in the initialization list. These lines ensure the label appears in the right place and that it has the correct font. In your plug-ins, you should have a similar pair of lines for each Label object.

The final lines handle the resizing of the editor window itself and the initialization of a timer that keeps the user interface synchronized with the parameter values even when the parameters are changed externally. The only line that may need to be changed in other plug-ins is this one:

```
resizeLimits_.setSizeLimits(370, 140, 500, 300);
```

This line defines the minimum and maximum size of the window in pixels. Here, the window can range from 370 × 140 at its smallest to 500 × 300 at its largest. The right size to use for any given plug-in will depend on the number of controls in the window.

Managing Parameters

PluginEditor.cpp implements two methods for keeping the on-screen controls synchronized with the values of each parameter in the `DelayAudioProcessor` object. The first method queries the current parameter values and changes the user interface to match:

```
void DelayAudioProcessorEditor::timerCallback()
{
    DelayAudioProcessor* ourProcessor = getProcessor();

    delayLengthSlider_.setValue(ourProcessor->delayLength_,
                                dontSendNotification);
    feedbackSlider_.setValue(ourProcessor->feedback_,
                             dontSendNotification);
    dryMixSlider_.setValue(ourProcessor->dryMix_,
                           dontSendNotification);
    wetMixSlider_.setValue(ourProcessor->wetMix_,
                           dontSendNotification);
}
```

In the constructor, a timer was started that causes this method to be called by the system every 50 ms. It is possible for the plug-in parameter values to be changed by some means other than the user interface, for example, by MIDI messages. This method ensures that the user interface always shows the actual current values of the parameters. One consequence of the `timerCallback()` method is that if in your plug-in you forget to save the values of parameter changes, either in `DelayAudioProcessorEditor::sliderValueChanged()` or in `DelayAudioProcessor::setParameter()`, you will find that every time you change a control, it immediately snaps back to its original value.

The second parameter management method is called every time the user changes the value of a slider:

```
void DelayAudioProcessorEditor::sliderValueChanged (Slider*
slider)
{
    // It's vital to use setParameterNotifyingHost to change
    // any parameters that are automatable
    // by the host, rather than just modifying them directly,
    // otherwise the host won't know
    // that they've changed.

    if (slider == &delayLengthSlider_)
    {
        getProcessor()->setParameterNotifyingHost
          (DelayAudioProcessor::kDelayLengthParam,
```

```
                            (float)delayLengthSlider_.getValue());
    }
    else if (slider == &feedbackSlider_)
    {
        getProcessor()->setParameterNotifyingHost
          (DelayAudioProcessor::kFeedbackParam,
                             float)feedbackSlider_.getValue());
    }
    else if (slider == &dryMixSlider_)
    {
        getProcessor()->setParameterNotifyingHost
          (DelayAudioProcessor::kDryMixParam,
                             (float)dryMixSlider_.getValue());
    }
    else if (slider == &wetMixSlider_)
    {
        getProcessor()->setParameterNotifyingHost
         (DelayAudioProcessor::kWetMixParam,
                             (float)wetMixSlider_.getValue());
    }
}
```

This method first queries which `Slider` object generated the call. It then queries the current value of the slider and updates the audio processor object accordingly. Notice that this method uses the parameter indices declared in the `enum` statement inside PluginProcessor.h. In your plug-ins, you should have one `if` statement for each slider, and each slider should correspond uniquely to one of the `enum` values. The `setParameterNotifyingHost()` method is provided by JUCE and will ultimately result in a call to the `setParameter()` method declared in PluginProcessor.cpp.

If your plug-in uses other types of controls besides sliders, an analogous method to `sliderValueChanged()` will need to be implemented for each type of control.

Resizing

Depending on the values provided to `resizeLimits_.setSizeLimits()` in the constructor, the user may be able to change the size of the editor window. Whenever the window size changes (and at least once on start-up), the `resized()` method will be called:

```
void DelayAudioProcessorEditor::resized()
{
    delayLengthSlider_.setBounds (20, 20, 150, 40);
    feedbackSlider_.setBounds (200, 20, 150, 40);
    dryMixSlider_.setBounds(20, 80, 150, 40);
```

```
    wetMixSlider_.setBounds(200, 80, 150, 40);

    resizer_->setBounds(getWidth() - 16, getHeight() - 16, 16, 16);

    getProcessor()->lastUIWidth_ = getWidth();
    getProcessor()->lastUIHeight_ = getHeight();
}
```

This method is responsible for placing all the sliders in the appropriate locations and informing the plug-in processor of the new window size. The pixel locations may have to be worked out experimentally to make the interface look right; alternatively, the Introjucer can be used to graphically construct an interface that automates some of the processes in PluginEditor.cpp.

Cleanup

When the plug-in is removed by the host environment, the destructor will be called. Any objects that were manually allocated using `new` or `malloc()` need to be released with `delete` or `free()`, respectively. In this case, no such allocation has taken place, so the destructor is empty.

```
DelayAudioProcessorEditor::~DelayAudioProcessorEditor()
{
}
```

Summary

This section has examined the code for an example plug-in that implements a delay with feedback. Four source files were required, two related to the audio processor and two related to the user interface. The most important task for the audio processor is to implement the *audio callback* function `processBlock()`, which the system calls every time it needs a new block of audio. Since audio is processed in small blocks, it is necessary to remember the state of the effect between callbacks, so *instance variables* were declared in PluginProcessor.h to record information that persists beyond the duration of `processBlock()`.

The other important task was the management of effect parameters, which required careful coordination between all four files. Implementing parameters required an ordered list of parameter indices to be declared in PluginProcessor.h alongside instance variables to hold their values. Controls to change their values were declared in PluginEditor.h. Both PluginProcessor.cpp and PluginEditor.cpp implemented methods for getting and setting parameters, which were ultimately used by the `processBlock()` method in PluginProcessor.cpp to render the effect.

Advanced Topics

Efficiency Considerations

For more complex effects, it is useful to consider how the audio processing can be most efficiently implemented. This is especially true for effects on mobile or embedded devices, but computational cost is even a concern for the fastest of computers when many effects are used together. A standard metric of computational cost used in digital signal processing is *multiplies per sample*: How many multiplications does the computer have to perform for each audio sample? Though it is not a perfect metric of processing complexity, it provides a useful overall guide to how an effect can be made more efficient.

A straightforward example of considering multiplies per sample is filtering. A finite impulse response (FIR) filter of length N will require N multiplies per sample to implement; for long filters, this can become quite expensive. A particularly troublesome example is *convolutional reverb*, where the input signal must be *convolved* with an impulse response that could potentially exceed 100,000 samples. Aside from shortening the filter, a variety of tricks are possible to improve efficiency using the fast Fourier transform. These are further discussed in Chapter 11.

Another example of managing computational complexity can be found in the *wah-wah* effect. Here, the effect is generated by a second-order infinite impulse response (IIR) filter whose coefficients change whenever the user adjusts a control. Applying the filter is inexpensive, requiring only five multiplications per sample. However, calculating the coefficients involves a complicated formula including trigonometric functions that require many more multiplications to implement. It is not efficient to recalculate the coefficients of the filter at each sample based on the current value of the cutoff frequency. Instead, a more efficient approach will recalculate the coefficients *only* when they are changed by the user, typically within the `setParameter()` method, and save these values for future use by the callback. This significantly reduces calculations but has the potential to introduce a subtle bug, discussed in the next section.

A third example is the calculation of low-frequency oscillators (LFOs). In an *auto-wah* effect, the cutoff frequency of the filter changes continuously over time under the control of an LFO. It might appear that recalculating coefficients every sample is necessary. However, with most LFOs, the change in value from one audio sample to the next is so subtle that the filter coefficients can be updated less frequently, for example, every 16 or 32 samples, with no audible change in performance.

A final example concerns the use of complex mathematical functions. Suppose a *phaser* effect wanted to implement a complicated exponential LFO waveform to vary the location of the allpass filters. Calculating the value of this function each sample might require a large number of multiplies since internally, exponential functions are much more complex to calculate than basic multiplications. However, it might be possible to generate a *lookup table* with all the values of the function precalculated and stored in a block of memory. Then on each sample, rather than running the calculation, the callback function could simply access the table to determine its value. If greater precision is needed, *interpolation* between values in the lookup table could be used while still maintaining a significant efficiency improvement over raw calculations. See Chapter 2 for further details on interpolating within buffers.

Thread Safety

Most audio plug-ins are *multithreaded*. This means that two different methods could be running simultaneously in different threads of execution, with no guarantee that one method finishes before the other begins. In particular, the thread that runs the audio callback function is often different from the thread that handles changing parameters. This results in the potential for subtle bugs and even outright crashes.

Consider the case of a phase vocoder plug-in that needs to gather samples in a buffer before performing a fast Fourier transform. Suppose that the user changes the window size of the effect using one of the graphical controls. When this happens, a call to `setParameter()` will be generated, and because the window size has changed, the plug-in may reallocate the window buffer to hold a different number of samples. In a multithreaded environment, the call to `setParameter()` might happen *at the same time* as the callback `processBlock()` is running. The callback function will be unaware that the buffer is about to change size, so it may attempt to access an invalid index and cause the plug-in to crash, potentially bringing down the entire DAW. Similar problems may occur on recalculating coefficients for filters and other situations where memory is allocated or deallocated while the effect is running.

One solution is to provide a way of ensuring that *only one* of `setParameter()` and `processBlock()` can run at a time. If `processBlock()` is running and `setParameter()` wants to change a buffer size, it must wait until `processBlock()` finishes, and the same is true in reverse if `setParameter()` begins first. This behavior can be achieved using a special variable type called a *mutex* (short for mutually exclusive). When one thread locks the mutex, the other thread must wait until it has been unlocked before continuing. Consider the following example code from a phase vocoder effect. First, in PluginProcessor.h, the mutex variable is defined within the audio processor class:

```
// Spin lock that prevents the FFT settings from changing
// in the middle of the audio thread.
SpinLock fftSpinLock_;
```

SpinLock is a type of lock object provided by JUCE. At the beginning of processBlock(), the method acquires the lock before beginning its processing and releases it upon completion:

```
void PVOCPassthroughAudioProcessor::processBlock(
    AudioSampleBuffer& buffer, MidiBuffer& midiMessages)
{
    // Helpful information about this block of samples:
        // How many input channels for our effect?
    const int numInputChannels = getNumInputChannels();
        // How many output channels for our effect?
    const int numOutputChannels = getNumOutputChannels();
        // How many samples in the buffer for this block?
    const int numSamples = buffer.getNumSamples();

    int channel, inwritepos, sampsincefft;
    int outreadpos, outwritepos;

    // Grab the lock that prevents the FFT settings from
        // changing
    fftSpinLock_.enter();

    // [...]
    // **** Phase Vocoder processing goes here
    // [...]

    fftSpinLock_.exit();
}
```

Meanwhile, any call that changes the window size or invalidates the internal buffers will also acquire the lock. If one thread holds the lock and a second tries to acquire it, the second thread *blocks* (waits) until the lock has been released. This ensures that no two threads act on the same resources in incompatible ways. However, if the mutex is locked when the audio thread tries to run, the audio thread will be delayed, which could result in dropouts. For this reason, some programmers consider mutexes in audio code to be bad form. At minimum, whenever a non-audio thread holds the mutex, keep any activity in that thread as short as possible.

Multithreaded programming can be quite subtle and challenging, particularly as the number of threads and number of shared resources increase. Several good texts exist on the subject, e.g., [107].

Conclusion

This chapter has shown how to put the principles of building audio effects into practice through the creation of audio plug-ins. The JUCE framework is a convenient environment for creating audio plug-ins since it allows the same code to be compiled into multiple plug-in formats on multiple operating systems. However, the general principles of writing audio callback functions, managing parameters, allocating resources, and creating a user interface are similar across many plug-in formats. The example code included with the book offers templates from which you can start building your own effects, including examples from most chapters and a blank plug-in into which you can add your own code.

References

1. J. O. Smith, *Physical Audio Signal Processing*, W3K Publishing, 2010.
2. J. O. Smith, *Spectral Audio Signal Processing*, W3K Publishing 2011.
3. A. V. Oppenheim and R. W. Schafer, *Discrete-Time Signal Processing*, 3rd ed., Englewood Cliffs, NJ: Prentice Hall, 2009.
4. S. J. Orfanidis, *Introduction to Signal Processing*, Prentice Hall, 2010.
5. U. Zolzer, *Digital Audio Signal Processing*, 2nd ed., New York: John Wiley & Sons, 2008.
6. G. Milner, *Perfecting Sound Forever: The Story of Recorded Music*, London: Granta Books, 2010.
7. T. Laasko et al., Splitting the Unit Delay [FIR/allpass filters design], *IEEE Signal Processing Magazine*, 13.1, 1996, pp. 30–60.
8. O. Niemitalo, Polynomial Interpolators for High-Quality Resampling of Oversampled Audio, October 2001, http://yehar.com/blog/wp-content/uploads/2009/08/deip.pdf
9. A. M. Stark et al., Real-Time Beat-Synchronous Audio Effects, presented at New Interfaces for Musical Expression (NIME), New York, 2007.
10. M. Lewisohn, *The Beatles Recording Sessions*, New York: Harmony Books (Crown Publishers), 1989.
11. G. Martin and W. Pearson, *Summer of Love: The Making of Sgt Pepper*, London: Pan Books, 1994.
12. J. D. Reiss, Design of Audio Parametric Equalizer Filters Directly in the Digital Domain, *IEEE Transactions on Audio, Speech and Language Processing*, vol. 19, pp. 1843–1848, 2011.
13. D. Self, *The Design of Active Crossover*, Oxford: Focal Press, 2011.
14. A. Case, *Mix Smart: Professional Techniques for the Home Studio*, Boca Raton, FL: CRC Press, 2012.
15. R. Izhaki, *Mixing Audio: Concepts, Practices and Tools*, New York: Focal Press, 2008.
16. E. Perez Gonzalez and J. D. Reiss, Automatic Equalization of Multi-Channel Audio Using Cross-Adaptive Methods, presented at 127th AES Convention, New York, 2009.
17. M. Holters and U. Zölzer, Graphic Equalizer Design Using Higher-Order Recursive Filters, presented at Digital Audio Effects (DAFx), Montreal, 2006.
18. ISO, ISO 266, *Acoustics—Preferred Frequencies for Measurements*, 1975.
19. G. Massenburg, Parametric Equalization, presented at 42nd AES Convention, 1972.
20. G. Massenburg, Did Massenburg Really Invent the Parametric EQ?, Dec. 1999, available from http://www.massenburg.com/wp-content/uploads/2011/12/GM_ParaEQ.pdf.
21. L. Bregitzer, *Secrets of Recording: Professional Tips, Tools and Techniques*, New York: Focal Press, 2009.

22. Z. Ma et al., Implementation of an Intelligent Equalization Tool Using Yule-Walker for Music Mixing and Mastering, presented at 134th AES Convention, Rome, 2013.
23. A. Loscos and T. Aussenac, The Wahwactor: A Voice Controlled Wah-Wah Pedal, in *New Interfaces for Musical Expression (NIME)*, 2005, pp. 172–175.
24. M. Vdovin, Artist Interview: Brad Plunkett, *Universal Audio WebZine*, vol. 3, October 2005.
25. R. G. Keen, Technology of Wah Pedals, September 1999, www.geofex.com/article_folders/wahpedl/wahped.htm
26. R. Parncutt, A Perceptual Model of Pulse Salience and Metrical Accent in Musical Rhythms, *Music Perception*, vol. 11, Summer 1994.
27. H. Fastl and E. Zwicker, *Psychoacoustics: Facts and Models*, 3rd ed., Berlin: Springer, 2007.
28. S. Rosen, Temporal Information in Speech: Acoustic, Auditory and Linguistic Aspects, *Philosophical Transactions of the Royal Society B*, vol. 336, 1992.
29. B. Lachaise and L. Daudet, Inverting Dynamics Compression with Minimal Side Information, presented at Digital Audio Effects Workshop (DAFx), Helsinki, 2008.
30. D. Giannoulis et al., A Tutorial on Digital Dynamic Range Compressor Design, *Journal of the Audio Engineering Society*, vol. 60, 2012.
31. B. Rudolf, 1176 Revision History, *Mix Magazine Online*, June 1, 2000.
32. D. Barchiesi and J. D. Reiss, Reverse Engineering the Mix, *Journal of the Audio Engineering Society*, vol. 58, pp. 563–576, 2010.
33. R. J. Cassidy, Level Detection Tunings and Techniques for the Dynamic Range Compression of Audio Signals, presented at 117th AES Convention, 2004.
34. J. S. Abel and D. P. Berners, On Peak-Detecting and RMS Feedback and Feedforward Compressors, presented at 115th AES Convention, 2003.
35. P. Dutilleux et al., Nonlinear Processing, in *Dafx: Digital Audio Effects*, ed. U. Zoelzer, 2nd ed., New York: John Wiley & Sons, 2011, p. 554.
36. J. Lethem, The Genius and Modern Times of Bob Dylan, *Rolling Stone Magazine*, September 7, 2006.
37. J. Bitzer and D. Schmidt, Parameter Estimation of Dynamic Range Compressors: Models, Procedures and Test Signals, presented at 120th AES Convention, 2006.
38. L. Lu, A Digital Realization of Audio Dynamic Range Control, in *Fourth International Conference on Signal Processing Proceedings (IEEE ICSP)*, 1998, pp. 1424–1427.
39. Sonnox, Dynamics Plug-In Manual, *Sonnox Oxford Plug-Ins*, April 1, 2007.
40. M. Zaunschirm et al., A Sub-Band Approach to Musical Transient Modification, *Computer Music Journal*, vol. 36, Summer 2012.
41. M. Senior, *Mixing Secrets for the Small Studio*, New York: Focal Press, 2011.
42. D. Gibson, *The Art of Mixing*, 2nd ed., artistpro.com LLC, 2005.
43. M. J. Terrell et al., Automatic Noise Gate Settings for Drum Recordings Containing Bleed from Secondary Sources, *EURASIP Journal on Advances in Signal Processing*, vol. 2010, pp. 1–9, 2010.
44. S. Gorlow and J. D. Reiss, Model-Based Inversion of Dynamic Range Compression, *IEEE Transactions on Audio, Speech and Language Processing*, vol. 21, 2013.
45. B. De Man and J. D. Reiss, An Intelligent Multiband Distortion Effect, presented at AES 53rd International Conference on Semantic Audio, London, 2014.

46. D. Yeh et al., Simulation of the Diode Limiter in Guitar Distortion Circuits by Numerical Solution of Ordinary Differential Equations, presented at Digital Audio Effects (DAFX), 2007.
47. V. Välimäki et al., Virtual Analog Effects, in *Dafx: Digital Audio Effects*, 2nd ed., New York: John Wiley & Sons, 2011.
48. D. Yeh et al., Numerical Methods for Simulation of Guitar Distortion Circuits, *Computer Music Journal*, vol. 32, pp. 23–42, 2008.
49. J. Pakarinen and D. Yeh, A Review of Digital Techniques for Modeling Vacuum-Tube Guitar Amplifiers, *Computer Music Journal*, vol. 33, pp. 85–100, 2009.
50. J. Pakarinen and M. Karjalainen, Enhanced Wave Digital Triode Model for Real-Time Tube Amplifier Emulation, *IEEE Transactions on Audio, Speech and Language Processing*, vol. 18, pp. 738–746, 2010.
51. W. M. J. Leach, SPICE Models for Vacuum-Tube Amplifiers, *Journal of the Audio Engineering Society*, vol. 43, pp. 117–126, 1995.
52. H. Shapiro and C. Glebbeek, *Jimi Hendrix: Electric Gypsy*, new and improved ed., New York: St. Martin's Press, 1995.
53. J. L. Flanagan and R. M. Golden, Phase Vocoder, *Bell System Technical Journal*, pp. 1493–1509, 1966.
54. M. Portnoff, Implementation of the Digital Phase Vocoder Using the Fast Fourier Transform, *IEEE Transactions on Acoustics, Speech and Signal Processing*, vol. 24, pp. 243–248, 1976.
55. J. Laroche and M. Dolson, Improved Phase Vocoder Timescale Modification of Audio, *IEEE Transactions on Speech and Audio Processing*, vol. 7, pp. 323–332, 1999.
56. M. Dolson, The Phase Vocoder: A Tutorial, *Computer Music Journal*, vol. 10, pp. 14–27, 1986.
57. J. Tyrangiel, Singer's Little Helper, *Time Magazine*, vol. 173 (6), pp. 49–51, 2009.
58. J. Vilkamo et al., Directional Audio Coding: Virtual Microphone-Based Synthesis and Subjective Evaluation, *Journal of the Audio Engineering Society*, vol. 57, 2009.
59. R. Alexander, *The Inventor of Stereo: The Life and Works of Alan Dower Blumlein*, CRC Press, 2000.
60. D. Beheng, Sound Perception, Deutche Welle, Radio Training Centre (DWRTC), Cologne 2002.
61. B. Bernfeld, Attempts for Better Understanding of the Directional Stereophonic Listening Mechanism, presented at 44th Audio Engineering Society Convention, 1973.
62. V. Pulkki, Virtual Sound Source Positioning Using Vector Base Amplitude Panning, *Journal of the Audio Engineering Society*, vol. 45, 1997.
63. D. G. Malham and A. Myatt, 3-D Sound Spatialization Using Ambisonic Techniques, *Computer Music Journal*, vol. 19, pp. 58–70, 1995.
64. J. S. Bamford, An Analysis of Ambisonics Sound Systems of First and Second Order, MSc, University of Waterloo, Waterloo, Ontario, Canada, 1995.
65. M. A. Poletti, Three-Dimensional Surround Sound Systems Based on Spherical Harmonics, *Journal of the Audio Engineering Society*, vol. 53, 2005.
66. E. G. Williams, *Fourier Acoustics: Sound Radiation and Nearfield Acoustical Holography*, London: Academic Press, 1999.
67. P. M. Morse and K. U. Ingard, *Theoretical Acoustics*, New York: McGraw-Hill, 1968.
68. M. Gerzon, Design of Ambisonic Decoders for Multispeaker Surround Sound, presented at 58th Audio Egineering Society Convention, 1977.

69. E. N. G. Verheijen, Sound Reproduction by Wave Field Synthesis, PhD, Delft University of Technology, 1998.
70. J. Blauert, *Spatial Hearing: The Psychophysics of Human Sound Localization*, Cambridge, MA: MIT Press, 1997.
71. F. Rumsey, *Spatial Audio*, New York: Focal Press, 2001.
72. J. W. Strutt, On Our Perception of Sound Direction, *Philosophical Magazine*, vol. 13, pp. 214–232, 1907.
73. V. R. Algazi et al., Motion-Tracked Binaural Sound, *Journal of the Audio Engineering Society*, vol. 52, 2004.
74. C. P. Brown and R. O. Duda, A Structural Model for Binaural Sound Synthesis, *IEEE Transactions on Speech and Audio Processing*, vol. 6, 1998.
75. R. O. Duda, 3-D Audio for HCI, Department of Electrical Engineering, San Jose State University, 2000, interface.cipic.ucdavis.edu/sound/tutorial/index.html
76. V. Pulkki, Spatial Sound Generation and Perception by Amplitude Panning Techniques, Electrical and Communications Engineering, Helsinki University of Technology, Helsinki, Finland, 2001.
77. D. de Vries et al., The Wave Field Synthesis Concept Applied to Sound Reinforcement: Restrictions and Solutions, presented at 96th Convention of the Audio Engineering Society, Amsterdam, 1994.
78. A. Farina, Simultaneous Measurement of Impulse Response and Distortion with a Swept-Sine Technique, presented at 108th AES Convention, 2000.
79. A. Pierce, *Acoustics: An Introduction to its Physical Principles and Applications*, College Park, MD: American Institute of Physics, 1989.
80. J. O. Smith, Doppler Simulation and the Leslie, presented at 5th International Conference on Digital Audio Effects (DafX), Hamburg, 2002.
81. B. G. Quinn, Doppler Speed and Range Estimation Using Frequency and Amplitude Estimates, *Journal of the Acoustical Society of America*, vol. 98, pp. 2560–2566, 1995.
82. A. R. Gondeck, Doppler Time Mapping, *Journal of the Acoustical Society of America*, vol. 73, pp. 1863–1864, 1983.
83. D. Rocchesso, Fractionally Addressed Delay Lines, *IEEE Transactions on Speech and Audio Processing*, vol. 8, 2000.
84. B. Burtt, Sound Designer of Star Wars, *Film Sound*, 2007, available from http://filmsound.org/starwars/burtt-interview.htm.
85. L. L. Beranek, Analysis of Sabine and Eyring Equations and Their Application to Concert Hall Audience and Chair Absorption, *Journal of the Acoustical Society of America*, vol. 120, 2006.
86. D. Howard and J. Angus, *Acoustics and Psychoacoustics*, 4th ed., New York: Focal Press, 2009.
87. D. Davis and E. Patronis, *Sound System Engineering*, 3rd ed., Amsterdam: Elsevier, 2006.
88. D. Davis, *A More Accurate Way of Calculating Critical Distance*, Altec TL-207, 1971.
89. J. Cage and D. Tudor, *Indeterminancy: New Aspect of Form in Instrumental and Electronic Music and Ninety Stories by John Cage, with Music*, Smithsonian/Folkways, 1959/1992.
90. J. Cage, *Silence: Lectures and Writings*, Wesleyan University Press, 1961.
91. M. R. Schroeder and B. F. Logan, Colorless Artificial Reverberation, *Journal of the Audio Engineering Society*, vol. 9, 1961.

92. M. R. Schroeder, Natural Sounding Artificial Reverberation, *Journal of the Audio Engineering Society*, vol. 10, 1962.
93. J. A. Moorer, About This Reverberation Business, *Computer Music Journal*, vol. 3, pp. 13–18, 1979.
94. J. Allen and D. Berkley, Image Method for Efficiently Simulating Small-Room Acoustics, *Journal of the Acoustical Society of America*, vol. 65, pp. 943–950, 1979.
95. E. Lehmann and A. Johansson, Prediction of Energy Decay in Room Impulse Responses Simulated with an Image-Source Model, *Journal of the Acoustical Society of America*, vol. 124, 2008.
96. P. Peterson, Simulating the Response of Multiple Microphones to a Single Acoustic Source in a Reverberant Room, *Journal of the Acoustical Society of America*, vol. 80, 1986.
97. W. G. Gardner, Efficient Convolution without Input-Output Delay, presented at 97th Convention of the Audio Engineering Society, San Francisco, 1994.
98. D. M. Huber and R. E. Runstein, *Modern Recording Techniques*, 7th ed., New York: Focal Press, 2010.
99. D. K. Wise, Concept, Design, and Implementation of a General Dynamic Parametric Equalizer, *Journal of the Audio Engineering Society*, vol. 57, pp. 16–28, 2009.
100. P. Pestana, Automatic Mixing Systems Using Adaptive Audio Effects, PhD, Universidade Catolica Portuguesa, Lisbon, Portugal, 2013.
101. P. D. Pestana and J. D. Reiss, Intelligent Audio Production Strategies Informed by Best Practices, presented at AES 53rd International Conference on Semantic Audio, London, 2014.
102. B. Stroustrup, *The C++ Programming Language*, Reading, MA: Addison Wesley, 2000.
103. A. Koenig and B. E. Moo, *Accelerated C++*, Reading, MA: Addison Wesley, 2000.
104. S. B. Lippman et al., *C++ Primer*, 5th ed., Reading, MA: Addison Wesley, 2012.
105. R. Boulanger et al., *The Audio Programming Book*, Cambridge, MA: MIT Press, 2010.
106. W. Pirkle, *Designing Audio Effect Plugins in C++ with Digital Signal Processing Theory*, Burlington: Focal Press, 2013.
107. M. Walmsley, *Multi-Threaded Programming in C++*, Berlin: Springer, 1999.

Index

F

G

Q

R

S

T